Kant made a number of highly original discoveries about the mind – about its ability to synthesize a single, coherent representation of self and world, about the unity it must have to do so, and about the mind's awareness of itself and the semantic apparatus it uses to achieve this awareness. The past fifty years have seen intense activity in research on human cognition. Even so, not only have Kant's discoveries not been superseded, some of them have not even been assimilated into current thinking. That is particularly true of his work on unity and on the semantic apparatus of self-awareness.

The first four chapters of the book present a comprehensive overview of Kant's model for nonspecialists, an overview largely unencumbered by detailed exegesis. The work then offers a close study of five major discussions of the mind in the *Critique of Pure Reason* and *Anthropology*.

Kant and the Mind is designed to appeal to contemporary cognitive scientists and philosophers of mind, as well as to students and scholars of Kant.

Kant and the Mind

Kant and the Mind

ANDREW BROOK
Professor of Philosophy
Carleton University

PUBLISHED BY THE PRESS SYNDICATE OF
THE UNIVERSITY OF CAMBRIDGE
The Pitt Building, Trumpington Street, Cambridge CB2 1RP

CAMBRIDGE UNIVERSITY PRESS
The Edinburgh Building, Cambridge CB2 2RU, United Kingdom
40 West 20th Street, New York, NY, 10011-4211, USA
10 Stamford Road, Oakleigh, Melbourne 3166, Australia

First published 1994
Reprinted 1995
First paperback edition 1997

Library of Congress Cataloging-in-Publication Data
Brook, Andrew.
Kant and the mind / Andrew Brook.
p. cm.
Includes bibliographical references and index.
ISBN 0-521-45036-5 (hard)
1. Kant, Immanuel, 1724–1804 – Contributions in philosophy of mind.
2. Philosophy of mind – History – 19th century. I. Title.
B2799.M52B76 1994
128'.2'092 – dc20 93-22703
CIP

A catalog record for this book is available from the British Library.

ISBN 0-521-45036-5 hardback
ISBN 0-521-57441-2 paperback

Transferred to digital printing 2001

For C.K., G.B., and D.B.

Contents

Preface

This book was written with two audiences in mind. The first is the community of cognitive scientists, philosophers of mind, and students of cognition in general. The second, of course, is the community of Kant scholars and those with a special interest in Kant. The case I want to make to the first audience is that some of Kant's thoughts and discoveries, as I put it in Chapter 1, not only have not been superseded by more recent work on the mind, but have not even been assimilated by it. I hope I will give this first audience reason to believe that Kant still has things to teach us. For the second audience, I will argue that some aspects of Kant's theory (better, theories) of mind have not been well understood, especially in recent English-language commentaries, and that some others have been missed altogether.

The book has been constructed with these dual objectives in view. For the first audience, Chapters 1–4 attempt to construct an overview of Kant's model of the mind as a whole, without a great deal of detailed exegesis or textual justification for the views ascribed to him. (I try to give just enough quotations and citations to show that Kant did say the things I attribute to him.) The ideas in Chapter 4 on Kant's theory of self-awareness are the part of the project that, as Kant put it in connection with his Transcendental Deduction, "have cost me the greatest labour", and I can only echo his comment: "– labour, as I hope, not unrewarded" (Axvii). Those who just want a straightforward account of Kant's theory can stop when they get to the end of these chapters. The remaining chapters are for Kant scholars. They are devoted to the hard work of exegesis needed to justify my attributions and show where I think the particular views ascribed to Kant in Chapters 1–4 arise in his work and how they fit into his general system. In my view, five discussions of the mind in the *Critique of Pure Reason* are particularly important, three in the first edition and two in the second. Chapters 6–10 take them up, one per chapter. In Kant, everything connects and there is a great deal that I do not discuss. To those who particularly feel the absence of one topic or another, I can only offer an apology.

The ideas in this book have had a long evolution. The first seeds were sown by P. F. (now Sir Peter) Strawson in a Kant seminar he gave at Oxford many years ago. I am not sure how much he would recognize in the ultimate fruits of the seeds he planted. Since then, successive generations of students in my own Kant seminars have challenged me and puzzled over Kant with me year after year; I owe these students a large debt. I have been fortunate to have had some extremely able graduate research assistants; three who made a major contribution to this project are Deborah Knight, Richard DeVidi, and Christopher Viger. Many colleagues and students have read parts of the work as it evolved and made invaluable comments and suggestions: Michael Blake, Douglas Dryer, Lorne Falkenstein, Jack Iwanicki, Timothy Kenyon, John Leyden, Hilmar Lorenz, Lorne Maclachlan, Roland Marshall, Gordon Nagel, Jim Ramsay, Daniel Shannon, Stephen Talmage, Martin Weatherston, and Philip Wright. Lorne Falkenstein and Christopher Viger both read the text in its entirety and between them saved me from a great deal of vagueness, confusion, and error. Terence Moore, executive editor, Mary Racine, production editor, and Robert Racine, copy editor, of Cambridge University Press did a splendid job of assessing, editing, and producing the book.

An intermediate stage in the evolution of the work was supported by a Social Science and Humanities Research Council Leave Fellowship. In the year 1991–2, I had the good fortune to be elected Marston Lafrance Research Fellow at Carleton University. That year free of teaching and administration gave me the time to put the work into its final form. Carleton University awards one of these fellowships every year in its Faculty of Arts, and it would be hard to think of a better way to support research in the humanities.

The three people who play the biggest role in my life are my wife, Christine Koggel, and my sons, George and David. All three of them have accepted the demands of this project with affection and enthusiasm. I do not know what I would do without them. Christine has also played a very large role in the project itself, extending even to the huge task of reading not one but two complete drafts of the work. Her eye for philosophical confusion and stylistic inelegance has made this a much better work than it would otherwise have been.

1

The contemporary relevance of Kant's work

1 Kant's contribution

There is a tendency to think of great philosophers of the past as cultural artefacts, intriguing and historically significant, perhaps, but long since superseded. In what must surely rank as one of the most patronizing comments in philosophy, William James expressed just that attitude toward Kant:

> Kant's mind is the rarest and most intricate of all possible antique bric-a-brac museums, and connoisseurs and dilettanti will always wish to visit it and see the wondrous and racy contents. The temper of the dear old man about his work is perfectly delectable. And yet he is really . . . at bottom a mere curio, a 'specimen'.[1]

But some earlier philosophers are more than cultural artefacts. Even with all that has happened this century, some philosophers of past centuries continue to be fellow workers. We read these philosophers not just as an archaeological dig into our roots but to see what we can still learn from them. Kant is one of these philosophers.

At any rate, I think that is true of Kant's work on the mind. Given what has happened to epistemic foundations and the idea of necessary or *a priori* truth in the past few decades, it could be argued at least that Kant's epistemology is now merely a cultural artefact. In my view, that is not true of his work on the mind. Even though Kant's epistemology is one of the pillars of his fame – his ethics is another – and his psychology was a mere by-product of his epistemology, a body of ideas that even he viewed as incomplete and inessential to his main project, I think that the discoveries he made about the mind not only were a contribution in their time, but continue to be important now.

Like other philosophers, Kant was interested primarily in four questions about the mind: What can it do? How does it do it? What is its awareness of itself like? And what is it like? (In connection with the last question, he thought that there are severe restrictions on how much we can know.) Not only have Kant's discoveries concerning each of these issues not been superseded by more recent work on the mind, they have not even been assimilated by it – or so I will argue. This chapter sketches Kant's objectives and the way his ideas on the mind relate to the work being done in our own time. Chapters 2–4 attempt to lay out an overview of the main features of his model: synthesis and unity in Chapter 2, awareness in all its varieties in Chapter 3, and self-awareness specifically in Chapter 4. Kant isolated and was the first to characterize an important form of self-awareness, namely, awareness of oneself as the subject of one's experiences. He also achieved some remarkable insights into the referential apparatus we use to attain it and what I will call its *representational base*. Closely connected to what he called apperception, this kind of self-awareness is quite different from our awareness of our psychological states. I will call it *apperceptive self-awareness* (ASA). The notion is introduced in Chapter 3, and Chapter 4 lays out Kant's complete theory.

With this, the overview of Kant's account is complete and we can turn to exegesis. Chapter 5 explores the surprisingly complicated question of where Kant discussed the mind in the two editions of the first *Critique*, and why. Chapters 6–10 then examine each of the major discussions, one per chapter. Perhaps Kant's best-known discoveries about the mind were the ones concerning the role of synthesis in its workings and about the place of the special kind of unity he called the unity of consciousness. We examine these ideas in Chapter 6. As we will see, there is a synchronic dimension to this unity as well as the more obvious diachronic one, a point that is sometimes overlooked (by Patricia Kitcher, for one important example) and about which Kant himself was not always as clear as one could wish.[2] In addition, Kant had important and original things to say about why the unity found in awareness – the unity of consciousness – does not dictate what a mind's structure must be like (Chapter 7) or how it must persist over time (Chapter 8). (He also gave a highly plausible diagnosis of why we are tempted to take the opposite view on both these points.) In the second edition, Kant sketched a radical theory of the mind as representation, a theory that holds that the mind not only has representations but is a representation, in part at least – a representation of a rather special sort, to be sure (Chapter 9). He also had some surprising things to say about awareness of the mind as it is (Chapter 10). The general conclusion will be that Kant had ideas from which we can still learn about the mind's synthesizing functions, its unity, its awareness of itself, and its status as a representational system. Far from having been assimilated and superseded by the work of contemporary philosophers and cognitive scientists, his ideas on these topics have seldom even been discussed by them. For that reason, we should still approach Kant as students, not as archaeologists.

Not everyone will recognize Kant in everything I have just sketched. Particularly with respect to his views on self-awareness and the representational status of the mind, I tend to find more in him than many others do. There has been a burst of studies of Kant and the mind in the past few years. Following Ameriks' lead of a decade ago, Kitcher, Waxman, and Powell have all recently written books devoted to the subject, and the commentaries by Allison, Guyer, and Aquila all have long discussions of it.[3] In my view, these writers have not exhausted the topic. They tend to focus either on what we might call the mind's front-line epistemic capacities, as laid out in the Transcendental Analytic of the *Critique of Pure Reason* – intuitions and the forms of intuition, the concepts of the understanding, the principles, and so on – or on what our awareness of ourselves does not tell us about questions concerning our nature, such as whether we are simple or immaterial. (The latter is one of the themes, but is often taken to be the only major theme, of the chapter on the Paralogisms of Pure Reason.) By contrast, my main interest is in something less frequently explored – the nature of what lies behind these front-line epistemic capacities and introspective limitations. For example, what are the general features of the combinatorial powers a mind needs if it is to apply concepts to intuitions? What sort of unity, at a time and across time, does the use of these powers require? What implications do these powers and the unity requirements of using them hold for the mind's representations of itself and for its status as a representational system? If awareness of self gives us little access to what we are like, what is this awareness itself like? Approaching Kant with these questions in mind has interesting results. Some of his remarks about the mind suddenly stand out in high relief, remarks often buried in discussions of other things. Thus, as well as arguing that some of Kant's ideas on the mind continue to have relevance, indeed that on some issues he saw further than anyone else, in his time or ours, I will also be making some claims about what those ideas were that do not entirely agree with influential interpretations. As a result, I will often be pushing in two directions at once: trying to show that the ideas I attribute to Kant are important, on the one hand, and that he did hold them, on the other.

Each new generation of philosophers approaches Kant with the preoccupations and positions of its time, the aim being to see how much contemporary sense he still makes. In our time, that is now beginning to happen in cognitive science; in connection with the mind, Patricia Kitcher's work is the leading example.[4] There is a danger in this approach: if any of Kant's major concepts or ideas have not been assimilated into the context being used to assess him, important things are apt to be missed. Kitcher's work illustrates both the strengths of the approach and the risk. On the one hand, applying contemporary concepts and ideas to Kant allows her to find a remarkable amount of contemporary good sense in some of his most criticized doctrines, the ideality of space and time and the idea that a multistage activity of synthesis is required to create representations being two examples. On the other hand, a limitation in the contemporary concepts with which she approaches him leads her to miss a vital feature of Kant's theory. The problem concerns unity.

In contemporary usage, 'unity' is often used to mean 'identity' or 'individuation', specifically identity or individuation across time. Kitcher reads this usage into Kant. Thus, when Kant talks about the unity of consciousness, for example, or the unity of apperception, she takes him to be talking about being one person (Kant would have spoken of one mind) across time or being individuated as a mind across time. Powell reads him this way, too.[5] But this is a serious misreading. By the unity of consciousness or apperception, Kant meant one of the mental requisites of being aware of a number of things together, as parts of a single complex representation ("one single experience" [A110]),[6] not being one mind across time. Far from the unity of consciousness being the same thing as being individuated as a mind or being one mind across time, Kant specifically insists, in a Parfit-like argument against the Third Paralogism, that being unified in awareness with an earlier mind (this would be via memory or something very much like memory) does not even *entail* that one is that earlier mind! Indeed, one could be unified in this way with a number of earlier minds (A363n)! It is not entirely clear that Kant thought unity of consciousness and being one mind always coincided even at a time! We will return to this issue in the next chapter and, in one way or another, practically every chapter after that.

As well as leading her to misunderstand Kant on unity, Kitcher's misreading has another serious consequence. Because she takes Kant's notion of unity to be largely or entirely a diachronic one, she completely overlooks the central role that being aware of a number of representations *at the same time,* that is to say, synchronic unity of consciousness, plays in his thought. To be sure, Kant colludes in this oversight. Though he relies on the idea repeatedly, as we will see in Chapter 6, he actually speaks directly about synchronic unity not more than a half-dozen times.[7]

In his study of the mind, as elsewhere, Kant limited himself to questions about which he thought genuine knowledge was possible. For him, only necessary and universal truths yield genuine knowledge. Necessary and universal truths are also *a priori,* as he saw it, so in connection with the mind he limited himself to the mind's *a priori* features – "the subjective sources which form the *a priori* foundation of the possibility of experience" (A97) – and ignored the empirical ones (except insofar as some things of which we can be empirically aware are also part of the *a priori* foundation). He delegated the study of purely empirical or *a posteriori* questions about the mind to anthropology and empirical, which for him meant introspective, psychology, the physiology of inner sense. (Kant thought that the products of empirical psychology fell short of being genuine knowledge in other ways, too, as we will see.)

For a cognitive feature to be *a priori,* we must acquire and/or become aware of it other than via sensible intuition. (For Kant, only cognitive features that are necessary for having experience can be acquired and/or known from other than sensible intuition.) Note that *a priori* cognitive features either can be *acquired* from a nonsensible source or can be *known* nonsensibly, that is, from other than the sensible element in experience. As Kant saw it, things can be both acquired *a priori* and known *a priori*. In addition, for Kant the *a priori* is necessary – necessary for something or necessarily true. This conceptual apparatus of the *a priori* (nonempirical) and necessary versus the *a posteriori* (empirical) and contingent, and the division of labour that goes with it, has caused no end of trouble in the history of philosophy. It has even been behind some remarkable claims about Kant. Strawson's claim in his 1966 book that "the entire theory [of synthesis] is best regarded as one of the aberrations into which Kant's explanatory model inevitably led him" is a good example. (Strawson no longer holds this view.)[8] Strawson levelled this charge because he thought at the time that by claiming that synthesis is an "antecedent condition of empirical knowledge", Kant has ruled out the possibility of empirical evidence for it.[9] However, if the *a priori* – empirical distinction on which Strawson relied has no validity, the charge collapses.

Fortunately, there is a better way of capturing what interested Kant. Stripped of the jargon of transcendental necessity, what interested him were the most general constraints on anything that could function as a mind – a mind, at least, that is dependent on sensible input as we are. Kant may have called these constraints transcendentally necessary conditions, but we do not need to follow him in this. Readings of Kant that take him to be talking about psychological realities of some kind in the way I am – not just abstract ('formal', 'logical', 'conceptual', or whatever) conditions that may or may not reflect any psychological reality – have become extremely controversial, especially since Strawson's work. However, psychological or anthropological readings of Kant go back to the beginning. As Kitcher documents, until Helmholtz and Frege, psychological readings, often mixed with metaphysical ones about transcendental conditions, were the rule, not the exception, and she has developed a powerful version of this reading herself. By 'psychological reading', I mean a reading that takes Kant to be making claims, perhaps rather abstract claims, about the actual nature and functioning of the mind, not just about some sort of 'logically necessary conditions' that may tell us little or nothing about what actually goes on in a mind. An example of the latter would be the 'formal' requirement that representations be someone's, a requirement that says nothing about how representations are connected to one another or to the person who has them.[10] Thus, I am using the term in a broad sense. Psychological readings of Kant's theory of representation have had a bad press this century because they are thought to commit the sin of psychologism – seeking to explain by causes what needs to be explained by reference either (a) to credentials and justification, (b) to conditions of something obtaining, or to both. Kant rejected accounts of this kind as mere "physiology" (Aix), scornfully taking Locke as his example (see A86 = B118–19). This is a complicated subject, one that Kitcher discusses in far greater detail in the first chapter of her book than I will here, but the charge cannot be made to stick.

Whatever the claims of normative logic and epistemology against their various naturalizing detractors, when we turn to what the mind must be like to reason and know, we are turning to description, to how the mind does and must work (in some sense of 'must'). We are not seeking a normative account of how it should work. In connection with Kant, even that has sometimes been denied, but it seems to me obvious that here we are not doing normative theorizing. So much for (a). It does not follow from this, however, that we will inevitably sin against (b). Our alternatives are not limited to 'logically' necessary conditions or psychologism. There is a third alternative: an account that explores *both* the necessary conditions of the mind's operation *and* the actual psychology of these operations and that does the latter precisely by doing the former. In the past few decades, some commentators have taken Kant's notion of the transcendental or logical to exclude the empirical, so that if *X* is a transcendental feature of *Y*, *X* cannot be an empirical fact about *Y*. I am not sure what is meant by the latter claim – perhaps that *X* cannot be an object of representation – but it was clearly not one that Kant accepted. Far from having our Strawsonian worries about the genetic fallacy, about confusing logical with causal priority, Kant clearly held that his 'logic' of the mind is part of what we would now call psychology:

> The lower cognitive power is characterized by the passivity of the inner sense of sensation; the higher by the *spontaneity* of apperception – that is, of pure consciousness of the activity that constitutes thinking – and belongs to *logic* (*a system of the rules of the understanding*), just as the former belongs to *psychology* (to a sum-total of all inner perceptions under laws of nature).[11]

We would now include both this logic and this psychology in psychology. Indeed, Kant went even further. If he thought that the abstract study of the mind is part of logic, he also thought that the structure of general logic, the structure of the basic forms of judgement and categories within which we think, is part of the structure of the mind, as the italicized phrase indicates. For Kant, to explore the logic of our concept of experience simply is to explore how the mind works. *X*'s being necessary for *Y* to occur is quite compatible with *X*'s being among the causes of *Y*.

There is a passage early in the first *Critique* that illustrates how two such different readings of Kant can get started:

> What I call applied logic . . . is a representation of the understanding and of the rules of its necessary employment *in concreto,* that is, under the accidental subjective conditions which may hinder or help its application, and which are all given only empirically. It treats of attention, its impediments and consequences, of the source of error, of the state of doubt, hesitation, and conviction, etc. Pure general logic stands to it in the same relation as pure ethics, which contains only the necessary moral laws of a free will in general, stands to the doctrine of the virtues. (A54–5 = B78–9)

What then is pure logic? The antipsychological readings I am contesting would see Kant as contrasting applied logic with something 'merely logical' that is, nonempirical, not a feature of actual minds as we observe them. Moreover, this reading would see Kant as applying the contrast both to logic itself and to the necessary features of a mind that uses it. The comparison with pure ethics might seem to point in that direction. However, I think Kant wants us to understand the difference between pure and applied logic in a different way.

If applied logic is a "representation of the understanding . . . " under "the accidental subjective conditions" of its operation, pure logic is a representation of the understanding and so on *abstracted from* the effect of these accidental subjective conditions; that is to say, it is a representation of its general and/or necessary features. Moreover, I think he is making a similar point about ethics: pure ethics identifies the 'moral laws of a free will in general'. These laws are not nonempirical, in the sense that we could not observe them in particular virtues. On the contrary, they are what is common to all virtues. To be sure, they are more than empirical, also being necessary, and it is also true that we cannot establish their necessity by empirical means. But they are still empirical, in the sense specified. The famous remark just before the passage quoted, that "pure logic . . . has nothing to do with empirical principles, and does not . . . borrow anything from psychology" (A54 = B78) is to be read in this light. Pure logic is not shaped by experience, and its necessity and universality cannot be established by experience, but it still specifies the general structure of experience, conceptual experience at any rate; it is still "a doctrine of the elements of the understanding" (A54 = B78). "The distinction between the transcendental and the empirical belongs therefore only to the critique of knowledge; it does not concern the relation of that knowledge to its objects" (A56–7 = B80–1).

In short, to avoid reductive, point-missing psychologism, Kant did not feel the need many have felt in this century to resort to an antiseptic separation of necessary from causal and other empirical conditions. He felt that the conditions he was exploring were both.[12] It is hard to see how he could have been wrong. If we go one step further and begin to doubt whether there even is a special kind of truth associated with the former, the case for not separating the two becomes still stronger. Whether the best theory of the constraints Kant postulated contains some special kind of *a priori* or necessary propositions quite different from the propositions of a high-level empirical theory would now cease to matter. What would matter would be whether these constraints are there and have the generality and importance that Kant said they have. If it be thought that this makes Kant's psychology too empirical to count any longer as philosophy, I can do no better than quote Kitcher's response to this charge:

> [Kant] is totally uninterested in the actual physical or psychological embodiments of particular mental processes; the only goal is to explore the requirements of [performing] various cognitive tasks. In this respect his work is centrally in epistemology [and, I would add, philosophy of mind] and very different from empirical psychology.[13]

The need for acts of synthesis and the unity required to perform them are the constraints that interested him most.

Not a single one of the ideas I have attributed to Kant plays any important role in contemporary work on the mind. This is not because they have been examined and found wanting. On the contrary, most contemporary workers have never even considered them. For a number of decades, theorists had what might be called a bias against the mind as a whole, though that is beginning to change. Students of cognition studied content: the nature of content, kinds of content, attitudes to content, ability to manipulate content, explanation of content, and so on. But they had little or nothing to say about the awareness of this content or about the thing that has this awareness. As Dennett has put it:

> Curiously enough, most of the major participants in the debates *about mental contents* . . . have been conspicuously silent on the topic of consciousness. No theory, or even theory-sketch, of consciousness is to be found in the writing of Fodor, Putnam, Davidson, Stich, Harman, Dretske, or Burge, for instance.[14]

In his 'First Law of the Non-Existence of Cognitive Science', Fodor suggests as a reason for this that "the more global (i.e., isotropic) a cognitive process is, the less anybody understands it". (A cognitive process is isotropic when the processing of a new cognitive item may draw on anything in a person's previously established field of beliefs and so on.)[15] Kant certainly had a theory of content. He held a version of the representational model of the mind, and not only is the representational model a theory of content, it is still the sovereign theory of content, recent connectionist pretenders notwithstanding. But he also had a theory of consciousness. Theory of synthesis, theory of unity, theory of self-awareness, theory of the mind as a representation – all of these are aspects of theory of consciousness. In fact, Kant's main interest in the mind was in its isotropic features, such as consciousness and the powers and unities required to be conscious. Some of his ideas still deserve our attention.

Whatever the interest of Kant's ideas about the mind, it is not easy to dig them out. Of the many reasons for this, here I will mention just three. First, most of Kant's remarks about the mind and its awareness of itself in the first *Critique* and other works are asides, made in the course of discussing other topics. Many of them are also too brief to be anything more than *obiter dicta*. What they mean is often extremely unclear. Worse, they are widely scattered throughout his texts, both in the first *Critique* and elsewhere. In the first *Critique,* the bulk of them occur in three places: the Transcendental Deduction (TD) in the two versions of the first two editions, the chapter on the Paralogisms in its first-edition version, and the Refutation of Idealism. Even in these places, they occur in discussions of quite different topics. But remarks on the mind and self-awareness occur in many other places, too: in the prefaces and introduction and in the chapters on the Aesthetic, the Antinomies, and the Doctrine of Method. There is not a single sustained discussion of either the mind or its awareness of itself anywhere in either edition of the first *Critique*.

The same is also true of most of the other works in which Kant touched on these topics. The only exception is his little *Anthropology from a Pragmatic Point of View,* from which we quoted earlier. This unjustly neglected work, first published in 1798 about six years before Kant's death, was a manual for popular lectures he gave for many years at the University of Königsberg. By 'anthropology' Kant meant in part the study of human beings from the point of view of their (psychologically controlled) behaviour, especially their behaviour toward one another, and of the things revealed in behaviour, such as character. Anthropology in this sense contrasts with what Kant understood as empirical psychology, namely, the physiology of inner sense – psychology based on introspective observation. Because there is no stable and persistent multidimensional structure in inner sense to be observed, Kant thought that empirical psychology could never gain 'knowledge of an object' (A381), that is to say, find underlying structure in the ever-changing contents of inner sense.[16] The same is not true, he thought, of behaviour, the field of study of anthropology. His critique of introspection and turn to behaviour have a very contemporary flavour. Thus, it is surprising that the *Anthropology* has received so little attention. In the past ten years, that has begun to change. For example, Allison, Guyer, and Kitcher all make some use of it.

Kant, it seems, thought that to make sense of behaviour, character, and so on, we must know something of the powers and faculties of the human mind (sensibility, understanding, feeling, and appetite), and the way it gains knowledge and chooses behaviour. Thus, before he can provide an anthropology of character (Anthropological Characterization, Part II), he must teach us something about the mind (Anthropological Didactic, Part I). In fact, this didactic ends up being three-quarters of the book. This is the part of the work that is interesting for our purposes; I will largely ignore Part II. Though clearly shaped by the same ideas as the first *Critique,* because Part I focuses squarely on the mind in a way neither edition of the *Critique* ever did, it expresses some of Kant's dark notions more clearly than either edition of the *Critique*. For our purposes this little lecture manual does have one serious limitation: being a manual for popular lectures, it lacks the depth and sophistication of the *Critique*. Thus, it can only supplement the latter work, not serve as a primary text, and is seldom studied in its own right. Even though I find it extremely helpful on some issues, I too will not do a full study of it.

A second reason it is difficult to get at what Kant thought about the mind is that he was so pessimistic about studying the mind empirically; he thought that empirical psychology could never be a science. Indeed, this pessimism runs so deep that it may be wondered what there is for a book on Kant and the mind to discuss! Kant thought that empirical psychology is a nonstarter for at least five reasons. Here the canonical text is neither the first *Critique* nor the *Anthropology,* but a well-known passage in *The Metaphysical Foundations of Natural Science.*[17] Kant begins the work by saying that "a twofold doctrine of nature is possible: a *doctrine of body* and a *doctrine of soul*" (Ak. IV:467). Next he tells us that science proper must be apodictic, therefore in part *a priori,* therefore mathematical, because expression in a mathematical model is the only way for a science to achieve necessity or certainty. He then turns to "the empirical doctrine of the soul" (Ak. IV:471) and tells us that it "must remain even further removed than chemistry from the rank of what may be called a natural science proper." (Kant's notorious remarks about chemistry were made before it had been reduced to a single quantified theory.) Recall that, for Kant, the domain of empirical psychology is introspective observation, the contents of inner sense. He now tells us that the contents of inner sense cannot be studied scientifically, in a passage that contains more than is generally recognized.

First, having only one universal dimension and one that they are only *represented* to have at that, namely, distribution in time, the contents of inner sense can be quantified in only one dimension; thus no informative mathematical model of them is possible. As he puts it in the *Critique,* the only universal element in this field of observation is the mind itself, and the mind as a whole cannot be studied empirically for another reason: it presents virtually no characteristic or universal properties to observe. ("In what we entitle 'soul', everything is in continual flux and there is nothing abiding except [if we must so express ourselves] the 'I'... its representation has no content, and therefore no manifold" [A381].) Second, "The manifold of internal observation is separated only by mere thought" (Ak. IV:471). That is to say, only the introspective observer distinguishes the items from one another; there are no real distinctions among them. Third, these items "cannot be kept separate" in a way that would allow us to connect them again "at will", by which Kant presumably means 'according to the dictates of our developing theory'. Fourth, "Another thinking subject [does not] submit to our investigations in such a way as to be conformable to our purposes" – the only thinking subject whose inner sense one can investigate is oneself. Finally and most damningly, "Even the observation itself alters and distorts the state of the object observed". (Little did Kant realize how general an issue in science that would become!) In fact, as Kant insists in the *Anthropology,* introspection is even bad for the health: it is a road to "mental illness" (*An* Ak. VII:161; at VII:133, he says it leads to one or the other of two conditions he calls 'Illuminism and Terrorism'!). Strangely enough, Kant seems never to have said whether he thought anthropology in his sense could be a science.

In the light of these strictures on the study of inner sense, what is left for a book on Kant and the mind to talk about? The answer is both straightforward and well known, as ideas of Kant's go, at least. If we cannot study the connections among the denizens of inner sense, lacking as they do either structures or patterns of relationships that are universal and necessary, we can study what the mind must be like and able to do to have them. Here we can find, if not mathematical models, at least universally true, that is to say, 'transcendental' psychological propositions.

A third reason why it is not easy to find out exactly what Kant had to say about the mind is that on two crucial issues in his transcendental psychology, he never seems to have reached a stable position. One is the relationship of synthesis to self-awareness. The other is what our representation of ourselves as subject is like and what exactly it is representing. In addition, he vacillated in his use of some key terms. The problems with the term 'transcendental apperception' (TA) are the best known. Indeed, the difficulties with the notion of TA are notorious in Kant studies. Apperception is a concept-using, judgement-making ability of some kind, parallel in some respects to perception (A94). When Kant first introduces TA, he introduces it as nothing more than a special form of this same ability (A107). However, in later passages, indeed as early as A108, he also says or implies that TA is (in addition?) a form of self-awareness, and this is how his notion of TA has usually been understood. Just to add to the confusion, he can also say that TA can occur *without* self-awareness (A117n), or at any rate without awareness of the representations that it generates (A103 and B132)! However, there are problems in Kant's usage of other terms, too. For example, as we will see in Chapter 3, his use of '*Bewußtsein*' (consciousness or awareness) is as confusing as his use of 'TA', indeed in much the same way. In addition to these instabilities and ambiguities, Kant's interesting idea that the mind is a representation first clearly appears only in the second edition; but other, equally interesting ideas – for example, ideas on self-reference and self-awareness – disappear! In short, to find out what Kant had to say about the mind is none too easy a task.[18]

As I said, Kant viewed his ideas on the mind as secondary to his main project. Descartes bequeathed at least two major issues to philosophy: (1) the nature of knowledge, where and how it is possible, and (2) what the mind and its awareness of itself is like. Kant wrote the first *Critique* to resolve the first issue, not the second. The mind enters only because one of Kant's strategies for dealing with the issue of knowledge was to examine what a mind must be like to have it. But even here his aim was not to understand the mind. As he put it, his enquiry into what he also calls the pure understanding is "not an essential part of my [main purpose]"; it is also "somewhat hypothetical in character" (Axvii). Nevertheless, this enquiry produced a number of remarkable insights, both into how the mind functions and into its awareness of itself. Many of these insights were lost again after his death and have not been entirely recovered or rediscovered to this day, at least in the English-speaking world. (It is curious that of what is living and what is dead in Kant, his asides on the mind are still living and much of what he said about knowledge now seems largely dead, his foundationalism in particular.)

Kant used a number of terms to refer to the mind, including 'self' (*Selbst*), 'mind' (*Gemüth*), 'subject' (as in subject of experience or awareness; note that he does not spell it *Subjekt*), 'thing which thinks' (*dieses Ich oder Er oder Es* (*das Ding*) *welches denkt* [A346 = B404]), and 'soul' (*Seele*). Kant used these terms pretty much as extensional equivalents. I will generally use 'mind' or 'subject', except when the context calls for 'self'. When we reach the Paralogisms, I will follow Kant and use 'soul'. With respect to '*Bewußtsein*' and '*Selbstbewußtsein*', things are not so straightforward. Kemp Smith usually translates these terms as 'consciousness' and 'self-consciousness'. When quoting his translation, I will follow his usage. Likewise, when I am using a term like 'unity of consciousness' that has become a standard term in Kant scholarship, I will follow standard usage. However, 'consciousness' and 'self-consciousness' have been so over-used that they make little impact; 'self-consciousness' also has a sense that has nothing to do with our concerns. Wherever possible I will use 'awareness' and 'self-awareness'. For one thing, they cannot be so readily hypostatized: 'awareness has the power to . . . ' would sound a little silly. But there is a problem with 'awareness', too: 'aware state' is not idiomatic English, and 'state of awareness' barely is. So when I am talking about what Kant termed '*Bewußtsein*',

I will on occasion have to use 'consciousness'. Fortunately, 'self-aware' and 'self-awareness' work in all contexts, so except in quotes from the Kemp Smith translation, I will always use these terms where Kant used or would have used '*Selbstbewußtsein*'.

2 Kant, functionalism, and cognitive science

If some of Kant's views on the mind have been neglected by contemporary workers, that is not true of all his thought. His views on knowledge and even his general conception of the mind have had a huge influence on contemporary thought, particularly cognitive science. Indeed, Kant has virtually been adopted as an intellectual godfather by cognitive science. Yet cognitive scientists seldom mention even the topics of the mind's synthesizing powers, or its unity, or the distinctive awareness it has of itself (as opposed to its states), let alone Kant's theories about them. This is a strange state of affairs. The fourth of his theories, that the mind is itself a representation, is not talked about either, but that is less surprising.

Among the notions that cognitive scientists and the philosophers associated with them have taken over from Kant, probably the most important is the doctrine that most representations require concepts as well as percepts – cognitive acts as well as deliverances of the senses. This doctrine has become as orthodox within cognitive science as it was central to Kant's critical philosophy. In addition, Kant's central methodological innovation, the method of transcendental argument, has become a major, perhaps the major, method of cognitive science. One way to describe the role of transcendental arguments is to say that they attempt to reveal the conditions necessary for some phenomenon to occur. (Other descriptions include: they reveal the constraints on any such phenomenon occurring, and they reveal what must be true of any possible system in relation to which that phenomenon could occur.)[19] This method has become influential in cognitive science because it provides a toe-hold on the barrier between observable behaviour and its unobservable psychological antecedents. Transcendental arguments are a way of finding constraints on what the unobservable antecedents could be like.

Strange as it may seem in light of what has been neglected, even Kant's conception of what we can and cannot capture in our models of the mind has been taken over by cognitive science and philosophers associated with it, at least in a general way. The functionalist version of the representational model of the mind is virtually the official philosophy of mind in cognitive science at the moment. The basic idea behind functionalism is that the way to model the mind is to model what it does and can do, its functions ('the mind is what the brain does'). The basic idea behind the representational model is that the function of a mind is to shape and transform representations. Kant too had a representational model of the mind (a rather radical one, if my reading of him is right), and his view of the mind as a system for applying concepts to percepts is entirely in line with functionalism.

The three basic moves underlying Kant's model of the mind are as follows. (i) Most or all representation is representation of objects; such objects are the result of acts of synthesis. (ii) For representations of objects to be anything to anyone, they must "belong with others to one consciousness" (A116); for this, the mind must synthesize its various objects of representation into what I will introduce in the next chapter as the *global object* of a special kind of single complex representation called a *global representation*. (iii) Synthesis into either individual or global objects requires the application of concepts. (For an elaboration of this schema, see Chapters 6 and 9.) These are the central elements of the model. What all three of these tenets describe are either 'functions' (that was Kant's term, too [A68 = B93, A94, and other places]), or conditions required for functions to operate, unified awareness in particular. In short, Kant's approach to the mind centred on how it works, as opposed, for example, to how it is built (whether abstractly or physically characterized) or its introspectible contents. To be sure, functionalism now comes in a number of flavours – in order of specificity, that mental functions can be specified only by their relation to other mental functions (together with input, output, and history), that explanation of mental functioning is a special sort of explanation (focusing on reasons for action), that explanation of mental functioning must be conducted in the language of psychology, that this vocabulary and the style of explanation conducted by using it has 'autonomy' (cannot be reduced to nonpsychological explanation), that this autonomy stems from such explanation being holistic in certain ways, and perhaps others. Unlike contemporary functionalists, Kant paid no attention to such specifics. Nor did he consider how to characterize functional states in terms of their relation to other functions, context, the person's behaviour, how the functions fit in the history of the person who has them, and so on. If Kant's theory is a version of contemporary functionalism, then his functionalism was of a rather general sort. Nevertheless, I think it is a version of functionalism.

The thought that Kant was a functionalist *avant le mot* is no longer new. Sellars was perhaps the first to read Kant as a functionalist or protofunctionalist; more recently Kitcher, Dennett, Meerbote, Powell, and others have joined him.[20] It is less often noticed that Kant was committed to a vital negative doctrine of functionalism, too, the dictum that function does not determine form. About the relation of function to form, functionalists maintain two things: (i) mental functioning could be realized in principle in objects of many different forms; and (ii) we know too little about the form or structure of the mind at present to say anything useful at this level in any case, except that mental functions will never be straightforwardly mapped onto any associated forms. Kant accepted a variant of both these positions. Concerning (ii), Kant maintained not just that we know little about the 'substrate' (A350) that underlies mental functioning, but that we know nothing (or we can never know that we know anything) about it. This is his doctrine of the unknowability of the noumenal mind. If the noumenal mind is unknowable, however, (i) immediately follows; the mind as it is could take different forms. Otherwise, how it functions would tell us how it is. Indeed, function imposes so few constraints on form that so far as we can infer from function, we cannot determine even something as basic as whether the mind is simple or complex (A353). Kant accepted a very strong version of the notion that function does not dictate form.

Indeed, his doctrine of the unknowability of the noumenal mind is little more than a strong version of that very idea. And this doctrine is no mere personal fancy in his system. On the contrary, it was absolutely vital to him. The very possibility of free will and immortality hang on it, and our belief in freedom and immortality are two of the three great practical beliefs whose possible truth Kant wrote the whole *Critique* to defend (Bxxx). (The third was belief in God's existence; the possibility of its truth depends on the unknowability of the noumenal too, but the noumenal world, not the noumenal mind.) The *Critique* has other goals too, of course, more positive, theory-justifying goals, but showing the unknowability of the noumenal is vital to the work's practical goals.

In short, three of Kant's most central insights have been embraced by cognitive science:

1. his epistemological insight into the relation of concepts and percepts;
2. his main method, the method of transcendental argument; and
3. his general picture of the mind as a system of concept-using functions for manipulating representations.

Indeed, some workers in cognitive science have even begun to explore the implications of more specific aspects of Kant's model of the mind for their work.[21] All this makes it exceedingly strange indeed that his ideas about synthesis, unity, and self-awareness have played so little role in contemporary work.

As we leave this section, notice something very interesting. Until a moment ago, it contained not a single word about self-awareness. Yet I have laid out all the essentials of Kant's model of the mind. This seems to suggest that a great deal of Kant's model has nothing to do with self-awareness, though he himself may not always have been as clear about that as one could wish. In my view, the idea that Kant argued in some obscure way that self-awareness is necessary for having experience is ripe for reappraisal. We will examine it in Part II of Chapter 6.

3 The resistance of materialists

One reason why Kant's model of the mind has not been more influential is that most contemporary theories of mind are materialist,[22] and Kant, as is well known, was implacably hostile to materialism, at least about the mind. For this reason, some people assume that Kant can have nothing to offer current workers. I think they are wrong. For one thing, it is easy to misplace this hostility. Kant's reasons for it were primarily nontheoretical: he thought that he had powerful practical reasons to believe in morality and immortality, and materialism endangered both of them. So far as theory goes, if he thought materialism could not explain, for example, the unity of apperceptive awareness, he also thought that immaterialism and the simplicity of the soul could not do so either (B415n).[23] For another, I think (1) Kant does have something to offer us, (2) materialism fits remarkably easily into his overall theory (if not into some beliefs for which he thought he could give a nontheoretical justification, namely, his beliefs about God, free will, and immortality), and (3) his observations and inferences concerning synthesis, unity, and self-awareness can quite easily be made to fit into materialist theories of mind, including contemporary ones.

1. It seems to me unlikely that the features of the mind he postulated are chimera. In my opinion (an opinion much of the rest of this book is devoted to trying to justify), we do have some ability to synthesize, we require a special unity to use this ability, we have the special kind of self-awareness I call *apperceptive self-awareness* (ASA), and we use peculiar referential apparatus to gain it. (The idea that the mind is a representation is less initially plausible, so I will not discuss it here.) If so, philosophers and cognitive scientists cannot continue to ignore these features of the mind, no matter what their theoretical persuasion. Nor does any theory I know of entail that no such features exist, that the concepts of synthesis, unity, and ASA are concepts for illusions (however much we may ultimately want to redescribe or reclassify what they purport to refer to). If so, whether one is a holistic (Davidson, Dennett) or a nonholistic functionalist (Fodor, Pylyshyn) or an antifunctionalist (the Churchlands, recent Putnam) about representation and mental activity; whether one is a realist (Fodor) or an instrumentalist (Dennett) about mental activity; whether one is a supporter (Fodor, Dennett) or an eliminator (the Churchlands, Stich) of intentional psychological discourse and theory (dismissively called folk psychology); whether one is a sententialist (Fodor, Pylyshyn) or an antisententialist (Dennett, the Churchlands) about the way the brain realizes representations – from any of these stances, one must at some point consider synthesis, unity, and ASA.

Especially with respect to unity, this may seem a strange thing to say. Surely, it will be objected, many theorists have now refuted Kant's claims about the unity of the mind in different ways; Fodor and the connectionists immediately come to mind. I am not so sure. As I see it, contemporary theorists have not so much refuted Kant's claims about unity as rejected a certain theory of it and reduced its scope. What Kant called unity and characterized in a purely abstract way got tied to a certain theory of how unity is realized, namely, in an executive control system in the mind. This theory has turned out to be uninformative. It also seems clear that any unified awareness in the mind extends over a smaller range of psychological states than was once thought. But neither point so much as touches Kant's original observations and inferences about synthesis, unity, and self-awareness, let alone refutes them.

2. Before I examine whether materialist theories of mind can accommodate synthesis or unity or ASA, I want to provide some brief support for

the second of the three claims I made: that Kant can accommodate materialism. Whatever Kant's personal views, his overall theory, I will argue, is quite compatible with materialism, especially his epistemology. Because *Kant* was so hostile to materialism about the mind, it is easy not to notice that much of *the general theory* he developed is not.

Kant held that we have immediate, noninferential awareness of only our representations. (As a result, he has been accused of being some kind of phenomenalist. Walker points out that Kant was not a classical phenomenalist, at any rate, because he did not believe that the content of beliefs about the world could be *reduced* to sensible representations.)[24] If we do not have immediate awareness of anything independent of our experience, then we can only make inferences to what such thing or things are like (something like inferences to the best explanation). And we can never know that our inferences are correct; indeed, Kant sometimes seems to say that these inferences could not be correct, that our beliefs can never correspond to the world as it is. All we can know is that our inferences cohere with one another and correspond to the (intentional) objects of our representations (A58–9 = B83–4 and A104–5). If so, something of major significance follows concerning the mind.

What follows is that, so far as the real nature of the mind is concerned, strict ontological neutrality has to be the order of the day, not just about the world as it is and other minds as they are but also about our own mind as it is. If there is a 'substrate' to the representational system that is our mind, as Kant clearly thought there is (A350), we can never know, or at least know that we know, what it is like. We can never know even something as basic as whether this substrate is material or not. Nor does what we know of our representations help us here, for we know them only as they as appear to us, too, and how they appear to us is not necessarily what they are like. What representations are in themselves like is just as unknowable as anything else about things as they are. Even the most basic things cannot be settled; for example, are they what Kant called substrate under another description, or something quite different? If so, and this is the crucial point, materialism has just as good a chance of being true of the mind-as-it-is and representations-as-they-are as any other theory – dualism, (standard, not transcendental) idealism, or whatever. Even the idea that the mind itself is a representation (the idea I am setting aside) would be compatible with materialism. This representation, too, could be material.

Against this point of view, it could be objected that for Kant, surely, representations at least *exist,* and exist immaterially ("the ideality of all appearances [is] established in the Transcendental Aesthetic" [A379]). But material objects *do not exist,* not as anything other than intentional objects; they are nothing more than the results of the mind's processing of its representations. Representations, however, are not a working up of representations. So representations, and presumably the mind that has them, could not be material. We could imagine Karl Ameriks making this objection.[25] Kant himself gives some weight to it by sometimes offering an account of matter as infinitely divisible, and the like, that seemed to him to imply that matter could only be a feature of appearances, never of anything as it is (see, e.g., *The Metaphysical Foundations of Natural Science,* Ak IV:503–8). Thus, he could say, in apparent contradiction of my view:

> Neither the *transcendental object* which underlies outer appearances nor that which underlies inner intuition, is in itself either matter or a thinking being, but a ground (to us unknown) of the appearances which supply to us the empirical concept of the former as well as of the latter mode of existence. (A379–80, his emphasis)

However, Kant is entitled to say this only on his own, very peculiar conception of matter, which simply implies that it is a property of representations. On any account of matter free of such an implication, he could not claim, if the ground of outer appearances and inner intuition is (or are) really unknown to us, that it is (or they are) neither matter nor a thinking being. They could be neither, but they could also be either – or both, should thinking things turn out to be material. On most accounts of matter or the mental, all three options would remain open.

There are other problems with the objection and the statements of Kant on which it is based. First, Kant is not entitled to any view about the real nature of appearances, any more than about anything else. Dennett has made a similar point, with great force, about mental images: we know our psychological states only as they appear to us, and that does not necessarily tell us how they are.[26] The only account Kant can allow us to give of things, *including representations,* as they are, is whatever turns out to give the best account of things, *including representations,* as they appear. Thus, if materialism turns out to give us the best account of representations as they appear to us, which is how things seem to be turning out, Kant would have to accept it.

Second, the objection overphenomenalizes Kant. Kant certainly thought that objects other than myself and my representations at least exist, and exist as more than objects of my representations. Kant was not a solipsist! (Whether he should have been, given his theory of perception, is another question.) Only the representation of an object is a result of the mind's activities. The object itself is not. Due to the contribution of the mind (together, as Kant unfortunately believed, with our being immediately aware only of representations), we can never know whether our representation of an object is like the object. But objects other than ourselves do exist. Once we see this, however, it is immediately obvious that materialism has just as good a chance of being true of objects as they are as any other theory, except on a bizarre account of matter such as Kant's. (Indeed, in the Refutation of Idealism Kant says things that imply that materialism is true of objects other than oneself, some of them at least [see B278]. But that may have been merely a slip.) In short, whether as a theory of representations as they are or of anything else as it is, including the mind, materialism has as good a chance as any other theory.

That Kant was what he called a transcendental idealist argues nothing to the contrary. Kant's transcendental idealism holds that the mind provides the spatial, temporal, and conceptual aspects of the objects of its representations, as part of what it does to find organization in the raw materials of representation (the manifold of intuitions). All of this is quite compatible with materialism; for materialism might turn out to be the best way of conceptualizing things as they appear, indeed as good a theory of representations, for example, as it has turned out to be for what we call the physical world. (We call the latter physics.) Nor does the mind's spontaneity argue anything to the contrary. 'In the exercise of some of its abilities', it will be objected, 'the mind manifests a spontaneity and creativity that cannot be reconciled with materialism'. This is like Pippin's objection to the functionalist reading of Kant discussed earlier.[27] The answer is simple: we no more have an adequate theory of the mind's spontaneity and creativity than Kant did. But we have every reason, indeed far more reason than Kant, to think that when we do get such a theory, it will be a materialist one. The conclusion is clear: as a theory of things as they appear, including mental things, materialism could clearly turn out to be the best theory.

As well as being useful in its own right, this conclusion about appearances also strengthens the conclusion we reached earlier about things in themselves. There we concluded that materialism has just as good a chance of being true of things as they are as any other theory. Now we can say more than that. Most theories of things as they appear to us *are* theories about how these things really are. For any theory of this sort, the best theory of things as they appear would not just be as good as any other theory of how things are; it would be the best theory of how things are. If Kant would not have wanted to agree with this stronger point, I do not see how he could have resisted the weaker one: his overall position is at least *compatible* with materialism. (At any rate, that is true of his theoretical position. I have already allowed that he thought he had good *practical* reasons for rejecting materialism about the mind.)

3. Now my third claim, that Kant's claims about synthesis, unity, and the like could be taken into contemporary materialism. The most radical position that we could derive from a combination of the various materialist positions just sketched would be a nonsententialist instrumentalism that eliminates intentional psychological discourse in favour of the discourse of the neurosciences: an instrumentalist, behaviourist, eliminative materialism. What would happen to synthesis, unity, and ASA in such a position? These features of the mind would now have to be understood rather differently from the way Kant understood them, of course. Rather than being seen as real states and activities existing in an entity called the mind, they would now be seen as states and activities either observed in or postulated to explain an 'order that is there' in behaviour.[28] Being eliminativist, presumably our radical position would also talk about them in a terminology rather different from Kant's. For example, the term 'self-awareness' might be replaced (or roughly replaced; the match would be anything but one to one) by some sort of information-feedback discourse. (Then again, it might not be; 'self-

awareness' might turn out to be theory neutral to a useful degree.) Would even a position as radical as this be incompatible with Kant's claims about synthesis, unity, or self-awareness (however redescribed)? Not at all. Nor would it necessarily eliminate them.

I can imagine the protests! 'Kant compatible with any form of behaviourism? You're not serious!' I am serious. Kant himself, of course, placed mental activities and states such as synthesis, unity, and ASA in a Cartesian mind, hidden and unobservable, something very different from behaviour. But we need not follow him in this. Indeed, we should ask whether he was entitled to distinguish between mind and behaviour in this way. If he meant it when he said we do not know how things really are, how could he be so sure that minds as they are, are not behaviour? But the real point we should be discussing is not whether Kant's own beliefs about the mind are compatible with behaviourism, but whether what he actually observed and/or inferred is compatible with it. Could Kant's observations and inferences be accommodated by a behaviourist account? Though the language Kant used would probably have to be modified radically, the answer to this question is yes, they could be. Kant was a thoroughgoing intentionalist, of course, indeed he would not have imagined in his wildest dreams of approaching perception and cognition nonintentionally. But that does not mean that his observations cannot be transposed into a nonintentional framework.

Suppose we reconceive Kant's work and substitute 'behaviour' and 'dispositions' for his 'representations, 'experience', 'awareness', and so on. Then suppose we think of Kant as offering a contingent theory of behaviour, especially linguistic behaviour, not an *a priori* 'analytic' of a hidden mental realm. This theory would explain behaviour by postulating a certain unity and certain synthesizing powers. All Kant's insights into unity and synthesis could easily survive even so radical a recasting. (I am not saying, of course, that there would be no other problems with it.) Unity might become a theory of how an organism can group behaviours into integrated systems and can refer to whole systems of behaviour as a single object (a person) in single acts of reference and single propositions, not just to individual behaviours. Synthesis would become a theory of what an organism must be able to do to achieve such integration, and the theory of ASA would become a theory about such behaviour as self-attributions, reports about oneself, expressions of memories about oneself.

Of anything in the general neighbourhood of behaviourism, Wittgenstein's remarks on mental 'states', 'processes', and so on are *prima facie* the most unlike Kant's. Though radically intentionalist, Wittgenstein's remarks are also radically unsympathetic to Cartesian inner realms. No doubt a number of things about Kant's work *as he himself conceived it* would have drawn Wittgenstein's thunder: the idea that mental states and activities are something quite different from human bodies and behaviour, the idea that this mental something exists in a realm that may very well be nonspatial, the idea that philosophy of mind explores the necessary structure of this realm, the idea that we have to use special *a priori* techniques to do so, normal empirical investigation being quite useless – all this and more Wittgenstein would have considered nonsense, literally. If, however, we remove the Cartesian framework from Kant's ideas and reconceive them as empirical explanations of speaking and acting, in the way just sketched, would Wittgenstein still have to object to them? I do not see why. I want to emphasize this point. Even if theories of mind turn out ultimately to have been talking about behaviour, Kant's observations about synthesis, unity, and self-awareness could still be sound and have a place in such theory. How he himself conceived of the mind would have to be jettisoned, of course, but many of his observations and inferences about it would not.

Here, however, I need to qualify what I am saying. Kant's observations about self-awareness could not survive all behaviourist recastings. In particular, if 'I' as used in behaviour such as self-attributions is nonreferential, as some say Wittgenstein held, then many of Kant's observations about ASA would have to go.[29] This has been denied; for example, Rosenberg has recently argued that Kant anticipated even the idea that certain uses of 'I' are nonreferring.[30] Kitcher and Powell seem to agree. But this seems wrong to me. Kant viewed reference to self as referential, so if the Wittgensteinian idea is right, he was wrong (see Chapter 4:4). Whether or not Kant's observations could fit comfortably into Wittgensteinian behaviourism, however, it seems to me that they could fit into other forms of behaviourism.

Indeed, even as radical a departure from the view of the mind Kant actually held as Putnamian wide content would not change the picture, it seems to me. Added to the eliminative behaviourism we already have, wide content would mean that whatever has replaced semantic or intentional content can be ascribed to whatever has replaced minds only if the mind replacement has a relationship to a world outside it. Even here, though I will not argue the point, it seems to me that the aspects of synthesis, unity, and ASA that interested Kant would still survive, all radically redescribed, of course.

There is one outcome that would be fatal for Kant's claims about synthesis, unity, and self-awareness. Suppose that the best theory in the end is a form of eliminative materialism that eliminates not just the terms 'synthesis', 'unity', and the like, but also anything remotely resembling what we took these terms to name. Here Kant would no longer have anything to say to us. Though possible, this outcome strikes me as improbable. But what would the status of Kant's work be if it did come about? Then he would have done the most searching of explorations of how the mind's processing of energy gradients on its sensitive surfaces (or whatever) and its processing of its access to itself were conceived of in the eliminated discourse. Even if it turns out that this is all Kant achieved, it would still be a considerable achievement. Moreover, since even the most ardent propagandists for eliminative materialism agree that we are going to be stuck with intentional psychological discourse for a long time, Kant's achievement would still continue to have value for a long time.

Certainly for anyone who still thinks that there is something to our 'folk' psychological discourse (e.g., Fodor and Dennett), Kant's concerns seem to me to be inescapable. I can imagine someone responding to what I have been arguing as follows: 'So Kant's ideas are compatible with materialism. So what? Is there any reason to care about them?' I will address this issue at some length in Chapter 2, but let me give a preview of why I think we do have reason to care about them. Use any part of the discourse of belief and desire and you will inevitably be led to ask questions such as these: How can we relate beliefs, desires, and the like to one another in the ways we do (synthesis)? What integration would be required for a person to do so (unity)? What sort of access do persons have to themselves (self-awareness)? And so on. Nor would adopting any form of radical materialism allow us to escape them.

Suppose that behaviourism is true. We may be able to explain some of the integration of behaviour as interacting outputs of otherwise unintegrated modules of some sort, but what about the phenomenon we now call being aware of a number of these outputs at the same time, or consciously comparing them, or being aware of oneself as the subject of (what we misleadingly label) one's 'experiences'? These are real puzzles about conscious mentality, and adopting a behaviourist stance would do nothing to remove them. Or suppose, as seems increasingly likely, that the brain is a neural network, containing nothing very much like either representations or rules for performing computations on representations as standardly conceived. There would still remain a level of activity where these ways of talking and the ways of talking to do with synthesis, unity, and self-awareness just described would continue to have point and cogency. (Even if our commonsense discourse about representations and so on turns out not to apply in useful ways to brains, it could hardly stop being a powerful way of talking about *persons*.) If the *prima facie* structure of this level of activity turns out to be radically unlike the structure of the brain, that does not mean the level would disappear. Quite the reverse. It would just become more mysterious. About the questions that would still arise, Kant would continue to have something to teach us.

Furthermore, any differences between Kant and materialist theories of mind are to a large extent balanced by a deep similarity. Except for some of the variants of behaviourism, Kant and nearly all the materialist positions I have mentioned share a Cartesian vision of self-awareness, eliminative materialism included. The only important difference between Kant and contemporary workers on this score is that the latter ignore ASA, indeed all awareness of oneself, and concentrate on awareness of psychological states and activities. In essence, the Cartesian picture models self-awareness on perception: self-awareness consists of representations of some kind (it used to be images) displayed before the eye of the 'I' in some system of relations, usually conceived as quasi-spatial (even by Kant, his claim that representations are nonspatial notwithstanding). Like Kant, most contemporary philosophers and cognitive scientists accept it. Whether functionalist or eliminativist about psychological discourse, whether realist or instrumentalist about mentality, whether sententialist or antisententialist about how the mind represents, we are all Cartesians about self-awareness. The appeal of this picture seems to be timeless.[31]

If Kant had something important to say about self-awareness, at least all theorists who accept some version of the Cartesian picture ought to be interested in his views. In Chapter 3:4, I will sketch what I think he added, and in Chapter 4 I will attempt to reconstruct the whole theory. None of it, I would claim, is either incompatible with or a candidate for elimination by contemporary materialism.

To conclude, Kant was not a materialist. Among other things, he thought that things as they are, including the mind, are neither spatial nor temporal and, as we saw earlier, neither material nor thinking (A380). The mind is nonspatial, he thought, even as we know it. He also thought that the mind has a self-legislating spontaneity that he could not have conceived to be the activity of a machine. And he advocated at least the possibility of immortality and free will, the existence of which he took to be incompatible with materialism. Even more awkwardly, he at least once seems to assert that, if the mind has unity, it has to be simple and without parts (B419), which would rule out its being material.[32]

It is possible to respond to these points. We could simply jettison Kant's positive account of the noumenal, his claim to know at least enough about things as they are to know that they are nonspatial and so on. That I would be quite happy to do. We could soften his denial of the spatiality of the mental and turn it into a claim that the mental merely does not *appear to us* to be spatial, a position that is more in line with his general position in any case. We could note that if Kant says that the unity of the soul entails that it is simple in one place in the second edition, he denies that we can know one way or the other in other places and in the first edition says flatly that the unity of the soul "may relate just as well to the collective unity of different substances acting together" as to a single simple soul (A353; the simplicity of the soul is the topic of Chapter 7). And about spontaneity we could say that Kant no more had a theory of what the noumenal machinery of the mind's cognitive and self-directing activity is actually like than anyone else does. But the important point is that I did not say Kant was a materialist or even that he could easily be turned into one. He was not and could not be. What I said was that in three important ways his views on the mind are not hostile to materialism.

First, Kant called himself an empirical realist. That means that he was committed to accepting whatever theory of the mind as it appears to the mind (to itself and to other minds) that these appearances support. Depending on how it was being done, Kant called this kind of theorizing either the physiology of inner sense or anthropology. Second, so far as the real nature of the mind is concerned, we are totally in the dark, so far as we know or can know. (At least, that would be Kant's position if we ignore the positive doctrine of noumena and his strange theory of matter.) Whether the way the mind appears to us reflects the way it is we cannot know. So barring his account of matter, materialism has at least as good a chance of being true of minds and their representations as they are as any other theory does. Third and perhaps most important, Kant's particular observations about synthesis, unity, and self-awareness can readily be transposed into the idioms of contemporary materialism.

To be sure, Kant thought that, so far as we can know, free will, immortality, and God (all incompatible with materialism, as he saw it) were possible, and he also thought that we have nontheoretical reasons to believe that they are all actual. This would entail that we have nontheoretical reasons to accept that materialism could not be the whole story. But so far as Kant's theoretical ideas about the mind go, many of the most important ones are not hostile to materialism. If Kant's positive theory of mind, to the extent that he had one, is a version of functionalism, as I urged in Section 2, that is exactly what we would expect. Functionalists need not be materialists, but their theory could hardly be incompatible with materialism, either. Functionalism, too, is ontologically neutral.

2

Kant's theory of the subject

At the beginning of Chapter 1, it was suggested that Kant made discoveries about four things to do with the mind: the role of synthesis, the unity of experience and consciousness, the special form of self-awareness I call apperceptive self-awareness (ASA), and the mind's status as a special kind of representation. Before we turn to the texts that lay out these ideas, it might be a good idea to construct an overview of Kant's model, one unencumbered by filigree of close exegesis. That is the task of this and the next two chapters; we will also attempt to display the relevance of some of Kant's ideas to contemporary research. This chapter takes up Kant's theory of synthesis and unity, Chapters 3 and 4 his views on awareness and self-awareness.

1 The need for a subject

Let us start with this question: Why do we suppose that experience needs a subject in the first place? The level of mental activity on which much current research into the mind focuses does not need a subject. To identify the level in question, let me use a personal example. As a result of having remarkably bad handwriting, I am all too often in the position of not being able to recognize a word I have written some time before. If, however, I take a careful look at the scrawl I put down and then go and do something else for a while, almost invariably I will eventually recognize what I wrote. (The word 'marginalized' was a recent example.) If the brain is a neural network, that is about what one would expect; the network needs time to settle on a solution. Many contemporary theoreticians are interested in what the neural process might be like that transforms the meaningless scrawl into a recognizable word. Here some form of the modularity thesis is very plausible, and there is no need to postulate a subject. However, at the end of this process of nonaware interpretation, a second level of activity commences; a representation comes to exist, I recognize the word, and I then set out to do whatever it is that I choose to do with the now-recognizable word. When we think of the activity of an aware mind, we are thinking of this second level of activity, not the first. At this second level, we need a subject, though exactly what that means is quite unclear.

Memory provides a second example of the same two levels in human cognition. The nature of memory in human beings is a topic of major interest at the moment, especially the highly distinctive features of our 'access' to it. An example is the way we can have a vague and general memory of something without any memory of the details, a phenomenon only too familiar to anyone who has ever written an exam. Memory in serial computers has nothing even vaguely comparable. The connectionist picture of memory as a parallel distributed processing system is attracting the most interest at the moment.[1] We can draw the same distinction of levels with respect to memory as we just drew concerning interpretation of handwriting and recognition of words. First the neural net produces a memory. Then we 'access' it. What is doing the accessing? What is the being aware of, the recognizing of a memory like? For example, how does being aware of a memory differ from just being affected by one behaviourally or affectively?

The second level of mental activity is the one in which Kant was most interested. He was certainly interested in the first level, too, the prior processes that generate recognizable representations – it is the target of much of his doctrine of synthesis. But his main interest was in the structure of the representations that synthesis generates, the recognitional and judgemental processes that then ensue and what a mind must be like to engage in these latter processes. To think about mental activity of the kind found at the second level, it seems that we have to postulate a subject.

Consider the following example. After hearing a commentary on a paper of mine once, I was unable to think of any response. My commentator looked at me expectantly. To break the silence, I said, "I am puzzled by your comments". It suddenly occurred to me that in this sentence I had what I was looking for. It displays the core of Kant's whole theory of the subject, including his reason for thinking that we must postulate that subjects exist. (It also contains the core of his theory of self-awareness, but that is the topic of the next chapters.) Let us examine it:

(1) I am puzzled by your comments.

This sentence displays what would seem to be one of the most basic structures of representations and awareness. When I said it, I expressed an experience, puzzlement at the comments, which seems to have or require the following elements:

(i) an object (intentional object or content), the comments as I perceived them;
(ii) acts of representing the comments, namely, hearing and being puzzled by them; and
(iii) a subject, namely, me, the person having the experience.

This tripartite structure is at the root of Kant's theory of representations and awareness. It has been argued that some states of awareness do not have an object – pains and mood states such as aimless anxiety, for example – but even here we can still distinguish state from subject. Before examining the need to postulate a subject displayed in (1), I should say a word about two other aspects of the example.

First, notice that I switched from representation talk to experience talk in the preceding paragraph. I did so for two reasons. As well as expressing a representation, (1) also expresses an attitude to what is represented. When Kant uses the terminology of experience and object, his adherence to the tripartite scheme is clear. When he uses the terminology of representations, however, the distinction between the representation itself and the object or content represented in it tends to get blurred. Thus, commentators who use this terminology tend to miss the extent to which Kant's work is built around this fundamental schema of intentionality (act of subject directed to object) and is concerned with objects as experienced, not our experience of them. Kitcher's earlier work is an example.[2] That being said, I will now switch back to talking about representations.

Second, I had better say a word about the object identified in (i). By 'object' I mean 'intentional object'. I am using the term here in a sense broad enough to encompass not just states of affairs, what could be described in a proposition, but also objects and events. Various questions can arise about what stands in the object position of statements of the form 'I see . . . ' and 'I want . . . '. For example, in the sentence 'I want something to eat', does 'something to eat' describe an object? It would take us far afield to deal with such problems; since Kant focused on the subject side of experience, I will do my best to skirt them. Note, however, that objects of representations do not have to be anything real. (This has important implications for the question of what kind of object Kant had in mind in his 'deduction of the object' in the Transcendental Deduction [TD], as we will see in Chapter 5:1.) In the experience expressed by (1), the object is something real, but that is an accidental feature of the situation. Another feature of (1) is accidental, too. As well as displaying the subject, (1) also refers to it – 'I am puzzled . . . '; the subject is represented in the experience (1) expresses. For our purposes here, that is irrelevant. Here we are exploring the fact that experiences have a subject. The subject's representation of itself is one of the topics of the next two chapters.

In the structure displayed by (1), act and object have received most of the attention for many years. For example, Paul Churchland, in his interesting theory that attitudes of intentionality (having a belief that *P*, having a desire that *P*) can be modelled on what he calls numerical attitudes (having a length$_m$ [m = metres] of *n*, having a charge$_c$ of *n*, and so on, where *n* stands for a number), does not even consider whether there might be a need for a subject when we are dealing with belief, hope, perception, and the like that is not present when we are dealing with mass and length![3] In general, recent work on the mind largely ignores the subject (pun intended).

Yet the subject cannot be ignored. There can be no awareness of something that is not *someone's*. Every representation *of* something represents it *to someone*. Every intention is intended *by someone*. Every action is the action of *some agent*. Everything meant by an utterance is meant *by someone*. That is why we must postulate a subject. In general, if we characterize an event or state of affairs in the language of intentionality, we must postulate that it is had by someone. As Dennett has put it, "Wherever a theory relies on . . . intentionality, there a little man is concealed".[4] If there were intrinsic representations – that is to say, states that represented, and represented one specific thing, no matter where they were, how they were connected to other representations, or whether they were related to minds – then this would not be the case; representations would not have to represent to someone. The classical empiricist theories of representation of Locke and Hume may be like this. But there is a well-known, compelling reason to deny that anything can be an intrinsic representation in this sense; anything can represent more than one thing in more than one way, depending on how it is taken. A 'taking' requires a 'taker'. Moreover, Kant would have been sympathetic to this argument: what something is representing gets determined, in his view, only when a judgement is made about it. In general, anything can be a representation only in a system of representations, all of them synthesized by a sensible and cognitive system. Indeed, as we saw in Section 1 of the preceding chapter, Kant knew that even something as basic as where one representation ends and another begins is often merely an artefact of judgement, not anything intrinsic to what is being judged.[5]

As we conceive it, the subject is the aspect of a system of representations that does the judging (interpreting) and recognizing of representations, something that can take representations up, let representations go, transform representations into new representations without itself changing in any essential way. It is able to refer to itself, indeed to itself as itself, knowing that it is itself to which it is referring, and to do so using distinctive acts of reference that yield the distinctive form of awareness I call *apperceptive self-awareness* (see Chapters 3 and 4). It is the thing that is aware of multiple objects as one object, a topic of the next section, and of itself as the thing that is aware of them all – in Kant's jargon, as their common subject (see Chapters 3 and 4 again). We conceive of this subject as separate from its representations, able to take some up, drop others, store yet others, without itself changing in any way significant to its being a subject and continuing to be the subject it is. Such a being would not be a person, not a full person at any rate; being a person requires representations, dispositions, competences, personality traits, and so on, as well as a unified thing that is aware of them.[6] In fact, the subject as we conceive it is a homunculus, though the homunculus to which I am referring when I refer to myself!

Even though each and every one of us probably ascribes one every time we ascribe a representation, to ourselves or to anyone else, the subject disappeared from research in the decades after World War II. One reason for this neglect, I suggested in Chapter 1, was a bias against the mind as a whole. Thus, the subject, awareness, and attendant things like unity and synthesis were all neglected. The same was true of Kant's views on these things. It was as though there was suddenly a taboo against talking about properties of the mind as a whole. About the only aspect of the mind as a whole that received regular attention in these years was its identity – what it is to be one person over time. Even here the question was usually raised in such a way as to minimize the fact that it was the identity of *the mind or person as a whole* that was being studied, not just particular causal continuities and the like. Moreover, only identity across time was studied; identity at a time was also ignored.

Recently, this history of neglect has begun to change. The change appeared first among cognitivists in other disciplines. Here I am thinking, for example, of Minsky's society of mind or the work on what Newell calls production systems such as Anderson's ACT* or his own Soar. In the past few years, philosophers have joined in, first in the form of the work of the Churchlands and others on how connectionist models might be able to account for large-scale integration of data and more recently in Dennett's multiple drafts model of awareness.[7] However, even these workers discuss the powers and abilities of the mind in isolation from the subject of experience. In most cases this is quite deliberate; the view is that the only hope for analysing the subject of experience is to analyse it away, model the properties ascribed to it in terms of something that is not a subject of experience. This, of course, is to analyse the powers of the mind in isolation from – the mind! Perhaps that is ultimately the right strategy, but so far no theory of how mental powers and abilities either depend on or even result in a subject of experience and no theory of full-blown awareness have emerged, certainly none to match the best available theories of mental powers and contents.

When contemporary philosophers and cognitive scientists ask questions about the mind as a whole, they tend to ask questions like the following: Are representations sententially structured in a language of thought, or do we represent in some other way? By what rules and using what kinds and how many levels of computations (and possibly other manipulations) does a cognitive system combine elements of representations into full representations and tie representations together so as to generate coherent patterns of action? Can states of ourselves have semantic or intentional content independent of a world? Do beliefs and other mental states exhibit semantic holism? And so on. Once upon a time, however, philosophers asked questions such as these: Does the mind have parts or is it simple? Could a mind end and if so how – by disintegrating or just by fading out? (Kant had a marvellous word for such fading: 'elanguescence' [*Elanguescenz,* B414].) What is it for something to be one mind at a given time? What is the mind's awareness of the world like? What is the mind's awareness of *itself* like? (The contrast is with its awareness both of the world and of its own particular states.) When I appear to myself as myself, how do I appear? What, if anything, does the way I appear to myself tell me about my nature?

Kant's questions are of this latter type. How must the mind synthesize representations so as to be aware of a number of them as the object of a single complex representation or to be aware of itself as their subject? What sort of unity is required to do this? Is the mind itself just a representation? To be sure, the activities and contents of the mind are eminently worthy of study, but the mind as a whole has properties, too. Some of them, moreover, have never been reduced to any combination of particular features, its various unities being a prime example. Indeed, the question of how the mind as a whole relates to its particular features is itself an interesting question; it is an instance of another general question that is out of favour: How does an object relate to its properties? (Kant raised this question, too, at least once, when he asked how 'successive determinations' get referred to 'the numerically identical self' in his introduction to the Third Paralogism [A362]; see Chapter 8.)

Now, as Dennett and others have quite rightly insisted, the little man cannot be left unexamined, an undischarged homunculus or exempt agent (exempt from capture in a theory).[8] Nor, I would add, can the questions about the mind as a whole that we associate with the subject of experience continue to go unasked. Here representational theories of mind face a grave danger. If representations *presuppose* a subject, it is hard to see how they could be used to say anything informative *about* the subject, to 'discharge' it. So, suggests Dennett hyperbolically, psychology is impossible! I am not so sure that representational theory is this impotent; indeed, I will argue that one kind of representational theory can meet the danger, namely, the kind Kant developed. (See Section 6 of this chapter and Chapter 9:5.) Instead of taking a high road such as this, however, most recent philosophers have attempted to circumvent the problem. Two strategies have been developed – eliminativism and homuncular functionalism.[9]

The eliminativists approach the problem of the subject by attempting to dissolve it. As they see it, the need to postulate a subject is merely an artefact of intentional language. Switch to some other vocabulary to describe the activities of the mind and the subject will disappear! The model of neural networks transforming vectors in a multidimensional phase space seems to be the currently favoured candidate.[10] Homuncular functionalists rather doubt that the 'real patterns' captured by intentional discourse could be mapped onto anything described in any other vocabulary, so they do not hold out much hope for the eliminativist programme.[11] If we keep intentional discourse, we must also keep the little man, of course, and they are prepared to do so. However, they insist that we need not remain stuck with one big, unanalysed homunculus per person. Quite the reverse. The one, big, smart homunculus can be reduced to a fleet of small, stupid homunculi flying in loose formation, each with a single or at most a small number of well-characterized functions.[12] Unfortunately, the mind is more complicated than is dreamt of in either philosophy. A few paragraphs back, we sketched a picture of the subject of experience as we tend to conceive of it: the subject is the thing that does the judging, is aware of itself, and so on. Perhaps it would be naive to expect everything in our folk picture to survive critical modelling, but some parts of that picture cannot be dismissed. No one has made much progress with capturing the parts we need to keep in any non-intentional language or homuncular decomposition.

Of the properties commonly attributed to the subject – the big homunculus – the following appear to create particular problems for either strategy. First, judgements are not only made in us by subagents; sometimes we make judgements, deliberately and aware of what we are doing. (What underlies these activities is another matter, of course.) That requires, second, that something in us be aware of a whole group of representations at the same time. Third, for at least many kinds of subject, the thing that is aware of whole groups of representations is also aware of itself as the common subject of these representations. It is hard to think that any of these phenomena are chimera, yet it is equally hard to see how to capture them in either eliminativism or homuncular functionalism. Dennett's recent attempt in *Consciousness Explained* to show how at least short-lived subjects could result from competition among multiple, draft narrative-fragments – the 'virtual captains', as he calls them – is perhaps the most heroic effort in that direction to date. Other less directly Kantian questions about the mind as a whole also press themselves on us. If various mental functions are performed by different systems in the brain or different simple-minded homunculi, what could the process be like that synthesizes these various activities into the single, simultaneously introspectible patterns of representation, belief, and behaviour so central to beings like us? How does this system integrate information that is located in it? (Moreover, just being located in it is not enough; the information must be of use to it – a point closely related to one Kant makes in TD, as we will see in Chapters 6 and 9.) How can such a system situate itself vis-à-vis its information in the ways that it does? How it is able to report on various bits of information in ways that relate them to other bits? And so on and so forth. In general, in aware mental life, no matter how described, aspects of the subject as traditionally conceived appear in a number of places. At least those aspects of the subject are not just an artefact of the language of intentionality.

If we recognize that the subject of awareness cannot be ignored, we must also not prejudge what it might be like. The someone to whom a representation is represented is probably not just a formal place holder on the model of 'It' in 'It is raining' (though even this unlikely view has been attributed to Kant!),[13] but it could in principle turn out to be almost anything else, ranging from Hume's bundle of representations and abilities (Dennett's multiple draft model is a new bundle theory) to some special sort of representation that in some way contains other representations, to a full-blooded 'thing that thinks' (material or immaterial). In particular, I urge that we not assume *ab initio* that the subject of representations has to be something radically unlike the representations it has. Kant's final view on the matter, it seems to me, was quite the reverse; the subject of representations is itself a representation, a special kind of representation that I will introduce shortly as a *global representation*. Recently, Fodor and Dennett have toyed with the idea of a self-representing representation, the thought being that we will never understand representations or discharge the homuncular subject until we devise a representation that can represent to itself.[14] As a response to the problem of the little man, this move has promise. However, if there are no intrinsic representations, if something can be a representation only if connected to a whole host of items similar to itself in an integrated cognitive system capable of judging and recognizing them, then any representation that could be self-representing would have to be very special. In particular, it would have to be a representation that is also the whole system of representations that represent to it. We will examine the requirements for an adequate self-representing representation in Chapter 9:1 and show how Kant's proposal meets these requirements in Chapter 9:5 (see also Section 6 of this chapter).

Kant had nothing to say about our inclination to postulate a homuncular subject; he would not have thought that there is anything in the inclination that needs to be explained. Equally, he had no interest in 'reducing' the subject – explaining its functioning in terms of nonaware, nonsubject events. Nor, of course, does he say anything about how the nonintentional machinery of the brain could generate something that could do the jobs that we ascribe to a subject of experience. Rather than attempting to model the subject's functioning in terms of simpler and less mysterious events, he focused on characterizing the subject as we find it and exploring the constraints on it. Ultimately, we would like to have a theory of the subject from the bottom up – from ensembles of neurons or some simple unit of behaviour or a small unit of information such as Dawkins' 'memes' – to a subject of experience. Even if we found such a theory, however, we would still have to work the other way, too, that is, from the top down, before we could know that it was adequate; we would have to characterize the functions of a subject and the constraints that having such functions impose and work out what *sort* of apparatus could realize these functions within these constraints. This is the part of the project where Kant can still help, because he did precisely this sort of top-down work. He identified some of the functions, inferred some of the constraints, and studied the implications of both for various forms of awareness and self-awareness. These functions and constraints and the forms of awareness and self-awareness they affect are the topics of this book.[15]

2 'One single experience': the unity of experience

As Kant saw it, the constraints on what a subject of awareness can be like are rather special. There are constraints on what its experience must be like and on what the subject itself must be like. To deal with experience first, a subject can have not only the experience that would be expressed by

(1) I am puzzled by your comments,

but also and at the same time experiences that would be expressed as follows:

(2) I love my wife.
(3) I am enjoying the music I hear outside.
(4) I believe our agreement was to meet at 6:00.
(5) Yesterday I thought I understood Kant's notion of the object.
(6) I wish the world was a fairer place.

We could generate a similar list out of examples Kant himself gives: I count up the number of some group of objects, see a triangle, recognize a physical object (A103–5), and understand a sentence (A352).

Moreover, and this is a crucial point, we can treat whole groups of experiences such as these in much the same way as we treat individual experiences. For example, in the same way that we can make judgements relating item to item within the object or content of a single representation, we can compare the objects or contents of one representation to the contents of other representations, and also one representation to another. For example, I can compare yesterday's clarity to today's bafflement, my enjoyment of the music to my sense that I should keep my appointment. (By 'object or content' I mean 'intentional object or content', of course.) When we make the latter two kinds of comparisons, we are aware of all the contents or representations being compared 'at the same time', as we are inclined to say, or, a better saying, as parts of the object of a single representation. We make them (and often many other things as well) into what Kant also called 'one knowledge' or 'one single experience' (A110). Indeed, Kant thought that in this one single experience "all perceptions are represented" (past as well as present? of everything in both inner and outer sense?). But let us stick to the less ambitious claim for the moment.

When the elements being compared are parts of the content or object of a single representation of the usual sort, the claim just made about the conditions of comparing items to one another is fairly clear. When we turn to comparisons of more than one representation or of the contents of more than one representation, however, the idea becomes quite murky. What could be meant by saying that here, too, the elements being compared must be parts of 'one single experience'? The notion of 'single experience' at work here is not easy to explicate, but the following might help a little. When two items are parts of a single experience, one can be aware of either of them without ceasing to be aware of the other; this makes possible the way of comparing them to one another to which I referred. (To the extent that this comment describes a single experience, it should be clear that it also describes a single object of experience.) This comment suffers, of course, from circularity, but that makes it neither useless nor, as we will see in the next chapter, particularly unusual, at least so far as concepts to do with unity and awareness are concerned.

Kant's thought, I will argue in Chapter 6, was that in the same way as a representation of the usual sort has a single object, individual representations and/or their objects become the single more complex object of "one single experience" (A110). To make sense of this idea, Kant postulated a special kind of experience, which he called a *general experience* (A110). This experience also has a single object, but its single object is many individual representations and/or their objects, "all of which belong to one and the same general experience" (A110). (Kant seems to have thought that we have only one general experience at a time or perhaps one altogether [see Chapter 4:3].) The person having the experience can be aware of many or all of these representations and objects as parts of the single object of this general experience. In my view, this notion is the key to his whole theory of the mind (and also, I would argue, his whole theory of experience). It is still of the highest interest.

Given the close relationship between at least some of his uses of 'experience' (*Erfahrung*) and 'representation' (*Vorstellung*), Kant could just as easily have spoken about a 'general representation' as a general experience.[16] I will call the thing in question a *global representation,* a name rather more distinctive than Kant's, and define the term as follows:

Global representation = ***df:*** a representation that has a number of particular representations and/or their objects or contents as its *single global object*.

I next define 'single global object' as follows:

Single global object = ***df:*** an intentional object that represents a number of intentional objects and/or the representations that represent them, such that to be aware of any of these objects and/or their representations is also to be aware of other objects and/or representations that make it up and of the collection of them as a single group.

Let me add four points. (1) A person need not be aware of the global representation he or she is having. As I will argue in Chapter 6:II:2, it is difficult to think of any kind of representation for which being aware of oneself is a requirement of having it. (2) However, if a person is aware of his or her global representation, I will suggest in Chapter 4:3 that he or she will be aware of only one global representation at a time. (3) It seems plausible to suggest that a person's global representation contains psychological states themselves, as well as the objects or contents of psychological states. (4) It may also be that one could only be aware of having representations whose objects are part of the object of the global representation that one is having at any given moment. We will return to these ideas in Chapter 9.

Perhaps I should explain why I have belaboured these definitions. It is customary to express the idea behind Kant's notion of the unity of experience and the closely related notion of the unity of consciousness (see Section 4) by talking about being aware of a number of things 'at the same time' or as parts of a 'single complex thought'.[17] However, this way of expressing the idea falls short in one crucial respect. One could be aware of two or more things at the same time and perhaps even as parts of a single thought, depending on how 'single thought' is defined, without being aware of any group of them together. (This way of putting the point is based on remarks Kant makes at B134. We will examine this passage in Chapter 9:4.) Another way to put the point would be to say that one can be aware of a number of things individually at one time without being aware of any multiple of them as a group.

I have found only one adequate way to capture what we mean by 'together' and 'collectively' here. In these cases, awareness of any one item *just is* awareness of other items and of a number of the items as a group, as a singularity made of a multiplicity – multiple items, one act of awareness. Thus, one can be aware of any one item while remaining aware *and aware that one is aware* of other items in the single object. There being only one act of awareness is also what makes it possible to be aware of a number of items 'at the same time'; but the latter is not sufficient for the former. (Equally, being aware that one is aware is not necessary for unified awareness of a number of items in a single object. That is so, at any rate, if awareness does not require self-awareness, as I will argue Kant held. I will defend this unorthodox reading in Chapters 3 and 6.) I have claimed that the notion of awareness of one item being awareness of other items and of groups of items as a singularity is the key to his theory. This is the notion I am attempting to capture in the concepts of the global representation and global object. The notion in cognitive psychology of 'chunking', of grouping a number of items so that one need represent or remember only one item to have access to them all, is a rough contemporary analogue.

Is there any evidence that we actually have global representations, are aware of a number of individual representations and/or their objects as the single object of a single representation? Go back to the experiences expressed by sentences (1) to (6). I can relate the objects of the representations these experiences include to one another. ('His comments are louder than the music I'm hearing'.) I can relate the experiences themselves to one another. ('I can't stay and listen to this music because of our agreement to meet at 6:00'.) And I can do these things in a number of different ways. The best way I can think of to account for our ability to do these things is to say that we are aware of them as a single object, in the sense of 'single object' just defined. Indeed, all thinking, imagining, doubting, and the like, which involve relating representations or objects of representations to other representations or objects of representations, seem to require that we have a global representation of them; I can think about more than one representation or object only if I am aware of all the representations or objects in question in a single representation – a 'higher-order' representation of which these representations and/or their objects are the object.

3 Kant's doctrine of synthesis

To explain both how the mind can generate objects for individual representations of the usual kind and how these representations and their objects can come to 'belong' to a global representation, Kant postulated a process that he called *synthesis*. As we saw at the beginning of Chapter 1, the notion of synthesis has sometimes been ridiculed by analytically oriented commentators, but the idea is neither very strange nor, at the level of generality at which Kant developed it, very controversial. The mind has to have *some* way to relate the various things it experiences to one another, and it would be highly unlikely, to say the least, that this process has nothing to do with its ability to have and recognize single representations and single objects of representation as parts of a single global representation. In light of the growing awareness of the importance of understanding 'ensembles' – groups of beliefs, groups of meanings, systems of representations, ensembles of neurons, 'frames' for determining relevancy, and so on – the question of how the mind connects psychological states to other psychological states in the vast number of ways it does deserves to receive more attention than it is receiving. Kant's doctrine of synthesis could be a good place to start.

Synthesis, as Kant saw it, is broadly two activities. It is the tying of elements together into a single object or unified content of a representation, and it is the tying of representations and their objects together into 'one knowledge'. Synthesis comes in three parts, namely, locating something in time and often in space (Kant calls this synthesis of apprehension), associating current representations with earlier ones (synthesis of reproduction), and unification of the various elements of a representation, or a number of representations, under concepts (synthesis of recognition in a concept). Such acts of synthesis are what make it possible for us to make judgements about a single representation and about groups of representations, judgements that relate item to item within the object or content of a single representation and that relate the contents of one representation to the contents of other representations, or representations to other representations, in a group of representations. Synthesis makes all this possible in the following way. To make comparisons, I urged in the preceding section, we must be aware of the elements compared 'at the same time', that is, as parts of the object of a single representation. For the elements compared to become parts of a single object, they must be 'tied together', related to one another; the activity of tying them together, relating them to one another, is what Kant called synthesis.

Not only is Kant's doctrine of synthesis not very strange, but both parts of it are again appearing in contemporary work. The first has reappeared as the notion of binding (in the psychological, not the linguistic sense). Colours, lines, shapes, textures, and the like are represented in widely dispersed areas of the brain. Somehow these dispersed representations get tied together into a representation of an object. This process is called *binding*. Treisman and her co-workers have even erected a very Kantian theory holding that three stages of visual processing are involved.[18] The three stages involve feature modules, a map of locations, and recognition network/object files; they parallel Kant's apprehension, reproduction, and recognition in concepts. It is a testimony to how little is known about Kant's work on synthesis that workers on these processes invented a new term instead of just continuing to use the one Kant used. As to the second part of Kant's doctrine of synthesis, aspects of the process of tying representations together into 'one knowledge' are now being studied by theorists as different as the production system cognitivists mentioned in Section 1 and semantic holists such as Davidson and Dennett. The very attempt to tie both kinds of synthesis together in a single theory marks Kant's contribution as significant. Few contemporary theorists even try to unite the two processes in a single theory.

When the elements being compared are parts of the content or object of an individual representation, the claim just made about the conditions of comparing items to one another is fairly clear. When I see a book, for example, I will have perceptions of various colours, shapes, textures, locations, materials, and the like. When I perceive distinct, individuated, persisting books, it is natural to think that relating properties of the kinds just listed to one another will have something to do with the creation of these perceptions. Of course, controversies can arise even here, as the debates about primary and secondary properties and whether there are distinctively phenomenal properties illustrate (debates I have tried to skirt in what I have just written). But the idea is at least fairly clear. When we turn to comparisons of representations of more than one object, however, the idea becomes less clear. When I compare one book to another book, by height or colour or interest, for example, what could it mean to say that here, too, the elements being compared must be parts of a single object of a single representation? Kant's thought seems to have been that in the same way as acts of synthesis tie elements of the content of an individual representation together into a single object of representation, they tie a number of individual representations and objects of representations together into a single more complex object of a global representation (see Chapter 6). Indeed, it was to make sense of this idea that Kant postulated the general experience.

As an example of the way questions related to synthesis have been neglected recently, especially synthesis of the second type, consider Lackner and Garrett's famous sentence-interpretation experiments. These experiments show that the interpretation of an ambiguous sentence consciously heard in one earphone is affected by hearing another, disambiguating sentence played in the opposite ear-phone even when the second sentence is played so softly that the subject is not aware of hearing it. (The interpretation of 'The officer put out the lantern to signal the attack' will be affected by playing 'He extinguished the lantern' in the other ear-phone even when the subject is not aware of hearing the second sentence.) In the many discussions of these experiments I have read, I have never come across even one that raises what would seem to be a central question – How is the mind able to bring its encounter with the second sentence to bear on its interpretation of the first? Theorists' interest in these experiments has stopped with the fact that the subject could not be aware of the mechanism connecting the two sentences. Yet the subject's lack of awareness of the second sentence is not even essential to the question I am raising, though it heightens the mystery: if the kind of comparison with awareness that synthesis often makes possible is not involved here, then just how do subjects manage to relate the two sentences to one another? Saying that the connecting mechanism, whatever it is, does not operate 'consciously' is not saying very much.

Consider another example. Many philosophers and cognitive scientists now believe that when reasons are the cause of an action, this cause will consist at minimum of both beliefs and a motive of some kind, connected to one another and to the action by the exercise of rational abilities. The nature, scope, and ontological status of this belief–desire holism, as it is called, are all hotly disputed. Do such holistic explanations really explain anything or will they eventually be eliminated? If they do explain something, how wide a range of psychological phenomena can they explain? Are reasons real states and/or events that could themselves be causally efficacious or are they merely instrumentally useful postulates? (Kant of course would have said they are real.) And so on. But few even ask how the mind can do what is necessary for holistic explanations to work, how it can actually bring beliefs and desires (or their underlying neural substrates) together under conditions of rationality and relate them to one another and to other psychological states so as to generate decisions and actions. How can the mind tie things together in this way? Moreover, when beliefs, desires, and actions are tied together in this way, we can usually be aware of the whole group of them in a single representation. Does the former have anything to do with making the latter possible? It appears that there is work to be done by a theory of synthesis.

The process of forming objects of awareness is what Kant called apperception; the specific part of apperception concerned with uniting a multiplicity of individual objects together into a global object is transcendental apperception (TA). Acts of apperception are acts of synthesis. (In the second edition, Kant got some mileage out of a concept of empirical apperception, too. Indeed, the term appears in the first edition [A107], but Kant does nothing with it there; moreover, it seems to have a different sense from the sense it has in the second edition. We will return to this difficult term in Chapter 10:3.) A subject of experience, at any rate a subject of an experience like ours, must have whatever it takes not just to have individual representations but to have global representations, in which many representations and their objects 'belong' to one representation. The theory that it is acts of synthesis by TA that do this does not seem too implausible.

4 The unity of consciousness

Having said something about experience and its unification in the global representation, let us turn to the constraints on what the subject of this representation can be like. What are some of the constraints on a subject able to perform acts of TA to generate global representations? In Kant's theory, the two most striking constraints are (1) that there must be a single common subject (A350) of all the representations and/or objects of representation united in a global representation and (2) that the awareness this subject has of these objects and/or representations must be unified. Kant refers to this unity in a number of ways at different places: unity of consciousness (A103), unity of apperception (A105 and A108), absolute unity of the thinking being (A353). He seems to have the following thought in mind: I am the subject not just of single states of awareness, but of a great many states of awareness in a single representation, and I am the same subject of each of them. The same unity is found in connection with actions; one and the same subject is the agent not just of single actions but of a great many actions, and the agent who coordinates and connects them is the single common agent of all of them. Note the synchronic dimension of this unity.

In addition, many global representations also have a temporal dimension. In such representations, as well as the current representation, there is also a component of retained earlier experience. Any representation that we acquire in a series of temporal steps, such as hearing a sentence, makes this clear. (We hear the words one after another.) Kant was well aware of this point (A104 and A352). We will explore the implications of this temporality for the composition and persistence of the mind in Chapters 3, 7, and 8. Kant says some surprising things about how little persistence is required in a subject to accommodate this dimension of its experience. In addition to the temporal dimension Kant considered, it has been argued more recently by Anscombe, Dennett, Wollheim, and others that there are constraints on the whole history, the whole biography, of a subject, but Kant did not get this far.[19]

The kind of unity that Kant called the unity of consciousness is the unity displayed when a person is aware of a number of representations and/or their objects, as we say, 'at the same time', by which, I suggested earlier, we really mean 'as a single object'. The particular single object Kant had in mind, of course, was the single object of a global representation. For Kant, being aware of a single object requires a single act of awareness. However, there is more to the unity in the consciousness than just being singular:

Unity of consciousness =*df:* (i) a single act of consciousness, which (ii) makes one aware of a number of representations and/or objects of representation in such a way that to be aware of any of this group is also to be aware of at least some others in the group and as a group.

As this definition makes clear, awareness being unified involves more than just being one state of awareness. The state of awareness is not just singular, it is unified. Indeed, simply being one is not even what is distinctive about a state of awareness being unified. The distinctive feature of awareness being unified is the same as the distinctive feature of global representations and global objects, namely, that in one act of awareness we are aware of a multiplicity of items as a single, grouped object.

The definition I have just given of the unity of consciousness is nonstandard in one respect. In the eyes of many commentators, Kant held that the presence of one, unified awareness requires identity of mind or person. Henrich and Allison both hold this view.[20] As I noted in Chapter 1:1, Kitcher restricts unity of consciousness even further, to oneness of mind *across time*. On my definition, by contrast, it is possible to have one, unified system of awareness without being one mind and certainly without being one person (as defined by any criterion other than having one or a unified system of awareness). At least for identity across time, Kant also argued for this possibility – or so I will argue in Chapter 8. Unity of consciousness may require identity of *consciousness* (B134), and identity of mind may require unity of consciousness (A108), but Kant nowhere says that unity of consciousness requires identity of mind. Both Henrich and Allison make something like this distinction between unity and identity; but unlike me, they both think that unity of consciousness does require identity of mind (for Henrich, only a 'moderate' identity, whatever that is!).[21]

Kant placed great emphasis on the unity of consciousness, both positively and negatively. Positively, he held that minds must be one and unified across a range of both contemporaneous representations and successive representations if they are to have conceptualized representation, of the kind that we have at any rate. Indeed, the unity that minds must have (note that I am carefully avoiding any suggestion that unity of consciousness requires being one mind, either at a time or across time) struck Kant as so considerable and he was so impressed with the idea that all one's representations 'belong' to this single experience that he could even speak of unified awareness as "the subjective form" of all our concepts and representations (A361). Some commentators have taken this remark and others like it to indicate that, for Kant, positing a subject is a purely formal requirement of the way we talk about states of awareness (sentences need subjects). Kitcher may be an example, but I will leave that possibility for Chapter 10:2. As will be clear by now, I disagree – but I will save my reasons for saying that for Chapter 10, too. When Kant suggested that unified awareness is part of the form of experience, I think he had something quite different and much more interesting in mind. Kant concluded by arguing that for unified awareness to be possible, objects or contents of conceptualized representation must be synthesized under concepts. (He also had a view as to which concepts we must use, namely, the concepts of Euclidean geometry and Newtonian mechanics. Not many people follow him as far as these detailed claims now.) Negatively, from a mind having the unity that unified awareness confers, nothing follows concerning its composition, its identity, especially its identity across time, or its materiality or immateriality, points he argued in his attacks on the Second, Third, and Fourth Paralogisms.

If awareness must be unified across a range of representations and can be unified only when objects of representation are linked by acts of synthesis, that should hold implications for the various sensible and cognitive abilities used to perform these acts of synthesis. In particular, one would expect that these abilities would have to be unified, too. Perceptual, linguistic, judgemental (identificatory and feature-placing), volitional, memory, and other competences are all used in forming and manipulating at least a great many of our representations. The kind of unity would be different – it would be integration of competences, not unity of consciousness – but it would seem that anything that could synthesize objects, especially global objects that connect representations and/or their objects to one another, would have to have a highly integrated control system. Kant gives us the framework for a theory here, too. First, for experience to be possible, sensibility, imagination, and understanding must all work together.[22] Second, the framework of concepts within which the understanding and imagination perform their acts of synthesis on the material of sensibility, that is to say, the 'forms of judgment', must itself form a unity. However, this is as far as Kant seems to have gone with this topic. In particular and most surprisingly, Kant never seems to have connected the integration of competences to the unity of consciousness.

To be aware of the objects of a number of representations as a global object, there must be a unified mind aware of all these objects. As I noted earlier, the unity of the mind has fallen into disfavor lately. When the idea of unity is mentioned at all, the aim is usually to heap scorn on it. Strangely enough, however, it seems as if everybody is talking about its *disunity!* Davidson, Fodor, Dennett, Pylyshyn, and the Churchlands come immediately to mind. The mind, it is said, is made up of 'modules' (a term Fodor has popularized), and many of them work out of the sight and control of the aware (meaning self-aware) mind.[23] Distinguishing two levels of mental activity as I did, I can readily accept this claim. It does seem to describe what goes on in the prerecognitional level. Does it entail that Kant was wrong about the need for unity of consciousness, for one unified mind? Not at all. For there is still the other level. The most the modularity claim does is to shrink the range over which the unity extends, shrink the little man, and identify a number of things that we cannot introspect. If something is out of the sight or control of the mind, we should ask, out of the sight or control of what? And when something else is within sight and control, what properties must the thing that has such sight and control have? It seems to me that practically anything that could be said about the unity of a mind conceived in the pre-twentieth-century way as having broad awareness and control of its states and events could also be said of the unity of the twentieth-century mind whose range of awareness and control has shrunk so dramatically. Modules there may be, but a unified mind there is, too.

Yet with the sole exceptions of Foder and more recently Dennett (in a way), not one of the philosophers just mentioned even raises the question of whether the mind needs unity or what its unity might be like; nor do Putnam, Shoemaker, Nagel, Parfit, Nozick, Dretske, Burge – the list could go on.[24] This is strange; it hardly seems controversial that the mind has (or is) unified awareness, at least in part, though how far this unity extends and over what can be debated. Indeed, without knowing what the unity of consciousness is, it is hard to see how we can even talk coherently about the situations so prominent at the moment where unity is absent or damaged: self-deception, repression, brain bisection cases, multiple personality disorder, our encapsulated cognitive modules, the kind of cases Dennett discusses where one says one thing to oneself and does the exact opposite ('I must be careful of this pan, it is very hot', reaching out and burning myself while I say it), and so on.[25] What are these cases missing that makes them cases of *disunity?* What would cases of *unity* be like?

5 The kind of unity we have

What this unity is like is a far from straightforward matter. The same unity appears to feature in the mind, awareness, acts of apperception, representations, and objects of representation, both global and particular. Kant thought that this kind of unity is unique. It is more than just being one and the same as oneself; mere numerical unity, being one of something and the same as itself, is '*analytic* unity'. This unity "is possible only under the presupposition of a certain *synthetic* unity" (B133 and B135; we will discuss this distinction further in Chapter 9:3). Unity becomes synthetic when it is a matter of being aware of a number of things as one thing, one represented object, in such a way that to be aware of any part of this one object is to be aware of others in the group and of at least some of them as a group (see the preceding definition of 'unity of consciousness'). The latter unity is shared by minds, global representations, global objects, acts of apperception and awareness, ordinary representations and objects, and perhaps even space and time. Even concepts being single and common to a variety of instances requires that these instances be tied together in a synthetic unity (B133n).

Because Kant says some quite remarkable things about synthetic unity and because what follows will be the only section of the book devoted to the people, we will pay more attention to Kant's actual words than we have in the rest of this chapter. His first gloss on the specialness of synthetic unity is to say that it is "not the category of unity" (B131). The category of unity is the unity of being numerically one. Synthetic unity is more than being one in *this* way. The reason from within Kant's own system, as he tells us late in the *Critique,* is that we cannot apply a category to an object unless "the schema of the category is given in sensible intuition" (A682 = B710). What he means, roughly, is that we can apply the categories only where we can individuate temporally located objects. We cannot do that with a subject of representations for at least two reasons, at least when we consider it from the point of view it has on itself. First, to be one of something is to be different from another of something. The oneness of the unity of consciousness is not a oneness which is experience dividing, which distinguishes self as subject from any other. (I will attempt to justify this claim in detail in Chapter 4:4.) Second, the unity I have is not the result of any individuating judgement, any application of the category of unity to myself. Indeed, my being one is a precondition of making any judgements (see Chapter 8:6). In these ways, my unity as one subject is different from the unity of a table as one table. As a result, my unity appears to be very special: I appear to myself to be one and never many (A107); noncomposite (simple), not complex (Chapter 7); and to persist in a special way (Chapter 8).

We can identify at least three special features of synthetic unity. The first is the point about it being a precondition; it is nicely captured in a remark of Bennett's. To think of myself as a plurality of things, he says, is to think of *my* being aware of this plurality, "and that pre-requires an undivided *me*".[26] Unlike one anything else, it is not optional that I think of myself as one (A107). By 'me' he means not just being one but also being the same one across my experience. Thus, it is impossible, for example, to imagine oneself not merely going into a fissioning machine but also changing into and coming out as two minds. I cannot think of myself going through fission because I cannot find any way to imagine myself being aware of two different intentional objects without combining them into a single intentional object; I must think of my experience as one. (We will discuss this thought experiment further in Chapter 7:3.) The second point is contained in what was just said. The oneness of synthetic unity is a matter of something being common to a number of particular representations tied together as one representation. Why can I not think of myself as a 'we', or not just a 'we'? (The idea that the mind is a 'we' is to be found in theories of mind from Plato to Freud, but in all of them I have to picture the 'we' as making up *me*.) The reason is the special singularity that representations and the contents of representations have: I cannot be aware of a representation or an intentional object *except as singular*. The third special feature of synthetic unity is that it requires integration of skills, representations, volitions, cognition, and who knows what else, a requirement we touched on in the preceding section. Representations are the result of an integration of capacities and competences of great complexity; think of representing oneself as subject.

In sum, there does seem to be something special about synthetic unity. Characterizing this specialness is strangely difficult. As Kant said, "This unity . . . is not the category of unity" (B131). That is to say, it is not a matter of being one of something (as opposed to two or ten or . . . of that kind of thing). If someone were to ask of this unity, 'One what?' or 'Unified as one in what way?' we have no ready answer; we are dealing with a representation that "does not contain in itself the least manifoldness" (B135; see Chapters 4 and 7:3). In general, "Of the . . . unity of this subject . . . I possess no concept whatsoever" (A340 = B398).

Perhaps some things Kant said about space and time can help to situate these remarks. The unity of (our intuitions of) space and time seems to be similar (B136n). Anyone who has ever tried to explain in virtue of what space and time are one will know how difficult it is to say anything informative. The idea that space and time are unitary certainly seems to mean something to us, but it is exceedingly difficult to *say* much about it. Our unity seems to put up exactly the same resistance. Perhaps Kant thought that there is something about the kind of unity they share that cannot be said (described, expressed in concepts). In the much-neglected section on the Amphiboly, Kant castigated Leibniz for treating sensible representations as mere confused concepts. An amphiboly is "confounding an object of pure understanding with appearance" (A270 = B326). Leibniz was forced by this confusion, says Kant, to treat the contents of the *concepts* of space and time "as likewise valid of [their] appearances" (A276 = B332), that is to say, as the sum-total of what space and time consist in, so that "if a certain distinction is not in the concept of a thing . . . , it is also not to be found in the things themselves" (A281 = B337). Thus, he clearly thought that what we are aware of when we are aware of space and time outstrips what we can capture in any description of what their concepts contain. That is why we need intuitions as well as concepts. He may well have felt the same about the unity of the mind.

More radically, it is possible that Kant felt that we can say very little about synthetic unity at all. Other philosophers have held this about other things – Wittgenstein: "What the solipsist *means* is quite correct; only it cannot be said, but makes itself manifest".[27] We can grasp what the solipsist means, but we cannot describe it. (Whether the solipsist is correct we need not discuss.) Even more apposite is Augustine's famous dictum that we know what time is until we try to say what it is and then we no longer know what it is. Kant did not go as far as these two. He thought that a number of things can be said about the way in which space, time, and the subject are one – that their singularity consists in part in their being representations that contain many representations (B136n) and that the latter are parts of a whole, not instances of a concept, for example. For each of us, in addition, there is only one space, one time, and one subject of which we are aware 'from the inside'. So at least something can be said about the singularity that space, time, and the subject have.[28] Nevertheless, Kant seems to have felt that there is something about synthetic unity that outstrips description; he did say that "of the . . . unity of the subject . . . I possess no concept whatsoever" (A340 = B398). Kant's reasons for such a view would have been very different from Wittgenstein's, of course; the gap would reflect the fact that space, time, and the self are parts of the form of representation, not what language can and cannot do. But in both cases we would have something that we can grasp, something that makes itself manifest, which we cannot completely describe.

Whatever cannot be said about the unity we have, one thing we can say is that this unity does not appear to be like the unity that a system of relations has. Kant says that the categories make up a perfectly unified system, a totality in which nothing is left out. We will examine what he might have meant by this in Chapter 5:1, but whatever he meant, the unity I have does not seem to be like that. The unity of the Categories consists of the way their semantic relations to one another make it possible to conceptualize any representation, and all representations together (see Chapter 5:1). As I appear to myself as the common subject of diverse objects united in a global object, my unity does not appear to be a system of relations connecting discrete particulars. It is not like the unity of integrated components of a system, but the unity of an intentional object. Beyond this 'definition by what it is not', however, it is difficult to say much about what synthetic unity is like.

6 Tying it all together: the mind as a representation

If I, my awareness, apperception, global representations, and global objects have unity of the same kind, perhaps we should wonder if we are really dealing with multiple instances of unity here or just one: perhaps me, my awareness, the global representation, and the global object are all one thing described in different ways. In all these cases, the unity consists of particular representations and/or objects standing together in a single representation, and the way particular representations and objects stand together in a global representation and the way they stand together in me are precisely the same. Perhaps the mind itself just *is* a global representation.

Representational theories of mind are not exactly a rarity in philosophy, of course. To a first approximation, what makes Kant's theory different is that he did not just think of the mind as *having* a system of representations; he also thought of it as *being* a representation, namely, the global representation, the single representation within which many of the usual denizens of a system of representations are all contained. The global representation is not something the mind *has,* it is what the mind *is;* the mind is a representation. (At any rate, that is what the mind is as characterized psychologically. But we can know nothing of the mind under any other kind of description, that is to say, as noumenal [neural?] substrate, so this qualification is not as significant as it might seem.) This idea that the mind is a representation appears more clearly in the second edition than the first and it does not appear very clearly even there. We will explore the evidence for these claims in Chapter 9:5.

If the mind is a representation, we can immediately discharge the big homunculus in a purely representational theory; we will return to this, too, in Chapter 9. The idea that the mind is a representation can do other work, too, work that is more important for our present purposes. We have been exploring synthesis and unity. Though we will not consider it properly until the next chapters, we also need to bring apperceptive self-awareness (ASA) back for a moment. By postulating that the mind is a representation, Kant was able to tie all three of them together in a single theory. Here is how. To synthesize a collection of representations and/or their objects into a global object, Kant believed, these representations must all be the representations of a single, unified mind; as Kant put it, they must have a common subject (A350). If the single, unified mind *is* a global representation, that ties synthesis and unity together. Now for ASA. The crucial part of the notion of ASA is that each of us is aware of him- or herself not just as the subject of individual representations, but also as the common subject of a great many representations, the same subject of each of them. For it to be possible for us to do so, these representations must be united in a global representation, Kant's 'one single experience'. If the subject *is* this global representation, then to be aware of this representation *just is* to be aware of oneself; that is to say, the theory of ASA and the theory of the global representation would be parts of a single theory. Of course, as well as the representation, we would also have to posit something that 'realizes' this representation/mind, but we have to do that for any theory of mind.

To summarize the results of this chapter:

1. A number of features of the way we think about representations, experience, and so on give us *prima facie* good reasons to postulate a subject of experience.

2. To explain the unity of experience, Kant proposed the special kind of representation that we are calling a global representation.
3. Kant's theory of synthesis offers an explanation of the mind's ability to make comparisons within and among representations.
4. As a term for our ability to be aware of a number of representations and/or their objects as the single object of a global representation, Kant introduced the 'unity of consciousness'.
5. The unity involved in the unity of experience, unity of consciousness, is more than just being one. This extra element is difficult to characterize.
6. Kant tied synthesis, unity, and also apperceptive self-awareness (ASA) together in the idea of the subject as a global representation.

We will return to synthesis in Chapter 6 and to the unity of experience and the unity of consciousness from time to time in every chapter from 6 to 10.

3

Kant's conception of awareness and self-awareness

Having said something about Kant's theory of the subject, I shall turn now to his views on awareness and self-awareness. Theory of the subject and theory of awareness cannot be completely separated, of course; theories of synthesis and of the *unity* of experience and awareness are parts of a theory of awareness. A number of general questions about awareness and self-awareness as such are so central to understanding Kant's ideas about the mind, however, that the topic deserves separate treatment. These questions include: To what did Kant use '*Bewußtsein*' (awareness) and '*Selbstbewußtsein*' (self-awareness) to refer? What sort of distinction did he take the two terms to mark? What did he understand the referent or referents of these terms to be like? How did he think awareness is related to self-awareness? As well as being interesting in their own right, these questions are also closely connected to the task of figuring out what Kant meant by his notions of inner and outer sense. There are difficulties associated with answering all of these questions. Unlike his treatment of synthesis, unity, and the like, Kant did not really have a *theory* of awareness or self-awareness. He took the notions as unproblematic and said little about them directly. Thus, our task is more to reconstruct what he must have believed than to lay out any theory he gave. It is not even easy to determine how many different forms of awareness Kant thought there were, let alone what characterized them.

One source of the difficulty is that the term '*Bewußtsein*' in German, 'consciousness' or 'awareness' in English, and their cognates can be used to refer to two different things. They can be used to refer to simple awareness, the kind of epistemic access we are attributing to something when we say that it is conscious or aware of its surroundings. But they can also be used, indeed nowadays are more frequently used, to refer to self-consciousness or introspection: awareness of oneself and one's psychological states. Because 'consciousness' is sometimes used as a term for simple awareness, sometimes as a term for self-awareness, confusion of the two is inevitable. Such a confusion is very prominent in contemporary work and also bedeviled Kant. Sorting out the difference between the two and how Kant saw the difference is vital not only to figuring out what he meant by '*Bewußtsein*', but also to resolving some long-standing exegetical puzzles, particularly the puzzle over whether Kant thought that at least conceptualized simple awareness (representation) of objects requires awareness of oneself. Was he able to distinguish the two, and if so, did he think they always go together, or did he have a more sophisticated picture of the relationship of awareness to self-awareness than that? That is, we need to sort out Kant's use of '*Bewußtsein*' to know something as basic as what is going on in the Transcendental Deduction (TD).

An ambiguity in the passage from Dennett quoted in Chapter 1 illustrates the potential for confusion. Dennett says that "most of the participants in the contemporary debate about mental contents . . . have been conspicuously silent on the topic of consciousness". What does he mean by 'consciousness'? Does he mean what I called *simple awareness,* bare sentience as such, something consisting of awareness of the world and perhaps in addition having such states of awareness as pains and hunger, or does he mean what would more exactly be called *self-awareness?* Unfortunately, it is not clear what he means. He probably means self-awareness, introspection, not simple awareness (unfortunately), but it is just not clear. And that illustrates the problem, one that troubled Kant's work more than it troubles Dennett's.[1] When Kant uses the word '*Bewußtsein*', over and over we want to ask, Is he referring to simple awareness or to self-awareness? Many commentators take him to be referring to self-awareness, but often it just seems unclear and sometimes he seems to be referring to simple awareness. (That is true of the first *Critique,* at any rate; in the *Anthropology,* he usually seems to be referring to self-awareness.) In fact, the problem is worse than I have indicated. It is not that Kant and contemporary workers have two, neatly separated uses for a single term. Rather, they run the two referents together so that one cannot clearly determine what they have in mind.

One consequence of running simple awareness and self-awareness together is that simple awareness tends to fall through the cracks. We talk about contents and we talk about consciousness, meaning awareness of oneself and one's contents (though these are seldom distinguished, either), and simple awareness of the world and simple states of awareness such as hunger and pain get lost, so lost that many people now have trouble even distinguishing between having a state of awareness such as hunger or pain, and being aware of having it. To understand Kant, it is vital that we be as clear as possible about the difference, because Kant himself was not always clear about it.

To begin to separate the two phenomena, consider this statement: 'Animals have conscious states, but they are not conscious of having them'. Here the duality is striking. The statement can be parsed as saying that animals are aware of the world, and perhaps that they have such states of awareness as hunger and pain, but are not aware of their states of awareness or of themselves. Clearly we are talking about two different kinds, or perhaps two different objects, of awareness. (The statement assumes that it is possible to be hungry or in pain without being aware of being so. I have no difficulty with that assumption in principle.)

1 Defining *'Bewußtsein'*: outer and inner sense

When I talk about awareness of the world and about states of awareness such as pain and hunger, I do not mean some anaemic surrogate, I mean full-bodied awareness. Dennett's awareness$_2$ is an example of an anaemic surrogate:

> *A* is aware$_2$ that *p* at time *t* if and only if *p* is the content of an internal event in *A* at time *t* that is effective in directing current behavior.[2]

One way to supplement Dennett's notion of awareness$_2$ in the direction of a more full-bodied concept would be to add some of the things that it lacks even from the standpoint of simple information processing. Let us introduce 'awareness^I' (for awareness, information processing) as a term for this supplemented notion:

Awareness^I of X ***=df:*** having access to information about *X* such that either behavioural reactions to *X* that bear information about *X* or dispositions to react to *X* that bear information about *X* are set up; dispositions can be either memories or dispositions other than memories.

There are problems pinning down the notion of information used in this definition, as many philosophers have noted. Indeed, Dennett suggests that corralling the notion of information may be about as difficult as corralling the notion of a proposition, because they are much the same problem.[3] Intuitively, something gives information when something about it can be used to form correct beliefs about something other than itself; it 'contains information' about something other than itself. I start with information processing both because it is a 'foundational' activity of minds and because the notion has been so central to research in artificial intelligence and cognitive science. Awareness^I includes some things that Dennett's awareness$_2$ leaves out: memory, other dispositions, and nonpropositional objects. (Unlike Dennett's 'that *p*', my '*X*' would allow objects as well as states of affairs; I accept nonreal as well as real values for our variables and I take it Dennett would, too.) However, awareness^I is still far short of full-bodied awareness. Intuitively, it seems clear that the conditions of awareness^I could be satisfied without any *awareness* at all. To get all the way to full-bodied awareness, I think we need to look away from the subintentional and in the direction of something more directly intentional.[4]

I know of no way to define the notion of being aware or being a state of awareness without circularity. That, however, need not be fatal because circular definitions can capture a notion, too. They just need to capture a difference the thing in question makes. In the case of awareness, one such difference can be caught by the distinction between how something is and how it is represented. Take, for example, an optical illusion such as the Müller–Lyer arrowhead illusion, in which two lines of equal length look to be of different lengths. If an organism's response to these lines can be explained only on the supposition that it is reacting as if the lines were of different lengths, then it is aware of the lines; awareness of the lines, not any other relationship to them, is what explains the behaviour.[5] The notion of awareness captured by this distinction might be called awareness^R (for awareness, representation):

Awareness^R of *X* =*df:* having access to *X* such that (i) awareness^I is present and, in addition, (ii) behavior with respect to *X* can be explained only by reference to how *X* is represented to someone, not by how *X* actually is.

This definition contains a thinly disguised circle (representations are states of awareness) and an only partially defined notion of access. Despite these flaws, it can still serve as an anchor for a concept of awareness. As a definition, it may not be as good as a noncircular, fully articulated one, but as the start of a theory of awareness, it is not useless. Theories exist for other things that no one has been able to define noncircularly – time, for instance. In actual cases, we can distinguish between how something is represented and how it is, whether we can define the difference noncircularly or the representational access fully or not. And the definition yields a full-bodied concept of awareness. It may appear that the definition captures a very limited range of cases – what about all the behaviours where we can explain the behaviour by simply referring to how *X* is? – but the range is broader than might first appear. For awareness of any *X*, if there is not already behavior that could be explained only by invoking the notion of how *X* is represented, we could easily imagine some.

What makes a representation a state of awareness? To fill out the definition of awareness^R, first note that it does not help with states such as being hungry and being in pain. The difference between how they are and how they are represented is too indistinct. Yet these are clearly states of awareness, too. So let us ask, What makes being hungry, being in pain, representing objects, representing states of affairs, and the like all states of awareness? Representations of objects and states of affairs are not entirely the same as states like being hungry or in pain. In the case of the former, the representational state and what is represented are distinct, in the case of the latter, not. However, the characteristics that *make them states of awareness* are generally the same. Three characteristics are particularly relevant, though we will not examine one of them, to do with what we use to become aware of them, until a bit later.

First, all these states are obviously information bearing, are states of awareness^I: from them an organism can learn something about its environment, itself, or both. Second, the information comes in the form of a 'manifold of sensible intuition,' to use Kant's term. What makes it a manifold is that what is conveyed comes with discriminable features related to one another in some system of temporal, qualitative, conceptual, and often spatial relations. That it is a *sensible* manifold is shown by the fact that we can make distinctions with it that we could not make using concepts alone. Such a manifold is what allows us, for example, to distinguish qualitatively indistinguishable objects or to recognize one experience cancelling another out in the way that pain can cancel out pleasure, something that has nothing to do with contradiction of concepts.[6] (This distinction between the sensible and the conceptual is based on the old point that experience outstrips description;

no description, for example, can replace a perception of a work of art, an attractive person etc.)

As a defining characteristic of awareness, the notion of a sensible manifold faces a problem; there are states that we would clearly consider to be representations that do not convey what they convey in anything sensible. Representations of abstract objects, concepts, and the like seem likely examples; though the *representation* has, or rather, as both Kant and Dennett insist, is *represented as having,* at least temporal structure, it is not clear that *what is represented* has even that much manifoldness.[7] Such states still present structured information to us, however, so they seem to have something that we treat as analogous to a sensible manifold. It is not easy to see how to characterize this element except in terms that suffer from the most blatant and unhelpful circularity. Sensible manifolds may even be our model for this sort of manifold; at any rate, I will call them both manifolds. For sensible manifolds Kant had his notion of the manifold of sensible intuition. He had nothing similar for the analogous kind of manifold. From now on I will distinguish them.

The notion of awareness^{R} is an improvement on the two definitions that preceded it. When filled out as just described, it does seem to capture something that we might be willing to call awareness. However, a great many states of awareness, to say nothing of states of self-awareness, contain something more – with *representation* goes *recognition.* Recall the two levels we distinguished in the process of coming to recognize a word in what at first appeared to be a meaningless scrawl (Chapter 2:1). The first level was a process of nonintrospectible interpretation. (Kant would have called it a nonconceptual process of synthesis in the first edition [A97–105], though he may have changed his mind in the second [§26].) It resulted in a representation of the word coming into being; this representation satisfies the definition of 'awareness^{R}'. However, another level of activity then ensued: I recognized the word and set out to do whatever it was that I wanted to do with it. The definition of 'awareness^{R}' contains nothing corresponding to this second level. Now not all states of awareness end up being recognized and they certainly do not need to be. In the case at hand, the representation of the word could have produced nothing more than a behavioural or dispositional response or no response at all. Neither would have required any process of recognition. Nevertheless, a lot of awareness does include a process of recognition, whether it is present or not makes a big difference, and our definitions should reflect it. Let us call this kind of awareness awareness^{RR} (for awareness, representation, and recognition):

Awareness^{RR} of *X* = *df:* being aware^{R} of *X,* plus recognizing *X.*

Here the worry about circular definitions is apt to become insistent. Even if circular definitions can sometimes be defended, is this one not so hopelessly circular that it is useless? I think not; we can often distinguish quite readily, for example, between a person being influenced by a representation and recognizing it.

We can even make this distinction in connection with states such as pain and hunger to which the notion of awareness^{R} does not apply. We can distinguish, for example, between simply *being* hungry or in pain and being *aware* of being hungry or in pain. Many nonhuman animals can be hungry or in pain, but it is far from clear that they can be aware of being in such states. Can they contemplate their pain, reflect on their hunger, compare the ache of today to the agony of yesterday? Some may quibble about calling being hungry or in pain a *representation* of pain or hunger, but they are clearly states of awareness of some kind – we do *feel* pain, *feel* hungry – and they are information-bearing states of awareness, so they are at least analogous to representations. Yet being in these states and recognizing them are two different things. (The same is true for being in them and recognizing that one is in them.) If so, then recognizing does not reduce to representing.

In fact, we need to distinguish three cases. The first stage of the meaningless scrawl example before the word was deciphered is one kind of case. Here the representation I had (of the scrawl) certainly contained information about a word, but I could not decipher it; I could not recognize what the word said. An example of a second kind of case can be found in the Garrett and Lackner experiments discussed in the preceding chapter. By contrast with the first kind of case, here the 'subliminal' words were recognized – recognized in a concept, as Kant would have put it. It was the semantic information in the words that influenced the interpretation of the other sentence, not anything else. The third kind of case is the normal one. Something is represented in us and we are 'conscious' of what. The difference between the second kind of case and the third seems to be the difference between the awareness Garrett and Lackner's subjects had of the ambiguous sentence (third case) and of the one that disambiguated it (second case). But what does this difference amount to?

That is none too easy a question to answer. Two different kinds of recognition seem to be involved, recognition in a *concept,* roughly, and what we might call, none too helpfully, recognition in *consciousness*. We might label these 'awareness$^{RR\text{-}CC}$' and 'awareness$^{RR\text{-}CS}$'. (There may be an important problem for Kant here; he may have failed to make this distinction in his central notion of recognition in a concept. We will return to this question in Chapter 6.) For awareness$^{RR\text{-}CC}$, perhaps Kant's insistence that recognition always involves concepts can give us a clue; it may simply consist in being able to apply one or more concepts to a representation. Thus, in the scribble case, recognizing the word represented by the scribble may simply be a matter of being able to apply the concept of that word to the representation of the scribble. In the Garrett and Lackner experiments, taking in the meaning of the disambiguating sentence would be a matter of applying concepts to it. By this approach, we could account for both representation of the sentence and this form of recognition of it in the absence of awareness$^{RR\text{-}CS}$. Part of what recognition in a concept does is to take a representation that is *in* us and make it something *to* us, to use another Kantian expression, one we will explore in Chapters 6 and 9. Is recognition in a concept just another level of representation, then, a representation that usually or always includes representation of semantic information? This suggestion seems to have promise; it is also along the lines of a suggestion in the second-edition Deduction that concept application is a matter of adding a representation to a representation (B131; see Chapter 9:3). If so, awareness$^{RR\text{-}CC}$ would reduce to two or more levels of awareness^{R}.

Awareness$^{RR\text{-}CS}$, conscious recognition, is trickier. It is tempting to think of awareness$^{RR\text{-}CS}$ as a form of *self*-awareness, awareness^{R} or awareness $^{RR\text{-}CC}$ of being aware$^{RR\text{-}CC}$ of something.[8] I am not sure that this approach takes us far. I am inclined to think that representations of all sorts, including representations of one's own representations, can exist without awareness$^{RR\text{-}CS}$, conscious recognition, of them. Nor can I see that being aware$^{RR\text{-}CC}$ of a representation, even a representation of a representation, would change that. If so, awareness$^{RR\text{-}CS}$ can be reduced neither to representations nor to awareness$^{RR\text{-}CC}$. I can think of two ways to pin down the difference, though neither gives us much insight into it. First, when we are aware$^{RR\text{-}CS}$ of something, we can report it.[9] However, circularity is again a danger, because to explicate the differences between reporting on something in this sense and just making noises that happen under some interpretation to fit, we might have to invoke the very notion of recognition we are trying to explicate. Second, we can invoke the example of blind sight and perhaps similar pathologies. In cases of blind sight, patients find nothing to report in a portion of their visual field. However, as with Garrett and Lackner's subjects, these patients use words presented to them in that part of their field to disambiguate other words, if told to reach blindly for something located in the 'blind' portion of their visual field, they tend to reach to the right place and so on. This pattern of behaviour seems to illustrate the difference that awareness$^{RR\text{-}CS}$ makes very clearly; these patients have awareness$^{RR\text{-}CC}$, to some degree at any rate, but lack awareness$^{RR\text{-}CS}$.

Earlier we looked at two characteristics of states of awareness: bearing information and conveying information in a sensible or analogous manifold. These states also have a third. The state itself is all we need *so far as representations are concerned* to become aware of one of these states and of oneself having it (one also needs some synthesizing and concept-using abilities), and when one of these states represents itself to us, the awareness it yields of itself is direct and noninferential. The awareness here would be awareness$^{RR\text{-}CS}$, of course. This third characteristic is crucial for Kant's picture of self-awareness as I see it, so let me combine it with the two characteristics discussed earlier to define a notion of a *representational state:*

X* is a representational state =*df: (i) *X* bears information, (ii) *X* has a sensible or analogous manifold, and (iii) to become aware of *X* or of oneself having it, the only representation one needs is the state itself.

Here, *esse est* (all the representation we need for) *percipi*. In addition, I suggested that the 'perception' will be direct and noninferential. Note that this definition is set up so that one can have representational states of which one is not aware^{RR}; a state representing itself and me recognizing that I have that representation or what is represented in it are two different things. Consider a pain of mine. If pain is a representational state, the pain would represent itself. As I have set things up, whether I recognize the pain, that I am in pain, and the like would remain a separate and open question.

As a final step, then, let us define the notion of being aware of a representational state by the representational state representing itself to us. Call this awareness^{H} (for awareness by having):

Awareness^{H} = *df:* recognizing a representational state one is having on the basis of having it.

The recognition here would be awareness$^{RR\text{-}CS}$. There is more to awareness of one's representational states than recognizing them, of course – feeling them, for example – but here I will let the part serve for the whole. Certainly Kant does not take us further than that. Otherwise, this definition seems to capture a good deal of what our awareness of our own representational states consists in. When I am aware of one of my perceptions, the perception itself is the representational state that makes me aware of it (usually at any rate), and of myself having it. If I am aware of a pain, the pain itself is usually the representational state that makes me aware of it, and of myself having it. And so on. The same is true of action. If I am aware of doing an action, the action is usually the representational state that makes me aware of it, and of myself doing it.

We can ask of awareness^{H}, as we did earlier of awareness^{RR}, what is this activity of recognizing a representational state, over and above representing it? The two do seem to be different. It seems possible in every case to have a representation of something, including one's own representational states, without being aware of having it, either aware$^{RR\text{-}CC}$ or aware$^{RR\text{-}CS}$, without, that is to say, recognizing the representation or what is represented by it.

Like the definition of 'awareness^{R}' and 'awareness^{RR}', the definition of 'awareness^{H}' is circular; it uses the notion of recognizing to define being aware. (The definition of a representational state is not similarly infected, thank goodness.) Nevertheless, the definition is not useless; it brings out a distinction central to the notion of awareness. Indeed, the notions of a representational state, as defined, and awareness^{H} together seem to me to capture something quite central to awareness as we understand it. What makes representational states states of awareness is that they represent themselves; that is how they can make us aware of themselves. As I said earlier, these seem to be features of all representational states, those that give us awareness^{R} and represent something other than themselves as much as states such as hunger and being in pain that do not. For example, perceptions can be states of awareness^{H} just as much as feelings of hunger and pain. If we become aware of a perception we are having, it is the perception itself that makes us aware of it; like feelings of hunger and pain, perceptions represent themselves. The same is true of desires, fears, hopes, imaginings, and anything else that I would want to call a state of awareness. The point I am making can also be made in the language of content. States such as perceptions and imaginings have whatever they are about as content. However, they have something else as content, too: themselves. And if states like feelings of hunger and pain represent only themselves, they have only one thing as content – themselves.

Let us now apply our results to Kant. The two concepts of awareness^{R} and a representational state can be applied fairly straightforwardly to Kant's notions of inner and outer sense. Here is a simple definition of inner sense:

Inner sense $=$***df:*** the totality of representational states.

If states of recognition in a concept (states of awareness$^{RR\text{-}CC}$) are representational, then they would also be in inner sense, as I think Kant envisaged; similarly, for states of outer sense. On what seems to be Kant's considered view, inner sense contains all states of awareness, states of recognition and outer sense included (see, e.g., A98–9); the only general exception seems to have been ASA (see *An* Ak. VII:141, discussed later). However, he could also contrast inner and outer sense; on this usage, a good deal more than ASA is excluded from inner sense. The view that all representations are in inner sense, except for those of ASA, is the one I will adopt. Kant also maintained, as we will see in Chapter 4, that having a state in inner sense is all the representation we need to become aware of having that state. My definition captures both these features. Now for outer sense. It is tempting to define it in terms of awareness^{R} and states of awareness^{RR} accompanying them – to define it, that is to say, as the totality of states that represent something other than themselves. The something would be an intentional object, of course, and so could be real or nonreal. But this would be a bit too broad, because we can have awareness^{R} and awareness^{RR} of representations, but only some representations could possibly be in outer sense. Kant's way to delimit outer sense was to limit it to representations whose objects have spatial properties, excluding even imagined spatial objects, which are merely *represented* as having spatial properties. Thus:

Outer sense $=$***df:*** the totality of states of awareness^{R} whose objects have spatial properties (see A373).

The distinction between representations and what they represent is central to Kant's notion of outer sense, and this definition captures that part of Kant's concept nicely.

Note that I have said nothing directly about self-awareness so far. In connection with pain, perception, and the like, I have been examining what makes these states states of awareness, not anything about them in relation to self-awareness. Now, it has turned out that what makes something a state of awareness is that it can be represented by itself. But 'can be' and 'is' are two different things. Recall our original distinction between simple awareness and self-awareness. In the notions of awareness^{R}, awareness^{RR}, and the representational state, it seems to me that we now have a full-bodied notion of awareness, not just an anaemic surrogate. Yet none of these need be any form of self-awareness. I think, and I think Kant thought (see Chapter 6), that it is entirely possible to represent the world and even to recognize the world in concepts (awareness$^{RR\text{-}CC}$) and make judgements about it without being aware (certainly aware$^{RR\text{-}CS}$) of (1) being aware of the world, (2) having these representations and/or making these judgements, or (3) oneself making them. If what we have explicated so far is simple awareness, how then did Kant see self-awareness? In the next section I will introduce his main ideas; Chapter 4 offers a fuller treatment.

2 Two forms of self-awareness

As I said in Chapter 1:3, Kant's underlying picture of self-awareness is similar in general shape to the picture underlying most contemporary accounts. Like most contemporary philosophers, some Wittgensteinians being the exception, Kant approached self-awareness within the Cartesian image: self-awareness as a form of perception. Unlike both Descartes and contemporary philosophers, however, Kant saw that our awareness of ourselves comes in two distinctly different forms. Indeed, as I suggested earlier, he seems to have been the first to articulate one central form of it, and he had insights of major importance into the referential apparatus we use to attain it. Before we can attempt to characterize self-awareness as Kant saw it, we need to distinguish these two forms. Only one of them is at all like normal perception.

The one that is more like normal perception is the awareness we have of particular representational states and events in ourselves. Kant had various terms for this form of self-awareness: 'empirical awareness of self' (*empirisch ... Bewußtsein seiner Selbst* [A107]), 'inner perception' (*innern Wahrnehmung* [A107]), and 'inner sense' (in the narrower of the two senses that he gave to this term). This form of self-awareness consists of awareness of particular psychological states such as perceptions, memories, and desires. The study of it is what Kant called the physiology of inner sense. Let us call it ESA, for empirical self-awareness.

Kant also described another kind of self-awareness, not awareness of particular states or acts of awareness, but awareness of oneself. Unlike ESA, it is quite different from normal perception, in part because it is not dependent on a particular kind of representation. Almost any representation or, to be more precise, any act of apperceptive representing (A108) makes it available. This is the kind of self-awareness introduced in Chapter 1 as apperceptive self-awareness (ASA); the name was chosen to honour its close connection to apperception. The distinction marked by the terms ESA and ASA is fairly subtle, but it is also vital. It marks the difference between, for example, being aware, of desiring *x*, on the one hand, and being aware of myself having the desire, on the other. When I am aware of myself in this latter way, I am aware not just that I am the subject of this one desire; I am also aware of myself as the common subject of other psychological states: that I, a single unified being, believe that *p*, am seeing *y*, fear *z*, and so on. It seems fairly clear that being aware of myself in this way is something more than being aware of individual psychological states such as a desire or a perception. If so, being aware of my desires, perceptions, and so on is not the same thing as being aware of myself as their subject and common subject.

That Kant distinguished between ESA and ASA in the way I am suggesting may not be obvious in the first *Critique,* but the *Anthropology* makes it clear:

> *The "I" of reflection* contains no manifold and is always the same in every judgment. . . . *Inner experience,* on the other hand, contains the matter of consciousness and a manifold of empirical inner intuition. (*An* Ak. VII:141–2; emphases in the original)

Here Kant is clearly distinguishing between awareness of oneself and awareness of one's representational states. "*The 'I' of reflection* [is] always the same in every judgment", I think, because the self is represented as nothing but me. If it is the same in every judgement, that further suggests, though does not require, that a representation of this 'I' is available, perhaps not in every judgement but in at least a great many of them. Unfortunately, Kant complicates the picture by immediately going on to label the representational states of which we are aware in 'inner experience' "the 'I' of apprehension" (*An* Ak. VII:142). The *I?* Suddenly the distinction between what I am calling ASA and ESA has become a distinction between two ways of being aware of *oneself!* ('Apprehension' here means 'sensible or analogous representation', or, roughly, 'experience'.) Well, the introduction of the 'I' in this second place is not as strange as it might at first seem. This ' "I" of apprehension' is oneself as one appears to oneself when appearing as the object of a representation – for example, a perception – rather than as the thing doing the perceiving. Looking at oneself in a mirror and thinking *about* oneself are two examples of being aware of oneself as the object of a representation in this way. This complication, adding awareness of oneself as the object of particular representations to ESA, is interesting. We will return to it in Chapter 4:1 and examine our ability to identify the self as object with the self we are aware of as subject in Chapter 8:7. The phenomenon does not negate the point I am making here, that Kant made a clear distinction between ASA and ESA.

With the exception of Allison (to be discussed in Chapter 4), few commentators in the English tradition of Kant scholarship have paid any attention to Kant's distinction between ASA and ESA. Strawson does not; Kitcher does not; even Powell does not, the title of his book notwithstanding.[10] Most commentators see that Kant distinguished between awareness of psychological states such as representations, on the one hand, and awareness of our acts of apperception, on the other – acts of what Kant called reflection in the passage from the *Anthropology* just quoted – and see that acts of apperception can make us aware of ourselves, but they miss the related point: the awareness of oneself that acts of apperception provide (or are) is a very special form of self-awareness. This is ASA, awareness of oneself as the common subject of one's representations. In Kant's view, it is profoundly different from awareness of our psychological states and is gained by use of highly unusual referential apparatus. It is also profoundly different from awareness of oneself as object. If Kant commentators miss ASA, few non-Kantians even seem to be aware that this form of self-awareness exists, so I had better say a bit more about it.

I have said that ESA is awareness of particular states and events in oneself: desires, fears, thoughts, bodily sensations, and the like. One attains this kind of self-awareness by having particular representations, representations appropriate to becoming aware of the states and events in question. When contemporary writers discuss self-awareness, almost invariably this is the kind of self-awareness and the only kind of self-awareness they discuss. But there is a way of becoming aware of oneself that requires no special representation; virtually any representation whatsoever will do. Here is how it works. Having a representation can make me aware of more than just the object or content of the representation. Having a representation can make me aware of that representation, and it can also make me aware of myself. For example, seeing my computer makes me aware of the computer. In addition, however, this perception can also make me aware of the act of seeing it, and it can also make me aware of myself – that I am seeing it. Awareness of myself of this sort is what I am calling ASA. (It has been said that I do not know who is seeing the computer when I know it is me. I touch on that objection in Chapter 4:4 and will not consider it here.) In this way, almost any representation, almost any state or act of awareness, can make me aware of myself; having virtually any representation gives me all the representation I need to be aware of myself as the subject of that representation. This makes ASA very different from any of the usual inhabitants of inner sense (see Section 4).

Let me now try to explicate the notion of ESA, awareness of our states of awareness. The simplest way to do so and one very much in the spirit of Kant as far it goes is to suggest that it simply consists of awareness$^{\text{RR-CS}}$ directed at one's own representational states – perceptions, pains, and so on. This explication has its attractions. It would immediately allow having a state of awareness to be distinguished from being aware of having it (and, *a fortiori,* being aware of oneself having it, from ASA). I think this is an important distinction, as I have said. This explication is also in line with his view that we are aware only of representations of even our own states of awareness, not the states themselves, in just the way we are aware only of representations of nonconscious events and states of affairs, not the events and states themselves. However, the suggested explication is not quite right. The problem is this. Representational states, as we have defined them, represent themselves. Thus, we do not need to represent them in another representation. States that represent themselves to us are at least as important a part of ESA as states that represent another representation to us. For Kant, ESA consists of representations of representational states of both kinds.

Now for ASA. It seems to me that ASA, as Kant understood it, is a form of awareness^H. In the broadest terms, in the same way that I am usually aware of a pain on the basis of it representing itself to me, I am aware of myself, and of myself *as myself,* on the basis of acts of apperception representing me as their subject (see Chapter 4). Here what is represented is a person, not a state of awareness, the person who is the subject of those states, so the parallel is not perfect. But there is a parallel. Furthermore, the way in which I am represented to myself in my actions and states of awareness is very different, *prima facie,* from the way whatever they are *about* is represented in them. I can, of course, represent myself as the object of a representation, too, but then I am representing myself as an item of ESA, not ASA. Further clarification of all this will have to await Chapter 4.

What I have said so far barely scratches the surface of ESA and ASA. For example, the cautious notion of 'all the representation I need' used a few paragraphs back needs to be unpacked; I will try to do that by introducing the notion of a *representational base* of self-awareness in Chapter 4:3; I will argue indeed that it is the centre-piece of Kant's theory of self-awareness. Similarly, I have said nothing about the relation between simple awareness and ESA and ASA, one of the central puzzles about TD; I will tackle that topic in Chapters 6 and 9. But perhaps I have said enough to give the concepts some preliminary content.

3 *'Bewußtsein':* awareness without self-awareness?

Is it so clear that Kant distinguished between simple awareness, simply having representational states (which, to be sure, provides at least an opportunity for ESA), and actual ESA in the way I have done? Did he distinguish awareness of the world from awareness of being aware of the world, being hungry or in pain from being aware of being hungry and in pain, in the way I have suggested? Or did he not think, rather, that all states of awareness are also states of ESA, and perhaps ASA? Did he not run recognizing the world and being aware of recognizing it, being in pain and recognizing one's pain, together? Though this set of questions has ramifications for a great many things in Kant, it is difficult to be sure what he thought. He was quite capable of distinguishing these things, as we will see in a moment, but he could also run them together, as thinkers have done from his time to ours, by using the term *'Bewußtsein'* to refer to self-awareness or to cover both.[11] The temptation to run them together is easy to understand: to be aware of a perception, that perception is all the representation we need; to be aware of having a pain, that pain is all the representation we need; and so on. Thus, it is natural to think that the two always occur together or are even the same event. If Kant thought either of these things, then he would not have treated such states of awareness as pain and hunger simply as part of simple awareness as I have done, but as part of ESA. At best, I think Kant was unclear on the matter. This unclarity clouds his whole theory of inner sense.[12]

If we are to sort out Kant's thinking on the issue, we need to keep ESA and ASA as distinct from simple awareness as possible, just because Kant himself did not always do so. The important question is this: Could representations provide awareness of objects without ESA or ASA? More simply, is awareness without self-awareness possible? In my view, the answer is yes. Even if most states of awareness represent themselves and, of course, can be represented by other states of awareness, there is no necessity that the bearer of such representations recognize them, in either of the ways in which we can recognize something delineated earlier. ESA, actual awareness of one's own representations, requires not only representation but also recognition. In this it is not different from recognitional awareness of anything else. If so, a representation of a state of awareness existing in us and us recognizing it are distinct.

In addition, we must not succumb to the common error of thinking that by *'Bewußtsein'* Kant always meant self-awareness. Reading him this way seriously distorts his thought. If Kant meant self-awareness every time he used *'Bewußtsein'*, then he had to be linking awareness of the world to self-awareness in some obscure, baffling way. Strawson reads him this way.[10] But that is not what Kant was doing. When he wanted to talk about self-awareness, specifically, he was quite capable of doing so (see A107, A108, A111, A113, A117n, and A122 for some examples). One place where Kant distinguished the two quite unmistakably was in a famous letter to Marcus Herz of May 26, 1789, where he allows that animals are aware not only without self-awareness but even without the cognitive capacities necessary to have conceptualized representations.[14] In fact, there was nothing novel about Kant making a distinction between awareness and self-awareness. We already find it laid out very clearly by Leibniz, whom Kant knew, of course, like no other philosopher. It is well, says Leibniz,

> to make a distinction between *perception,* which is the internal condition of the monad representing external things, and *apperception,* which is consciousness or the reflective knowledge of this internal state. . . . And it is for want of this distinction that the Cartesians have failed, taking no account of the perceptions of which we are not conscious.[15]

In this passage Leibniz is clearly distinguishing awareness and self-awareness.

The way he makes the distinction is also extremely interesting. For what I call awareness, he uses the term 'perception' (Kant sometimes used 'perception' this way, too, e.g., at A120), and for self-awareness, he uses 'consciousness'. Using the term 'consciousness' to refer to self-awareness, as Leibniz does, not just simple awareness, goes back a long way; Kant came by his tendency to use the term both ways honestly. Note that Leibniz also uses 'apperception' as a term for self-awareness. This usage is related to another terminological problem in Kant. In the context of Leibniz, we could put the problem this way. Is apperception, and the reflective knowledge that apperception gives us, knowledge of "external things", or is it knowledge of our own "internal states"? Clearly, I can have knowledge of both; but they are not the same thing. So far as use of the term 'apperception' is concerned, Kant goes both ways in response to this question. Sometimes he follows Leibniz's explicit words in this passage and treats apperception as making judgements about representations, that is to say, as a kind of self-awareness. Sometimes he uses apperception as the name for acts of judgement about what is represented in representations, judgements that are acts of simple awareness, not judgements about the representations themselves. Here acts of apperception, acts of synthesis, are aimed at the world as represented, not at representations of it. In fact, this is how Kant first introduces the term (A94). And sometimes he just runs the two together. This confusion about apperception mirrors his confused use of '*Bewußstein*' to refer to awareness, self-awareness, or sometimes both.

Because Kant faithfully reproduced all the confusions and perplexities of Leibniz's terminology and added some of his own, there can be no general answer to the question of whether he fully distinguished simple awareness, which has at least a potential for ESA, from full ESA, the realization of that potential. The answer could only be: sometimes he distinguished them, sometimes probably not, or not fully. Thus, there can be few questions about Kant on awareness and self-awareness more basic than the question of what he means by '*Bewußtsein*' on each occasion of its use.

What most stands in the way of our gaining a clear view of the matter is a long tradition of taking Kant to have simply meant self-awareness by the term. I have already mentioned Strawson as one example. Bennett is a second; indeed, he has made one of the strongest statements on the matter to be found in the literature. He flatly denies "that Kant is armed with an account of awareness, another of self-awareness, and an argument which links the two."[16] Guyer, a third, urges that a key argument of TD rests on "a mere conflation of the concepts of consciousness and self-consciousness"![17] Rosenberg is a fourth example, a particularly interesting one. At one point he begins a discussion with a citation from B137, the relevant part of which runs:

> All unification of representations requires unity of consciousness in their synthesis. It follows that it is the unity of consciousness. . . .[18]

Note that there is no reference to self-awareness here; the same is true of the text immediately surrounding it. Here is how Rosenberg glosses this text: "This passage formulates the [theme]: Conceptual representation . . . is possible only for *self-conscious* subjects" (his emphasis). This gloss is remarkable! In the text in question, Kant says not a word about self-awareness! All he says is that conceptual representation is possible only for a subject with unified consciousness. This claim, while perhaps still controversial, is vastly less controversial than a claim that conceptual representation requires self-awareness.

Kitcher also took Kant to be talking about self-awareness in her earlier work. She once said, for example:

> The crucial doctrine [of the TD] maintains that any being that has conscious experience, *in the sense of making judgments about its mental states,* must be able to think of those states as belonging to itself [my emphasis].[19]

Parsed, this comes down to not much more than the following: any being who is aware in the sense of being self-aware must be self-aware! That is true – trivially true; but is it Kant? I think not. Kant was not talking about judgements about mental states, but judgements about *the objects* of mental states, judgements that, often at least, unify them into global objects. These judgements *are* mental states, and they operate via uniting several mental states (or what could be several mental states), namely, individual representations, into a single mental state, a global representation of a global object, but they are *about* the world, not mental states. We need not be *aware* of the uniting process at all. At the time of writing this passage, Kitcher was simply assuming that the kind of experience of which Kant was talking is self-awareness of some kind. However, in her book she sees that many of the central arguments of TD have little do with self-awareness,[20] that even the making of judgements about representations is central only in the second-edition TD.[21]

Sometimes philosophers misread Kant in this way because they themselves do not distinguish between self-awareness and simple awareness. Sometimes, however, they read Kant this way even when they do make the distinction. Bennett, Guyer, Rosenberg, and Kitcher all make the distinction. In the case of Rosenberg, he seems to have immediately turned around and forgotten it again! With Bennett, Guyer, and Kitcher, the problem may have been that they read Kant through Cartesian glasses: though they distinguished awareness from self-awareness, they take it that Kant was either talking about the latter (Kitcher) or ran the two together (Bennett and Guyer). On either reading, the result is the same: it is taken for granted that he is not talking about simple awareness.

Kitcher no longer reads Kant this way, but the reason why she once made the mistake just noted is still important. Before the distinction between awareness of objects and awareness of representational states can be clear, the distinction between representational states and their objects must be clear. When Kant uses the terminology of experience, the latter distinction is clear. But when he uses the terminology of representations, it can be obscured; it seems to become easy to talk about 'representations' *simpliciter,* without being clear about whether one is talking about the representations themselves or their content (see Chapter 2:1). Commentators who prefer representation talk to experience talk have sometimes run representations and their contents together. Confusion about when Kant is talking about representations and when he is talking about the object or content of representations then becomes inevitable.[22] I think this temptation can be avoided; since I prefer representation talk, I am happy about that.

If Kant did distinguish between awareness and self-awareness, then it becomes significant that he used the term for self-awareness (*Selbstbewußtsein*) and its cognates relatively rarely, especially in the first edition.

On any of the six pages previously cited (A107, A108, A111, A113, A117n, and A122), self-awareness is mentioned only once or at most twice, and these are all the direct references there are to self-awareness in the whole forty-six pages of the first-edition TD! Likewise, 'I think', Kant's favourite term for ASA in the Paralogism chapter (the first version of which was written not so very long after the first version of TD), does not occur in the first-edition TD even once. On the other hand, the term '*Bewußtsein*' occurs dozens of times. When Kant used the latter term, then, it is quite likely that some of the time at least he meant what he said – simple awareness, not self-awareness! Of course, by '*Bewußtsein*' he meant something more than bare sentience, something involving judgement and concept usage. But he did not mean self-awareness, either ESA or ASA – not always, anyway. Doubtless, Kant had self-awareness in mind more often than his sparse use of '*Selbstbewußtsein*' and its cognates would indicate. But to anyone who thinks that Kant is arguing in TD that self-awareness is a condition of the possibility of knowledge, all of this ought to give pause.

If Kant did distinguish awareness from self-awareness and if it is also true that he did not use '*Selbstbewußtsein*' or its cognates very often, his work begins to take on a new shape. It begins to look as though what most interested him was simple awareness – sentience or intentionality as such – not awareness of self. (He was especially interested in conceptualized sentience or intentionality, of course.) Put slightly differently, what interested him was intentionality, not subjectivity. One indication of this is that a great deal of what he wrote raises no questions of the 'what would it be like to be that thing' sort, questions that Nagel has made central to subjectivity. For him, the central question was, How is knowledge of *objects* possible? Kant did not use the terms 'sentience' or 'intentionality', of course, but their referents are also part of the referent of 'knowledge of objects', though the latter term also includes other things.[23]

Awareness of self is prominent in Descartes' work, and it is easy to think that Kant simply worked in the Cartesian tradition. But Kant's interests were unusually independent of outside influences, at least in his critical period. Anybody who could write *Dreams of a Spirit-Seer* just as he was gaining some real prominence as an orthodox academic philosopher was not a slave to intellectual fashion! His problematic was not derived from any tradition, it was his own. What fascinated Kant was awareness of the world, especially conceptualized awareness such as mathematics and science, and what the mind must be like to achieve it, not awareness of self. Though Kant made discoveries about self-awareness of the greatest significance, it was a secondary interest.

Curiously enough, even though Dennett was probably thinking of self-awareness when he made the remark quoted at the beginning of this chapter, his comment would have been more true about simple awareness. About self-awareness, in fact, he is not entirely right. Even by the time Dennett wrote, 1987, Fodor had said things about one form of self-awareness, namely, awareness of our own mental states, as had others. Since Dennett's book appeared, there has been a burst of new activity concerning self-awareness: a number of interesting papers and collections of papers.[24] But on simple awareness, little had been done by the time of his book, and little has been done since.

That completes my reconstruction of the picture of '*Bewußtsein*' and '*Selbstbewußtsein*' that Kant brought to his work on the mind. As we have seen, the latter takes two forms, ESA and ASA. Before we leave this chapter, I want to sketch some of the specific features of ASA, to introduce the theory that we examine in Chapter 4.

4 What is special about apperceptive self-awareness?

As I said earlier, Kant began from what we now think of as the Cartesian picture (the picture probably goes back further than Descartes). In this picture, self-awareness is modelled on perception: self-awareness is pictured as consisting of representations of some kind displayed before the eye of the 'I' in some system of relations, usually quasi-spatial. In its contemporary manifestations, believers in the Cartesian picture hold that awareness of self, like awareness of things other than the self, involves applying apparatuses of reference and attribution to the output of a modality of direct, analogous-to-sensible awareness. This modality and what it is sensitive to are entirely inside us, of course, but otherwise it is like the sensible modalities of sight, hearing, and so on; awareness of oneself is similar to awareness of any other particular. Given the way this picture has come to be associated with Descartes, it is important to note that it is neutral with respect to dualism. In fact, it has survived the death of dualism quite nicely.

A few decades ago, the Cartesian picture of self-awareness fell under a cloud of suspicion. Perhaps the only practical manifestation of the suspicion was that for a time it became a *faux pas* to refer to self-awareness as a kind of perception, but at least for that time the Cartesian picture began to look less than self-evident, at any rate. It may be that the critiques mounted at the time began to reveal some real weaknesses in the mighty edifice, but it did not collapse and except in isolated quarters again holds sway, so totally in fact that many philosophers and cognitive scientists are again speaking of awareness of self as a kind of perception, often without even commenting on the fact.[25] As I said in Chapter 1:1, whether functionalist or eliminativist about psychological discourse, whether realist or instrumentalist about mentality, whether sententialist or antisententialist about how the mind represents, we are all Cartesians about self-awareness.

Currently, however, studies of self-awareness usually restrict themselves to awareness of particular states of awareness like pains and perceptions, that is to say, to ESA. As I hope is obvious by now, Kant thought there is more to self-awareness than that. Our proprioceptive awareness of states of our body provides a nice illustration of this extra element. In addition to awareness of individual proprioceptive states, I am also aware of something else: that these states are mine, that is, that I have them and am aware of them.

The latter, it seems to me, is not awareness of another state of myself (see Chapter 4). If so, there is something missing in current inner perception accounts of self-awareness such as we find in the Churchlands. What is missing is ASA. At present, as I have said, few non-Kantians even seem to be aware that it exists.

If the study of self-awareness is currently restricted to ESA, that has not always been true. Awareness of oneself as subject played an important role, for example, in Descartes' thought, the *cogito* part of *cogito, ergo sum* being an obvious example. For Kant, it was the only form of self-awareness of any philosophical interest; what is studied as self-awareness nowadays he consigned to the physiology of inner sense and dismissed as empirical. (As we noted in Chapter 1:1, because there is nothing stable or constant in it, he also thought there could not be a science of ESA [A382].) So let us try to sketch some of the main lineaments of ASA as Kant saw it.

Recall the sentences we used to draw out Kant's theory of the subject in the previous chapter. They can also show us what ASA is like. Recall (1):

(1) I am puzzled by your comments.

This sentence, I claimed, displays a basic structure of awareness. In saying it, I expressed (a) an experience (puzzlement at the comments) that (b) has an object, namely, the comments as I perceived them, and (c) has a subject, namely, me, the person having the experience. I can also be aware of each of these items. If I have the experience at all, I must, of course, be aware of

(i) its object, the comments (as I perceive them).

In addition, however, I can be aware of

(ii) the experience itself: the hearing of the comments and the puzzlement about them; and
(iii) myself.

In my terminology, (i) is simple awareness, (ii) is ESA, and (iii) is ASA. ESA and ASA are strikingly different. In the experience expressed by (1), to have ESA is to be aware of perceiving and being puzzled. For this I need an experience specific to the psychological state of which I am aware. To have ASA is to be aware of myself, as myself and as the subject of that and other experiences. (Obviously I think these two are distinguishable and that ASA provides both.) For ASA, virtually any experience will do, no matter what it is like or what its object is. I call it *apperceptive* self-awareness, as I said in Section 2, because Kant thought that we gain it by performing acts of apperception.

As in the preceding chapter, I have switched from talking about representation to talking about experiences. The reason again is that what is expressed in (1) is more than a representation, strictly described; (1) also expresses attitudes to what is represented. I will now switch back to talking about representations. Because this section is only an introduction to ASA's special features, not a full treatment of it, I will proceed fairly impressionistically, making little use of the definitions introduced in Section 1. The next chapter contains a fuller treatment.

Chapter 2 introduced the theory of the mind as a global subject that has a global representation of a global object. As I have just said, we can also be *aware* of each of these. Having an intentional object is the same thing as being aware of it and the same is true of a global object. But having and being aware of a global representation and being and being aware of oneself as a global subject are not the same thing. Moreover, we can distinguish between being aware of a particular object and being aware of a global object, being aware of a particular representation and being aware of a global representation, and being aware of oneself as the subject of a single representation or action and being aware of oneself as the common subject of a number of representations. This last difference is crucial for understanding ASA. It may be more difficult to imagine than the other two, but Kant certainly thought that he could do so (B134). Awareness of oneself as the common subject of all of one's experience is the heart of ASA.

Recall the sentences from Chapter 2:2:

(1) I am puzzled by your comments.
(2) I love my wife.
(3) I am enjoying the music I hear outside.
(4) I believe our agreement was to meet at 6:00.
(5) Yesterday I thought I understood Kant's notion of the object.
(6) I wish the world was a fairer place.

I am aware of the objects of all the experiences expressed by these sentences (sometimes it may be by an associated perception or memory). And I am aware of them not just individually but also all together, as parts of a single, global object of a global representation. This form of awareness is, again, simple awareness. I can also be aware of these experiences themselves, and I can be aware of them both individually and as parts of a global representation. This is ESA. (At any rate, that is true of the part of it to do with individual representations. Being aware of having a global representation may not be just ESA.) Finally, being aware of having a global representation, I am also aware of myself – as myself and as the subject of each included experience and the common subject of them all. This at last is ASA; it is quite different from any awareness of individual experiences.

There are important questions about the relationship between the global representation and the subject of experience, but they will have to be left for later. In particular, do the terms refer to two different items or are they just two names for the same thing? This question will turn out to be central to understanding Kant's final position on the general nature of the mind, and we will consider it in Chapter 9. There I will argue that Kant's answer, flowing from his view of the mind as a global representation, was: the same thing. We could also ask whether I could be aware of a global representation by having it and *not know* that it is myself who has it, not know that it is mine. We consider this question briefly in Section 3 of the next chapter.

In the classical Cartesian picture, when I am aware of myself, this self is the object of a representation. If so, like other objects, the self should display a sensible or analogous manifold, so that if it does not, that would say something exciting about its nature. We examined the notion of a sensible manifold, the reasons for calling it sensible, and the idea of a nonsensible analogue in Section 1. As Kant saw it, to be a manifold is to have discriminable features represented as related to one another in temporal and other relations (not necessarily including spatial ones; in the example of comparing a desire to stay and listen to music with a feeling of being obliged to keep an agreement to be elsewhere, these feelings do not display any spatial relations). Kant did not accept this classical picture in its entirety. He certainly accepted the general idea that self-awareness is awareness of an entity and states of an entity of some kind, and he accepted some notion of both a sensible manifold and an analogous manifold of discriminable items represented as related to one another. But he did not accept either of the specific claims just mentioned. When I am aware of myself as subject, it is not via my being an object of a representation (B429–30). And when I am aware of myself as subject, no manifoldness is represented. ("Through the 'I', as simple representation, nothing manifold is given" [B135; see A381–2].) This would be true whether I, as I actually am, have a manifold of features or not. Contrary to the Cartesian picture, ASA is quite different from normal perception. However, Kant did not go as far in the opposite direction as some contemporary Wittgensteinians do. He always viewed ASA as a representation of some kind and a representation of an entity of some kind.

Kant made both positive and negative contributions to our picture of ASA. His negative contributions are well known. They consist of attacks on inferences that are very tempting within the Cartesian picture. The key inferences are that the mind or soul is simple and that it has some form of strict and absolute persistence. The chapter on the Paralogisms is a devastating critique of these inferences. We will explore it in Chapters 7 and 8. By contrast, some of Kant's positive contributions are not well known at all. They address six topics: (1) the varieties of self-awareness, ESA and ASA, (2) the cognitive and semantic machinery used to obtain ASA, (3) the representational base of ASA, (4) how we appear to ourselves in ASA, (5) the unity of ASA, its best-known property, and (6) what ASA makes us aware of. Here I will introduce them; the next chapter will lay out the theory Kant used to explain them.

1. Concerning the varieties of self-awareness, Kant made a fundamental distinction between two varieties, ESA and ASA, as we have seen. In ASA, I am aware of myself as myself, and as the common subject of my representations. I am not aware of myself as the object of any representation. In ESA, I am aware of particular psychological states and activities, states and activities that are in fact mine, though it is questionable whether I need be aware of that. ESA also includes all the ways in which I am aware of myself

as an object – for example, by looking in mirrors, hearing my voice, seeing that I am the object of another's awareness, and so on. That ESA extends in these ways is not something about which Kant was very clear. (The distinction between the transcendental and empirical aspects of the mind connects here; we will examine the distinction and the connection in Chapter 4:5.)

2. With respect to cognitive and semantic machinery, Kant made a major discovery concerning the nature of the referential apparatus we use to obtain ASA. We use a very special kind of reference. Kant says that when we refer to ourselves in the way we do in ASA, we 'denote' but do not 'represent' (A382), or we designate ourselves 'only transcendentally', without noting in ourselves 'any quality whatsoever' (A355). What Kant is isolating here bears a striking resemblance to Shoemaker's notion of self-reference without identification.[26] Shoemaker attributes the core of the idea to Wittgenstein, but I think it goes all the way back to Kant.

3. Kant also had an explanation for these peculiarities. I call this part of his theory the theory of the *representational base* of ASA. Kant never laid this theory out all together in any one place, so it is easy to miss it, but it is there. The fundamental idea behind it is this. In Section 1, I introduced the notion of the *representational state;* one of its features was that we do not need any representation other than the state itself (we also need some general cognitive skills) to become aware of it, even if the object of the representation is something quite different. In the same way, virtually any representational state can make us aware of ourselves as its subject. I will call any representational state of which that is true the *representational base* of ASA. No philosopher since has developed any similar general explanation of the peculiar semantics of reference to self; the theory of the representational base goes farther than anyone else to date.

4. Kant thought that the way we appear to ourselves in ASA is peculiar. As we appear to ourselves in ASA, "nothing manifold is given" (B135). As well as explaining the peculiarities of self-reference without identification, the theory of the representational base of self-awareness explains this peculiar poverty, too.

5. The unity of ASA is best displayed in the awareness it provides of oneself as the common subject of a number of representations. The unity of this awareness goes with the unity that it represents the self as having. Together, these instances of unity are perhaps the main source of our sense of ourselves as being unified in a special way. These instances of unity strongly resist explication by the resources of any existing theory of mental contents – representational, connectionist, or otherwise – and are a main source of the tenacity of the problem of the little man, the undischarged homunculus. Coming to understand the unity of ASA and of the self will play a vital part in sorting out some long-standing puzzle cases – that old saw of antifunctionalism, the mind whose 'neurons' are members of the population of China, being a good example. As an objection to functionalism, the story often goes something as follows: 'If what defines a mind is func-

tional organization, then size has to be irrelevant. If so, then the people of China could be one mind. All that would be required is that they be hooked up to one another so as to exhibit the right functional organization'. And that is supposed to be manifestly absurd. It is interesting to reflect on how Kant might have reacted to this story.

I imagine he would have reacted along the following lines. To find out whether the Chinese population could be a single mind, we need to determine two things. First, could the information realized in the relationships among the members of this population, some of it at least, be integrated so as to become a single object of a global representation? Second, could we imagine the spread-out entity composed of this population having the powers needed to be aware (i) of such an object, (ii) of the global representation of this object, and (iii) of itself, as itself and the common subject of the elements making up this representation? I do not know how to answer these questions, and I am not sure Kant did either. What Kant can offer is the questions; his notions of the unity of experience, the unity of awareness, and the awareness of oneself as the common subject of one's representations clarify enormously the issue of what the Chinese population *would have to have* to be a mind.

One objection sometimes made to the idea of the population of China as a single mind is that individual Chinese would continue to be aware of themselves as single subjects and that this would rule out any possibility of the population as a whole being aware of itself as a single subject. Kant's concepts allow us to break into this objection very nicely. What makes it impossible for the entity consisting of the whole population to have awareness unified in the way an individual's awareness of him- or herself is? Alternatively, what would a genuine 'group mind' – a mind aware of itself as a single mind that is made up of many minds aware of themselves as single minds – have to have? Until we understand what one normal person has when he or she has unified experience and is aware of him- or herself as its single common subject, we have no idea whether the objection is serious or not.

6. If ASA is awareness of a representation, am I aware only of this representation, presumably concept-laden and mind-shaped like all other representations, or am I aware of my actual self? Before recent work such as the Churchlands', philosophers generally took it for granted that we are aware of ourselves and ourselves as we are. Almost alone among pre-twentieth-century philosophers, Kant rejected this assumption; he would have been firmly on the side of the Churchlands on this issue (B153–4). We "know even ourselves only through inner sense, and therefore as appearance" (A278 = B334). Even ASA is a form of awareness^{R}. However, there is a twist to Kant's rejection. He certainly thought that we have no *knowledge* of ourselves as we are. But he may have thought that we nevertheless do have a *bare awareness* of ourselves as we are, a "consciousness of self [which is] very far from being a knowledge of the self" (B158). This twist is enough by itself to make his version of the 'no direct awareness of self' thesis considerably more interesting than the current ones (Chapter 10).

To summarize, Kant's work on self-awareness makes six important contributions:

(1) The distinction between apperceptive and empirical self-awareness
(2) The discovery of self-reference without identification
(3) The theory of the representational base of ASA
(4) The depiction and explanation of the peculiar barrenness of ASA
(5) The doctrine of the unity of ASA
(6) The idea that we do not represent ourselves as we are

We will explore the first four as a group in the next chapter. The fifth also appears there, as well as in Chapters 7 and 8. The sixth is fairly unrelated to the other five; we will consider it separately in Chapter 10:4–5.

Not one of Kant's ideas in these six areas has been taken up by later philosophers in the Anglo-American tradition. In particular, the distinction between ASA and ESA, the account of the referential machinery by which we acquire ASA, the account of the representational base of it, and Kant's work on the barrenness of the representation of self that it yields have all been ignored. Even his version of the idea that we do not know ourselves as we are has been ignored, despite the fact that the same idea has reappeared in the work of others recently. Even when observations that he made reappear, the fact that he had already made them over two hundred years ago continues to go unnoticed. We just saw this pattern in connection with what we know of ourselves. Shoemaker is another example. He credits the core of his ideas about self-reference to Wittgenstein but seems not to know that Kant articulated the same basic idea.[27] As a general theorist of awareness, Kant is no mere cultural artefact. As we will see in the next chapter, the same is true of his specific theory of ASA.

4

Kant's theory of apperceptive self-awareness

Given the history of commentary on the topic, we should note to begin with that here we are discussing what Kant thought ASA is like, not the role it plays in the subjective deduction. The latter is a topic for Part II of Chapter 6 and Chapter 9. Most of Kant's discussion of ASA is in two places: the chapter on the Paralogisms in the first edition and TD in the second, much of the treatment of the topic having moved from the former to the latter in the meantime. Here we will consider the doctrine that emerges and will not pay much attention to why it emerges in just these passages or what role they play in the overall project of the *Critique*. Commentators on Kant have not taken much notice of his ideas about how either ASA or the referential apparatus we use to achieve it is special; neither topic is even mentioned by Strawson, Walker, Ameriks, Guyer, or Kitcher. Among recent writers, Allison is one of the few who clearly recognizes that Kant at least identified ASA, and Rosenberg talks about what are in fact some aspects of it. Remarkably enough, even Powell does not discuss it.[1] That is partly because Kant's treatment of the topic is extraordinarily forbidding, even by his standards. However, few philosophers have paid much attention to ASA outside the circle of Kant scholarship, either. In this chapter, I will try to lay out Kant's complete theory.

Recall the six contributions to our understanding of self-awareness just sketched:

(1) The distinction between apperceptive self-awareness (ASA) and empirical self-awareness (ESA)
(2) The discovery that ASA uses self-reference without identification, a remarkable form of reference
(3) The theory of the representational base of ASA
(4) The depiction and explanation of the peculiar barrenness of ASA
(5) The doctrine of the unity of ASA
(6) The idea that we do not represent ourselves as we are

We will begin in Section 1 with the peculiar barrenness of ASA – in it, says Kant, "nothing manifold is given" (B135) – and examine the kind of reference we use to achieve it. Section 2 enlarges our earlier account of how ASA is distinct from ESA (Chapter 3:2). Section 3 is devoted to the theory of the representational base, and in Section 4 we put the theory to work to explain the barrenness of the representation of oneself in ASA. The doctrine of the unity of ASA, (5), is an application of the doctrine of the unity of consciousness to the special case of ASA and appears from time to time in this and subsequent chapters. We will leave the idea that we do not represent ourselves to ourselves as we are until Chapter 10. The final section of the current chapter looks at Kant's distinction between transcendental and empirical aspects of the self. There is nothing comparable to (3) or (4) in contemporary thought.

In Chapter III, we developed a framework of definitions to try to capture Kant's view of the various forms of awareness: the definitions of awareness^R, awareness^{RR}, and awareness^H. I will not repeat those definitions here. We also distinguished three different targets of awareness: objects (via awareness^R or awareness^{RR}), our own psychological states (ESA via awareness^{RR} or awareness^H), and ourselves (ASA, which, I will argue, is always via awareness^H). In Chapter 3:4, I argued that the sentence

(1) I am puzzled by your comments

displays a basic structure of awareness and self-awareness. Here I will argue that the representation of the object of (1), the comments, was all the representation I needed to become aware of the following: the comments, or the comments as remembered (the object); my representation of them and my puzzlement about them (ESA); and myself, the person who has the representation (ASA). The one representation of an object provided all the representation I needed to do all three jobs. Equally, when I am aware of many objects and/or representations of them as the single object of a global representation, the latter representation is all the representation I need to be aware not just of the global object, but also of the global representation itself (the 'one consciousness' I have of these objects), and of myself as the common subject of its constituent representations. The representation in (1) and this global representation are examples of what I call the *representational base* of being aware of these various things. In this chapter, I will not discuss Kant's general conception of awareness further. Instead, I will focus on ASA; his view of the referential machinery, cognitive capacities, and representational base used to attain it; and how Kant thought one appears to oneself in it.

1 Transcendental designation: the referential base of self-awareness

Of the peculiar features of ASA, one's awareness of oneself as subject, perhaps the most striking is that it is *nonascriptive* in a certain way. Kant put it this way: "Through the 'I', as simple representation, nothing manifold is given" (B135). He gives a two-level account of this feature. At the first level, which we will examine in this section, he argues (1) that we refer to ourselves "transcendentally" (A355), a kind of reference that is nonascriptive, and (2) that because the subject of representations must 'presuppose' itself to think about itself, we must be nonascriptively aware of ourselves, and of ourselves as ourselves, to ascribe things to ourselves. Then, at a deeper level, he explains (1) and at least aspects of (2) by an analysis of the nature of the representational base of ASA and of the apperceptive acts we perform on that base. We will examine this level in Sections 3 and 4.

If awareness of self as subject is nonascriptive, the reason, of course, is not that the self is some strange, indefinable being; as Kant brilliantly perceived, it is because of the nature of the acts of reference we use to become aware of ourselves in this way (see Chapters 7 and 8). And I am constrained to use such acts of reference, in turn, because of the way I become aware of myself as subject, namely, by being aware of doing apperceptive acts by doing them and because of the constraints the representational base imposes on this activity. Acts of referring in which we refer to ourselves as subject have attracted some attention this century. Wittgenstein looked into the topic in the *Blue Book,* and more recently Castañeda, Shoemaker, and others have worked on it. Kant spoke of this kind of referring only a few times, but when he did, he achieved powerful insights into it. In this section, we will explore nonascriptive awareness of self and the kind of reference involved. Recent workers have rediscovered some of the interesting things he discovered, but he discovered them first, and his theory of how the representational base of ASA imposes these features on ASA goes further than anything has gone since, as we will see in Sections 3 and 4.

For Kant's discoveries about the kind of reference involved, the crucial text is A355 of the first-edition attack on the Second Paralogism. The doctrine also appears at B157 of the second-edition Deduction, though not by name. It is clearer on A355 than anywhere in the second edition:

> In attaching 'I' to our thoughts [in using 'I' to refer to myself as me, as the subject of my thoughts] we designate the subject . . . only transcendentally, without noting in it any quality whatsoever – in fact, without knowing anything of it either by direct awareness or by reasoning.[2]

The central notion here is the idea that I can refer to myself as 'I', as myself, without 'noting . . . any quality whatsoever' in myself. Kant says that here we are designating ourselves 'transcendentally'. One can refer to oneself in a variety of ways: as the person in the mirror, as the person born on such and such a date or in such and such a place, as the first person to do *X,* and so on, but one way of referring to oneself seems to be special. I can refer to myself as the subject of a representation by being aware of that act of representing by doing it, thus being aware that it is mine, that I am its subject. By 'attaching "I" to my thoughts', it seems to me that Kant had this way of referring to myself in mind.

Let me now single out something that Kant seems to have taken for granted. In this special form of reference to self, I am not only referring to myself; I am referring to myself *as myself.* Even if I note no quality of myself, in ASA I do know that it is me of which I am aware; indeed, as we will see a bit later, Kant argued that that is something I must presuppose to know that anything else is true of myself.

When I refer to myself by 'attaching "I" to my thoughts', nothing about *how* I am appears in the awareness of myself that results. I just appear as me, not as a kind of thing. Compare Kant's description of this form of reference to some observations by Shoemaker on what he calls self-reference without identification:

My use of the word 'I' as the subject of [statements such as 'I feel pain' or 'I see a canary'] is not due to my having identified as myself something [otherwise recognized] of which I know, or believe, or wish to say, that the predicate of my statement applies to it.[3]

That is to say, I am aware of myself, as myself, without inferring this from any other feature of myself. If so, that the referent is myself is something I know independently of knowing anything else. If so, I must be able to refer to myself as myself independently of 'noting any quality' in myself, just as Kant said. I can be aware of myself as myself without being aware of myself as anything except – myself. (Being myself is not a 'quality' of me; not something I and other things have in common.)

Another way to bring out the force of what Kant is saying is to compare his remarks on reference to his doctrine that existence is not a predicate (A598 = B626). In the same way that being aware of myself as myself is something over and above being aware of qualities of myself – something that can neither be inferred from nor analysed into awareness of any such qualities – being aware that something exists is not as such to be aware of any feature of it either. As part of his criticism of Leibniz's Amphiboly, Kant says that space and time have the same feature, too. Being aware of space and time is something over and above anything we could analyse out of the concepts of space and time (A276 = B332; see A281 = B337).

Some will be inclined to ask, Did Kant really discover central features of self-reference without identification, or had he merely happened onto something – something that we can identify in retrospect as self-reference without identification – without having more than the vaguest idea what he had stumbled on? It is now pretty clear, thanks to the work of Shoemaker and Castañeda, that the indicator 'I' has unusual semantic features when used to refer to oneself as oneself. (A number of other philosophers have worked on this sort of reference to self in the past few decades, too.)[4] If Kant was aware of some of these semantic features, that would be good evidence that he knew what he had discovered. I think he was.

Kant certainly knew that such acts of reference require no identification of the referent via a description. In his words, the use of 'I' to refer to oneself as subject designates "only transcendentally . . . without knowing anything of [the subject]" (A355). It "denotes" but does not "represent" (A382). The referent of 'I think' is as ubiquitous in experience as the referent of any categorical concept, so, says Kant, it is a perfectly good transcendental concept. It is not like other concepts, however, because "it can have no special designation" (A341 = B399) – it does not pick out its referent as one kind of thing rather than another or even as one object rather than another at all.[5] (This last idea will be central in the next section.) In short, Kant believed that self-reference occurs without ascription of properties to oneself. That seems to be the core of Shoemaker's idea that it can occur without, in his sense, identification. In fact, I think the terms 'self-reference without ascription' or 'nonascriptive reference to self' would capture the main peculiarity of this sort of reference better than Shoemaker's 'self-reference without identification'.[6]

So much for (1), the claim that 'transcendental' (A355) reference to self is nonascriptive, hence 'contains no manifold'. Nagel, Castañeda, and Shoemaker argue that some references to oneself not only are but must be nonascriptive. Though Kant seems not to have thought of this point himself, it is very much in the spirit of his analysis. Shoemaker puts it this way:

> No matter how detailed a token-reflexive-free description of a person is, . . . it cannot possibly entail that I am that person.[7]

Or as Putnam has put it in the course of developing his theory of meaning:

> The word 'I' is indexical. . . . It is not synonymous with a description.[8]

(Putnam then goes on to say that the same is true of 'water', but we cannot pursue that suggestion here.)

Let us now look at (2), the presupposition claim. To support (2), Kant actually uses something like the argument just cited. For this peculiarity of the semantics of self-reference, let us begin with something else from Shoemaker. In addition to urging that token-reflexive-free descriptions of properties could never entail that they are mine, Shoemaker also argues that if I can refer to myself by ascribing a property, I am also "potentially capable" of referring to myself nonascriptively, that is, simply as myself.[9] This sounds exactly like what Kant was saying in the following obscure passage:

> The subject of the categories cannot by thinking the categories [i.e., applying them to objects] acquire a concept of itself as an object of the categories. For in order to think them, its pure self-consciousness, which is what was to be explained, must itself be presupposed. (B422)

Judgements about oneself "presuppose" "pure self-consciousness". Shoemaker makes the point more cautiously than Kant. According to him, ascription of properties to oneself makes one "potentially capable" of referring to oneself nonascriptively. 'Potentially capable' is weaker than 'presupposes', but otherwise the two claims seem to be the same: ascriptive references to self have a substructure of nonascriptive ones. (Note that, for Kant, it is only judgements about *oneself* that presuppose 'pure self-consciousness', not judgements of any sort; this ought to give pause to those who think self-awareness is at the centre of TD. Neither Kant nor Shoemaker is making any claim that we must be aware of ourselves; all they are doing is exploring what is available in ASA when in fact we are.)

My claim that Kant made much the same point as Shoemaker here rests on a far from certain interpretation of two passages. Both are short on lucidity. The first is part of Kant's concluding remarks at the end of the introduction to the chapter on the Paralogisms. The passage begins with a famous variant on the pivotal 'no manifold' doctrine:

> Through this I or he or it (the thing) which thinks, nothing further is represented than a transcendental subject of the thoughts = *X*.

It then goes on:

> It is known only through the thoughts which are its predicates, and of it, apart from them, we cannot have any concept whatsoever, but can only revolve in a perpetual circle, since any judgment upon it has always already made use of its representation. (A346 = B404)

We will examine this passage as a whole in Chapter 7. Here I am interested only in the last clause, "any judgment upon it has always already made use of its representation." Kant seems to be saying two things here. On the one hand, to know that anything is true of me, I must first know that it is me of whom it is true. That would seem to require some awareness of myself that could not be derived from any knowledge of (what are in fact my) properties. I must know of myself as myself to know that any self-referential statement ascribing a 'predicate' is true of me. On the other hand (a point that will become vital later), this awareness of myself as myself is not via some independent representation of myself, some representation other than the representations of objects I have. We do not have '*Ich-Vorstellungen*' of the sort envisioned by Frege or Husserl. Awareness of self is somehow part of representations of objects.

The second obscure passage is the one from B422 already quoted. It is from the second-edition version of the Paralogisms chapter. We find a similar claim in the first-edition version: "It is . . . very evident that I cannot know as an object that which I must presuppose to know any object" (A402). It seems likely that 'pure self-consciousness' of myself is awareness of myself as myself or awareness of myself as subject and that knowing myself as other than an object is being aware of myself as subject. If so, then these passages are saying that in order to 'apply the categories' to oneself, in order to make 'any judgement upon' oneself or know oneself as an object, one must already and independently be aware of oneself as oneself, as subject, too. Kant seems to have in mind here judgements that I know to apply to myself, not just those that do in fact apply to myself. Judgements are ascriptions of properties. To know, of any property, that it can be ascribed to me, that is to say, to know myself 'as an object', presupposes that I am already aware of myself as myself or as subject. That it is me that I am aware of, then, could not be inferred from any properties of which I am aware, even those that are in fact properties of myself, unless I already know that it is me who has those properties, or so the argument would strongly suggest, if not actually entail. In short, Kant seems to be claiming not only that ascriptive awareness of self makes nonascriptive awareness of self possible, but that the former genuinely *presupposes* the latter. Moreover, his argument for the claim seems to be that no awareness of properties of myself described in a token-reflexive-free way could entail that I am the person who has them.

To summarize our results so far. Kant seems to have been aware of two features of reference to self that Shoemaker views as distinctive:

(1) when we designate the subject 'transcendentally', we are aware of the subject "without noting in it any properties whatsoever" (A355); and
(2) ascriptive awareness of self, awareness of properties as properties of oneself, 'presupposes' (Kant) or makes one 'potentially capable of' (Shoemaker) awareness of oneself simply as oneself, nonascriptive awareness of self.

(1) is supported by the Nagel–Castañeda–Shoemaker argument that to be aware of any property as a property of oneself, one must be aware of oneself in a way that is independent of awareness of properties. Kant actually seems to have used a version of that argument to defend his claims about (2). In short, he saw very far into the nature of reference to self. If self-awareness outstrips what can be known through properties, that explains why "through the 'I' as simple representation", that is to say, in awareness of self as subject, "nothing manifold is given" (B135). Awareness of myself as subject, as myself, has to be *something more than* awareness of properties of myself, no matter what the properties; I must be able to be aware of myself *simply* as myself – no properties, no manifold.

The general morals of the story so far are twofold. First, nonascriptive uses of 'I' play a role in access to ourselves that no form of awareness of changing and contingent psychological states could ever replace (A381–2). Second and even more striking, no psychological feature or cluster of features need figure in such awareness of self, none common to all occasions of it at any rate. This distinction between awareness of changing states and awareness of self is, indeed, a large part of the content of Kant's distinction between the transcendental and empirical aspects of the self (see Section 5). For Kant's destructive purposes in the Paralogisms chapter, the second point is crucial. Another idea (one that has been important in the work of Thomas Nagel) would go naturally with Kant's thought here, the idea that nonascriptive awareness of self cannot be analysed in terms of ascribed properties of any sort. Kant seems not to have thought of this point.

A small problem needs to be resolved. I say that nonascriptive reference to myself as myself outstrips any awareness of my qualities; yet I also say that referring to myself simply as myself is referring to myself 'as subject'. I would reconcile these two points in the following way. Even so little as that I am a subject of experience is not something that I need *know* in order to refer to myself as myself. Thus, in my usage I can refer to myself 'as subject' without necessarily knowing that I am a subject. Reference to oneself as subject is reference to oneself of a sort that is possible only because one is a subject of experience. Thus, I call it reference to self as subject. But one need not know that one is such a subject.

Even the bare possibility of referring to anything 'without noting in it any quality whatsoever' has been denied. Whatever is possible elsewhere, with respect to the self Kant held that such nonascriptive reference is not only possible but, if reference to self occurs at all, ineliminable. In this, as we have seen, he is in good company. Strangely enough, few of Kant's students have viewed his work on transcendental designation as significant.[10] Doubtless there are many reasons for this. Kant managed to give only one *clear* statement of what he thought about the topic in the whole *Critique,* namely, A355. Not only is the description exceedingly brief, but he dropped both it and the term in the second edition. It is also buried in the middle of an obscure paragraph on what may seem to be a rather parochial discussion of the simplicity of the soul. Perhaps most important, the remarkable insights that Kant sketched into the mechanics of reference to and awareness of self were not taken up by any of his students, indeed appeared again at the earliest only with Wittgenstein, in his notion of the use of 'I' as subject. Then it lapsed again until Shoemaker took it up more recently in his notion of self-reference without identification.[11] Finally, it seems to me unlikely that anyone could have recognized what Kant was saying about self-reference without the advantage of Shoemaker's and Castañeda's work on the topic; certainly Kant did not have concepts adequate to describe his discoveries. Indeed, it is not easy to determine whether Kant was even aware of what he had discovered; such a blind spot would be quite in line with his general lack of interest in how reference and concept application are actually accomplished. Like everyone else, philosophers can depict and be influenced by things of which they are not fully aware.

2 The sources of self-awareness

Whether or not he was aware of doing so, Kant managed to spot some of the distinctive features of nonascriptive self-reference. He also and even more remarkably found a theory to explain the most striking of them. To grasp it, we need some understanding of how Kant saw two preliminary issues. First, how does a representation make us aware not only of its object but also of itself and its subject, the person who has it? Second, is awareness of oneself as subject similar to or different from awareness of something as an object (even oneself)?

These are both questions for the doctrine of inner sense. It would be good to begin our investigation with a full account of that doctrine, but that would be a very big job, and I am not going to do it here. Whether or not TD is a bog, as some claim, the doctrine of inner sense certainly is.[12] Kant insists that all representational states are in inner sense, including those representing the objects of outer sense (spatially located objects),[13] but he also says that the object of inner sense is the soul, the object of outer sense is body (including one's own). He comes close to denying that we can be aware of the denizens of inner sense – they do not represent inner objects and have no manifold of their own. Yet he also says that we can be – representations can themselves be objects of representations – and that representations can make us aware of themselves. As will be clear from my definition of inner sense and a representational state in Chapter 3, I take the latter two positions to be his considered view. In its role as a form of or means to awareness of oneself, apperception ought to be part of inner sense, on the first characterization of it just given. Yet Kant regularly contrasted apperception, a means to awareness of oneself and one's acts of thinking, with inner sense as a means to awareness of – what? Presumably, particular representations: perceptions, imaginings, memories, and so on; that is to say, what I call ESA. Here is a passage from the *Anthropology:*

> §24. Inner sense is not pure apperception, consciousness of what we are doing; for this belongs to the power of thinking. It is, rather, consciousness of what we undergo as we are affected by the play of our own thoughts. This consciousness rests on inner intuition, and so on the relation of ideas (as they are either simultaneous or successive). (*An* Ak. VII:161; note the reference to a synchronic element)

In short, Kant's doctrine of inner sense is a mess, and to sort it out would take more space than the task is worth.

Let me single out three points from this quotation that I will use. The first is the distinction between apperception, as awareness of 'what we are doing', and awareness in 'inner intuition' of 'what we undergo', that is, awareness of our representational states. Here is one of Kant's clearest statements of the distinction, stripped of Kemp Smith's emendations:

> The I that I think is distinct from the I that it, itself, intuits . . . ; I am given to myself beyond that which is given in intuition, and yet know myself, like other phenomena, only as I appear to myself, not as I am. (B155)[14]

This distinction between the 'I that I think' and the 'I' that this I 'intuits' seems to be our distinction between ASA and ESA. Note that only the latter is in any obvious way a form of *appearance.* The second point is the idea that apperceptive awareness of self is "consciousness of what we are doing". And the third is an idea only implied in the *An* quote but amply supported by other passages to be considered later, that in apperceptive awareness of oneself as subject, one's awareness of oneself is very different from the awareness one has of represented objects. Together, these three claims contain the basics of a theory of the sources of ESA and ASA and how, as a result, they differ from one another.

To flesh out the first and second ideas, return to the idea of an object. For Kant, we are aware of most items as the *object* of a representation. Such objects begin in a manifold of intuition and come into being when we perform an apperceptive act synthesizing this manifold into a coherent, recognizable, reidentifiable particular, an act yielding first a representation of an object (awareness^{R}) and then the two forms of recognition of it (awareness$^{RR\text{-}CC}$ and awareness$^{RR\text{-}CS}$). There are many different kinds of represented objects, and they can be represented by many different kinds of representation: objects perceived, objects imagined, objects introspected, and even abstract objects whose presentation involves no sensible modalities (no size, shape, sound, smell, etc.) at all. Represented objects include the spatial, smellable objects of outer sense, as well as the imaginary, the abstract, the introspectible, and so on (see A104, Kant's clearest statement about what he meant by 'object' and the discussion of the topic in Chapter 5:1).

Our standard way of becoming aware of an *act of representing* is quite different from the way we become aware of any *object* of a representation. We become aware of acts of representing not by receiving intuitions but by doing them: "Synthesis . . . , as an act, . . . is conscious to itself, even without sensibility" (B153); "This representation is an act of *spontaneity,* that is, it cannot be regarded as belonging to sensibility" (B132). This is awareness^{H} (see Chapter 3:1) and Kant tells us that it does not operate by forming a representation of an object. That is not to say that acts of representing are not themselves represented in inner sense; they certainly are. It is just that they are not the *object* of a representation. How then are we aware of these acts? The act itself, the representation it forms, makes us aware of it. In Kant's words, the awareness of them is given "not indeed in, but with . . . intuitions" (B161). We can be aware of an act of representing as the object of a representation, of course; but what is special about them is that we can also be aware of them just by doing them, just by representing something – awareness^{H}. Another way of capturing what Kant had in mind here would be to distinguish between 'awareness by doing' and 'awareness by having an image'. That distinction fits his thinking fairly well, too, because for him we are aware of all intentional objects in images (A120) – he even thought that all intentional objects are represented spatially (B154–5, B156, B158–9). On the other hand, he most assuredly thought that we do not represent representational acts in images, as the passage from B153 just cited makes clear.

Doing an act of representing is also what standardly makes me aware of myself as the agent of that act, the subject of that representation. When I am aware of myself as the subject of a representation, I am aware of myself not as a represented object but by doing an act of representing. One can of course be aware of oneself as an object of representation, too, by seeing oneself, for example, in a mirror. This is the way in which one becomes aware of one's size, shape, colour, and so on. But when one is aware of oneself as the subject of one's representations or agent of one's acts, it is by being aware of acts of representing by doing them. This distinction between awareness of oneself as subject by doing acts of representing and awareness of objects of representations is the heart of Kant's distinction between awareness via apperception (ASA) and awareness via intuition-based inner sense (ESA). We will offer further support for it in Sections 3 and 4.

When the act that makes me aware of myself is an act of global representing, I am aware of myself, not just as the subject of a single representation, but as the common subject of all of the representations included in the global object of that act of representing; focusing on or paying attention to any one of them makes me aware of myself and that I am the subject of these representations. This awareness of myself as the common subject of multiple representations is the core of ASA. As I said in Chapter 3:2, I call it *apperceptive* because the acts of representing that yield it are acts of apperception, synthesizing acts of recognition. When these acts are acts of global representing, the apperceiving act is an act of *transcendental* apperception (TA); it unites a multiplicity of objects of representation and often the representations of them in one global object. (Here and elsewhere I adjure the sense of the term 'transcendental apperception' in which it itself refers to self-awareness; we will return to this term in Chapter 6:I:5.) ASA is the awareness of self that performing acts of apperception give us, primarily acts of TA; as Kant put it, the "consciousness of the identity of the self" is given by a consciousness of the "identity of function whereby it synthetically combines [the manifold] in one knowledge" (A108). I am aware of acts of TA and of myself as their subject not by sensing them as the object of a representation but by *doing* them.[15] Awareness of oneself as subject is not awareness of that self as an *object* of a representation. (We will return to this last point in Section 4.)

For Kant, this distinction is of fundamental importance – when one is aware of oneself by doing cognitive and perceptual acts, one is aware of oneself as spontaneous, rational, self-legislating, free – as the doer of deeds, not just a passive receptacle for representations: "I exist as an intelligence which is conscious solely of its power of combination" (B158–9), of "the activity of the self" (B68).[16] To summarize: we have two ways of becoming aware of ourselves and our representational acts – by working intuitions up into intentional objects and by being aware of acts of representing and of oneself as their subject by doing them. The former makes us aware of ourselves as a represented object, the latter as the subject and agent of an act of representing. These ideas are the keel of the theory by which Kant explained the peculiarities of ASA.

3 The global representation: theory of the representational base

We now turn to the second level of Kant's theory of ASA. When the medium of awareness of oneself is the doing of acts of representing, the medium itself imposes strict constraints on what this awareness can be like, constraints that explain the nonascriptiveness of ASA and show just how different being aware of oneself as subject is from being aware of oneself as an intentional object. That Kant spotted many of the distinctive features of nonascriptive self-reference is remarkable enough. It is even more remarkable that he also had a theory to explain some of them. Neither Shoemaker nor Castañeda nor anyone else who has worked with the semantics of self-reference has ever gotten anywhere near as close as Kant got to explaining why some of its features are as they are. By what means is nonascriptive reference to self and the manifold-free awareness that it yields possible? How can such reference be achieved without any description, any awareness of features of oneself? How does this sort of awareness relate to normal representation? Is the lack of manifoldness an optional feature of this form of self-awareness or a constraint imposed by the very nature of the medium of awareness? Kant's theory answers all of these questions. The theory he offers provokes some thoughts about another question, too. What is the self, this thing of which nonascriptive self-reference makes us aware?

Kant's theory is neither easy to spot nor simple to unravel. He never laid it out completely; indeed, he only hints at some of its most important features and in a number of different places. Thus, any reconstruction of it must of necessity be somewhat speculative. The key component of the theory, not surprisingly, is the global representation. If A355 is the crucial text for Kant's view of ASA and the kind of reference that yields it, A108 is the crucial text for the theory of what is behind it. Indeed, between them these two cryptic pages contain the entire core of Kant's view of self-awareness. Regrettably, they could hardly be more obscure. As we will see in Part II of Chapter 6, A108 plays a fascinating role in another context, too.

To show how this theory develops, we need to return to the notion of the representational base introduced in Chapter 3:4. Recall the definition of a representational state from Chapter 3:1:

X* is a representational state** =df:*** (i) *X* bears information, (ii) *X* has a manifold, sensible or analogous, and (iii) to become aware of *X* or of oneself having it, the only representation one needs is the state itself.

Now recall the notion of awareness^{H}:

Awareness^{H} =***df:*** recognizing a representational state one is having on the basis of having it.

I argued in Chapter 3:1 that we have representational states of which we are not aware. In addition, we can be aware of a representational state as the object of another representational state. However, representational states also represent themselves. When they do, they make awareness^{H} possible. Here is how it seems to work. Right now I am looking at and so am aware^{R} and aware^{RR} of the computer in front of me. If I now turn my attention to my perception of it, what makes me aware of this perception? Nothing is available but the perception itself. This perception is what I called the *representational base* of my being aware that I am seeing the computer in Chapter 3:4. It is also the representational base of being aware that it is *me* seeing the computer; having such a representational state is all I need by way of representations to be aware of myself. Kant's theory starts with this idea.

So far as awareness^{H} is concerned, it does not matter what sort of object is being represented. Imagining Pegasus will do just as well as perceiving external objects such as computers. Indeed, representational states that have no object such as pains or feelings of hunger will also do. Nor does a representation have to be recognized to provide the representational base for awareness$^{H.}$ Just recognizing the *object* of a representation allows me to recognize that it is me who is aware of it. And when one is aware not just of the object and oneself but also of representing the object, it would seem that this representation is the representational base of all three acts of recognition, all three acts of awareness^{RR}. Having the representational base for recognition of a state is not actually recognizing it or myself, but it is having all the *representation* I need.

Though Kant never said so in so many words, there are strong indications that what I have just described reflects his view of the basis of ASA pretty closely – that he saw it as consisting of representations of objects, not a separate *Ich-Vorstellung* of oneself. We now need to add another element. To serve as the representational base of awareness of oneself, Kant tells us that a representation must be the result of an act of TA, an act of representing tying multiple objects and often the representations of them into a 'general experience'. Here is his description:

When we speak of different experiences, we can refer only to the various perceptions, all of which, as such, belong to one and the same general experience. This thoroughgoing synthetic unity of perceptions is indeed the form of experience; it is nothing else than the synthetic unity of appearances in accordance with concepts. (A110)

This general experience is our global representation. Now, what is the evidence that Kant thought that global representations are the representational base of ASA? He seems to say exactly this on A108:

The mind could never think its identity in the manifoldness of its representations . . . if it did not have before its eyes the identity of its act, whereby it subordinates all [the manifold] . . . to a transcendental unity. (A108)

Kant seems to mean that what allows me to become aware of my identity as the common subject of all my various representations is that I can be aware of the single, unified acts of TA by which I combine these representations and their objects into a global object. I think he was expressing the same idea when he said in the second edition that I am aware of myself as single common subject by being aware of "the identity of the consciousness in . . . [conjoined] representations" (B133); the conjoined representations seem to be the global representation. Kant's fullest statement comes later in the *Critique:*

Man, . . . who knows the rest of nature solely through the senses, knows himself also through pure apperception; and this, indeed, in acts and inner determinations which he cannot regard as impressions of the senses. (A546 = B574)

He described the 'bare consciousness' of self that results a number of times: A342 = B400, B155, B157, and B161. A108 is the first description of the foundation of the theory of ASA in the whole *Critique*. It is also where ASA enters the deduction of the categories for the first time, and a most ungainly entry it is, as we will see in Chapter 6:I:5.

Why can only a global representation generated by an act of TA serve as the representational base of ASA? Kant thought that synthesis into global objects is *a necessary condition* of ASA. Without objects of representation being tied together as a single complex object of a single representation, we might conceive of the subject of each such representation being aware of itself, but we could never conceive of the subject of one such representation becoming aware that it was the subject of any other such representation. Rather, "I should have as many-coloured and diverse a self as I have representations of which I am conscious" (B134) – as are had by the being who is *in fact* me, for I would not, of course, be aware that it was me. Thus, only a global representation that has many of the objects and representations that are currently recognized in me as its object could serve as the representational base of ASA. Indeed, this is one of the central claims of the second-edition subjective deduction, and we will examine it further in Part II of Chapter 6 and in Chapter 9:4. The 'synthesis of all appearance' being necessary for ASA, no other synthetic acts could be the representational base of ASA.[17]

Are acts of TA also sufficient for ASA? No; as we saw in Chapter 3:3 and will explore in more detail in Chapter 6, Kant was clear that one could engage in acts of TA without being aware of oneself (A113, A117n, B132). By the second edition, Kant may have thought that the mind simply is a global representation, one that represents itself to itself as both representation and subject of that representation. Even on this supposition, it would not follow that acts of TA by what would now be a global representation must result in it having ASA. As I noted a few pages earlier, one can have representations that one does not recognize, maybe even could not recognize. I cannot see why the same would not hold for global representations. All Kant's argument requires is that nothing *representational* could be lacking. If an act of TA does not make me aware of myself, what is missing might be directing attention in the right way or even some cognitive apparatus necessary for taking advantage of the representational opportunities available to me. (Something like the latter may explain why the higher animals are not aware of themselves as subjects.)[18] But it could not be anything representational. Strawson, Allison, and others talk about representation of objects providing a potential for ASA, a possibility for " 'I think' to accompany all my representations" (B131). As we will see in Chapters 6:II:2 and 9:4–5, the notion of the representational base may give Kant a way to ground this otherwise woolly claim.

At any one time, there will be one largest act of representing of which we can be aware by doing it. That is one's current global representation. One can be aware of more than one act of representing by doing it. However, to become aware of any one of them is for it to join with all the other representations of which one is similarly aware in one's current global representation. It is the latter that gives me my awareness of myself as myself. How otherwise could I be aware of myself as the *common* subject of all the representations thus conjoined?[19] It also seems, then, that each of us could have only one global representation at one time. If so, to use a phrase of Wittgenstein's, it has no neighbour; if there is only one global representation at any one time, one could not have any other simultaneous representation from which to distinguish it.[20] It stands alone. This uniqueness will prove to be important when we turn in the next section to how the theory of the representational base of ASA explains some of the peculiarities of ASA.

The global representation is not only alone, it is one. In fact, it is the home of the unity of consciousness. The unity here is important because it is a model for – in fact, may be – the unity of the subject or mind. Any act in which a complex of items is recognized as a single intentional object must itself be a single, unifying act. As we saw earlier, Kant spoke of the act by which one becomes aware of a single object as the act "whereby [a mind] synthetically combines" various elements into a representation (A108). The act being a single act (he also speaks of the 'identity' of the act [A108]), the mind is "conscious of the identity of function whereby it synthetically combines [the manifold] in one knowledge [one global object]" (A108). The unity of acts of global representing is what makes one aware of the unity of the subject; one is able to 'think one's identity', as Kant put it, by being aware of the identity of acts of global representing.[21] It is notoriously difficult to elucidate this kind of unity, as we saw in Chapter 2:5. We should keep in mind that both in acts of apperception and in the awareness of act and self that they make possible, the unity has both synchronic and diachronic dimensions. We will consider the former in Chapter 6:I:6, the latter in Chapter 8.

When I am aware of a global representation and myself by having it, am I aware of distinct items? I think not. Being aware of an act of global representing by doing it may *simply be* to be aware of oneself as its subject. The same is not so obviously true, however, of being aware of individual representations. It seems to me that we could imagine cases in which one was aware of a pain or a feeling of hunger by being in or feeling it, without being aware of oneself feeling the pain or hunger. That we can even draw this distinction may need some argument. To show that awareness of the subject is really a separate piece of information here, one would have to show that one could be aware of a pain or a feeling of hunger by being in or having it and yet not be aware of who is having it. That might happen if, as a result of some interesting wiring or some other technology, one were aware of feelings as though one had them – of intentional objects as though one were representing them – but the representation of these objects was in every other respect associated with other people. For example, they were seen through others' eyes, these others can report representing them just as I can, and so forth. Being aware of a representation by having it is not enough to render the question of whose representation it is trivial. We return to this issue briefly near the end of Chapter 6:I:5.

It follows from Kant's position that most representations representing the self have something else as their object. Indeed, there may be no representations that just represent oneself as oneself, no *Ich-Vorstellung.* If so, one could not be aware of oneself except by representing objects (or, perhaps, by having states like pain and hunger). It does not follow from this, however, that to be aware of oneself as subject, one must be aware of objects *other than oneself.* The objects could be oneself and one's own states; both the subject and the object of a representation could be oneself. By the time of the second edition, Kant had become aware of this possibility. Thus, when he became concerned about something like 'the problem of the external world' in the second edition (see Chapter 5:1), he devised separate arguments that ASA requires awareness of objects *other than oneself.* In an argument in TD, he presumes that ASA requires representation of manifoldness, argues that, barring supersensible intuition, the manifoldness of representations is always derived from the spatial properties they represent (B154–5, B156, B158–9), and concludes that representation of objects other than oneself is needed for ASA.[22] In the Refutation of Idealism, he argues for the same conclusion, roughly, by arguing that I could not locate my representational states nor therefore myself in time unless I had recognitional awareness of things other than myself. How this might refute some forms of idealism is obvious.

To summarize, one's global representation is the representational base of being aware of objects, of the representation itself, and of oneself as its subject. Do the characteristics of this representational base explain important peculiarities of our awareness of ourselves as the common subject of our representations? Is ASA constrained to be the way it is by its representational base?

4 Why apperceptive self-awareness is the way it is

Let us begin by reminding ourselves that ASA is not the only form of awareness of self we have. One can also be aware of oneself by seeing oneself in a mirror, by acts and states of inner sense such as feelings, thoughts, and so on being the object of representations, by inferring things about oneself from other things of which one is aware, by being aware of oneself through perceptions of one's body, behaviour, and so on in outer sense, and perhaps in other ways. In all these cases, one would be aware of oneself as the object of a representation. ASA, awareness of oneself as subject, is different. In both editions, Kant claims that when one is aware of oneself as subject by doing acts of TA, one is not aware of oneself as a represented object. Here are some passages: "It is . . . very evident that I cannot know as an object that which I must presuppose to know any object" (A402). "[The representation] 'I' is . . . as little an intuition as it is a concept of any object" (A382). "The proposition, 'I think', in so far as it amounts to the assertion, '*I exist thinking*' . . . determines the subject (which is *then* at the same time object) in respect of existence" (B429; second emphasis mine). To be aware of myself as an object requires not only "spontaneity of thought", that is, acts of TA, but also "receptivity of intuition"; that is, it requires "the thought of myself applied to the empirical intuition of myself" (B430–1). Finally, there is a passage we cited earlier:

> Man, . . . who knows the rest of nature solely through the senses, knows himself also through pure apperception; and this, indeed, in acts and inner determinations which he cannot regard as impressions of the senses. (A546 = B574)

Other things suggest that Kant saw one's awareness of oneself in ASA as not being awareness of an object of a representation. (By 'object' I mean intentional object throughout.) He tended to tie awareness of objects very closely to sensibility, to appearances and intuitions (see A104); all awareness of objects seems to be via sensibility. But, as Kant put it, "Synthesis . . . , as an act, . . . is conscious to itself, even without sensibility" (B153); being aware of an act of representing by doing it is not being aware of it by receiving intuitions of it, having an image of it. In addition, he says that the "unity of the synthesis of the manifold" (i.e., that we are representing the manifold in a single representation) is given "not indeed in, but with . . . intuitions". Since one is aware of oneself as subject by being aware of acts of representing by doing them, not via intuitions in sensibility (B430), it would follow that one is not aware of oneself as a represented object. On the other hand, at A342 = B400 and A361, Kant does say that the subject is an object, the 'transcendental' object (*Gegenstand*) of inner sense. I take this to be a loose way of talking about objects that does not negate the useful distinction he drew in the passages quoted earlier, so let us explore the distinction.

If any global representation no matter what it represents can be the representational base of ASA, that alone would make ASA very different from awareness of an object. To be aware of myself as an object, I need a special representation, a representation of which I, rather than something else, am the object. However, any representation of which I am aware presents the same subject to me and, to the extent that it represents me as me, in the same way. If so, I could not distinguish the self presented in one representation from the self presented in any other representation; there would be no representation in which the subject appears differently or from which it is absent.[23] As a result, when one is aware of oneself as oneself, as subject, this awareness is not 'experience-dividing', to use a term of Bennett's – "i.e. [statements expressing it have] no direct implications of the form 'I shall experience C rather than D' ".[24] In a statement such as

(1) I am puzzled by your comments,

the verb expression or the object expression may divide experience, but the subject expression does not. In this, ASA is unlike all other awareness.

Kant himself seems to express something very close to Bennett's thought: "If I want to observe the mere 'I' in the change of all representations, I have no other *correlatum* to use in my comparisons except again myself" (A366; see A346 = B404 and B422). To see the parallel, turn once more to the notion of the representational base. If any representation provides the possibility of recognizing it as mine, recognizing myself as its subject, awareness of self on this base would not divide our experience. We could not compare it or contrast it with what is presented in representations in which it does not appear. Any representation of which I am aware by having it does provide that possibility, even representations that might be somebody else's by any other criterion.

Another reason that not dividing experience rules out being an intentional object is that a representation is individuated, differentiated from other representations, by its object. But no representation of mine is made different from any other representation of mine by the fact that it makes me aware of myself as its subject. Indeed, to represent something as an object is at least to individuate it, to place it vis-à-vis other objects. It is also, of course, usually to ascribe properties to it. Thus, to appear in a representation as subject of it is not to appear as object and is quite different from appearing as object, just as Kant said (A342 = B400).[25]

In addition to being experience dividing and representation individuating, does awareness of objects have other characteristics that awareness of oneself as oneself lacks? One more can be derived from remarks Kant makes about Leibniz in The Amphiboly of the Concepts of Reflection. (We will consider the passage itself near the end of Chapter 6:1:5.) Any given represented object will conflict in various ways with at least some other possible represented objects: if this thing is here, it cannot simultaneously be somewhere else; severe pain cancels out even great pleasure; and so on. In addition, as Kant also said there, any represented object can be distinguished from any other represented object, even one qualitatively indistinguishable from it. But no awareness of self as subject conflicts with any other awareness of self as subject, and no such awareness distinguishes one self from another (see A360 and A366). To use Wittgenstein's phrase again, awareness of oneself as oneself has no neighbour. For a variety of reasons, then, Kant's idea that when I am aware of myself as subject, I am not aware of myself as an intentional object seems to have merit.

Let us now put the theory of the representational base to work to explain some of the peculiarities of ASA. The first was that in awareness of self as subject 'nothing manifold is given'. I said Kant had two levels of explanation for this. At the first, examined in Section 1, we saw his arguments that (1) 'transcendental designation' is nonascriptive, and (2) any ascriptive awareness of self presupposes (Kant) or makes one potentially capable of (Shoemaker) nonascriptive awareness of oneself. We also saw that Shoemaker's argument –

> No matter how detailed a token-reflexive-free description of a person is, . . . it cannot possibly entail that I am that person –

supported (1) and actually seems to have been used by Kant in connection with (2).[26]

At the second level, if any representation can serve as the representational base for awareness of myself as subject, so that awareness of self as subject is not experience dividing, the lack of manifold and the nonascriptiveness that yields it are easy to explain: such awareness of oneself must be independent of recognition of or ascription to oneself of properties or features. The argument goes like this. To recognize oneself as subject holds no implications that one will or will not experience any other entity or properties of any particular kind and does not differentiate this entity from what is presented by other representations. But recognizing properties of oneself would have such implications and result in such differentiation. Thus, awareness of self as subject does not involve recognition of properties. As subject,

I appear in the same way in each and every representation. If so, I do not really appear as anything, not even as having a spatial location – just as Kant said, "Through the 'I', as simple representation [or 'bare consciousness' (A346 = B404 and B158)], nothing manifold is given" (B135). This argument immediately explains why reference to self on the basis of having a global representation cannot be "accompanied by any further representation" (B132), why 'I' can only 'denote', not 'represent' (A382), why it designates "only transcendentally" (A355), and why it cannot be like other concepts because "it can have no special designation" (A341 = B399–400).

It follows, of course, that no recognition of properties is *required* for reference to oneself as oneself, either. Because ascribing properties distinguishes one thing from another and awareness of oneself as subject does not, using 'I' to refer to oneself on the basis of having a global representation could not be tied to ascribing properties. Awareness of myself as subject is awareness of myself as nothing more than – myself. Surely, if acts of reference to self as subject are always made as part of representing an object, which can be described, it might be objected that such reference is ascriptive. The answer is that though the reference to the object is ascriptive, any accompanying reference to oneself as subject is not. That Kant even saw that 'I' behaves like this was a breakthrough. Having a theory to explain it is truly remarkable. Recent work showing that uses of 'I' and its cognates cannot be replaced by descriptions expresses the same basic insight, it seems to me, but that work has not yet been able to explain it.

Recently, some commentators have started to read Kant's rejection of intuitional object awareness of ourselves as a claim that ASA is not awareness of a being at all, all (noninferential) awareness being intuition of objects (intentional objects). If so, we could not be aware of ourselves, only our representational states, and the subject would be something we must infer. Far from 'I think' being a nonascriptive referring expression, it is not a referring expression at all. Allison, Rosenberg, Kitcher, and Powell all subscribe to some variant of this view. As Allison puts it, " 'I' designates only 'something in general', which is to say that it does not refer to anything at all".[27] This view of self-'reference' has been attached to the name of Wittgenstein in some quarters. As an account of Kant, it has nothing to be said for it, and it is very implausible in its own right. As Shoemaker says, "In making a judgment like 'I feel pain' one is aware of [no]thing less than the fact that one does, oneself, feel pain."[28] In fact, I think the view often rests on nothing more than a simple confusion, the confusion of nonascriptive reference with no reference. As a reading of Kant, it rests on the further mistake of assuming that he thought that all reference occurs via ascription of properties. As A355 makes abundantly clear, he thought the exact opposite. Kant sometimes spoke of nonascriptive self-awareness by saying that it gives us a "consciousness of self" that is "very far from being a knowledge of the self" (B158). Allison notes this striking passage, but does not see its connection to the notion of nonascriptive self-awareness or its implications for his reading of Kant.[29] The distinction will play a big role in Chapter

10:4–5, when we come to sort out whether Kant thought that we have any direct awareness of ourselves as we are.

The theory of the representational base explains both why in ASA 'nothing manifold is given' and that the kind of reference used to attain it is nonascriptive, point (1) from the first level of explanation. What about (2), that ascriptive awareness of self presupposes (Shoemaker: makes one 'potentially capable' of) nonascriptive awareness of oneself as oneself? In the language of reference, Kant's stronger version of the claim is such that to make references to self via ascribing properties, we must be able to make references to self that do not ascribe properties. Castañeda seems to hold that this feature of ASA cannot be further explained; putting his argument into Kantian terms, anything that could explain it would already presuppose it.[30] That is to say, it is just a brute fact of self-awareness that cannot be further explained.

Castañeda may be right, but Kant's theory can explain something else and thereby at least clarify and narrow the element of brute fact. Indeed, Kant's theory can explain this other thing away. The other thing is Shoemaker's claim that token-reflexive-free descriptions of properties could never entail, nor tell me, that I am the person of whom they are true. I am not sure that Shoemaker is right. It seems to me that the reason Shoemaker seems to be right is that descriptions of properties usually do not specify the point of view from which one is meant to be aware of the property. If the point of view is specified, Shoemaker's claim collapses, for some properties at least. Take the property of feeling a pain. Specify whether I am aware of that pain by feeling it or by observing behaviour or other evidence for it, and instantly I know whether it is my pain or someone else's. Yet the pain was described nontoken-reflexively! This analysis does not do away with the presupposition claim, however; it just narrows it. It does not do away with it because knowing that a pain I am (in fact) feeling is mine requires that I be aware of myself – Kant's, and I think Castañeda's, point. It narrows it because once I am aware of myself, there is a way of knowing whether a pain is mine or not that does not depend on having a token-reflexive description of it. This analysis would be impossible without the distinction at the heart of Kant's theory between being aware of something by observing it and being aware of it by feeling or doing it.

The same distinction can explain other putative peculiarities of self-awareness, peculiarities of a kind Kant himself would never have considered. Shoemaker has argued that certain uses of 'I' could not be mistaken in referring to someone as myself. He calls this 'immunity to error through misidentification' and claims to have found at least the core of the idea in Wittgenstein.[31] I think Kant would say – certainly I would say – that there is even the appearance of such immunity only so long as I am aware of a person as the subject of representations and agent of actions that I am aware of by having or doing them. For if it is ever true that there is a way in which I can identify a person as myself and never be wrong, it could be only when I am aware of somebody in that way. (Nor, perhaps, can I be aware of this person *in that way* and not take him or her to be myself.) Shoemaker's point loses all plausibility, however, when I am aware of the person on any other representational base. In addition, if the states or acts of which one is aware on the basis of having or doing them could include states or acts of others, judged by other criteria, Shoemaker's claim may be wrong even on that base. I touched on this idea near the end of Section 3.[32]

Intriguingly, the barrenness of awareness of self as subject appears even phenomenologically. One can easily observe in oneself that having a representation gives one information about itself and its object (what type of representation it is, how it was formed, what we are representing by it, etc.), but it merely presents the subject. Beyond the information about the subject that being aware of having that representation with that object conveys, namely that it is *me* who is representing that object, the representation tells me nothing about myself. This barrenness in one's awareness of oneself as subject was perhaps one of the things that lead Hume to think that no subject is to be found in introspection at all.

The basis in theory for Kant's insistence that being aware of oneself as subject tells one almost nothing about oneself is now clear. Kant allowed that we can distinguish the subject from all objects (A342 = B400) (though how we can do so is not clear; perhaps we use the two quite different ways in which we are aware of each). But we cannot compare it to, contrast it with, one subject *rather than another*. So we can know nothing about it. Here, how we know fixes what we know. Something of great interest follows from the fact that ASA is not experience-dividing, does not distinguish me from or identify me with anything in the world of which I could be aware as an object. It follows that, *so far as anything my awareness of myself as subject could tell me*, I could be *any object* or *any compilation of objects* or *any succession of objects* whatsoever. Not by accident do these three possibilities parallel the first three Paralogisms. For one of the mistakes the rational psychologist makes is precisely the mistake of taking the barrenness of the awareness of self as subject to be direct awareness that the self has a very special simplicity and kind of persistence. Kant, by contrast, insists that ASA gives us no knowledge of what we are like at all (A355; B156). As we will see in Chapters 7 and 8, Kant's theory of ASA is one of the things that underpins his attack on the Paralogisms.

5 Coda: transcendental and empirical aspects of the self

I want to close this chapter with a kind of coda, a look at Kant's distinction between the transcendental and empirical aspects of the mind. Did he think we have two selves or just one? And how do these two sides of the self relate to the distinction between empirical awareness of ourselves as an object and apperceptive awareness of ourselves as a subject? These are purely interpretive questions of little ultimate philosophical importance, but they are interesting.

The transcendental aspect of the self consists of the powers and properties it *must* have in order to have certain kinds of representations, namely, global representations of objects and the representational base of ASA they provide. The crucial powers are the powers described in the doctrine of synthesis, and the crucial property is the property of being the common, 'necessarily identical' subject of all one's representations (all the representations that could be something, at any rate), unified in such a way that to be aware of any representation included in the object of one's current global representation is also to be aware of other representations included in it and of at least some of them as a group. (See the definition of unity of consciousness in Chapter 2:4.) Kant also speaks of this transcendental aspect as the subjective form of experience (A361), the form of apperception (A354). His thought seems to be that in roughly the way space and time are the forms of intuition, the transcendental aspect of the self is the form of representations (A110, A125, A346 = B404) (see Chapter 8:6). If this captures the transcendental aspect of the self, presumably the empirical aspect is simply everything else – all the qualities, traits, feelings, actions, and so on that make one up and, of course, all one's representational states. So far, this seems straightforward. Does the sort of Humean bundle just described exhaust the empirical side of the self? Kant seems to think so; he says the empirical unity of consciousness is just an "association of representations" (B139–40).

We have seen that when we are aware of ourselves as subject (ASA), Kant holds that we are not the object of a representation. It is the transcendental aspect of the self that we are aware of in ASA. About our awareness of this aspect of ourselves, Kant seems to claim something even stronger than that we can have nonobject awareness of it. He seems to claim that we cannot have anything else.

> No fixed and abiding self can present itself in the flux of inner . . . sense. . . . What has *necessarily* to be represented as numerically identical cannot be thought as such through empirical data. (A107)

How abiding the self actually has to be is a question we will examine in Chapter 8. If we cannot be aware of this self as unified by studying any flux of representations, it is hard to see how it could be an object of a representation at all, as we understood an object in the previous section. We can be aware^{H} of it only through acts of TA of which we are aware by doing them. That also seems to be the message of this passage: "This representation [of the self as common subject of all of its representations] is an act of *spontaneity, . . .* it cannot be regarded as belonging to sensibility" (B132). But is Kant right about that? Is it impossible to be aware of our transcendental aspect as the object of a representation? Indeed, is even the reverse the case? Does ASA make us aware of *only* our transcendental aspect?

The first question first. Is it impossible for "empirical data" to make us aware of our fixed and abiding self? I do not see that it is. Everything to do with the mind as a whole, *including its transcendental aspect,* can appear to itself as an intentional object. Take an example:

(1) I notice that I am a middle-sized organism and ask if I could instead have been something else – a computer, a blue cheese mould, whatever.

Consider the first clause, 'I notice that I am a middle-sized organism'. In the awareness via which the first use of 'I' achieves reference, I appear as subject, not as object. (Indeed, this use of 'I' is not even the grammatical object of the sentence.) But in the representation via which the second use of 'I' and the rest of the sentence achieves reference to me, I appear as an intentional object. Yet it is me that appears, not just properties or aspects of me, and that me *includes my transcendental aspect.* If Kant's thought had been simply that ASA is the only way of coming to know that one's transcendental aspect *is transcendental,* that is, a necessary condition of experience, one could have no quarrel. The same would be true if he insisted that any awareness of the self as object either presupposes or creates a potential for nonobject awareness, indeed that unique form of nonobject awareness in which I am aware of myself as myself.[33] But this unique nonobject awareness is not the only way of becoming aware of one's transcendental aspect.

By the second edition at least, Kant himself may have had some sensitivity to the point that one can have empirical awareness of one's transcendental aspect.

> The proposition, 'I think', in so far as it amounts to the assertion, *'I exist thinking'* ... determines the subject (which is then at the same time object) in respect of existence, and cannot take place without inner sense, the intuition of which presents the object not as thing in itself but merely as appearance. There is here, therefore, not simply spontaneity of thought, but also receptivity of intuition, that is, the thought of myself applied to the empirical intuition of myself. (B430–1)

This passage seems to be saying not only that the 'I' as subject of representation can appear as object, but indeed that it must when the representation of it contains even the information that it exists. Kant seems to have changed his mind. Likewise, we can be aware of perfectly empirical states of ourselves as other than objects of representation. For we can be aware[H] of individual acts, by doing them, and of individual representations, by having them. Thus (i) we can be aware of all aspects of the self, transcendental and empirical, as object; and (ii) we can be aware of many empirical states of ourselves in the nonobject way. If Kant failed to make these distinctions, it may be because he tended to run the distinction between empirical and transcendental aspects of the self, a metaphysical distinction, in tandem with the distinction between being represented empirically via intuitions as an object and being represented in a global act of representing, an epistemological distinction. That is a double mistake. We can be aware of any aspect of ourselves, including the transcendental one, as an intentional object, that is to say, empirically, and we can be aware of some nontranscendental aspects of ourselves, namely, acts of representing, by doing them, that is to say, nonempirically.

I have said little about one of the standard questions in connection with

Kant on the transcendental and empirical self. Did Kant think we have one self or two – or three?[34] I have not raised it because it is not very important and there can be only one answer: Kant thought each of us is exactly and precisely one self, a self that has a transcendental aspect and an empirical aspect. This no more implies two selves than the distinction between the self as it appears to itself and the self as it is implies two selves. It is all one self. In the course of making a different point, Kant makes that clear:

> How the I that I think, can be distinct from the I that it, itself, intuits . . . , and yet, *as being the same subject*. . . . (B155; my emphasis)[35]

The 'I' that thinks and the 'I' known as an object are "the same subject". He seems to be saying the same thing in the *Anthropology*: "Man's 'I' is indeed twofold in terms of form (manner of representation) but not in terms of matter (content)" (*An* Ak. VII:134n). (One of these forms of representation is presumably nonobject representation.) I know of no text that contradicts this view. We will come back to the interesting circumstance of one thing being aware of itself in two such very different ways in Chapter 8:7.

There is one important issue about ASA that has not been raised in this chapter. When we are talking about reference to self – the representational base of ASA, how the self appears to itself, and so on – we are talking about the self as represented to itself. The additional issue is this. Do these representations ever make us aware of the self itself or merely of representations of it? Kant's attitude to this question is cautious and complicated and the issue deserves unhurried treatment; we will return to it in Chapter 10:4–5.

In Chapter 3, I suggested that Kant started from the Cartesian picture of self-awareness. As we now see, he also added to it in major ways. The result is arguably the richest and most sophisticated version of the theory to date. Kant did not address every issue that such a theory should address, and he worked at a level of stunning generality, but he did manage to address many issues and to generate an array of new ideas – struggles and eccentricities of exposition notwithstanding. No picture anywhere near as comprehensive exists in contemporary philosophy of mind or cognitive science. Moreover, Kant's conclusions are cautiously advanced and carefully drawn, surprisingly so given the carelessness of his exposition of them. In particular, he took great care to avoid the temptations that seduced both his rationalist and his empiricist predecessors (see Chapters 7 and 8). So broadly and cautiously did Kant supplement and correct the Cartesian picture of self-awareness that if he is substantially wrong, probably the whole picture is wrong, and we should be looking to alternatives as radically different as the one credited to Wittgenstein, in which uses of 'I' and its cognates are viewed as not being referential activities, nor therefore representational activities, nor therefore activities of awareness of any standard sort at all, but some different sort of speech act all together – the so-called noncognitivist thesis.

As a response to the excesses of the Cartesian tradition, Kant's work compares interestingly to Dennett's. Like Kant, Dennett vigorously assaults some of the tradition's worst mistakes and omissions – and like Kant, he never challenges the basic picture of self-awareness as a referential, representational activity. One of the excesses Dennett attempts to root out is the idea that in addition to space and fictional space (space depicted in fiction), we are aware of a third, inner, phenomenological quasi-space in ourselves: the space of the theatre of the mind where our sensible and analogous images are located. In a number of places and a number of ways, Dennett attempts to show that the very idea is nonsense.[36] But like Kant, he mounts this argument within what I earlier called the Cartesian image. Just as Kant's attack on the inferences drawn from the Cartesian picture of self-awareness never challenges the underlying picture itself, the picture of self-awareness as referential and representational, so Dennett treats our awareness of our self and its states as closely analogous to perception. Because of parallels like this between Kant and contemporary theorists, Kant's views on ASA should be readily accessible to contemporary theorists, and where he still has contributions to make to contemporary research it should be fairly easy to incorporate these contributions. Before any alternative account is accepted, contemporary workers should at least consider the theory Kant left us. It is more than just an outdated stage in our intellectual history – far more.

5

The mind in the *Critique of Pure Reason*

This chapter is for those who would like a sketch of Kant's overall programme in the *Critique of Pure Reason,* how the mind fits into it, where he discusses the topic, and some of the main exegetical problems. Nowhere in the first *Critique,* indeed nowhere in any major work except the *Anthropology,* does Kant offer a sustained, single-minded discussion of the mind. When Kant does discuss the mind, it is invariably in the context of other issues, and he says only as much as he needs to say to serve his immediate need. The same is true of the *Critique of Pure Reason;* in both editions the mind and its awareness of itself are mentioned in many places but properly discussed in none. Recall the view Kant himself took of the status of his enquiry into the mind in the preface to the first edition: "This enquiry . . . [into] the pure understanding itself, its possibility and the cognitive faculties upon which it rests . . . is of great importance for my chief purpose, . . . [but] does not form an essential part of it" (Axvii). In effect, he is warning us not to expect any sustained discussion of the mind in the work to follow. (Kant did not retain this passage in the second edition, but the sentiment it expresses continued to apply.) How the mind and its awareness of itself fit into the overall structure of the *Critique* is more complicated than might at first be expected. This is true both of where these topics are to be found in the fabric of the *Critique* and of how they fit into the logic of the work.

After a preface and introduction, the *Critique of Pure Reason* begins with a short section called the 'Transcendental Aesthetic', which is about space and time (the contrast is with anaesthetic). It is followed by a middle section, which takes up two-thirds of the book, called the 'Transcendental Logic'. The third and last section of the work is called the 'Transcendental Doctrine of Method'; it is more interesting, especially on the mind, than is usually credited. Most of what interests us is in the Logic. Kant divides it into two parts, a constructive one called the 'Transcendental Analytic,' the most famous chapter of which is the 'Transcendental Deduction' (TD), and a critical one called the 'Transcendental Dialectic,' of which the chapter on the Paralogisms is the most important for our purposes. In both editions of the *Critique,* most of the discussions of the mind take place in TD and the chapter on the Paralogisms, though more of the discussion is concentrated in TD in the second edition than in the first. TD is mainly about the conceptual and other cognitive conditions of having representations of objects, as well as what the mind must as a consequence be like. (We will examine why Kant constructed this account in a moment.) The chapter on the Paralogisms is an attack on some rationalist arguments that reach implausibly strong conclusions about the mind, arguments that Kant called Paralogisms. How Kant distributed the things he had to say about the nature of the mind and its awareness of itself over these two chapters is extremely interesting, as is the way he changed this distribution in the second edition.

What was rewritten and what was left untouched for the second edition in these two chapters follows a similar pattern. Kant completely rewrote the main body of both chapters, yet he left the introductions to both of them alone. These introductions are sometimes overlooked, but Kant at least must have been content with them. The introduction to the Paralogisms chapter seems to me to be especially important, but the introduction to TD is not insignificant either. Though Kant did not rewrite the latter, he did add a few pages at the end of it, pages that make some interesting remarks about Locke and Hume. Additional discussions of the mind, discussions that remained the same in both editions, can be found in the chapter on the Amphiboly, the chapter on the Antinomies, especially the Third Antinomy, and in the Doctrine of Method. We also find the mind discussed in two passages that did not exist in the first edition, a passage added to the end of the Aesthetics chapter, and a new passage called the Refutation of Idealism. To complicate matters further, discussions of the mind and its awareness of itself are quite differently distributed in the two editions. Kant also changed his mind about some things in subtle but interesting ways in the second edition, and he dropped some important ideas altogether. In one respect, the second edition is easier to understand than the first – discussions of the mind are not as widely dispersed – but in some other respects it is even harder. In both editions, the texts abound in interpretive perplexities.

1 Kant's critical project and how the mind fits into it

Before we look at what these various discussions contain, I will try to say something about the role of the mind in Kant's critical project (Chapter 6 discusses this topic, too). Kant's programme in the Analytic bears an interesting resemblance to the programme of modern cognitive science. His target is human knowledge, that is to say, objectively valid perception and belief, and he was a successor to Descartes, Berkeley, and Hume. However, his concerns were strikingly different from theirs. Unlike this tradition, his main concerns are far removed from scepticism or grounding knowledge of the external world. On the contrary, he takes it for granted that we have knowledge: *a priori* knowledge about conceptual structures, synthetic perceptual knowledge about things outside ourselves, and even knowledge that is both *a priori* and synthetic. What interested him is how these various types of knowledge hang together. In his work, this interest took a specific form: How are all these kinds of knowledge possible? He saw no need to ask this question about traditional, analytic *a priori* knowledge, but he certainly asked it of the other two forms of knowledge: perceptual (synthetic *a posteriori*) knowledge, and synthetic *a priori* knowledge. It is easy, especially for philosophers, to misunderstand this 'How is it possible?' question. It is *not* a question about whether the kind of knowledge in question exists, nor is Kant looking for a proof that it does. That we have the kind of knowledge in question he takes as obvious (B20–1). He is asking, rather, what representations must be like and what we must be like if we are to have them. In this, he is closer to contemporary cognitive science, which also focuses on how perception and cognition work and tends to be blissfully unconcerned with many traditional philosophical problems about knowledge, than he is to traditional epistemology. Kant had concerns that go beyond those of contemporary cognitive science, of course. In particular, he wanted to show the limits of each kind of knowledge, in order to make room for faith (Bxxx). But this interest just extends the cognitive science–like programme into new areas, it does not conflict with it.

To be sure, Kant did eventually become interested in traditional scepticism – after the publication of the first edition. As is well known, in a review of the first-edition *Critique,* Garve and Feder accused Kant of Berkeleyanism, as they understood it, probably incorrectly. For Kant, that implied scepticism, or solipsism. Kant was so stung by this charge that he wrote the only completely new section of the second edition in response – the Refutation of Idealism![1] I am inclined to think that he was not only stung, he was startled. I suspect that taking the validity of our beliefs and perceptions pretty much for granted as he did, at least as they are found in mathematics and science and apply to the world as we represent it, he was caught quite off guard by this accusation that his work implied a *denial* of their validity! When he then said that it is a "scandal to philosophy . . . that the existence of things outside us (from which we derive the whole material of knowledge, even for our inner sense) must be accepted *on faith*" (Bxl, n), he was commenting on his own former practice as much as anyone else's. For much of the first-edition *Critique* (not to mention earlier), he himself 'accepted on faith' that much of our knowledge is as sound and objective as we think it is. Moreover, for his purposes, there was nothing wrong with him doing so.

As some support for what I have just said, let me cite Kant's treatment of precisely this issue of objectivity. Over and over he tells us that he is concerned with objective validity. Yet, notoriously, nowhere in the whole first edition is there anything like an argument that either our conceptual or our perceptual beliefs have objective validity, are true of something more than our own representations. The only exception may be the attack on the Fourth Paralogism.[2] Writers have puzzled over this; indeed, some commentators have even tried to read such an argument into him, assuming that such an argument just has to be there somewhere. (Strawson, for example, reads something like the argument of the Refutation of Idealism back into TD.) If what I said just previously is right, however, the absence of such an argument is not at all surprising. Whether we have objective knowledge was just not something that Kant saw any reason to doubt. Even when he does confront sceptics such as Hume (as he does in the second edition, e.g., at B20), the sceptical arguments he discusses are arguments that the kind of knowledge in question (in this case, *a priori* truths about causes) is *impossible,* and in response he is quite content to show merely that it is *possible*. He feels no need to show, in addition, that it actually exists. As he says about pure mathematics and pure science of nature (physics) a page later, "Since these sciences actually exist, it is quite proper to ask *how* they are possible; for that they must be possible is proven by the fact that they already exist" (B20–1). He took that as given. Indeed, in the passage on B20, he tells us that Hume himself would have recognized this truth, had he just envisaged the problem he was raising for the possibility of *a priori* knowledge in all its generality. If he had, he would have seen that, by his argument, "pure mathematics . . . would also not be possible; and from such an assertion his good sense would have saved him." That is to say, it is obvious that pure mathematics is *a priori;* even Hume would not have denied that! This was pretty much Kant's attitude to the other major kinds of knowledge, too.

What interested Kant, rather, was how various forms of objective knowledge hang together and what is required for them to be possible. What are the constraints on a representation that represents objects other than oneself? What distinctions must we be able to make to have such representations? Can *a priori* knowledge of any sort be objective, or put the other way around, can objective knowledge of any sort be *a priori?* Even more generally, what do we mean by 'objective knowledge' – what are the defining characteristics (*Merkmal*) of representations that have this character? Considered as answers to questions like these, most of Kant's remarks on objective validity that are puzzling from other points of view suddenly make perfectly good sense. For example, a remark like 'Objective validity and necessary universality (for everyone) are equivalent terms' is pretty hard to understand if it is considered to be a remark about the meaning of, or sufficient conditions of, objective validity, but it makes perfect sense if read as a remark about one of the things necessary for objective validity.[3] The same is true of his belief that a proof that the Categories apply to the objects of sensible representations would be enough to establish their objective validity; that would indeed be true for sensible representations that themselves have objective validity. Kant simply seems to take it for granted that sensible experience is the, or at least a, foundation of knowledge.

His theory of truth as correspondence between belief and experience (A57 = B82ff.) evidences the same acceptance. In Kant's view, for a belief or a proposition to have objective validity, it is enough that it "agree with its object" (A58 = B83); and this requires only that "there is an intuition corresponding to the concepts" (A279 = B335; see A286 = B342). For a concept or belief to have objective validity, as Kant saw it, it is enough that it correspond to objects of representation. There is one other route to objectivity – if something can "furnish conditions of the possibility of all knowledge of objects", that is also enough to give it objectivity (A89 = B122) – but the important point here is that there is no further question about objects of representation corresponding to anything else.[4] There is another way to bring out what did – and did not – interest Kant about objectivity. For him, objectivity is the absence of subjectivity, unverified judgement, whim. He was aware, of course, that some objects of representation are more subjective and less under the control of experience than others – fictions and the contents of dreams, for example. He sought to sift out the good from the bad. The most important condition of reliability is that we be able to distinguish 'subjective' and 'objective' time orders – the order in which our representations occur and the order we find in their objects (Second Analogy).[5] From this point of view, there is no need to put objects of representation as such into question; in particular, whether anything independent of objects of sensible representation corresponds to them is something about which we can neither know nor have any reason to care (A286 = B342).

To be sure, this is not the whole story. The common-sense realist dispositions I have been describing notwithstanding, Kant also espoused transcendental idealism. As Guyer documents in a thorough and penetrating discussion, the common-sense realism of Kant's overall starting point and the idealism of his developed philosophy coexist in an uneasy truce. However hard Kant tried to keep common-sense (he calls it 'empirical') realism in his system of transcendental idealism, the latter keeps infecting the former. One of the most dangerous toxins was Kant's phenomenalist theory of perception ("Matter is with [the transcendental idealist] only a species of representations (intuition)" [A370]); the danger is that it threatens to infect the theory with scepticism and even solipsism.

The argument of the Analytic has two sides, though Kant never treats them separately. Here I do not mean the division into an Analytic of Concepts and an Analytic of Principles. The argument as a whole has two sides, what Kant once called the objective and the subjective deductions (Axvii).[6] The subjective deduction is what mainly interests us; it takes place largely in TD. However, the objective deduction is far better developed. Officially, it is an examination of the possibility of the only kind of knowledge that counted as true *knowledge* for Kant, synthetic *a priori* knowledge, but it proceeds by way of an investigation into the conditions of having knowledge of objects of any sort (and of any sort of object, or so I will argue). *A priori* knowledge ranked high in Kant's eyes not because it is *a priori,* strictly speaking, that is to say, known or knowable independently of experience, but because it contains necessary truth, though Kant tended to run the two together and use the term '*a priori*' to refer to both of them indiscriminately. Kant retained enough from his rationalist roots to think that necessary truths were superior to contingent ones. (Actually, most philosophers thought this until recently.)[7] Exactly how the objective deduction goes is highly controversial, a controversy that I will gratefully side-step, but the general story is something like this.

Kant had at least three closely related reasons to investigate synthetic *a priori* knowledge:

1. Mathematics and physics are knowledge of this type, in Kant's view. He thought that their credentials as knowledge were beyond any doubt, but he also thought that we need to show how knowledge of this excellent type

is possible. As Kant saw it, human knowledge is composed of elements of two kinds: inference forms (the forms of judgement) and concepts (the Categories, including their expression in the Principles), on the one hand, and sensibility, on the other. The structure of these forms of judgement is *a priori,* that is to say, not derived from experience, and the Categories are merely a specific form of these forms. Thus, the concept of causality is a specific form of the if–then relation, of hypothetical judgements; the concept of existence is a specific form of assertoric judgements; and so on. (Whether any of the details of this are right does not matter for present purposes.) Now, at least some of the propositions that these Categories help us to arrive at are 'necessary and universal', that is to say, state necessary truths, notably the propositions of mathematics and physics. If we cannot gain new knowledge from the *a priori* Categories and the Principles they generate, the only other possibility, in Kant's view, is from sensible representation, representation founded on intuition. However, intuitions by themselves cannot yield knowledge that is universal and necessary; experience could never teach us that anything must be so. Indeed, intuitions by themselves may not have enough organization and determinateness to yield propositions that could be true or false at all; "Thoughts without [intuitional] content are empty, intuitions without concepts are blind" (A51 = B75). Thus, mathematics and physics would be impossible, indeed all knowledge of the excellent type would be impossible, if the Categories and Principles were not *a priori.*[8] Though this is by far the best known of his reasons for exploring the synthetic *a priori,* the various elements of it were first clearly articulated only in the second edition. There are two others.

2. The second reason arises out of Kant's attack on the rationalist dogma that analytic *a priori* propositions can contain knowledge of things, indeed universal and necessary knowledge of things. We can get *a priori* propositions out of concepts alone in two ways: by analysing the concepts in propositions and by combining these propositions inferentially into arguments, via application of the forms of judgement. (The concepts that interested Kant were the Categories.) The trouble is, neither kind of analysis could ever tell us anything we do not already know; nor could either give us anything against which to test the truth or falsity of what they yield. "In the *mere concept* of a thing no mark of its existence is to be found" (A225 = B272; see Bxvii–xviii). That is why analysis is useless for establishing the doctrines of traditional metaphysics such as God, free will, and immortality, as Kant argues in the Dialectic. If analytic *a priori* propositions get us nowhere, however, and yet the most important kind of knowledge contains necessity, then synthetic necessity and therefore synthetic *a prioricity* have to exist.

3. No one would be inclined to disagree with Kant's harsh verdict on analytic *a priori* propositions. In addition to the general problem of delineating the alternative, however, this critique gave rise to a specific problem, as Guyer notes. If sensible intuition by itself contains no element of necessity, how is it so much as possible to apply *a priori* inference forms and concepts to *a posteriori* sensibility, so as to "provide insight into objects

which exist independently of [us]"?[9] Leave aside the element of necessity, how can we even *apply a priori* concepts to sensible representation? This is the question that actually begins the objective deduction, the famous question of right (*quid juris* [A84 = B116]): With what right do we apply the Categories, that is, concepts embodying necessary relationships, to the contents of sensible intuition?

Kant's problem here is not as arcane as it might seem. Behind the jargon lies an important issue: How can the world as we experience it conform to our logic, to the basic structure of our mind and its innate conceptual apparatus? In briefest form, Kant thought that the trick to showing how it is *possible* for synthetic knowledge to have an *a priori* element was to show that it is *necessary* for it to have such an element. And the way he set out to show the latter was to show that all representation of objects of any kind must have such an element, mere intentional objects as much as real objects that we represent in perception. The only objects it would not include would be objects of which we could have no experience, not an important exception, practically speaking. The aim of TD, then, is to deduce how categorial concepts, which are not acquired from the sensible element in experience, could nevertheless 'relate to objects' of sensible experience (A85 = B117).

Did Kant really mean *all possible* objects of experience, even fictional ones, as well as the objects of mathematics and physics that centrally concerned him? I think he did: "Once I am in possession of the pure concepts of the understanding [the Categories], I can think objects which may be impossible." Later in the same passage (in a different though still related context), Kant speaks "even of capricious and incongruent fictions" (A96). Similarly, right at the end of the Analytic (A290 = B346–7), Kant says that the distinguishing of any object, "whether it is something or nothing, will proceed according to . . . the categories." If this was Kant's strategy, we can immediately explain one of the more puzzling features of TD. As has often been noted, Kant repeatedly talks about knowledge, experience, or representation of objects without specifying in any way whether he means intentional objects or objects existing independently of our representation of them. Indeed, he even tells us that his concern in TD is only with intentional objects. ("We have to deal only with the manifold of our representations and . . . [the] *x* (the object) which corresponds to them is nothing to us" [A105].) If I am right about his strategy, that is perfectly understandable. His concern is with all objects of knowledge, experience, representation of whatever kind, merely intentional as well as the most real of the real. If we can show that experience of all objects of any kind has an *a priori* element, then it will of course follow that all objectively valid experience has an *a priori* element, and to repeat, he is not concerned to show that we have the latter sort of experience; he takes that for granted.

This question of the kind of object Kant is talking about in TD is important because there has been sharp disagreement about it. As I have just said, if we take his remarks early in the first-edition TD as definitive, he is exploring intentional objects. He asks what we mean by "the expression 'an object (*Gegenstandes*) of representations' " and answers that "sensible representations . . . must not be taken as [referring to] an object (*Gegenstande*) capable of existing outside our power of representation" (A104, Kemp Smith's translation modified slightly; see A96 and A129). Fictitious objects would do as well as 'real' ones. Kant does talk about 'real' objects, "objects corresponding to, and consequently distinct from, our knowledge" (A104; see A68 = B93), too, but these objects are a 'something in general', a 'transcendental object = *x*', and if they/it have/has qualities, we cannot know (or know that we know) about them. With the objects Kant is speaking of when he talks about objects of experience or representation, on the other hand, we are aware of qualities of every conceivable sort. Thus, Kant's objects of representation have to be intentional objects. If so, Kant was not exploring the specific conditions of objectively valid experience, not in TD at any rate.[10] He was exploring the conditions of representing objects as such – merely intentional objects of the imagination, for example – as much as objectively existing ones.

This is how Walker reads the objective deduction; indeed, he may see it as confined only to the consideration of intentional objects.[11] At the other end of the spectrum, we find Strawson, who has Kant mounting an opaque argument about 'objective' experience of some kind, an argument that something (Strawson's candidate is the form of self-awareness I call ASA) requires such experience. No recent English commentator has followed Strawson in this reading; it fits the Refutation of Idealism of the second edition better than either version of TD. (The close parallel between this reading and Strawson's own analysis in "Persons" has not been lost on his readers.)[12] I see TD the way Walker does; Kant is talking about any possible intentional object. That of course would include objects that exist independently of us, but would not be restricted to them.

What *a priori* element must all objects of representation have? For Kant, it was not enough that objects of representation must have some *a priori* element; he wanted to be able to demonstrate that that element was the Categories and the Principles derived from them. How he attempted to show that is a question that we can leave. However, the fact that Guyer, Allison, and Kitcher come up with very different readings of this 'deduction' (and all conclude that Kant failed) indicates something of the difficulty of the task and the obscurity of his argument. Another important question is, How can propositions be both synthetic and *a priori?* Kant wants propositions to be *a priori* so that they can be necessary, but most philosophers have thought that all synthetic propositions are contingent. We could also ask this: Even if making use of the Categories and Principles is necessary to generate the propositions of mathematics and physics, how does having this element (together with a contribution from something we have not mentioned yet, *a priori* intuition, temporal and/or spatial form) turn them into necessary propositions, necessary truths? In connection with the last two questions, I have argued elsewhere that Kant does not get around to answering this question until the Transcendental Doctrine of Method, and even then only sketchily and incompletely. One question that I do need to answer here is this. If Kant's question in TD is a *quaestio juris,* how can I treat the picture of the mind that he develops in it as a *quaestio facti?* The answer is as follows: the conditions necessary for certain knowledge claims to be justified may include, and in the case of the mind do include, certain factual conditions. This is how I would marry a justificatory, normative account of Kant on knowledge, an account such as we find in Allison, to a descriptive account of the mind. Recall the discussion of these issues in Chapter 1:1.[13]

Kant's answer to the *quid juris* question has at least three stages. First and before even asking the question, he analyses the structure of the forms of judgement to find what concepts actually embody necessity in one way or another. This he once referred to as the metaphysical deduction (B159); so far as I can see, the argument here is something very close to orthodox conceptual analysis as it was done in the decades after World War II. In the second stage, he asks the *quid juris* question and develops TD. The third stage is the schematized (temporalized) Principles. The mind plays a central role in the first stage and, of course, in the better-known second one. It plays no special role at the third stage, which we will not discuss.

Analytic a priori *propositions and the mind*

Because Kant was the first to introduce synthetic *a priori* propositions, it is easy to miss the fact that he also discussed and made heavy use of ordinary analytic propositions. They play a major role in his parallel pictures of the conceptual structure of knowledge and of the mind. In Kant's thought about the mind there is not one central movement but two, corresponding to the 'Metaphysical' and the Transcendental Deductions – the first two of the three stages just mentioned. Everybody is aware of the second one, the move up from objects of representation to their necessary conditions. But this move does not take place until TD. Before that, there is a movement down from our store of forms of judgement (also the two forms of intuition, space and time) to the concepts that shape all experience, the Categories. This earlier movement is not a transcendental inference to the necessary conditions of experience having objects, it is a straightforward piece of conceptual analysis. It takes place in 'The Clue to the Discovery of All Pure Concepts of the Understanding' (the chapter Kant called the 'metaphysical deduction' [B159]). Despite being the first parts of the Transcendental Analytic, this analysis has received very little attention.

The first clue is that the Transcendental Analytic begins not with experience but logic: the logic of Aristotelian syllogisms and the Aristotelian categories. Taking it for granted that the structure of Aristotelian logic is the structure of all thought (including irrational thought?), Kant proceeds by analysis to draw out the implications of this logic for the conceptual structure within which all thought and experience must take place. The structure in question is the system of the forms of judgement; the resulting theory is the theory of the Categories, and later, of the Principles. The fundamental idea behind all this, an idea that took flight with Hegel, is that the structure of logic is the structure of the higher cognitive powers of the mind. Here is how Kant made the point in the passage from the *Anthropology* examined in Chapter 1. He is distinguishing the higher cognitive powers from the lower one of sensibility.

> The lower cognitive power is characterized by the passivity of the inner sense of sensations; the higher, by the *spontaneity* of apperception. . . . [The latter] *belongs to logic* (*a system of the rules of the understanding*), just as the former belongs to *psychology* (to a sum-total of all inner perceptions under laws of nature). (*An* Ak. VII:140–1; second emphasis mine)

Kant did not have the minimalist and conventionalist image of logic – of inference and semantic relationships – that we with our empiricist roots tend to have today. His roots were in rationalism. For rationalism, the exploration of meanings and patterns of inference was also the exploration of the deepest structures of mind and world. These explorations were the task of metaphysics, and metaphysics as Spinoza, Leibniz, and Wolff conceived it was a purely deductive, meaning-exploring activity. It is a mistake to think that Kant had anything but the utmost respect for this activity. It explored the conceptual structure of all experience, indeed all knowledge, we have or could have. Kant did think it suffers from a small weakness – it could never discover anything new – but it still reveals the structure of all knowledge.

One of Kant's more dramatic ways of expressing the role of the Categories in representation is to say that the mind's categorial structure is part of the form of knowledge, in the same way that the 'pure intuitions' of time and space are (see, e.g., A122). It is clear that by 'form' here Kant meant something like a framework within which all the various objects of representation are located, in some sense of 'located'. This notion of mind as form plays a number of important roles in Kant's thought; we will examine it in Chapter 8:6–7. For example, one of the ways to mark the difference between the transcendental and the empirical aspects of the mind is to distinguish between the mind's form and its inner-sense contents.

As Kant saw it, the structure of concepts and forms of judgement that make up the conceptual framework of mind and knowledge constitute a system. He speaks of this structure as a system, and of the unity and totality of this system, in a number of places. ("Pure reason is, indeed, so perfect a unity" [Axiii; see Axix, A13 = B27, Bxxxvii–xxxviii].) This unified system creates a space where representation can happen, an *n*-dimensional conceptual space with the 'multiplicity' necessary to represent all possible objects.[14] Kant may have thought that the unity of this system has some important relationship to the very different kind of unity central to consciousness (see Chapter 2:5). If so, it is not clear what he had in mind. Whatever it was, he thought he could deduce the conceptual structure of experience from the components of this system. This deduction, to repeat, is not inference up from experience but deduction down from conceptual structures of the most abstract kind. In fact, the chapter containing the TD, which is where inference up from experience first occurs, is Chapter II of the Analytic; Chapter I, The Clue to the Discovery of All Pure Concepts of the Understanding, is all deduction down. For Kant, as I have said, the clue to the conceptual structure of experience is Aristotelian logic. By analysing the 'forms of judgment' of this logic and the concepts used in these forms, we can find the inference forms and concepts common to all experience (A12 = B25). In short, analytic propositions play a huge role in Kant's thought.

Synthetic a priori *propositions and the mind*

Then we arrive at TD. In this chapter, inference up from objects of representation to their conditions rises to meet deduction down. Note that deduction down of the sort just discussed is not synthetic. It is a process of spelling out and detailing what is already there in Aristotelian logic. Having spelled out the conceptual structure of possible experience, we are now ready to synthesize a picture of the complete *a priori* structure of it. Kant begins with the momentous suggestion that launches the objective and subjective deductions: if sensible representation by itself could yield only contingent knowledge and yet we can have no knowledge at all without it, perhaps the way to demonstrate that it has an *a priori* element is to examine the necessary conditions of having it. The specific aspect of our representations that Kant chooses to examine is that they have objects. Kant then argues roughly as follows: our representations could not have objects, be about anything, unless these objects were discrete, unified particulars. For that to occur, the mind must find order in intuitions. The mind could not find order in intuitions without the use of just those concepts, the Categories, that give the conceptual structure of experience (plus, of course, temporal and spatial systems of relations, which Kant thought to be nonconceptual). Not only are the concepts dictated by the forms of judgement of Aristotelian logic the only concepts we have, we have no choice but to apply them. Notice that even if these things are necessary for experience, it is a hypothetical necessity – just the sort of necessity, in fact, that one would expect to find in a scientific theory.

The deduction should now be complete. Strangely enough, however, the chapter has just nicely got started. In the first-edition version, for example, we have only reached A106, which is about one-third of the way through the chapter. Does Kant think that something in the official project remains to be done? I think so; but first we need some more groundwork. The moves Kant makes next catch one by surprise. Kant suddenly argues that the mind could not use concepts so as to have unified objects of representation if it were not itself unified (A107–8). Wait a minute; we want to ask, What is the mind or its unity doing here? We were after whatever element of necessity there is in experiential knowledge. We have found that element of necessity in the concepts we have to apply. So who cares if, in addition, something else – for example, the mind being unified – is also required? This is an important question. As Walker and Guyer both show, Kant wrote versions of the deduction of the Categories that make no reference to the mind or its unity at all.[15] Yet in the *Critique* he deliberately chooses a route that takes him through the mind; he defines his project as deducing "the subjective sources which form the *a priori* foundation of the possibility of experience." (A97).

Of the various philosophers who have written commentaries on TD in the last few decades, only the Henrich–Guyer theory of the two starting points seems to me to begin to do justice to the variety of quite different arguments to be found in TD. They point out that Kant had two ways of beginning a deduction of the Categories, one starting from objects of representation, the other from self-awareness (in fact, ASA). Guyer suggests that Kant was deeply ambivalent about which was better.[16] Clearly, I have emphasized the first starting point so far. It may appear that I am now describing Kant's first switch to the second one. However, that would not be quite right. The other starting point they identify is the conditions of a subject of experience being aware of itself. That is not what Kant switches to on A107, not initially at least. What he switches to first is the unity of *consciousness,* not the unity of self-consciousness or anything else to do with self-consciousness, and only moves to the latter a bit later (for the first time, clearly at least, on A108) and, at first glance, quite arbitrarily.

I think Kant suddenly introduces the fact that a unified mind is necessary for concept application on A107 because he felt that some of the things necessary for being a unified mind are of direct interest to the objective deduction, and he could not see any other way to demonstrate that these things are required for experience. The most important of these additional things are certain relational concepts and specifically the concept of causality. The importance of showing that we must apply the concept of causality to objects of experience is that this opens the way to the Second Analogy and a proof that Newtonian physics is not only synthetic and *a priori,* but also true of all objects of experience, in the same way that geometry (Euclidean geometry) is necessarily true of all space. And that is why Kant introduces first the unity of consciousness and then, on A108, the unity of ASA, the things necessary for consciousness to be unified also being necessary for the unity of ASA. Students of Kant will recognize that the past few paragraphs skate over many, many problems. The next chapter will have more to say about the relational Categories.

Now that we understand why Kant introduced the subjective deduction, why did he then say that it was inessential (Axvii)? Since the objective deduction is about the conditions of representations having objects, a better name for it might have been 'deduction of the object'. Similarly, a better name for the subjective deduction might have been 'the deduction of the subject' or 'the deduction of the subject's nature'. This enquiry was inessential to Kant's main critical project, defending the synthetic *a priori* credentials of physics in the objective deduction. From this point of view, anything uncovered about the nature and functioning of the mind would be a happy accident.[17] Kant's conviction that empirical psychology is impossible (see

Chapter 1:1) may also have dampened his interest in the abstract, necessary structure of the mind; since there can be no empirical psychology, constructing a general conceptual framework to rationalize and justify it would not contribute to any science. (For the distinction between the transcendental and empirical aspects of experience, see Chapter 10:3.) The subjective deduction, as I said, plays a prominent role only in the TD chapter. In the 'metaphysical deduction' and the Analytic of Principles, the objective deduction and its various ramifications dominate. Despite all this, the claims Kant makes about the mind in it are extremely interesting. Furthermore, the topics of the subjective deduction do appear from time to time elsewhere (e.g., at A161 = B201), and Kant did say very clearly that his choice to argue the objective deduction by invoking the mind was deliberate, as we just saw.

It is of the utmost importance, so far as understanding Kant's overall objectives in writing the *Critique of Pure Reason* are concerned, to understand that the objective deduction reaches not just one general conclusion about the nature and extent of possible knowledge, but two. One was positive, the other negative. We have been examining the positive one, that some synthetic *a priori* knowledge is possible in connection with experience. An extremely important negative conclusion goes with this: we can have no possible synthetic *a priori* knowledge of anything that we cannot experience. This negative conclusion is important because it is the main weapon that Kant will wield against traditional transexperiential (transcendent) metaphysics in the Dialectic. He wields this weapon with devastating effect. Some of the most honoured metaphysical beliefs of the Western tradition about the soul, free will, and God go down; they all turn out to require evidence that no experience could provide, and they most certainly are not talking about necessary conditions of having experience. However, in Kant's eyes, having no experiential evidence for them is not a reason to disbelieve them. It is a reason for intellectual agnosticism. The intellect is simply impotent to decide one way or the other. What makes this conclusion so important is that room is thereby left for faith, which can give us reasons of a more practical kind (Bxxx). When Kant spoke in the first-edition preface of his 'main critical project', he was referring to this whole complex of positive and critical arguments and conclusions.

I will close this section with a comment on the Henrich–Guyer two starting points interpretation. Notice that I have just managed, in a way that parallels my account of Kant and cognitive science in Chapter 1, to sketch the whole of the subjective deduction in the first edition without saying a word about self-awareness, the second starting point that Guyer identifies. Kant does, of course, make remarks about self-awareness in the first edition TD, starting on A108. The question, however, is whether anything in his argument required him to do so. My answer is a little complicated. As he developed the deduction in the first edition, I cannot see that he had any good reason to mention the topic. He does have good reason to introduce the mind's capacity to synthesize and its unity, but not its awareness of itself. However, he did introduce it. In the second version of TD, self-awareness is far more prominent, appearing in the first sentence of the second section of the rewritten part of TD (§16, B131–2). Here is how I see the order of the two strategies in the two editions. In the first edition, Kant begins with representation of objects, then moves to the unity of consciousness – consciousness, not self-consciousness. These are his only topics until A107. Then suddenly on A108, ASA appears, apparently as a new and separate starting point. The Henrich–Guyer hypothesis should alert us to the possibility that a new argument, one beginning from ASA, may be breaking through. In the second edition, by contrast, Kant gives ASA rather than simple awareness pride of place almost from the start. If so, Kant could be seen as having three strategies available to him, not just two: one beginning from knowledge of objects, one beginning from the unity of the mind, and one beginning from ASA. We will explore all this in Chapters 6 and 9. There I will argue that Kant did not bounce from one to another, from objects to unity to self-awareness, as an unresolved ambivalence would require. In the second edition at least, he integrated the three strategies into a single argument.

2 The location of the subjective deduction in the first edition

Where Kant's main discussions of the mind are to be found and what is contained in each of them is a surprisingly complicated matter. I will begin with the first edition and TD. In that chapter, there are two main discussions of the mind, in parts 1–3 of Section 2 (A98–108) and in the whole of Section 3 (A115–27). In Section 2, Kant lays out three kinds of synthesis, looks into the nature of the apperceptive acts that do the synthesizing, and then examines the implications of these things for the unity of the mind. This passage is where Kant introduces the notion of 'transcendental apperception'; when he first introduces the term, he uses it as the name for an ability of the mind to tie a multiplicity of objects of representation together into one global object. By some mysterious process, however, a connection to our ability to be aware of ourselves as the common subject of our representations soon creeps in. Section 3 pretty much repeats the material of Section 2, indeed twice, once beginning at A115 and a second time beginning just before A120. Kant runs through the doctrine of synthesis again and goes into a bit more detail about the unity of the mind and its being the single common subject of its experiences. In light of the distinction in Chapter 2:4 between unity and identity across time, a distinction that Kant seems to draw in his attack on the inference from unity to identity central to the Third Paralogism, it is striking that he here speaks of the mind's unity as an 'identity'. He may have had primarily its identity *at a time* in mind at this point. With the exception of the attacks on the Paralogisms and a few remarks here and there in the Principles, in the first edition pretty well everything Kant has to say about synthesis and unity is located in TD.

As with synthesis and unity, Kant's main discussions of self-awareness are also all in TD and the chapter on the Paralogisms. In connection with this topic, a number of perplexing problems of interpretation arise. Exactly where and exactly why does self-awareness come into the Deduction? What is Kant trying to say about its nature? Behind these perplexities lie two more general ones.

Does 'Bewußtsein' *refer to self-awareness in Kant?*

The first concerns the very meaning Kant assigned to '*Bewußtsein*' and '*Selbstbewußtsein*', the problem we examined in Chapter 3:3. As I said there, if one takes Kant literally, it would be natural to conclude that he says very little about self-awareness in the first edition. To be sure, Kant likely had self-awareness in mind more often than his sparse use of '*Selbstbewußtsein*' or its cognates would indicate. The term '*Bewußtsein*' appears very frequently, and sometimes, at least, Kant seems to have meant self-awareness by it or, at the very least, to be running awareness and self-awareness together. However, he could distinguish them, as we saw. The argument of TD in general and the nature of Kant's ideas on self-awareness in particular can easily become indecipherable if we do not keep awareness and self-awareness as distinct as possible. As we will see in the next chapter, if we read him to mean simply awareness by '*Bewußtsein*' wherever possible, not self-awareness, some major interpretive advantages accrue. One of these advantages arises very directly in connection with the second perplexity surrounding what Kant thought about self-awareness in TD.

Does awareness of objects require awareness of self or vice-versa?

This is the perplexity shared by most commentators over how Kant saw the relationship between simple awareness of objects (conceptualized awareness, at least) and awareness of self (ASA). This is really two perplexities: Does awareness of objects require ASA, and does ASA require awareness of objects? Concerning the first, if we read Kant as meaning simple awareness by '*Bewußtsein*' most of the time, then he is connecting awareness of objects to the unity of consciousness (*Bewußtsein*), not to self-awareness (*Selbstbewußtsein*), most of the time. This produces an argument that is vastly more plausible and vastly less mysterious than those found on any other reading. His key doctrine becomes the relatively uncontroversial claim that conceptual representation requires unified consciousness, as we just saw, which is far more plausible than saying that it requires self-awareness. Indeed, the argument becomes clear and plausible – by Kantian standards.

The received wisdom, however, is that when Kant talked about awareness being a condition of experience, he meant self-awareness or at least (as Strawson cagily puts it)[18] a potential for self-awareness. The interpretive question, of course, is, Who is right here? There are problems with the received view. It ascribes to Kant a claim that is not at all plausible, Kant himself seems specifically to deny that it is his view (A103, A117n, B132), it is almost impossible to find anything in TD or anywhere else that is clearly even a putative argument for the view, and so on. In general, what Kant thought he was trying to do becomes a huge mystery; but that of course is not enough to show that the received view is wrong. This question is so central to the issue of what Kant thought the mind must be like in order to have experience that the whole of Part II of the next chapter is devoted to it.

Concerning the second part of the perplexity, whether ASA requires awareness of objects, it is possible, as I said previously, that at one point in his argument (A108), Kant begins the deduction anew with self-awareness as the datum. At any rate, that is a possible reading of the first edition; as we will see in Chapter 9, the same cannot plausibly be said about the second. However, reading self-awareness into the structure of the first-edition TD up to A107 turns it into a hash.

3 The attack on the Paralogisms in the first edition: synthesis and self-awareness

In the first edition, Kant seems to have achieved a stable position on self-awareness only as late as the chapter on the Paralogisms. Certainly his position was not stable in TD. In fact, in the whole of the first-edition Analytic there is not a single sustained discussion of the topic at all, merely hints and intimations of things that become clear only in the later discussion. We have just examined some of the consequences of this instability. Kant could get away with being unclear about self-awareness in the Analytic because it was never a central issue there. When he got to the Paralogisms, he could no longer do so; self-awareness and specifically ASA figured prominently in the rationalist doctrines about the mind he was attacking, so he was forced to consider it. That is not to say that self-awareness is the only topic under discussion in the chapter. Contrary to the impression of some commentators, misuses of self-awareness and how they can lead us astray are only one of the kinds of rationalist mistake under discussion. Strawson treats the Paralogisms chapter, for example, as if misguided appeals to self-awareness are the only thing Kant attacks. Most of the time, Bennett makes the same assumption.[19] However, Kant's attack on how the rationalists used self-awareness in their arguments concerning the nature of the mind is only part of his critique; indeed, it is not even the largest part of it. Nevertheless, it is of great significance. It is where, as part of laying out his new wrinkles on the Cartesian picture of self-awareness, Kant first advanced his ideas about what is special in reference to self and in how the self appears to itself in the ASA yielded by reference to self.

The chapter on the Paralogisms is the first of the three parts of the destructive side of Kant's project and is devoted to the soul. The other two, on the Antinomies and the Ideal, take up free will (in a discussion of the world) and God. The rationalists had made a number of metaphysical claims about the soul; Kant called the whole package rational psychology (RPsy).

These claims were transcendent, that is to say, beyond what any possible experience could confirm, including awareness of self. As a result, they were unwarranted. There could be no possible reason to believe them (or, Kant thought, to disbelieve them either). Such reasons could be of two kinds, experiential or *a priori*. It is obvious why there could not be experiential reasons. There could not be *a priori* reasons because in the absence of experience, they could not be synthetic. Thus, the only kind of *a priori* argument available would be one based on the analysis of concepts. However, the analysis of concepts by itself cannot give us any reason to think that anything corresponds to the concepts we are analysing.

The introduction to the chapter, which remained the same in both editions, takes up the interesting question of how RPsy could argue for its claims. Kant held that RPsy has only two possible foundations: *a priori* arguments or experience. That Kant posited *two* foundations for RPsy is often overlooked. He then turns to the doctrines themselves. Here begins the part of the chapter that he completely rewrote for the second edition. As Kant saw it, RPsy makes primarily three claims. (I will consider the Fourth Paralogism later.) They are that the mind (or soul, as he refers to it here) is a thing (a substance), a simple thing, and a thing that persists in a special 'strict and philosophical' way, to use a famous phrase of Butler's. With each claim, Kant thought, goes a characteristic argument. Kant tries to capture each of them in a syllogism. Because these syllogisms are faulty, he calls them Paralogisms. His aim in the chapter is to show that we have no reason either to believe *or disbelieve* the conclusions of any of these syllogisms. In all cases, the conclusions are reached by an over-interpretation of the mind's unity and powers of synthesis. Set the First Paralogism on one side. Kant begins his attack on the second by showing that unity does not entail that the soul is simple (has no parts) – how it appears to itself perhaps to the contrary – and then goes on to make some interesting remarks about how our unity and singleness, as these appear to us in our apperceptive awareness of ourselves, make it easy for us to conclude that we are simple. It is in this latter discussion that he makes his striking observations about the special features of reference to self. Kant's attack on the Third Paralogism makes some interesting observations about unity, too, now in the context of the unity across time that we must have to have experience. He argues that this unity has no implications for the nature of our persistence or identity across time, indeed does not even imply that we do persist.

I shall argue that the subjective part of TD and the chapter on the Paralogisms are closely connected – that the claims about the soul that it is the purpose of the Paralogisms chapter to undermine are direct and natural over-interpretations of central claims from the subjective deduction. When Kant said that "even the wisest of men" cannot free himself from the illusion that inspired the Paralogisms, an illusion "which unceasingly mocks and torments him", it was because he saw this illusion as a natural over-interpretation of a doctrine about the mind that he himself placed at the centre of things, the doctrine of the mind's synchronic and diachronic unity (A339 = B397; see A341 = B399). These unities seem to entail exactly what RPsy wants, that the soul is a thing, a simple thing, and a thing that persists in a special 'strict and philosophical' way. Of course, if we can know any of this about the soul, the unknowability of the noumenal mind would be undercut and Kant's defence of the possibility of immortality and free will would collapse. So he has to attack these putative entailments. The connection between the fruits of the subjective deduction and the target of the attack on the Paralogisms is extremely close and, I will argue in Chapter 7, extremely important.

Keeping this connection in mind, let us return to Kant's six contributions to our understanding of ASA. Not surprisingly, they are spread over both TD and the chapter on the Paralogisms, at least in the first edition. The distribution is interesting – three of them occur in TD, three of them in the chapter on the Paralogisms. TD contains most of what Kant has to say about topic (1), ESA and ASA (though this distinction becomes really clear only in §25 of the second edition) and the related distinction between the transcendental and the empirical aspects of the mind. It also contains the essentials of topic (3), the theory of the representational base of ASA and topic (5), the doctrine of the unity of ASA. Kant's remarks on the other three – topic (2) being the peculiar features of reference to self, topic (4) being the barrenness of ASA, and topic (6) being the mind as knowing even itself only as it appears – occur mostly in the chapter on the Paralogisms. There too we find remarks on another aspect of topic (1), the distinction between appearing as the subject and as an object of a representation, and further discussion of the implications of the mind's unity. As we will see, in the second edition Kant takes all that remains of these six items into TD.

One reason why the chapter on the Paralogisms goes much further with the topic of self-awareness than TD is that, in attacking the Paralogisms, Kant was not content merely to undermine the arguments of rational psychologists. He also tried to diagnose and dissolve our temptation to believe their conclusions. (Another philosopher who held diagnostic work to be vital in philosophy was, of course, Wittgenstein.) Diagnosing our temptation to accept RPsy enabled Kant to see very deeply into the nature of our awareness of ourselves. This is why the Paralogisms chapter goes further with self-awareness than TD ever does. Once Kant looked at the topic squarely and single-mindedly, he rapidly achieved remarkable insights into topics (2), (4), and (6). He also clarified his thoughts further on topics (1) and (5). The key passage in the Paralogisms chapter is four paragraphs on A353 and A354 in the heart of the attack on the Second Paralogism.

The nature and limits of self-awareness

Kant's attack on the Paralogisms is where the question, What exactly did he take ASA to be like? arises most acutely, as does the question, How did he think this view of ASA cuts against RPsy? If the awareness we have of ourselves in ASA appears to reveal us to ourselves as simple and persistent in some special way but does not actually do so, why not? And if we nevertheless appear in ASA to have these special features, why do we appear this way? Nor are these questions about Kant and ASA and how he used his picture of it against RPsy merely of historical interest. The rationalist view of the persistence of the mind over time is still alive and well in our time; for example, Chisholm and Swinburne have both defended aspects of it.[20]

To summarize, in the first edition, TD contains most of what Kant had to say about synthesis and unity but little on the nature of ASA or indeed on self-awareness generally. The chapter on the Paralogisms, by contrast, contains most of what he has to say about ASA and exposes certain tempting misinterpretations of the implications of the mind's unity. In addition to the Second and Third Paralogisms just discussed, there are two others. Kant's attack on the First Paralogism will not receive separate treatment; the points he makes in it can be treated in concert with the Second and Third. (I will say a bit more about this topic at the beginning of Chapter 7.) The more complicated issue of the Fourth Paralogism and its fate in the second edition will return later.

In addition to the passages we have been discussing, shorter discussions of synthesis and unity can be found in a number of places in the first *Critique*, mostly in passages that remained the same in both editions, and remarks about them can be found throughout the work. There is the treatment of the Amphiboly mentioned earlier. The discussion of the Second Antinomy contains some interesting remarks about the simplicity of the soul. The Solution to the Third Antinomy offers some obscure but fascinating remarks about free will in relation to desire and other human motivation. Finally, a couple of interesting glosses of the attack on the Paralogisms are to be found in the Doctrine of Method (A784 = B812 is the most important). With tiny exceptions such as the note added to A162 = B201, which introduces new distinctions between composition and connection, and between aggregation and coalition, into the doctrine of synthesis, all of these passages remained the same in both editions. TD and the chapter on the Paralogisms changed, however.

4 The mind and its awareness of itself in the second edition

In fact, Kant rewrote both TD and the chapter on the Paralogisms almost completely, leaving only their introductions intact. In the course of doing so, he moved his treatment of ASA from the chapter on the Paralogisms to the new TD, and built the new version of the Paralogisms chapter around a completely new strategy. In sharp contrast to the first version, Kant does not try to undermine the rational psychologist's warrant for saying that the soul is simple and so on, now. Indeed, he accepts the claims of RPsy for the sake of argument. Instead, he tries to show that even if the soul were these things, the bigger claim about immortality that the doctrines of RPsy were designed to justify would not follow. The new strategy required little discussion of either the nature of the mind or its awareness of itself, so he moved his main treatment of these issues to TD. Kant continued to insist that we have no knowledge that the mind or soul is simple, nor of anything else about it as it is (B409), but this too becomes a secondary issue and the main discussion of it moves to TD, too.

The new strategy had an important advantage. It allowed Kant to make the point he wanted to make, that RPsy has no warrant for its conclusions about immortality, while avoiding the risk of certain misunderstandings to which the version of the chapter found in the first edition is prone. The most important of these misunderstandings was that Kant was rejecting the simplicity of the soul.[21] That was not what he was doing at all. Indeed, he himself probably believed that the soul is simple. What he was rejecting was the idea that we can demonstrate that it is – or that it is not. The new strategy allowed Kant to aim this attack directly at the issue that mattered most to him, namely, immortality (A345 = B403, B424–5, etc.), and show that we have no reason to believe or disbelieve it occurs, without running any risk of being misunderstood on the simplicity of the soul. Kant made some use of the same strategy in the first edition, too, though in a different context (see A357–61).

Because of the new strategy, Kant was now free to pull his whole treatment of self-awareness out of the Paralogisms chapter and move it to TD. And that is what he did, except for scattered remarks (B408, B422, B423n) and a brief summary of his theory added as a kind of supplement to the main analysis near the end (B429–30). Because this change makes the new version of the Paralogisms chapter much less interesting for our purposes, I will not devote a chapter to it.

In other new material prepared for the second edition, both the mind in general and self-awareness in particular receive more detailed attention than in the first. We find a first gloss on the topic of self-awareness as early as the Aesthetic, in a discussion Kant added there of how self-awareness might threaten his claim that the mind is unknowable (B68). In TD, two passages are particularly important. The first begins on the first page of §15, B129, and runs to B140. In connection with the mind, it deals with the whole panoply of issues that interested Kant, including synthesis, unity, and ASA. Self-awareness is front and centre from the first page of §16. The second is found near the end of the new TD, where it seems to have been added as a kind of supplement (B153–9); it deals almost entirely with issues to do with self-awareness. In the new material from B129 to B140, Kant makes some things clearer than they ever were in the first edition: the mechanism of synthesis, how ASA connects to synthesis, and how any representation makes ASA available. The interpretive problems common to both versions of TD, such as whether acts of synthesis require at least possible ASA and whether ASA requires acts of synthesis, continue and two others become prominent.

Unity

The first problem concerns the sort of unity Kant had in mind when he talked about the unity of consciousness and so on. Kant referred to the mind's unity in the first edition, of course: unity of consciousness (A103), unity of apperception (A105, A108), absolute unity of the thinking being (A353). The famous argument (the Unity Argument, as I will later refer to it) at the beginning of the first-edition attack on the Second Paralogism (A352) is another example (see Chapter 7), and the Third Paralogism is built on a claim about cross-temporal unity. However, the second-edition TD (B130–1) contains remarks on unity that are unlike anything in the first edition: "This unity . . . is not the category of unity" (B131), for example. It also makes claims that help to clarify the nature of this unity – for example, the claims that even a thoroughly disunified mind could still be aware of objects (B134) (and in which of the senses of 'aware' delineated in Chapter 3:1). We discussed the mind's unity in Chapter 2:4–5, and it will figure in every chapter from now on.

Kant on the nature of the mind

The second interpretive issue is the question of how Kant saw the mind's overall structure and composition, to the extent that he thought we can know anything about these things at all. This question arises in the passage beginning on B129 and hardly anywhere else. As I said in Chapter 1, Kant does seem to have had views about the nature of the mind, views that make contact with functionalism and the representational model of the mind. Functions are inferred, not known directly, and representations have to do with the mind as it appears to itself, not as it is, so views like these could, perhaps, be reconciled with the unknowability of the mind as it is. However, Kant also seems to have views about what the mind is like, or at least what it could not be like, in itself. Widely varying accounts have been given of these views, ranging from suggestions that he held that the mind is immaterial and a substantial being with a specific, strong sort of identity over time, all the way to suggestions that he viewed the mind, in Kitcher's words, as nothing more than a Humean "system of informationally [or, as she now puts it, contentually] interdependent states" – a new associationism.[22] This question arises particularly sharply in B129–40 because that is where exciting new ideas about the mind as representation seem to appear most clearly: the mind not only has representations; it is a representation, a global representation, at least as we can know it. Not only is this idea important in its own right, it might help to clarify some other obscurities – for example, Kant's tendency, especially in the second edition, to treat apperception as a representation of self while continuing to view it as a capacity to make judgements. This idea that the mind is a global representation will be a central topic of Chapter 9. If Kant held such a view, that would lead to another question: Is holding the mind to be a representation not inconsistent with denying that we know (or know that we know) the mind as it is? We will address this question in Chapter 10:4–5, where I will argue that there is no inconsistency.

The main issue of the second new passage, the one from B153 to B159, is closely connected to the one just discussed. It is this: Does ASA make us aware of mere appearances of the self or of the self itself? Though this question was always in the background, Kant did not address it directly anywhere in the first edition. In the years after the first edition was published, he did confront the issue, perhaps because of the tension between the stark implausibility of claiming that we have no awareness of ourselves at all, only of representations, on the one hand, an implausibility of which Kant was well aware (B68 and B152–3), and his view that the noumenal self is unknowable, on the other. He could not give up the view; but how could he maintain it? I suspect the urgency of this problem was one reason Kant moved his whole treatment of self-awareness to TD for the second edition.

Both the structure and the location of the passage from B153 to B159 are so awkward that we should go through it step by step. Wedged between the first half of section §24 and the notorious section §26, its contents are not obviously connected to anything before or after. Nor is anything like it to be found in the first edition. The passage has two main parts. The first begins after three asterisks, in both the original and the English translation, half-way through §24. It addresses the problem of whether we can have knowledge of ourselves as we are, in the particular form of a problem about how an active subject can be passive to its own appearances of itself in inner sense (B153–7; see B68). To solve this problem Kant gives a more detailed account of the distinction between self-awareness via apperception (ASA) and self-awareness via other aspects of inner sense (ESA) than he ever gives anywhere else. Then he suddenly jumps without warning, still in the same §24 of the Deduction, to something that seems quite different. We suddenly find him launching an argument that a kind of non-concept-using synthesis is required prior to any experience. Though this issue connects to some of the material in the surrounding sections of TD, how it connects to the topic of the active mind passively affecting itself is not, to say the least, obvious.

Next comes the second part of the supplement (B157–9) and another jump. This part has its own section number, §25, but no title, itself uncharacteristic of Kant. Here he finally takes up the crucial problem: Is one aware of one's real self? This issue turns out to be connected to another one, how one appears to oneself in ASA. Kant then handles both issues more clearly than he did anywhere in his treatment of them in the first edition. His treatment of these issues is also strangely over-simplified by comparison with the first edition. In particular, the new ideas he laid out in the first edition about reference to self almost disappear. Moreover, how this section is supposed to connect to the material in §24 about non-concept-using synthesis is far from clear. Kant then wades off into the murky waters of §26. This is not a happy state of affairs; the whole passage strikes one as more a mislocated appendix than anything else. As we have seen, the passage gives rise to a distinctive interpretive problem.

Am I aware of myself?

The problem is this. Did Kant hold that we are aware of our actual selves in ASA or just highly doctored representations (appearances) of self? The latter would seem more consistent with his position on the unknowability of the mind as it is,[23] but Kant seems to say both that we are aware of our actual selves and that we have no knowledge of the mind's actual qualities (B157; see B68). We will investigate how these views can be reconciled in Chapter 10. The solution is to be found in Kant's ideas about reference to and awareness of self.

In the two passages from B129 to B140 and from B153 to B159, Kant pulls together in one chapter most of what he has to say about the nature of the mind and about its awareness of itself. The passages in the Antinomies and the Doctrine of Method are still there, of course. There is the new passage I mentioned earlier at the end of the Aesthetic. But it remains true nevertheless that in the second edition most of what Kant has to say about the mind is found in TD. The only significant exception is the new Refutation of Idealism.

5 The Fourth Paralogism and the Refutation of Idealism

Kant wrote the new Refutation of Idealism to answer the charge that his theory of perception was a form of subjective idealism containing a tendency to scepticism and solipsism. Kant's refutation consists of an attempt to tie the possibility of one sort of awareness of self to awareness of permanence in something other than ourselves. The argument utilizes self-awareness in a highly original way.

It used to be orthodox to say that this new Refutation of Idealism replaces the argument against the Fourth Paralogism of the first edition, which Kant then dropped.[24] I do not think that this is entirely right. There are striking similarities of content between the two passages, but there are also striking differences: the first-edition attack on the Fourth Paralogism contains nothing like the discussion of the conditions under which we could have a sense of our own permanence, the discussion that dominates the new Refutation. The most important reason for doubting the received view, however, is that the second edition still has a separate Fourth Paralogism (B409)! Far from excising it, Kant retained it and again attacked it. Though he refocused both the Paralogism and his attack to make the connection to immortality more obvious, it is still there, to the same extent that any of the other Paralogisms are still there as separate Paralogisms. Since he also added a Refutation of Idealism, he must have thought of his attack on the Fourth Paralogism and his new Refutation as making distinct contributions. It would take us far afield to discuss these complicated passages here; I examine them elsewhere.[25]

6 Interpretive perplexities

In the course of this chapter, I have singled out six questions about which Kant's texts are particularly elusive. All six of them are constantly in the background of Kant's discussions of the mind, and it is important to have them in the back of our minds. Most of them have already been discussed once and will be again.

1. When Kant used the term '*Bewußtsein*', what exactly did he mean by it? Did he distinguish it from '*Selbstbewußtsein*'? Does the answer to this question throw any light on the way he used the term 'transcendental apperception' both as a name for judgements of a certain sort and to refer to self-awareness (Chapters 3 and 4)?
2. To be aware of objects, must one also be aware of oneself or have some kind of potential for awareness of self? Conversely, must one have a certain sort of awareness of objects to be aware of oneself (Chapters 6 and 9)?
3. What did Kant think ASA is like (Chapter 4), and by what means do we obtain it? How did he think his view of ASA cuts against RPsy (Chapters 7 and 8)?
4. What kind of unity did Kant think was at work in the unity of consciousness, unity of apperception, and so on (Chapters 2:4 and 6:I:5)? What sort of unity does a mind appear to itself to have (Chapters 7, 8, and 9)?
5. How did Kant view the mind's composition or structure, and how does this relate to his functionalism or protofunctionalism? How was he entitled to any such views, given his doctrine of the unknowability of the noumenal mind (Chapter 10)?
6. In our awareness of ourselves, are we ever aware of our actual self or just of appearances of ourselves (Chapter 10)?

Note that synthesis is not mentioned in any of these questions. Whatever one may think of Kant's doctrine of synthesis, it has not at any rate generated classic and long-standing problems of interpretation in the way other pronouncements have; it does arise, of course, as an issue in connection with question 2. On each of these six issues, Kant's exact views are notoriously difficult to pin down. We have some intellectual archaeology ahead of us if we want to discover what he still has to say to us about the mind. In the five remaining chapters, I will examine the five major discussions, one per chapter.

6

The first-edition subjective deduction: the object of 'one experience'

Having sketched the geography, both conceptual and textual, of Kant's work on the mind and marked out some of the bogs, it is time to get down to work. In an introductory section, we begin with a brief look at what a subjective deduction is about and why Kant included one. In the remainder of Part I we will examine some aspects of Kant's views on the synthesis of objects of representation and the uniting of a multiplicity of representations into what he called 'one experience' (A108), that is, one global representation. Part II is concerned with a more exegetical matter: the perplexing business of how Kant connected these things to self-awareness and why. Though Kant's ideas about synthesis and unity, the heart of his theory of mind, are parts of a theory of awareness of objects, he also connected these things to awareness of self. Part II examines this perplexing connection. (We have already discussed self-awareness itself in Chapter 4.) As I said earlier, my interest is in uncovering what Kant has to tell us about the mind; thus, I am less interested in whether TD managed to do anything that might be called 'deducing the Categories'.

As I said in Chapter 5:1, I view TD as primarily an argument from awareness of objects, Guyer's first starting point, not awareness of self, his second.[1] This is clearer in the first edition than in the second. Indeed, in the first edition, self-awareness does not even make an appearance until A107, two-thirds of the way through the first, Section 2 statement of the argument (A95–114). However, the second edition takes off from the first starting point, too. Even though self-awareness is front and centre from the beginning of §16, the best-known part of the chapter, §15 is the first part of the deduction, not §16, and it is about the conditions of anything being "combined in the object" (B130). Though §15 is radically shorter than the comparable discussion in the first edition, it is still about the conditions of representation of objects. The only difference between these sections in the two editions that might be significant is that Kant focuses more on *making judgements* about objects in the second edition than on *representation* of objects. (Kitcher make a lot of this difference, perhaps more than is warranted.) Nevertheless, self-awareness is more prominent in the second edition than the first. The investigation of these conditions of representing objects yields more insights into the nature of synthesis and the mind's unity than the conditions of self-awareness yield, so we will focus on the first-edition TD here and leave the second-edition version for Chapter 9. For many commentators, the first-edition TD is a swamp, a jungle, a morass, a patchwork, even a botch.[2] Strawson and Allison largely avoid it. By contrast, because the first starting-point argument is clearer and developed in more detail in the first edition than the second and this is the argument that yields the most interesting insights into synthesis and unity, I prefer it. The only topic on which the second version of TD is superior to the first is self-awareness; but on this topic, the first-edition attack on the Paralogisms is superior to both. Like Guyer and Kitcher, I think there are things to be learned in both versions of TD, but the first version has the edge, Section 2 in particular.

I SYNTHESIS AND UNITY

1 What is a subjective deduction, and why did Kant offer one?

The version of the deduction in the first *Critique* actually contains two deductions, as I indicated in the preceding chapter. In addition to the objective deduction justifying the application of the Categories to objects of representation, there is a subjective deduction of what the mind must be like to do so. The former deduction was by far the more important one for Kant, being the royal road, as he saw it, to an understanding of how physics can be synthetic *a priori* knowledge. As Henrich, Walker, and Guyer have described, versions of TD exist in other works that do not so much as mention what the mind must be like.[3] So what is a subjective deduction and why have one?

The subjective and objective deductions are not separate arguments; the former is part of the latter. The objective deduction is about the conceptual requisites of representing objects, making judgements, namely, the application of categorial concepts to the raw material of represented objects. The subjective deduction is about what the mind must be like in order to do so – the competences it must have and the chief mental requisite it must have, namely, being unified. Since the Categories must be *applied,* there will always be a subjective element, implicitly or explicitly, in any objective deduction. To the extent that the subjective deduction can be isolated as a separate line of argument, however, it can be viewed as containing one, two, or all three of the following:

(i) a doctrine of synthesis, of how concepts get applied;
(ii) a doctrine of what a synthesizer, a mind, must be like (here unity is the central notion);
(iii) a doctrine of the relation of the mind's awareness of itself to unity, to synthesis and/or to the application of concepts to objects.

These three possible parts of a subjective deduction are nested, earlier ones being *prima facie* independent of later ones. Each of them is also different from the others; the power to synthesize is not the same thing as being a unified subject, and synthesis and unity are not the same thing as self-awareness. The power to synthesize is a key part of the strategy that starts from representation or judgement of objects; self-awareness is the starting point of the other strategy Henrich and Guyer identify; and unity is central to what could have been a third. I have carefully separated the three for another reason, too. As I will argue in this chapter, we could be unified and use our power to synthesize without being aware of ourselves. Indeed, awareness of oneself is not even tightly connected to unity and the power to synthesize. Moreover, some of the time at least, this seems to have been Kant's view, too.

Beyond the doctrines of synthesis and the faculties of the mind (sensibility, imagination, understanding, and reason, if reason was a separate faculty for Kant), there is little agreement on what should be included under the label 'subjective deduction'. Kemp Smith, for example, seems to place the mind's unity and its awareness of itself, ASA at any rate, in the objective deduction. In my view, this issue is not important, because everything in the subjective deduction is part of the objective deduction as Kant developed it in the *Critique*. It is important, however, not to allocate things in a way that hides the close links between functions (the doctrine of synthesis) and nonfunctional properties of the mind (unity) in Kant's theory. Separating synthesis off from the others would also make it easier to think that synthesis largely disappears in the second edition, when in fact it does not do so, as we will see in Chapter 9.[4]

As we saw in Chapter 5:1, the subjective deduction enters the main line of TD in the following way. In order to show how the Categories could be about anything, could have objects, Kant is led to the conditions of *representations* having objects. He puts it this way. To "prove that by [the use of the categorial concepts] alone an object can be thought" (A97), he will not examine these concepts directly. Instead, he will examine the "subjective sources which form the *a priori* foundation of the possibility of experience", that is to say, the capacities we use to be aware of objects. Thus, he 'deduces' the Categories by asking what capacities or competences a mind must have if it is to represent objects. This investigation will lead him to his ideas about synthesis, unity, and also, as we will see, to his theory of the representational base of ASA. Kant thought of the mind as a system of concept-employing functions ("concepts rest on functions" [A68 = B93]) that generate and manipulate a system of representations. (In the radical representationalism of the second edition, he seems to have come to think of the functions as activities of a representation, too; see Chapter 9.) Not all of the mind's functions are concept using, not directly at least, but some of the essential ones are; for Kant, the concepts they use must include those of number, quality, relationship, and existence status (possible, actual, necessary) – the Categories.[5] In this way, the subjective deduction becomes the core of the objective deduction, too.

These 'subjective sources' turn out to be three special abilities to synthesize and the unity required to use them. The doctrine of synthesis has two parts. The first, which takes up over half of Section 2 (A97–105), is concerned with synthesis of individual objects. The second part follows immediately (A105–8). It is an argument that as well as synthesizing individual objects of representation, the mind must also be able to synthesize groups of objects and representations of them into 'one experience'. At this point, the unities enter; the mind must be able to be aware of numerous things as one object, and to do that it must be the single common subject of the representations of all these objects. On A108, a further element enters the picture, namely, ASA, and Kant makes some key remarks on the representational base of having it (see Part II and Chapter 4:3). Kant finishes Section 2 with what still remains to be done in the objective deduction (A109–14). Then in Section 3 (A115–27), he goes over much the same material again, indeed twice, first sketching the argument (A115–19) and then giving a full restatement of it (starting just before A120). I will focus on Section 2.

2 Kitcher and Kant's doctrine of synthesis

Kant's doctrine of synthesis has been an object of scorn, Strawson's attitude being the most famous example. (We examined two of his remarks in Chapter 1.) In a decade of publications culminating in her book, Kitcher has powerfully reclaimed the doctrine for contemporary theory. For my part, I do not see how we could make sense of the cognitive powers of the mind without some such doctrine. The ability we have to locate the stuff of our experience spatially and temporally, find units (intentional objects) in it, and relate these objects and our experience of them to one another in a myriad of ways seems to me to be absolutely central to being aware or thinking. In favour of Kant's doctrine, Kitcher seems to me to establish a number of points quite conclusively. (1) Whatever order or divisions there may be in things in the world, the perturbations of the sensitive surfaces of our body (retinas, ear-drums, finger-tips), which are the basis of sensible representation, are not preordered, certainly not with the order of the world. Thus, for our experience to have organized, unified objects, we need a rich ability to structure and organize sensible stimuli.[6] As Kant put it late in his life to Beck in a letter, "We must *synthesize* if we are to recognize anything as *synthesized* (even space and time)".[7] Even if things in the world have order, we need an ability that is independent of that order to recognize it. (This constructivism is also the answer to the charge that Kant's whole doctrine of synthesis is built on an archaic, atomistic theory of sensible stimulation, and captures a lot of what is still living in transcendental idealism.) (2) The limitations on what objects of representation are possible are far more stringent than could be explained by any temporal order in representations or spatiotemporal order in their objects. (3) Because practically anything can become associated with anything else (because, as Kitcher puts it, associations can be too promiscuous), associationism cannot account for what needs to be explained in either (1) or (2). Thus, associationism cannot explain our ability to form or find objects of representation.[8]

Rather than re-cover ground Kitcher has covered well, I will focus on some things she does not cover so well. As Kitcher recognizes, "Two synthetic unities are required for cognition, . . . of a representation [and] among cognitive states." By the latter, she means synthesis *among* representations, that is to say, synthesis of a number of representations into something bigger. These two unities correspond to a fundamental division in the doctrine of synthesis.[9] One part is concerned to identify the conditions under which individual objects of perception and belief are formed. The other and even more important part is concerned to identify what we must do to be aware of groups of objects collectively, as single global objects. However, Kitcher does no more than acknowledge the division and makes little of the second part of it. The second unity is always in large part synchronic, so Kitcher's scanting the second part may be connected to her thinking that the unity here, the unity of consciousness, is an across-time unity, related to personal identity or individuation.[10] That Kant thought the second part to be vital is indicated by the fact that he introduces the notions of transcendental apperception (TA) and what I call the global representation and global object in connection with it.

The first part of Kant's doctrine of synthesis consists of an argument that three cognitive abilities are required to represent objects, namely, apprehending, reproducing, and recognizing in concepts, and that each uses a distinct form of synthesis (A97–105). The third kind of synthesis also requires recognitional ability, of course. Somewhat surprisingly, Kitcher completely ignores recognition in her reconstruction of Kant's argument. This gap may be connected to the first one: Kant uses recognition to introduce precisely the second part of the doctrine of synthesis that Kitcher scants. The move from synthesizing individual objects to the second great part of Kant's doctrine of synthesis, the synthesizing of multiple representations and/or their objects into 'one experience', is a move from one target of acts of recognition to another. Here is how he makes it.

The syntheses of apprehension, reproduction, and recognition of single objects (a triangle [A105], a material object [A106], a sentence in a verse [A352]) march in a single temporal line. On describing recognition of individual objects, at A106 Kant suddenly makes a kind of 90° turn; from following the retention, reproduction, and recognition of a representation across time, he suddenly starts discussing a form of recognition that requires the unification and recognition of representations all existing *at the same time.* I mean the recognition of multiple objects and the representation of them in one representation. He moves from the first synthetic unity to the second, from the unity of acts of recognition of individual objects to the unity of acts of global recognition of multiple objects which "stand along side one another in one experience" (A108).[11] Around this right turn pivots a fundamental difference between Kitcher's vision of how Kant pictured the mind and mine. For Kitcher, Kant's picture is diachronic – a vision of a stream of successive representation elements – and the question is, How do earlier ones and later ones get tied together into representations of objects? For me, synchronic activity, a mind aware of a range of things at the same time, figures at least as centrally in Kant's picture as the diachronic, and one major question is, How can a multiplicity of *simultaneous* representation elements get tied together into representations of objects? I am interested in the diachronic dimension of representation, too, of course, but am quite content to let it wait until Chapter 8 to make an exclusive appearance. Interestingly enough, both visions can find some succour in Kant's texts, but an exclusively diachronic reading also faces sizable problems there.

In none of Kitcher, Bennett, Wilkerson,[12] Walker, Allison,[13] or Guyer (I think) does recognition of a number of simultaneous representations at the same time get much play. Even Strawson, who certainly gives the recognitional component of representation its due, does not identify this global form of it separately, though that is what he is in fact discussing sometimes. Likewise, this form of recognition plays little role in current research. That is true of even the large-scale cognitive systems like Act* and Soar that deal with simultaneous representations. They may make room for simultaneous representations, but they do not even discuss recognition. The same is true of binding theory and most other theories of smaller-scale phenomena. One partial exception is Treisman's model; it talks about recognition, but only recognition of individual objects. (All these theories were introduced in Chapter 2:1 and 2:3.) The only empirical work that touches on this form of recognition is Gestalt research; in fact, it has many points of contact with Kant's doctrine.[14] One might think that psychic holism theorists in philosophy might be interested in the form of recognition we are discussing, being concerned with ensembles of representations and so on, but nothing in these theories comes even close. They deal with what is recognized, not recognition – with content, not consciousness.

3 Apprehension, reproduction, and recognition in concepts

Kant lays out his three kinds of syntheses in three distinct discussions. Few commentators consider these discussions separately. Any object of representation has what Kant called a manifold (*Mannigfaltigen*), a notion we considered in Chapter 3:1. For a mind to represent an object, Kant tells us in the first part of his theory of synthesis, these elements must be recognizable as a single intentional object. This requires synthesis.

> By *synthesis,* in its most general sense, I understand the act of putting different representations together, and of grasping what is manifold in them in one knowledge. (A77 = B103; Kemp Smith's interpolation removed)

Each of the three kinds of synthesis, synthesis of apprehension in intuition, synthesis of reproduction in imagination, and synthesis of recognition in a concept, relates to a different aspect of Kant's fundamental duality of intuition and concept. Synthesis of apprehension concerns intuitions, synthesis of recognition concerns concepts, and synthesis of reproduction, or rather synthetic imagination as a whole including productive imagination, allows the mind to go from the one to the other. In different terms, one is the province of sensibility, one is the province of understanding, and the one in the middle is the province of a faculty that has a far less settled position than the other two, imagination (see A120). The first two, apprehension and reproduction, are inseparable; one cannot occur without the other (A102). The third, recognition, requires the other two but is not required by them. My terms 'awareness^{R}' and 'awareness^{RR}' were designed to capture the difference between the first two and the third. It seems that only the third requires the use of concepts; non-concept-using syntheses and their relationship to use of the Categories becomes a substantial issue in the second edition (see B150–65), where Kant tries to save the universality of the objective deduction by arguing that all three kinds of syntheses are required to represent objects. We will return to this issue toward the end of Section 5.

Acts of synthesis are performed on that to which we are passive in experience, namely, intuitions. A great deal of work has been done on Kant's notion of intuition (*Anschauung*), and I will not try to redo it here. In general terms, intuitions are quite different from sense-data as classically understood; we can recognize intuitions only after acts of synthesis, not as they come to us. Thus, they are something more like theoretical entities (or better, events) postulated to explain something in what we do recognize.[15] What they explain is that there is an element in representations over which we have no control. Actually, there are two elements over which we have no control, a conceptual one and a nonconceptual one.[16] The postulation of intuitions explains the nonconceptual element, the idea that we have to use the Categories explains the conceptual one. Intuition is the element in representation that forces certain representations on us; it determines therefore how our representations will serve to confirm or refute theories, aid or impede our efforts to reach various goals. It is also probably the element that yields pleasure and pain.

According to Kant, something happens to intuitions even prior to acts of synthesis, namely, a *synopsis* in inner sense. Kant speaks of synopsis only twice in the whole first edition (A94–5 and A97), the notion disappears in the second, and it seems not to recur anywhere else in his work. Thus, it is hard to know what he meant by it. My best guess is that a synopsis is simply a number of intuitions becoming either a coexistent or temporally arrayed but otherwise undifferentiated manifold. If so, it is just a manifold of intuition by another name.[17] At any rate, three kinds of synthesis are performed on this synopsis, beginning with the synthesis of apprehension in intuition.

Synthesis of apprehension in intuition

The synthesis of apprehension is also a somewhat shadowy notion. In the second edition, the idea does not even appear until §26, that is, until late in

TD. At A120, Kant tells us that apprehending impressions is taking them up into the activity of imagination, that is, into the faculty of the mind that becomes aware of images. He tells us that we can achieve the kind of differentiation we need to take them up only "in so far as the mind distinguishes the time in the sequence of one impression upon another" (A99). Kant uses the term 'impression' (*Eindrucke*) rarely; it seems to be in the same camp as 'appearance' (*Erscheinung*) and 'intuition' (*Anschauung*). The idea behind the strange saying just quoted seems to be this. Kant seems to have believed that we can become aware of only one new item at a time. Thus, a group of simultaneous 'impressions' all arriving at the same time would be indistinguishable, "for each representation (*Vorstellung*), *in so far as it is contained in a single moment,* can never be anything but absolute unity" (A99, his emphasis). Kant's use of *'Vorstellung',* with its suggestion of synthesized, conceptualized organization, may have been unfortunate, but what I think he meant is this. Prior to synthesis and conceptual organization, the only distinction we could draw in a manifold of intuitions would be a temporal one, so that a coexistent manifold would be an undifferentiated unit, a seamless, buzzing confusion. (This view of how many new impressions we can take in at once plays a role in the Second Analogy, too.) Thus, the only way to distinguish one impression from another would be to locate them separately in time. If so, this synthesis of apprehension is closely related to the Transcendental Aesthetic. It is the imposing of organization within the pure manifold of time by locating each intuition at a specific point in that manifold. Moreover, says Kant, we must do the same to time (and to space) itself, in a pure synthesis of apprehension. I think he means that just having a sense of undifferentiated time and space is not enough; we must also impose a metric on them.[18]

What happens, then, to simultaneous intuitions and to intuitions that we fix as occurring at the same time? Kant would not have denied that either exists. If a manifold of intuitions includes such things as colour, shape, size, and so on, then many manifolds of intuition contain coexisting elements. Moreover, without coexisting intuitions, nothing could be located in space, this requiring the idea of simultaneous items having different locations. The answer, I think, is that in order to distinguish different representations in simultaneous intuitions, we have to use the more discriminating kind of synthesis that Kant called recognition in a concept. We cannot do it with apprehension alone. Likewise, intuitions can be fixed as *occurring* at the same time, in the absence of a more sophisticated synthesis, only if *we have them* at different times. The view that we can experience only one item at a time, a view Kitcher shares, may have contributed to her impression that Kant's doctrine of synthesis is largely or entirely about across-time acts of unifying.[19] (As we will see shortly, what synthesis of reproduction is about contributes to this impression.) It is vitally important to see, however, that Kant is talking here only of presynthesized intuitions. The extent to which they can coexist and the extent to which representations with fully synthesized objects could coexist might be two very different things. We will return to this point.

Synthesis of reproduction in imagination

The synthesis of reproduction in imagination has two elements, a synthesis proper and associations necessary for performing that synthesis. (Kant explicitly treats them as separate on A125: "recognition, reproduction, association, apprehension".) Both start from the appearances, as Kant now calls them, which the synthesis of apprehension has located in time. At first glance, the element of synthesis in the synthesis of reproduction looks very much like memory; however, it is actually quite different from memory. It is a matter of retaining earlier intuitions in such a way that certain other representations can "bring about a transition of the mind" to these earlier representations, even in the absence of any current representation of them (A100). Such transitions are simply the result of acquiring an association (which, moreover, could be entirely nonconscious). This is not memory and does not even require memory. Likewise, no recognition of any sort need be involved; that the earlier representations have become associated with later ones is not something we need recognize, by either of the kinds of recognition distinguished in Chapter 3:1. Memory and recognition are both the job of synthesis of recognition, yet to come.

The necessary condition of performing these acts of associative reproduction is that we be able to find in appearances "a co-existence or sequence tak[ing] place in conformity with certain rules" (A100). Appearances must exhibit regularity in their relations to one another. Note that Kant speaks of a *coexistence* or sequence – these regularities may be at one time or across time or both. Thus, even though the synthesis of reproduction is obviously a diachronic activity, it yields synchronic results.

To our ears at least, it is a little strange to find Kant calling this activity of reproduction and the activity of apprehension acts of 'imagination'. Is it not just some form of automatic repetition? The answer is that it is not just repetition, if by repetition we mean merely the reintroduction of an old appearance into the present. The unordered flow of intuition is not simply repeated, it is connected to other things in some orderly way. That requires construction as well as repetition. Imagination is not just reproductive; it is also productive, a process of forming pictures and finding organization in intuition. This connecting is a connecting of elements by forming an image: "Imagination has to bring the manifold of intuitions into the form of an image" (A120). If 'imagination' is understood in its root sense of image making and we see imagination not as opposed to but as part of perception, Kant's choice of term is less peculiar. Kant describes the function he had in mind as "a blind but indispensable function of the soul" (A78 = B103), so he certainly had something rather different from what we think of as imagination in mind. In fact, the sense of the term 'imagination' seems to have been different in Kant's time from what it is in ours, or so at any rate Kant certainly thought (A120n).[20]

Apprehension and imagination, Kant also tells us, are required for awareness of more than the objects of empirical representation. Even such purely *a priori* representations as "the purest and most elementary representations of space and time" (A102) require acts of apprehension and reproduction. What exactly Kant means here is not entirely clear, but I will stand by my earlier suggestion: that he is talking about something to do with temporal and spatial metrics (see the second-edition opening of the Axioms of Intuition [B202–3]). As I noted earlier, Kant says apprehension and reproduction go together: "The synthesis of apprehension is . . . inseparably bound up with the synthesis of reproduction" (A102). For the object of a representation to have a determinant place, we have to be able to reproduce earlier representations or simultaneous but different representations of the thing so that the first representation is "set in a relation" (A100) to other representations of it.

Synthesis of recognition in a concept

The third kind of synthesis is synthesis of recognition in a concept. To introduce it, recall the two levels I distinguished in the process of coming to recognize what I had written in the piece of bad handwriting (see the opening of Chapters 2 and 3) and the definitions of different kinds of awareness introduced to delineate them. The first level, finding a representation of a word in the scrawl of the handwriting, required no recognition and was called awareness^{R}:

Awareness^{R} of ***X*** **=*df:*** having access to *X* such that (i) awareness^{I} (accessing information) is present and, in addition, (ii) behaviour with respect to *X* can be explained only by reference to how *X* is represented to someone, not by how *X* actually is.

Awareness^{R} is meant to correspond to Kant's syntheses of apprehension and recollection. The second level was recognizing the word thus represented. For this I coined the term awareness^{RR}.

Awareness^{RR} of ***X*** **=*df:*** being aware^{R} of *X*, plus recognizing *X*.

Awareness^{RR} corresponds to Kant's recognition in a concept. Note that I had to use a concept to recognize the squiggle as a word, namely, the concept expressed by the word written in the scrawl.

Kant held that I had to use many more concepts than that; indeed, this is the crucial claim of the objective deduction. Kant argued that I had to locate the scrawl temporally and in this case also spatially (which, however, may not require use of concepts in his view), and then had to use at least the following kinds of concepts: concepts of quantity (it is one scribble, is made up of curves, and so on), of quality (the curves and so on add up to a particular shape, make up a particular word), and of modality (it is a real scribble, not an imagined one). These, of course, are concepts from three of the four kinds of Categories. That recognizing the word required the use of concepts like these is Kant's fundamental reason for thinking that we must use the Categories, the main claim of TD. Note that I did not mention use of any relational concepts.

In Kant's view, recognition requires memory; if synthesis of reproduction is not memory, true memory does enter with the synthesis of recognition. The argument goes as follows. An appearance causing another appearance to reenter awareness would never be enough by itself for the two of them to become elements in a single object of representation. Perhaps each of them could be a momentary object by itself, but no object of representation of any connectedness or temporal depth could result, and that is tantamount to saying that no object of representation of any cognitive use to us could result.

> [A merely reproduced] manifold of representation would never . . . form a whole, since it would lack that unity which only consciousness can impart to it. If, in counting, I forget that the units, which now hover before me, have been added to one another in succession, I should never know that a total is being produced through this successive addition of unit to unit. (A103; see A78 = B104)

As this passage makes clear, synthesis by recognition requires two things. One is memory – true memory, that is to say, recovery and recognition of past representations as past, not just associative reproduction. The other, of course, is 'consciousness', that is to say, recognition – something in the past representations must be recognized as related to present ones. As Kant tells us and as I think is obvious, forgetting earlier representations would render impossible any form of synthesis that requires recognition of connections between earlier and later. Then comes the move that is crucial to deducing the Categories: to recognize that earlier and later representations are both representing a single object, we must use a concept, a rule (A121 and A126), or rather we must use a number of concepts: a concept of number, a concept of quality, a concept of modality, and of course, the specific empirical concept for the object we are recognizing.

Note Kant's equation of recognition and awareness. In Chapter 3, I suggested that Kant may run recognition in a *concept* and recognition in *consciousness* together, and this passage seems to contain a prime example. I introduced the distinction between awareness$^{RR\text{-}CC}$ and awareness$^{RR\text{-}CS}$ to tag the difference between these two. It is the difference between the conceptual content of a representation affecting me semantically, inferentially, and so on and my being able to report what it looks like and so on. Awareness$^{RR\text{-}CS}$ is what we have that blind-sight patients lack who find nothing to report in a portion of their visual field despite using words that are presented there and only there to disambiguate other words, or reaching in the right place for something if told to reach for something presented only in the 'blind' portion of their visual field and so on. Kant seems to run these two kinds of awareness together. In addition, he seems to think that the earlier kinds of synthesis are not acts of awareness at all. I disagree with him on all counts; where he sees one kind of awareness, I see three. Apprehension and reproduction are awareness^{R}. Recognition adds something new. However, this new recognitional element can be either awareness$^{RR\text{-}CC}$ or awareness$^{RR\text{-}CS}$.

Note that we are not talking about any form of self-awareness in any of the three cases just distinguished, not ESA of the act of recognition itself and certainly not ASA; in all three cases, we are talking about different forms of simple awareness of objects. I think that is the point Kant is making when he says, somewhat quaintly, that an act of recognition may be so faint that "we do not connect [our awareness] to the act itself, that is, . . . to the *generation* of the representation, but only to the outcome" (A103–4; Kemp Smith's translation modified slightly), though there is a problem with the passage to which we will return later. We can be aware of the object that results without being aware of the act of recognition that produced it. For Kant, recognitional awareness and even ESA are not the same thing, let alone ASA. In my view, no distinction is more important for an understanding of the argument in TD. Self-awareness does enter TD eventually, in fact in a most peculiar way, a point to which we will return in Part II. But the vital point is that Kant did not take it to go with all recognition in a concept. It is not there from the beginning.

4 Apperception and the unity of individual objects

It is time to wheel the unity of consciousness back onto the stage. The unity of consciousness is found in all acts of recognition; they are all awareness in one act of various elements tied together into an object of a representation – for example, three straight lines as a triangle, or shape and impenetrability as a physical object (A106): "The [unified] object makes necessary a unity which can be nothing else than the formal unity of consciousness" (A105; translation modified slightly). What makes unified acts of awareness yielding unified objects possible is the "synthesis of the manifold of representations" (A105). The unity of which Kant is speaking here does not contain everything included in the definition of the unity of consciousness in Chapter 2:

The unity of consciousness =*df:* (i) a single act of consciousness, which (ii) makes one aware of a number of representations and/or objects of representation in such a way that to be aware of any of this group is also to be aware of at least some others in the group and as a group.

At A105 Kant is talking only about unified awareness of individual objects, but the definition also includes unity across a representation of multiple objects. This may be why Kant calls the unity of which he is speaking here a 'formal unity'. Though it is more than the analytic unity we discussed in Chapter 2:5, it is less than the synthetic unity across a number of represented objects that we distinguished there. However, the difference between formal and full synthetic unity seems to be merely a difference of scope.

Now bring apperception back. Immediately after introducing recognition, Kant reintroduces apperception (he had mentioned it once before at A94) and first mentions the unity of apperception. (In the second edition, apperception is mentioned still earlier, at B68.) By apperception, here as at A94, Kant means what he means by awareness: the faculty or capacity for judging in accord with a rule, for applying concepts – the faculty that produces acts of awareness[RR]. Apperception is simply the faculty that performs syntheses of recognition (see A115); Kant also extends the term to the acts that this faculty performs. Apperception in this sense has nothing directly to do with awareness of self or even *awareness* of acts of apperceiving. Apperceiving is here conceived as an activity necessary for and parallel to perceiving (see A120). This is one of the senses in which Leibniz used the term, too.[21] To achieve unified awareness, unified recognition of a unified object, the mind must perform an act of judgement; it must find how various represented elements are connected to one another. This judgement is an act of apperception; the unity of apperception expresses the idea that for a single mind to range over a number of represented elements and be aware of them as one object, an act of judgement is needed to connect them under a concept. Unity of apperception is necessary for unity of acts of recognition and so for unity of consciousness. Note that we are not dealing here with *transcendental* apperception; nor, because we are dealing with representations of individual objects, are we dealing yet with global representations or global objects. The two points are connected, as we will see in the next section.

Kant's project in TD is to find out how categorial concepts could apply to anything, could have objects (A85 = B117), and he pursues it by asking how there could be objects of representation of any sort, how there could be anything for representations to be about. Yet, remarkably enough, when the crunch comes, and it comes with the synthesis of recognition, he actually says very little about objects. He says a lot about representations and about connecting representations, but little about objects. As we discussed in Chapter 5:1, he does tell us that he is talking about what we would now call intentional objects, not 'objective' objects of any sort (A104), and that real objects corresponding to intentional objects remain beyond our grasp; they are the realm of his transcendental object = *x*. But he says little about the objects that synthesis brings into being. However, talk about synthesis can easily be translated into talk about objects, so this omission is not terribly significant.

What we carry away from Kant's doctrine of synthesis thus far is primarily the idea that having objects (intentional objects) requires acts of recognition, acts of awareness – content requires consciousness – and acts of recognition must apply concepts to what representations present. Material from the pre-recognitional level of representation is not enough for a theory of mind. In addition, we carry away the intriguing suggestion (for we have not taken it further than that) that objects of representation all have a certain general structure. They are all some number of something, they all have qualities, and they all have an existence status. In fact, put this way, Kant's basic claims about the Categories begin to look quite plausible. When he gets to Leibniz's Amphiboly, he develops these claims further. The concept of number gets developed into the concept of identity, and Kant connects it to the concept of quality to yield the idea that qualitative identity is compatible with difference of number. (Kant is attacking Leibniz's principle of the identity of indiscernibles.) Similarly, the concept of existence status unfolds into a distinction between existing as a concept of the understanding and existing as an appearance or intuition, the only existence status that can confer objective validity (A279 = B335). I think that both central ideas of the doctrine of synthesis – the idea that recognition or awareness is central to representations having objects, content, and the idea that intentional objects have a certain general structure in common – deserve a bigger place in contemporary theory than they currently have.

5 Transcendental apperception: the unity of 'all appearances'

With the synthesis of recognition, that is, remembering and recognizing represented objects, Kant's discussion of the two conditions necessary to have objects of representation, namely, ability to synthesize and the unity to use it, should be complete. These notions immediately yield an objective deduction; memory and recognition are possible, Kant argues, only if we can unite what is presented in earlier with what is presented in later representations to form a single object of representation, and we can do this in turn only if the various things presented can be connected in some regular, rule-governed way, that is, under a concept. The concepts we use, he then goes on to argue, must include the categories (A110–14 and again twice later). And that should be that.

But that is not that; for, to pick up the story begun in Section 1, between the passage on recognition and the passage beginning on A110 on the use of the categorial concepts in recognition, we find a notoriously difficult passage on TA, the unity and identity of the mind, and the mind's awareness of itself as the subject of all its representations (A106–8). I think that this passage introduces a new line of argument. Here I do not mean one starting from self-awareness, one of the Henrich–Guyer starting points, but one that does not correspond perfectly either to representation of objects or to self-awareness. Recall that the relational Categories were left out of the analysis earlier. One can see how recognition of represented objects might at least seem to require the use of the other three kinds of category: quantity, quality, and modality. Kant gives three examples of synthesis of recognition, adding up units (A103), tying three straight lines together into a triangle, and binding representations of extension, shape, and impenetrability into a representation of a body (A106). They all seem to involve quantitative, qualitative, and modal concepts. But where are the relational Categories?

For Kant, that is a problem. The relational Categories and causality in particular were central to Kant's concerns; showing that we must apply an *a priori* concept of causal connection if we are to have objects of representation is one of the things he most wanted TD to do. In fact, he probably cared more about this category than about all the others put together. And to be sure, by A112 causality is indeed front and centre. Yet up to A106 Kant has not even mentioned the concept of causality, nor any other relational concept. It seems natural to suppose, then, that the material between A106 and A111 contains Kant's solution to this problem, even though he himself does not say so.

I think the solution is to be found in the 90° turn mentioned earlier; from following the retention, reproduction, and recognition of a representation across time, Kant suddenly takes up a form of recognition that requires the unification and recognition of a number of representations existing *at the same time,* that is to say, the unification and recognition of global objects. The shift occurs at the end of A106. In the doctrine of synthesis so far, Kant has talked about representation of nothing but normal individual objects: a triangle, a body, (at A352) a verse. The only exception is counting up units, and it is a very modest one. At A107, however, he suddenly begins to talk about tying together multiple represented objects, indeed "all possible appearances, which can stand alongside one another in one experience" (A108). The solution to the problem of showing that we have to use the Category of causality must lie somewhere in this activity of tying multiple objects together.

At the same time as he introduces the notion of tying multiple objects together, Kant introduces TA. If apperception is the ability to tie elements such as straight lines together into single represented objects such as triangles, TA should be the ability to tie 'all appearances' together into 'one experience'. And that is what it is. "This transcendental unity of apperception forms out of all possible appearances, which can stand alongside one another in one experience, a connection of all these representations according to laws" (A108). It works by a "synthesis of all appearances according to concepts", "whereby it subordinates *all* synthesis of apprehension . . . to a transcendental unity" (A108; my emphasis).

Tie these appearances together into what? Into a representation that is "one experience" of "all possible appearances, which can stand alongside one another in one experience" (A108), "one and the same general experience" of "all . . . the various perceptions" (A110), "a connected whole of human knowledge" (A121). Our term for what these phrases describe is 'global representation', defined in Chapter 2:2 this way:

Global representation $=$***df:*** a representation that has a number of particular representations and/or their objects or contents as its *single global object,*

where 'single global object' was defined as follows:

Single global object =*df:* an intentional object that represents a number of intentional objects and/or the representations that represent them, such that to be aware of any of these objects and/or their representations is also to be aware of other objects and/or representations that make it up and of the collection of them as a single group.

If these notions are unclear, it might help to refer back to the array of six sentences with which I introduced them. The global representation is the representation of which it was argued in Chapter 4:3 that each of us has only one at any given time, the representation that was said to be the home of the unity of consciousness.

Kant's ostensible reason for his shift (from representation of individual objects to representation of a number of objects as one) does not inspire confidence. Nor does it have anything to do with causality or any other relational category. If unified apperceptive acts are a necessary condition of single objects of representation coming to be, there is also, he suddenly tells us, a necessary condition of this necessary condition (A106), one moreover that does not itself have conditions![22] Aside from this obscure idea, Kant slides into this new discussion without any introduction; nor, most atypically, does he give the new topic a subheading of its own. What Kant is introducing with this strange move is TA. However bizarre the move to get to it, both it and the notion of unified awareness of 'all appearances' are vital to the objective deduction. Forming an object of an individual representation (in the normal sense: a single act of seeing, tasting, imagining, etc.) out of elements such as lines or units is different from forming a global object out of individual representations and/or objects in one crucial respect: with multiple objects and/or representations, there is at least a clear place for an argument that causal concepts are involved, that to "stand along side one another in one experience" (A108), objects must be connected causally.

If I am right about this, Kant's overall strategy suddenly becomes clear. It is revealed as consisting of three steps. Kant starts with

(1) representation of individual objects;

argues that

(2) such representations and/or their objects or some vital subclass of them must 'stand along side one another in one experience' and that this requires synthesis by TA into one experience in one consciousness;

and then infers that

(3) TA must use causal concepts to do so.

Here all Kant offers to take him from (1) to the claim that 'all appearances' must be unified in 'one experience' for individual representations of single objects to exist is his unconvincing condition of a condition argument (A106). Does he have anything better to link (1) to (2) elsewhere? I think he does; indeed, except for one small modification, he uses *exactly the same* linking principle in both editions, a point that astonished me when I first noticed it.

Before we examine it, we must make explicit an implicit qualification introduced into (2). Does Kant really mean *all* appearances, *all* representations, or did he have something a little smaller in mind? Put in other words, must *all* one's representations be tied together under concepts as a single global object if one is to represent objects at all? One would think not; indeed, Kant himself seems to say not, at least twice. Animals have representations, or at any rate sense-data that affect 'feeling and desire', that are connected by nothing more than empirical laws of association – that is to say, by something like the connections among representations in the synthesis of reproduction, and in the second edition he seems to allow that even we could have representations that are not transcendentally synthesized with other representations (B132). It would merely be impossible to be aware of more than one such representation at a time.[23] Perhaps he had things like dreams in mind. So TA is not necessary for all representation of objects. Kant might appear to say something different:

> The numerical unity of this apperception is . . . the *a priori* ground of all *concepts,* just as the manifold of space and time is the *a priori* ground of the intuitions of sensibility. (A107)

All concepts. However, the unity he is speaking of here may be merely the unity necessary even for representation of a normal individual object, not the broader unity of TA. Perhaps, however, there is some narrower set of representations crucial to cognition for which unity into a global object by an act of TA is essential.[24]

Here is one of Kant's statements of the principle taking us from (1) to (2) in the first edition:

> [Representations] can represent something to me only in so far as they belong with all others to one consciousness. Therefore, they must at least be capable of being so connected. (A116)[25]

For 'connected', Kant also uses 'taken up into one consciousness'. The crucial phrase is 'something to me'. The opposite of it seems to be 'nothing for me' (cf. A120). What Kant tells us with this phrase is that he is *not* dealing with representations of objects of any sort, he is dealing just with representations that represent 'something *to me*'. Let us give the linking principle forged out of this notion the name LP:

(LP) Representations can represent something to me only in so far as they belong with others to (can be connected in, can be taken up into) one consciousness.

What is it for a representation to represent something to me? A represented object becomes something to me, I think, when it becomes something that I could recognize, when one or both kinds of awareness[RR] of it becomes possible. LP forges a link between (1) representation of individual objects, *as restricted to represented objects that are something to me,* and (2) representations 'standing along side one another', a far better one than the condition of a condition claim could begin to achieve. Kant is then free go on to (3), that we need to use causal concepts, and he does so on A112–14, an argument that we do not need to follow.

As we will see in Chapter 9:4, the comparable principle in the second edition is LP′:

(LP′) Representations can represent something to me only in so far as it is possible for " 'I think' to accompany them", for them to "stand together in one universal self-consciousness". (B131 and B132)

The one small modification mentioned previously is that where LP refers to 'one consciousness', LP′ refers to 'one self-consciousness'. This change reflects the more central role of ASA in the second edition; we will consider its significance in Chapter 9. It is important, as I said, that LP does not link all representations of objects to (2), only those representations that could be 'something to me'. The same is true of LP′. Note that the whole of (1), LP, (2), and (3) makes no reference to self-awareness and that this is the form Kant's argument took in first edition.

The claim that LP is Kant's link between (1) and (2) is open to a textual objection. Kant makes the transition from (1) to (2) somewhere between A106 and A108, but the passage I just quoted is from A116. Something is indeed wrong. At the very least, I have to allow that Kant messed up the order of presentation of his argument. Actually, things are not quite this bad. The crucial linking claim first appears on A113, not A116. A113 is at least still in the same section of TD. I quoted the version on A116 because the one on A113 connects individual representations of objects to unified awareness via unified *self*-awareness, that is, via something like LP′, and I wanted to avoid that complication here. Every other statement of the principle I am calling LP in the first edition refers only to awareness (A116, A119, A120, A122, and maybe A123–4); if A123–4 is ambiguous, A119 makes the link only to possible *experience,* which is even more clearly not self-awareness. Nevertheless, if I am right about the structure of the argument, Kant's presentation of it is muddled. Two considerations support my interpretation of the structure. (i) At the point where Kant actually makes the move from (1) to (2), he offers us nothing except the curious condition of a condition claim. (ii) The same argument is repeated twice in Section 3, on A115–16 and from just before A120 to A123, and both times Kant uses exactly the structure I am claiming for Section 2: Step 1, LP, Step 2, Step 3. Anyway, even in Section 2 a full statement of LP appears at most five pages out of place and still within the same argument. There is one difference between the argument of Section 2 as I have reconstructed it and the argument of Section 3, but it is not important. In the latter Kant does not present the doctrine of the three kinds of synthesis at the beginning of the argument and in the context of individual objects. Instead, he moves immediately from representations of individual objects to the 'belonging' claim ("relation to a consciousness that is at least possible") and only then lays out the three kinds of synthesis, treating synthesis of individual represented objects and synthesis of representations and objects into "a connected whole of human knowledge" together. This merger renders his argument less perspicuous than it could be, but the kinds of synthesis are the same in both cases. (As we have seen, Kitcher follows him in this, with the same loss of perspicuity.) Moreover, the structure in Section 3 is exactly the structure we find in the second edition. The only difference is that LP gets modified to LP′. Thus, I am inclined to think that LP is Kant's real principle for linking (1) to (2) in the first edition, too, its misplaced first introduction notwithstanding.

I introduced TA as an ability, the ability to synthesize global objects, but Kant builds more into the notion than that. Here I do not mean self-awareness. When Kant introduces TA at A107, he does not introduce it as a form of self-awareness (I justify this statement in Part II:1), though the idea soon sneaks in (A108). I mean unity of consciousness (see Chapter 2:4). Having global objects requires unity of consciousness of wide scope. To recognize a single object, we use a single act of recognition. To recognize a global object requires more than that. It requires not just that the being aware of each object or representation be one consciousness, but (i) that the being aware of each object or representation in the global object be *unified with the being or beings* aware of every other bit of that global object (this is not the same as being the *same* being), and (ii) that the unified being have recognized the global object in one act of recognition, which will have the contents of the whole global object as its single collective object. "This pure original unchangeable consciousness I shall name *transcendental apperception*" (A107). Both 'identity of the self', as Kant also and unfortunately refers to this unity, and 'identity of function' are required, and they go together (A108). In fact, despite Kant's comments at A108 and A116 about 'identity of self', it is not belonging to one *person or mind* that interests him, but belonging to one *system of awareness,* one global representation whose object is recognized in one act of awareness. He carefully sorts out this distinction in his attack on the Third Paralogism, at least for identity across time (see Chapter 8). (The relation between global acts of recognition and being one mind *at a time* is closer.) In short, TA is the name for both a unified recognitional ability and the unity of consciousness. (As I said, I will consider how TA gets connected to ASA later.) The root idea behind Kant's model is an isomorphism of unity: one apperceptive act of recognition creating one state of awareness; one global representation having one global object.

The picture of TD I have developed differs from Guyer's increasingly influential model in one respect. It might be tempting to try to map my move from (1) to (2) onto Henrich's and Guyer's two starting points, taking my move to be a move from representation of objects to their second starting point, self-awareness. That would be a complete misunderstanding of my view: my (2) has nothing to do with self-awareness. Kant may make a shift to self-awareness, too (in fact, as early as A108, as we will see in Part II), but that is a separate matter. The move from (1) to (2) is a move within the first starting point in the Henrich–Guyer scheme. However, what happens at step (2) is very different from what happens at (1), and Guyer actually describes the first starting point as containing nothing but (1).[26] Thus, I prefer to think of them as separate. I therefore think of Kant as having three starting points, not two (see Chapter 5:1). In fact, I am not sure Kant treated self-awareness (ASA) as a new starting point at all, not in the *Critique* at any rate. It may appear that ASA is clearly a separate starting point in the second edition, but even there I am not so sure (see Chapter 9:4). ASA is certainly central, indeed Kant uses it in the new form of LP, LP′, but that is not the same as it being a new starting point. At any rate, in the first edition the argument from (1) to (3) does not invoke self-awareness. Thus, on the Henrich–Guyer scheme, all of it is within the first starting point.

What is it for appearances to "belong . . . to one consciousness" (A116; see B132) or 'stand alongside one another in one experience'? Moreover, why is it that only appearances that belong or can belong to one experience can be synthesized by TA into a global object of representation? Sometimes Kant is taken to be making merely the trivial claim here that the experiences a person can have must all belong to that person. He has even been taken to be making some claim about self-ascription or its possibility.[27] However, Kant had something more interesting than stale ideas like these in mind. He is interested in the conditions of a representation being recognizable, being something to someone, not its merely being someone's. To be recognizable by me, he argues, a representation must be synthesizable with representations that are already recognized by me – must be able to become part of 'one consciousness', one global representation, a representation whose parts I recognize in one object of one act of awareness.[28] This unified global representation is the representational base of ASA laid out in Chapter 4:3, the representational base of being aware of oneself as a single, common subject.

Being parts of the common object of a single, unified act of recognition requires that objects of particular representations and/or the representations of them be linked, so that they 'stand together in one experience'; one recognizes them as one object, not just *A* and, separately, *B* and, separately, *C*, but *A* and *B* and *C* as a group, collectively, as the complex but single global object of a single global representation. The final step in Kant's argument, step (3), is to argue that, to do this linking, to produce "synthetic products . . . contentually dependent on synthetic progenitors", as Kitcher puts it, we must use concepts, especially the concept of causality.[29]

Kant stopped this analysis here, but I want to carry it one step further. What representations can a person synthesize in this way? In general, I think a person can synthesize into a global object only representations and what can be inferred from representations that the person him- or herself has, where the relevant feature of this kind of 'having' is that the representations themselves are the representational base of being aware of these representations and/or the objects they represent. The analogue for actions is that doing the action provides all the representation that is needed to be aware of the action. (This is just the Chapter 4:3 notion of the representational base again in a different application.) Having all the representations that are *needed* does not guarantee that one is actually aware of these representations, actually recognizes them in either of the ways delineated earlier; other things might be missing. However, when a person is aware of the representations or that he or she has them, it is the representations themselves that are doing the representing. Shoemaker's useful metaphor of being aware 'from the inside' applies to being aware of a representation in this way (see Chapter 8). Put yet another way, my awareness of the objects of such representations is from the point of view of perceiving them (or imagining them). It is hard to see how I could synthesize anything from a representation or represented object that I came to recognize in any other way.

All of this is clearly something quite different from the trivial point that I have (only) my experiences. Even the kind of having is different. We are not talking about 'having' in the sense in which my skin has cells; having a representation is at least being aware^{R} of its object, not just the representation being one of my properties. Second, it may not even be the case that I can be aware of only my own representations by having them. Is it so clear I could not have a representation that is in other respects another person's (perhaps it is causally dependent on that person's eyes, not mine, for point of view, continued perception, etc.)?[30] Finally, Kant is not talking about the conditions of a representation being mine, he is talking about the conditions of a representation representing an object in a way that is something to me – though this more demanding condition is clearly articulated only in the second edition. LP specifies a condition of a representation being of cognitive use to me, not of it being mine. A representation that is not "capable of being taken up into one consciousness" (A116) may influence my beliefs, ways of seeing, and so on in various ways, but I could no more deliberately make use of it than I could deliberately make use of the state of the lining of my stomach. I have representations of the lining of my stomach and they play various roles in my biological economy, but I cannot make deliberate use of them. Nor, *a fortiori,* could I use them 'consciously', that is, recognizing what I am doing (deliberately is not the same as consciously). Kant's way of putting this point was to say, "Nothing could come of [this] knowledge" (A113); such representations would be "nothing to us" (A116 and A120).[31] We will return to this notion in Chapter 9. To repeat the key point. For a representation to 'belong to one consciousness' is for it to be represented to me by itself. What this allows is that I can become aware of this representation, aware^{RR} of it, by having it, by being aware^{H} of it, in the jargon of Chapter 3. (For awareness^{H}, see Chapter 3:1.)[32]

If, in the part of TD after the 90° turn, Kant's interest narrowed to representations that are something to me and 'belong' to my unified awareness, a class smaller than the class of all representations that have objects, how significant a loss of generality would that be? Generality with respect to what? – The scope of the category of causality. Categories of the other three kinds may be needed for all representation of objects, but the Categories of relation have to apply only to the narrower set of representations that are or at least could be something to me. Kant was well aware that not all representations are in this class, as we saw earlier: neither the representations of (nonhuman) animals nor those whose possibility is entertained on B134 would be in it. In fact, a representation and/or its object can relate in a whole host of different ways to a person's unified awareness and its global object. It can appear in the global representation only vaguely and generally.[33] One's awareness^{R} (and even awareness^{RR}?) of it could be 'on the periphery' of one's global awareness^{RR}, hardly available to the focused awareness^{RR} called attention. (Kant speaks of attention on B156n.)[34] Finally, a representation could be fully 'unconscious' in the psychoanalytic sense, that is to say, we could lack all awareness^{RR} of it, and yet still give us awareness^{R} and even awareness^{RR} of its object – a form of representation to which we are far more sensitive than Kant was.

Kant was aware that he did not have to restrict his argument for causal concepts to representations that actually are something to someone. His argument applies to representations that are even *capable* of being taken up into a global representation. To have so much as this capacity, they must be synthesized with other representations and/or the objects of same. However, the vagueness of the word 'capable' puts LP at risk, indeed threatens to evacuate it of meaning (a criticism that can be levelled at Strawson, too, as we will see in Part II:2). One way to reduce the vagueness would be to say that by 'capable', Kant meant or should have meant that these representations provide everything needed *on the side of the representation and its relationships to other representations* to be included in a global object and be something to me; anything lacking is on the side of recognition. Again we are in the realm of the representational base. How many representations would still be outside the argument because they are not even *capable* of being taken up or becoming something to someone? Perhaps not very many, though special techniques such as the techniques of psychoanalysis may be needed for them actually to enter a global object. If so, the loss in generality of the argument for the necessity of causal connectedness would not be very significant.[35] In any case, even if the demonstration of the necessity of applying causal concepts worked only for representations that are something to someone, that would still be an impressive achievement, especially if the other three types of categories must be applied to all represented objects of any sort.[36]

We are now ready to leave the analysis of TD. Before we do, I want to touch on one additional reason why Kant might have developed the second part of his doctrine of synthesis, the synthesis by TA of global objects in global representations. His main reason, I have urged, was the need to justify our use of *a priori* relational categories and specifically the category of causality. However, I think he may have had another reason. The second part of his doctrine seems to provide ammunition for his argument against Leibniz and the rationalist theory of knowledge. Return again to The Amphiboly of the Concepts of Reflection. Kant tells that an amphiboly is "a confounding of an object of pure understanding with appearance" (A270 = B326); the section is devoted to demonstrating why Leibniz was wrong to do so. Kant's argument is that the mind has recognitional capacities that it could not have if it were aware only of concepts. His conclusion, of course, is that in addition to concepts, the mind must also have sensible or analogous intuition (analogous in the way explained in Chapter 3:1). First, without intuition, the mind could not distinguish qualitatively indistinguishable objects as it does. Second, it could not recognize experiences cancelling each other out in the ways that have nothing to do with contradiction of concepts – the way pain can cancel pleasure, for example. (These two arguments work well; Kant also gives two others, to do with inner nature and external relations, and with form and matter, that work less well.) This line of argument depends on the subjective deduction in the following way. There Kant had argued that to have experience at all, the mind must have certain recognitional capacities. He now argues, against Leibniz, that to use these recognitional capacities as it does, the mind must also have intuition. The appendix on the Amphiboly thus takes up where the subjective deduction left off. It is important for another reason, too: it is about the only argument that is more than bald assertion in the whole *Critique* for the crucial claim that knowledge requires intuition.

6 Synchronic unity

It is time now to defend a claim I have made a number of times, that synchronic unity plays a central role in Kant's model. The remark on A99 that we examined in Section 3 does not support me in this, but Kant referred to synchronic unity in more places than that. We need look only as far as A100, where he writes of "a co-existence" as well as a sequence of representations, or A103, where he says that multiple numbers "hover before me", presumably at the same time, or A108, where he describes appearances "which can stand along side one another in one experience". Or consider A352, where he examines the conditions of being aware of all the words of a verse together. Kitcher underplays the role of the synchronic and overplays the diachronic as severely as anyone ever has, yet even she recognizes that Kant did at least address "the question of the 'unity' of a mental state occurring at a moment in time". However, says she, "his discussion is quite hopeless".[37] That remark might better apply to Kitcher's comment. She has in mind the remark on A99 and seems to think that that is all there is to Kant on unity at a time. She is doubly wrong! First, she overloads A99: Kant is not talking about anything that is unified at all on A99, let alone unified at a time.[38] Synthesis is required for unity. Second and far more important, Kant does talk about unity at a time in other places. Even Hume, whom Kitcher takes to be Kant's main target in TD, included the synchronic in his sceptical attack: "There is properly *no simplicity in the mind at one time,* nor identity in different" (my emphasis).[39] In her book, Kitcher describes an example very much like Kant's verse example, "listening to the first few measures of '*Für Elise*' " and recognizes that we must represent this temporally disparate information "in a single moment".[40] This representation 'in a single moment' is also a single *representation,* with multiple *coexisting* parts. Because it is so obviously and widely generalizable, this simple example of synchronic unity is disastrous for any purely across-time analysis, though Kitcher seems not to see this.

It is also true, however, that Kant never singles out synchronic unity for separate treatment. In fact, in the first *Critique,* he refers to it at all only about a half-dozen times, explicitly at least. That is why I allowed at the end of Section 2 that Kitcher could also find some succour in Kant's texts; she might also cite A121 on reproduction in her favour. However, it would be dangerous to draw conclusions from the fact that Kant did not single something out or refer to it frequently. On this principle, we could argue that Kant meant *only* synchronic identity when he spoke of identity. He never *says* that the concept includes identity across time! Needless to say, I do not think that Kitcher used such a principle of interpretation; in fact, it is hard to find any argument in her work for focusing exclusively on diachronic unity. However, the scarcity of references to synchronic unity might be explained precisely by the fact that it is so pervasive in awareness. Kant might have felt that it did not need to be singled out – it is present everywhere.

Not seeing that Kant was concerned with synchronic unity just as much as with diachronic goes with not giving the unifying of multiple objects and representations to produce global objects and representations its due. Certainly all synthesis of recognition, even of single objects, requires synchronic as well as diachronic unity. In synthesis of recognition, elements are recognized in a single act of recognition, and for that, they must all be recognized at the same time. Certainly there is a diachronic element – earlier representations must be retained and brought forward to be linked to current ones – but synthesis could not take place without simultaneous recognition. As Kant puts it in the example of counting, the units I retain "hover before me"; that is to say, they are all there at the same time. Certainly we would not be able to locate objects in space without awareness of them as coexistent. The synchronic aspect of global objects and representations is even more obvious. Moreover, the acts of recognition here must "necessarily be represented as numerically identical" as much as the representer (A107). The identity here is identity across the simultaneously appearing representations, that is, identity at a time; indeed, at a time, unity may be enough to ensure identity. At any rate, both unity and identity have a clear synchronic dimension in Kant.

Though Kitcher's picture of Kant and mine have a similar overall shape, we disagree on more than the role of synchronic unity. Let me close this section by trying to pull these disagreements together. (In the next few paragraphs, page references will be to her book.) Like me, Kitcher sees two objects of synthetic unity, individual represented objects and multiples of representations and objects (p. 104). Likewise, her notion of the synthetic product (p. 117) bears a resemblance to my notion of either the global object or global representation (it is hard to know which). Perhaps because she sees connections among representations as primarily a diachronic affair, however, she never gets the idea that the products of synthesis must be single representations into focus; nor does she see that they have single complex objects, the parts of which coexist. Whether the multiple representations that are her progenitors or their objects or both are intended to be the (intentional) *object* of the synthetic product is also unclear. Perhaps the most serious gap in her work from my point of view, however, is that she never separates awareness out as an independent element. It may be that her own view of the matter is that awareness is not something separate, that it should be reduced to her synthetic products or something similar (p. 119 suggests this). However, awareness cannot be left out, especially recognitional awareness, and her account of synthesis and products of synthesis does not begin to capture it: not awareness^{RR} of objects, not the unity of awareness, not the subject of awareness, nor the subject's awareness^{H} and awareness^{RR} of itself and its states. At the very least, a purely representational account like hers needs substantial enrichment.

In addition to these differences on Kant's theory, we disagree about three things in the structure of Kant's argument. (i) Kitcher's account touches (e.g., on p. 144) on all three of the steps I lay out in my scheme but neither identifies them individually nor sees them as parts of a single argument scheme. (ii) She does not view the 'belonging' requirement as a principle linking two parts of the argument (my LP) but simply as a condition of TA. (iii) Connected to (ii) and despite Kant's own words, she takes TA, not representation of individual objects, to be the starting point of the deduction (p. 96). That is to say, she views the unity of apperception and its possibility as the first premise of the deduction, not as a connecting link between representation of individual objects and unified awareness of global objects (Kant's 'connected whole of human knowledge' [A121]).

To summarize, as we leave TA and its unity we carry away a number of ideas. First, there is the idea of unifying multiple objects and representations into a single global object of a single representation. Second, there is the idea that, to do so, the objects must be unified with other objects in a global object. Third, there is the isomorphism of unity: one global object, one global representation, one global act of recognition, one global awareness. These are the unity constraints on anything that could represent in the way we do. None of them has much profile at present. Doubtless there are modules in us of which we are not aware, as Fodor has argued, but we also have unified awareness capable of unifying acts of recognition. Whether these unities must always be in one mind is a question; at a time, unity and identity are at the very least closely related.

II THE STRANGE CASE OF SELF-AWARENESS AND THE DEDUCTION

Our discussion of the central ideas of the subjective deduction is now finished. However, the subjective deduction has also generated some enduring puzzles. The most prominent are those about the role of self-awareness in the deduction (Chapter 5:2). How does self-awareness relate to TA? Did Kant think that self-awareness or a potential for self-awareness is necessary for representation of objects or some particular form of representation of objects? Did Kant think that something else, in turn, is necessary for self-awareness? In every case, the kind of self-awareness in question is ASA, awareness of oneself as the common subject of one's experience. We have already examined the extraordinarily interesting things that Kant had to say about ASA in Chapter 4, so here we can restrict ourselves to its role in TD.

The argument scheme for the Categories laid out in Part I does not invoke self-awareness. In it, Kant begins with (1) individual representations of objects, infers, via LP, that (2) such representations must belong to one awareness and must be synthesized into 'one experience' by TA to do so, and then argues that (3) causal concepts must be used to achieve this synthesis. We found backing in Kant's text for each step, backing of the sort that he generally took to be adequate, though we said little about (3). Yet he clearly brought self-awareness into the argument, certainly by A108 and perhaps earlier, and it is prominent in the second edition. Why? And why did he eventually put it into LP to generate LP′, its second-edition replacement? Let us start with how self-awareness actually enters TD. It is not a pretty picture.

1 Apperception and self-awareness

To the end of A106, self-awareness is not even mentioned. By then the whole theory of synthesis is finished. Even TA is not linked to self-awareness when first introduced on A107 but to a 'fixed and abiding self', an 'original consciousness' necessary for representation of objects. (The very first lines of A107 may appear to belie this claim; I will consider them in the next paragraph.) As we saw in Part I, Kant can construct a complete deduction going from representation of objects all the way to the relational categories without self-awareness. Yet for as long as philosophers have written about Kant, the received view has been that TA is a form of self-awareness, at least in part. Among English-speaking writers, we find this view as far back as Meiklejohn and as recently as Allison. Walker introduces TA as, "the transcendental unity of apperception, or self-consciousness".[41] Yet as I noted in Chapter 3, in the first-edition TD Kant refers to self-awareness by name only eight times in connection with anything, and the references are all very brief. Only a short passage on A108 and perhaps a remark in A117n link it to TA – one or two remarks in forty-six pages! Remarks on A122, A108, and A117n linking TA to something else all link it simply to awareness.

It is easy to read A107, Kant's first mention of TA, so as to miss this point and think that he links TA to self-awareness from the first mention of it. Indeed, when Guyer quotes Kant as introducing TA as a "consciousness of self" on A107, he is not even misquoting him – misunderstanding him, but not misquoting him.[42] The 'consciousness of self' Kant is talking about is *empirical* awareness, of items of inner sense – 'empirical apperception' (*empirische Apperception*). This remark is the only time Kant mentions empirical apperception in the whole first edition, but it seems to be a matter of representations being associated with one another in inner sense, representations that are in fact one's own, though one would not know that: Hume's bundle. (The notion makes an appearance in the second edition and in a fascinating passage in the Anthropology [Ak. VII:134n]; we will return to it in Chapter 9.) Such association is not enough, Kant thought, to allow awareness of representations as a group. For that, something more is required: unified awareness, awareness of them all together as a single intentional object. That is to say, TA is required. Perhaps the single biggest gap in Kitcher's account of Kant is her failure to see that in addition to representations connected by patterns of rule-governed association to produce "synthetic products . . . contentually dependent on synthetic progenitors",[43] Kant also insisted that we require in addition a unified awareness. Empirical apperception is not enough. The important point here, however, is that, on this reading, which seems textually accurate, Kant clearly need not be read as saying that TA is a form of awareness of self in this passage on A107.

In the first sentences of A107, it is unclear what exactly is meant by 'transcendental apperception'. Thus it is also unclear what the contrast with empirical apperception is. Both points come clear in the next paragraph. TA is "unity of *consciousness*", "original unchangeable *consciousness*" (my emphases). Thus, contrary to what Guyer and a host of other readers have thought, Kant is not contrasting TA with empirical apperception *as two contrasting forms of self-awareness*. So why does he bring empirical self-awareness into the first paragraph? To explain his use of the word 'transcendental'. What he is claiming about "this flux of inner appearances" and our empirical awareness of it is that *we cannot get TA from them;* TA must have a transcendental, that is, *a priori,* source. Nothing in this implies that TA is itself a form of self-awareness. In fact, Kant clearly links TA to self-awareness (*Selbstbewußtsein*) only once in the whole first-edition TD, as I said, on A108.[44] Even at A122, where he explicitly links apperception to awareness, he links it to *awareness*. The phrase he uses is "one consciousness (*Bewußtsein*) (original apperception)". If TA is our capacity to tie inner appearances together into one unified global object and, by extension (A107), our being the sort of fixed and abiding self that can do so, I cannot see that it either is or requires self-awareness, any more than apperception of a single object does. Kant originally introduced the term 'apperception' as the name for a faculty and activity of synthesis – synthesis of recognition in a concept (A94). He continued to treat it as the name for a faculty and activity through to A107 and the introduction of TA, and again on A115, presumably still including TA in the characterization. As he says on A107, TA is pure original unchanging *consciousness!* Unfortunately, however, that does not settle the matter. It is also clear that Kant does present TA as (or confuse it with) self-awareness. The passage at A108 would not show this by itself, but he said similar things a number of times thereafter, especially in the second edition and the *Anthropology*.

Where does he get this idea that TA is a form of self-awareness? The way self-awareness first appears when it suddenly slides onto the stage on A108 is very strange. The first three sentences of A108 run as follows (I will number them):

> [1] The transcendental unity of apperception forms out of all possible appearances, which can stand alongside one another in one experience, a connection of all these representations according to laws. [2] For this unity of consciousness would be impossible if the mind in knowledge of the manifold could not become conscious of the identity of function whereby it synthetically combines it in one knowledge. [3] The original and necessary consciousness of identity on the side of the self is thus at the same time a consciousness of an equally necessary unity of the synthesis of appearances according to concepts, that is, according to rules. (A108)[45]

Put together, these sentences are simply baffling. Sentence (1) seems to be just a summary of the basic idea behind apperceiving synthesis: synthesis of a multiplicity of appearances requires unity of subject. In light of what has preceded on A105–7, one would expect the next two sentences to argue as follows. 'Unity of TA or unity of consciousness requires acts of synthesis that unify objects. For this, the objects of synthesis must be brought under concepts.' No self-awareness in any of this. But that is not what happens at all. Instead, Kant suddenly introduces a reference to the mind's *awareness* of its acts in (2) and to its *awareness* of its identity throughout its acts in (3)! These references to self-awareness appear completely out of the blue.

The clue to what has happened may be in sentence (2). The only way to make sense of it, especially in combination with (3), is to take Kant to be talking about *awareness* of the unity of consciousness in it, not unity of consciousness itself. Read thus, (3) follows on without any problem. However, this reading also reflects back on (1). If 'unity of consciousness' in (2) is talking about self-awareness, then 'transcendental unity of apperception' in (1) must be talking about self-awareness, too, about 'the original and necessary consciousness of identity on the side of the self' of (3). In short, on A108 Kant may suddenly *switch* to taking TA to be a kind of self-awareness! In addition to, or instead of, its earlier role as the mind's synthesizing power? That is not clear, but I think in addition to – Kant just uses the term to talk about two different things (Guyer and Kitcher agree).[46]

How can we explain this slide? Unfortunately, it may be nothing more than Kant falling victim to the general and rather witless tendency to conflate awareness of objects and awareness of self explored in Chapter 3:1. Both meanings for the term 'apperception' were found in Kant's philosophical milieu – Leibniz, for example, seems to have used the term in both senses – and on occasion Kant clearly could conflate the two kinds of awareness, as so many other philosophers have done. Clear examples are relatively rare in the *Critique,* thank goodness, but when they occur they are striking.[47] The clearest one I know of is on A103. Kant has been talking about the conditions of recognizing, becoming aware of, objects. Suddenly he says:

> This consciousness may often be only faint, so that we do not connect it with the act itself, that is . . . with the *generation* of the representation, but only with the outcome.

He has suddenly switched to talking about awareness of the act of experiencing, not awareness of its object, it seems without the slightest sense of having done so. The trouble with this explanation of the slide is, first, that such clear examples are extremely rare, and second, that Kant was also quite capable of keeping the two apart when he wanted to. Indeed, in the first edition he says specifically, twice, that awareness of objects does not require awareness of self, and he says the same thing in the second edition, too (B132). On A113, he says, "All possible appearances . . . belong to . . . a *possible* self-consciousness" (emphasis mine) – possible, not actual. In the long footnote to A117, he says, talking about our representation of ourselves as subject, "Whether this representation is clear (empirical consciousness) or obscure, or even whether it ever actually occurs, need not here concern us". (I take it that actually being aware of ourselves is what Kant means by empirical awareness here.) Since awareness of objects, at least the sort of awareness of objects he is talking about on A113 and A117, does require TA, it is clear that Kant did not always think of TA as a form of self-awareness, not actual self-awareness at any rate. Indeed, it is not clear that the act of 'original apperception' mentioned on A113 is an act of self-awareness at all; it may merely be the act of forming the mind into a 'numerical identity' – that is, the act of unifying the system of awareness into a single unified system. The footnote on A117 may be a place where Kant runs TA and self-awareness together, however.

In one of the wondrous incongruities that makes Kant so fascinating as an author, the obscure remarks so obscurely placed on A108 first introduce his arresting new theory of ASA, the one discussed in Chapter 4. There is something wonderful about remarks so opaque laying out something so important! In fact, these remarks, all one paragraph of them, and Kant's critique of the Second Paralogism together constitute his most extended exposition of the theory!

2 Why did Kant introduce self-awareness into the deduction?

Whether or not we can explain how Kant was able to slide from viewing TA as a recognitional, synthesizing ability to viewing it as a form of self-awareness and henceforth to conflate the two things in it, why did he want to introduce self-awareness into TD in the first place? I speculate that he may have had a vague sense that ASA, awareness of oneself as the common subject of multiple representations, could be a new datum, a new starting point for a deduction. Perhaps he thought that ASA, either by itself or as a replacement for unified consciousness in LP to generate LP′, could either strengthen the argument from Step (1) to Step (2) or simply begin a new argument from a new starting point. Either way, its introduction would strengthen his case. He did not manage to get this thought clear or introduce ASA into his account very cleanly because he tended to run ASA together with simple awareness.[48]

The idea that Kant thought that something like the *cogito* could start the deduction has had an interesting history. For many years, the received view was that it was Kant's (only) starting point. Strawson, Bennett, and Kitcher in her early work on Kant all advocated this view. However, Kitcher for one now disparages the idea that it was even one of Kant's starting points![49] Earlier we saw that at least a plausible deduction of the relational categories could be built on the idea that to have a unified awareness of representations and their objects as a global object, we must find causal relations among them. The problem is, this argument does not apply to all representations of objects, only to those capable of being something to someone, as we saw in Section 5. There is another kind of awareness that is as good a base for deducing the relational concepts as unified awareness: ASA. As a new starting-point, ASA would stand alone and so avoid the problem that unified awareness is not needed for all representation of objects. That might explain why ASA suddenly appears on A108; and Kant's inclination to conflate it with simple awareness might explain why it does so with such awkwardness. To be sure, this account faces problems. The main one is that, in the *Critique* at least, A108 is the only place where Kant mounts more than the merest sketch of such an argument, and even on A108 the whole thing takes but one short paragraph. To be sure, it is a fascinating and important paragraph because it contains the basics of his whole theory of ASA and for the first time in the *Critique,* but it is just one paragraph. The second-edition deduction may appear to be built on such an argument, but there, too, Kant starts from representations of objects (§15) and makes only a few remarks on ASA at the beginning of §16 before moving on to unified awareness of objects (see Chapter 9:3–4). There the remarks on ASA are clearly a bridge (LP′) to get from one to the other, not a new starting-point. How might ASA play a linking role in a deduction of the Categories?

Two questions arise. The first concerns how Kant might have seen ASA in relation to the 'belonging' move. Here we can do no more than speculate. The requirement that all representations that could be anything to me belong to one unified system of awareness links representations of individual objects to unified awareness of multiple objects. In the second edition, however, Kant links the former first to self-awareness (LP′) and only then to unified awareness (LP). If so, he may have half-thought he was doing the same thing in the first edition. This explanation, if right, would reflect very directly on the Henrich–Guyer notion of two starting points; it would follow from it that even in arguments using LP′, Kant saw the task of ASA to be the linking of representation of objects to unified awareness, not starting the argument over again using self-awareness as a new starting-point. In Chapter 5, we canvassed the possibility that Kant tied the two starting-points into a single argument; this is how he would have done so. Whatever its other merits, this reading casts doubt on the idea that Kant viewed ASA as a second starting-point, at least in the *Critique* (for more on this suggestion, see Chapter 9:4).

The second question is, Does the introduction of ASA confer any advantages? Kant must have thought it did or why would he have substituted LP′ for LP in the second edition, using the conditions of ASA as his argument for (3)? The argument there goes as follows: if the multiplicity of objects of representation are not tied together into one object, we might conceive of the subject of each given representation being aware of itself, but we could not conceive of the subject of one such representation becoming aware that it was the subject of any other. Rather, "I should have as many-coloured and diverse a self as I have representations of which I am conscious" (B134) – conscious of their object, not conscious of self; though the representations are in fact had by me, I could not be aware of that, either (see Chapters 4:3 and 9:4). Indeed, Kant seems to introduce a very compressed version of the same argument at A108. The very next sentence after the three quoted in the preceding section runs as follows:

> [4] For the mind could never think its identity in the manifoldness of its representations, . . . if it did not have before its eyes the identity of its act, whereby it subordinates all synthesis of apprehension (which is empirical [!]), to a transcendental unity, thereby rendering possible their interconnection according to *a priori* rules.

From exploring conditions of a representation being something to me, Kant suddenly switches here to exploring the conditions of the mind 'thinking its identity'! The main condition of the mind thinking its identity, he tells us, is that it tie all its appearances together 'according to *a priori* rules'. Kant then goes on to claim (some think he argues) that among such relational rules, the rule of causal connectedness is preeminent. There may be a brief allusion to the same argument on A113. Note that in the argument that most closely parallels B134, the one at A122, Kant returns to talk about the conditions of consciousness of *perceptions!* In an extension of the incongruity just introduced, this sentence (4) of A108, so puzzling as to the role it plays in TD, is Kant's first use in the *Critique* of the idea that synthesized representations of objects are what we have called the *representational base* of ASA (also of ESA; see Chapter 4:2–3).

Whatever Kant may have thought, does ASA have advantages over unified awareness, as either a new starting point or a step in the deduction? I think not. Consider it as a separate starting point first. If the fact that we so clearly have ASA seems to speak in favour of the idea, the fact that not all representation of objects requires it speaks against it. What reason is there to think that all – or even any – representations of objects *must* be "the experiences of a self-conscious subject", even, as Strawson puts it, "potentially"?[50] First, what does Strawson's 'potentially' or Kant's 'possible' (A113) mean here? In some sense of the word 'potentially', even an earth-worm's representations are *potentially* the representations of a self-aware subject! Perhaps we would need to add a few little things like a transcendentally unified subject and an ability to use concepts – but that is just the point. How far short of actuality can an experience fall without losing the potential Strawson has in mind? This strikes me as a major problem with Strawson's analysis. He says that, for Kant, "unity of consciousness . . . implies . . . the *possibility* of self-ascription" (p. 98). 'Possible' goes with 'actual under certain additional conditions'. What additional conditions would make a potentially self-aware subject into an actually self-aware subject? The range of possible answers runs from 'a shift of attention from one's objects to oneself' to 'an entirely different kind of mind'. In short, it is not clear that Strawson has said anything very much. Kant faces the same problem at A113, A116, and in §16 of the second edition, but he may have a solution, in the notion of the *representational base* examined in Chapter 4 and discussed again in Part I:5.

Second, as I argued in Part I:5, self-awareness is not required for all or even most representation of objects (Descartes notwithstanding) and Kant knew it, as we also saw.[51] Self-awareness is not even required for all representations that are 'something to me'; what about the ones that are integrated into and have an effect on processes of deliberate thought and perception without my ever recognizing them (see Part I:5)? We even make judgements about mental states, millions of them in fact, that we never recognize. For example, every time I leave a building, I change and therefore make judgements about a huge number of beliefs about where I am in relation to things around me. It is difficult to think of so much as a single type of representation for which being aware of oneself is even a *prima facie* requisite of having it. If so, basing the necessity of using the Categories on ASA or its possibility would mean that for a huge range of representations, we have been shown no need to apply the Categories. In any case, Kant himself repeatedly rejected the idea that ASA is required to represent objects (A113 and A117n; see A103 and B132).[52] Third, surely anything to be inferred from ASA could be inferred just as well from unified awareness, which is broader than ASA and which ASA itself requires in any case (see §16 in the second edition). Anything self-awareness can do, awareness can do – if not better, at least as well.

As a step in the deduction, self-awareness enters as a replacement for unified awareness in LP to generate LP′. LP′ is a claim that all appearances that are anything to anyone must belong to "a possible self-consciousness" (A113 and §16 of the second edition); LP links them to "one consciousness" (A116 and A122). I cannot think of any reason to prefer LP′ to LP as a way of getting from (1) to (2). The argument of Part I:5 about the conditions of being something to someone and part of a global representation could apply equally to either of them, but it would have wider scope when applied to unified awareness than to ASA. As I have just said, anything we can infer from ASA we can also infer from unified awareness alone. In short, self-awareness has advantages neither as a replacement for awareness in LP to create LP′ nor as a stand-alone starting point. (This issue will return in Chapter 9.)

Return at last to the questions with which we began Part II. Kant introduced self-awareness as a replacement for unified awareness in LP, to argue that at least the capacity for being an item of self-awareness is necessary for a representation to be part of a global object or for it to be anything to anyone. That allows a ready answer to the question about whether self-awareness is necessary for anything else. Self-awareness or at least the capacity for it would indeed be necessary for some representation of objects. Similarly for the question of whether anything is necessary for self-awareness: application of the relational Categories to representations would be necessary. If we consider ASA as a stand-alone first premise, the latter point would still apply, though of course the former one would not.

There is one final reason why Kant may have let self-awareness slide onto the stage on A108. The idea that unified awareness, unified apperception, is itself a representation, the idea that the mind not only has but is a global representation, may have been starting to push its way to the surface of his thought. As a claim about the first edition, any such suggestion must of necessity be highly speculative. However, in the second edition, Kant either propounds or comes close to propounding such a view. If so, the idea may have been playing some role in his thought earlier. Now carry the idea one step further: What if a global representation also represents itself (Chapters 4:3 and 9:4)? If the mind is such a representation, then the mind would represent itself. We can also apply the idea to the puzzle about TA. TA is a power of the mind; if the mind is a representation, then TA would be a power of this representation. If this representation includes a representation of itself, TA would be linked to self-representation. Notice – a vital point – that it would not follow from all of this that TA is full self-awareness – one can have representations of which one is not aware, even representations of oneself. Indeed, we have countless representations of self of which we are not aware – memories of oneself, for example. With this distinction, in turn, we could understand how Kant could hold *both* that TA is a form of self-awareness *and* that "whether this representation [of the 'I'] is clear or obscure or even . . . actually occurs" (A117n) is an open question (see Chapter 9).

In Part II of this chapter, we have examined the role of ASA in TD. That the remarks which first introduce the powerful theory of ASA examined in Chapter 4 enter the *Critique* in such an ungainly way leaves me bemused. Not only do they not fit at all comfortably into the line of the argument of TD up to that point, they are less than one paragraph long! For many commentators, the most interesting thing about these remarks is what they are taken to tell us about Kant's view of the relationship between representation of objects and awareness of self (ASA). As Chapter 4 demonstrates, what interests me about them, by contrast, are the insights they contain into ASA itself. We turn now to the way Kant used these insights and some other things to demolish what he called the Paralogisms of rational psychology.

7

Kant's diagnosis of the Second Paralogism

Kant's chapter on the Paralogisms is a devastating attack on rationalism's theory of mind, the theory he called rational psychology (hereafter, RPsy), presumably after Wolff's *Psychologia Rationalis*. That theory has largely drifted off into the mists of history, unlamented (though remnants of it can still be found in such philosophers as Chisholm and Swinburne, as was noted in Chapter 5:3). Nevertheless, Kant's attack on it still has value. In the course of diagnosing the illusions behind RPsy, Kant gains major insights into three issues of great contemporary interest. We discussed two of them in Chapter 4: the nature of nonascriptive self-reference and its role in ASA. The third is how little we can infer about the mind's structural nature from its functions and awareness of itself. I will take the earlier discussions of the first two as read and focus on the third.

As many commentators have noted, Kant's thought has a strong functionalist strain (see Chapter 1:2–3). Nowhere does this show through more clearly than in his attack on the Paralogisms; even a function as central as TA turns out to tell us little about the mind's structure, not even about such basic features of structure as composition and mode of persistence. The fundamental tenet of functionalism is that function does not determine form. Kant's thinking adheres to this tenet throughout but nowhere more forcefully than in his attack on RPsy, one long argument that how the mind functions tells us virtually nothing about its structure, not even whether it is simple or complex. In fact, the tenet might have been one of Kant's main supports for the whole doctrine of the unknowability of the noumenal mind. For many philosophers, function is not nature; for them, a thing's nature is its structure (composition and persistence), and a functional account of the mind would not describe the mind as it really is. If Kant made a similar supposition about structure making up what a thing is (in itself), his much-maligned claim that we can know nothing about the mind as it really is becomes not only intelligible but even plausible, given how little we know about the brain.

Functionalism or protofunctionalism is not Kant's only argument for the unknowability of the noumenal mind, of course. If we cannot *infer* the mind's structure from its functions, we might still be able to *observe* it. Normal experience is forbidden to rationalism, but it is allowed a certain kind of appeal to ASA. (I will show why that is so in Section 3.) Kant thought that avenue goes nowhere, too. Our awareness of ourselves in ASA does not reveal our structure. It is in the course of justifying this claim about self-awareness and diagnosing our temptation to think otherwise that Kant achieves the important insights into reference to and awareness of self in the doctrine of transcendental designation examined in Chapter 4:1 – that reference to self requires no identification of the referent under concepts, and the insight concerning the manifoldlessness of ASA. The latter emptiness plays an important role in the attack on the Paralogisms because rationalists (and other philosophers, too) mistook this emptiness for some profound revelation of the mind's nature, namely, that it is simple and without parts. In general, Kant's important contributions to the theory of ASA are in the chapter on the paralogisms. They are as fresh and penetrating today as they were in 1781. We explored the structure of them in Chapter 4. Now we will see them in their original context, Kant's attack on RPsy.

To prevent a possible misunderstanding, let me say that just because the chapter contains important insights into ASA, it does not follow that Kant's attack on the Paralogisms is primarily about self-awareness, though commentators otherwise as diverse as Strawson, Bennett, and Allison all maintain that it is (Kitcher and Powell do not). In my opinion, this reading is seriously mistaken. Far from RPsy being based on appeals to self-awareness, *in the case of every single paralogism* the argument that Kant treats as the major or even the sole argument for the conclusion in question makes no appeal to self-awareness whatsoever! Rather, they all begin from the unity a mind must have to function as it does. From this one ought to conclude that RPsy's attempt to infer structure from function concerned Kant at least as much as its use of self-awareness. It just happens that it was his investigation of the latter that led Kant to his insights into self-reference and the manifoldlessness of ASA.

A great deal has been written about Kant on the Paralogisms.[1] Thus it is striking that no consensus has emerged on what he is saying against them. In my opinion, there are two main reasons for that. One is the mistake of thinking that Kant is only attacking mistakes about self-awareness. The other is that no one has got to the bottom of what he is saying about self-awareness. In particular, no one has understood his comments on self-reference and on why what I will call *self-appearance* is as it is. ('Self-appearance' is a useful shorthand term for how a person appears to him- or herself, what a person appears to him- or herself to be like. The interesting and problematic kind of self-appearance is the manifoldlessness of how we appear to ourselves in ASA.) There are other reasons, too. Though many commentators see that the attack on the Paralogisms is connected to the subjective deduction in TD, a point to which I will return, I am of the view that no one has quite got those connections right. It seems likely that these connections were the reason or at least were among the reasons why the Paralogisms worried Kant so much, a point to which we will also return. The size of the recent literature on Kant and the Paralogisms poses a problem for me. A number of writings on the Paralogisms make contact in many different ways with my view of them, Kitcher's and Powell's recent books in particular. The trouble is, the connections are so dense that it would take a book just to explore them. (Indeed, a number of books have been written just on the Paralogisms chapter, including Mijuskovic's, Ameriks', and Powell's; Chisholm's book probably belongs in this category, too.) This being impossible, I will take the opposite approach. With some exceptions, I will simply lay out my view and the evidence for it and leave the connections to others' work unexplored. I also think that there are things in Kant's analysis of the Paralogisms that no commentator has explored so far, things of considerable importance. In broad approach, the work of Kitcher and Powell is closest to my own but even they leave important things unexamined.

As I said in Chapter 4, Kant laid out his discoveries of a kind of self-reference that requires no identification and the implications of this for the emptiness of self-appearance in ASA only once – in enough detail to be clearly identifiable at any rate – in four key paragraphs on A354 and A355. Though there are anticipations earlier in TD (e.g., on A117n) and though Kant makes further use of the notion later in the first and in a number of places in the second edition, these paragraphs are the only place where Kant actually describes what he had discovered. The second edition, from which Kant excised these paragraphs, contains not a single description of these discoveries at all, even though he continued to use the notions in the new version of TD (e.g., B157). Even in these four paragraphs it is not easy to grasp what Kant is driving at. That they are about reference to self is clear, but that is about all that is clear. As I argued in Chapter 4, I think they depict insights into the mechanics of reference to self and the emptiness of self-appearance of the utmost interest. In showing in this chapter how Kant used them in his overall attack on the Paralogisms, I will take the analysis of Chapter 4 as read.

As I also said in Chapter 4, these insights into self-reference and self-appearance seem not to have been taken up by any of Kant's immediate successors. The central insight into self-reference did eventually reappear, as we saw, but Kant's central insights into self-appearance seem never to have made another appearance. The strange history of these insights might explain why the Paralogisms chapter has remained so murky for so long. Until A354 and A355 are no longer a mystery, how could anyone understand Kant's disposition of the Paralogisms – or, therefore, his overall theory of mind? Of the various terms Kant used to refer to the mind, he most often used 'soul' or 'subject' in the Paralogisms chapter; I will follow him.

1 The Paralogisms

If we skip Kant's architectonic scaffolding, the special faulty arguments that Kant calls paralogisms lay out arguments for three doctrines about the nature of the soul: that it is a substance, that it is simple and without parts, and that it persists in a manner that, in Bishop Butler's phrase, is 'strict and philosophical'; Kant's terms were 'incorruptible' (A345 = B403) and 'absolute persistence' (B415). (I am setting aside the Fourth Paralogism.) These doctrines were all prominent in Kant's time, especially among the rationalists. Kant called them *rational* psychology because they were supposedly derived by the use of reason alone from purely analytic propositions, without any recourse to experiential evidence. What exactly reason is supposed to be applied to here and how the use of nonexperiential or 'pure' reason is consistent with making use of self-awareness, a kind of experience, are issues to which we will return in Section 3.

This chapter is limited to the Second Paralogism and Kant's attack on it, and even then only as found in the first edition. I will not examine the First Paralogism separately, though issues from it come up in Section 3 of this chapter and in Chapter 8, which takes up the Third Paralogism; I will say no more about the Fourth Paralogism than was said in Chapter 5:5.[2] The Second Paralogism argues that the soul is simple. As the opening paragraphs of Kant's discussion make clear, that means that it is not a composite, has no parts, is not a plurality of things. In Kant's opinion, the idea that the soul is simple is the foundation of all RPsy. This makes it "the Achilles of all dialectical inferences in the pure doctrine of the soul" (A351). (In Kant's terminology, a dialectical inference is a special kind of tempting but ultimately invalid inference, of which a paralogism is one form.) Simplicity of the soul is the root doctrine of RPsy (Axiv, Bxxix; see A443 = B471) because being simple would be sufficient for the soul to be a substance, the conclusion of the First Paralogism (this could be argued in other ways, too, of course), and necessary for personal identity to be absolute, the conclusion of the Third Paralogism. Since absolute identity is necessary in turn for immortality, being simple would be necessary for immortality, the real topic behind at least the Third Paralogism. (Kant addresses the topic of immortality directly only in the second edition, but A345 = B403 make it clear that it preoccupied Kant in the first edition too.) These entailment relations are enough to show that the simplicity of the soul and Second Paralogism are indeed 'the Achilles' of RPsy. If the idea is groundless, the First Paralogism suddenly hangs in the air and the third is in much deeper trouble than that.

I will concentrate on the first edition because Kant's attack on the Second Paralogism is far richer there than in the second edition, where he disposes of it in exactly one paragraph (the same is true of the other three). In addition, in the second edition the attack on the Paralogisms is no longer the place where Kant discusses self-reference and self-appearance. He made a radical change in the strategy he adopted against the Paralogisms, as we will see in Section 5, and the new strategy did not require discussion of these issues. For this and other reasons, Kant moved what remained of his analysis of self-reference and self-appearance to TD, where it became the centrepiece of his defence of the unknowability of the mind as it is against the objection that in ASA we are aware of the self itself, not just representations of it (see Chapter 10).

The attack on the Paralogisms has sometimes been thought to depend on the unknowability doctrine, indeed to be merely a parochial restatement of that doctrine, to the effect that there is nothing wrong with RPsy's views as such, but they are only true of appearances and tell us nothing about how we really are. If Kant's discussion were in fact nothing more than a claim that RPsy is all right so long as it is restricted to appearances, it would hold little interest. But this would be a gross misreading. Far from arguing anything as vapid and *parti pris* as that the doctrine of noumena shows the claims of RPsy to be true but only of appearances, Kant argues that we cannot know the claims of RPsy to be true of *anything*. What troubled Kant about the claims of RPsy and made them worth attacking is that they contradict the unknowability of the noumenal. Since the whole point of Kant's attack is to defend the unknowability of the noumenal (B412), if it presupposes this same unknowability, it is hopelessly circular. It should appeal to something neutral, and it does. It appeals to two things: first, to what the conditions of the mind functioning as it does actually imply concerning its nature and, second, to how little the way that the mind appears in ASA actually reveals concerning its nature.

2 Three claims from the subjective deduction

It is generally agreed that Kant's attack on the Paralogisms leaves little standing of the principal Cartesian and Leibnizian doctrines concerning the mind. Exactly which philosopher Kant is attacking in any given passage may sometimes be unclear (though consulting the appendix on the Amphiboly of Concepts of Reflection makes this less unclear; Kant's discussion there of Leibniz's doctrine that what exists is "simple beings endowed with representations" [A283 = B340] strongly suggests that he had this doctrine in mind in his attack on the Second Paralogism, too). In addition, the exact details of some of Kant's moves may be obscure. But it is agreed that the overall impact of his attack is devastating. Less widely recognized is the fact that Kant had a major personal stake in undermining RPsy. I do not mean the obvious one, his desire to protect his doctrine that the mind as it is is unknowable; I mean something more specific. Kant felt the allure of RPsy to be as powerfully present in the heart of his own account of the mind as in the work of any of his predecessors. The very doctrines that give the subjective deduction its Critical bite can readily seem to point to the doctrines of RPsy, indeed have been taken to point to these doctrines by some of Kant's own disciples, Paton, for example. In fact, I think this appearance is the illusion Kant had in mind when he wrote at the beginning of the Paralogisms chapter that RPsy takes off from an "illusion which cannot be avoided" (A341 = B399). The critical philosophy can seduce the unwary into the embrace of RPsy with the threat it poses for the unknowability of the noumenal mind at least as readily as any of the doctrines that Kant was rejecting. That, I think, was Kant's most important reason for diagnosing and dissolving these temptations in the Paralogisms chapter.

That the attack on the Paralogism is related to TD in some way is not controversial.[3] However, exactly how the illusion behind the Paralogisms grows out of the subjective deduction is not well understood. Nor is it well understood that Kant's *arguments against* RPsy also come straight from the subjective deduction. RPsy used two kinds of argument, one based on certain of our concepts for the mind and one based on our awareness of ourselves. The attacks on both arguments come straight from the subjective deduction. In mounting these attacks, Kant gets his theory of mind properly articulated for the very first time. They are also the only place in the *Critique* where Kant situates his view on the mind vis-à-vis positions he rejects. In fact, to the extent that Kant's arguments against the Paralogisms remain cloudy, his whole theory of mind remains cloudy. If Kant's chapter on the Paralogisms is related to his overall conception of the mind in these ways, that by itself would be enough to show that his dispute with the rationalists about the mind was by no means a parochial one.

If Kant thought that the conclusion of the Second Paralogism that the soul is simple (like the conclusions of the First and Third Paralogisms that the soul is a substance and persists in some 'strict and philosophical' way) is the result of "an illusion which cannot be avoided", he must have had some good reason for saying this. Yet few commentators have ever ventured even to speculate on what he may have had in mind. Here is my suggestion. In the subjective deduction Kant lays out some claims about the mind's functions and unity, as well as some claims about how it must be represented. These claims about the mind's function and how we must represent it seem to hold the most direct implications for its structure (its composition, how it persists). Indeed, they seem to imply RPsy; they seem to show that the mind is a substance that is simple and persists in some specially absolute way. In my view, this is the "illusion which cannot be avoided", and I think Kant wrote the Paralogisms chapter to undermine it, to the extent that any argument can do so. How something functions and how it can be represented need not reveal anything about its structure; the illusion to the contrary may be unavoidable, but it is profoundly mistaken.

At least three different claims made in or implied by the subjective deduction give rise to the illusion. The first of them contains two parts. One part takes off from the conclusion of one of the central arguments of the subjective deduction, which I will now call the *unity argument* (UA), the conclusion that a multiplicity of representations can be synthesized into the object of a single representation only if they have a single common subject. (That is true for concurrent representations, at least. The situation is more complicated for representations spread across time, as the attack on the Third Paralogism makes clear [see Chapter 8].) It is extremely interesting that UA is the only argument that Kant represents RPsy as using to support the Second Paralogism.[4] The other part takes off from another claim of the subjective deduction. As well as being one, when we think of a subject in the act of representing something (perceiving, having a thought, imagining something, etc.), we can *represent* it only as being one. This limitation arises only when a subject is representing something in a way that is *something to it,* but carefully noting that qualification throughout would make for complicated sentences. It will turn out that only visualization, representing by direct awareness and imagining, suffers this constraint; description does not.

Now, anything or any collection of things can be pictured as one of some sort, but Kant had something more in mind. When he said the subject "has *necessarily* to be represented as numerically identical" (A107; see A116, A122, B132), he meant that *we cannot but* picture a subject of representations as one, as a unit.[5] As Kant makes clear only in the Paralogisms chapter in a table on A344 = B402, we cannot picture a mind or subject of representations as a composite or a system of parts working together, a plurality. Normally, when we conceive of anything as one thing, we can also conceive of it as a plurality, more than one, usually in many different ways. When we think of a subject of representations in the act of representing, however, the option of conceiving of it as many, as composite, seems not to be there. Since we can certainly picture other things both as one and as composite, this limitation is special to subjects. Though I barely mentioned this restriction on how a subject can be pictured in Chapter 6 because it plays little or no role in Kant's theory of the unity of apperception and consciousness, it is central to his attack on the Paralogisms.

I will treat these two claims, the one about unity and the one about picturability, as parts of a single claim:

(1) To represent a multiplicity of representations as the object of a single representation, they must all have a single common subject. Furthermore, when we think of a subject in the act of representing, we must picture it as being one and cannot picture it as a plurality of any sort.[6]

My reason for putting these two claims together is that Kant treats them together; they both figure in his treatment of UA and its relation to the Second Paralogism (see Section 4). Either part of (1) might seem to run a risk of violating the unknowability of the noumenal. Concerning the part of the claim to do with unity, Kant will suggest in effect that the requirement that the subject be single is specified functionally and implies nothing about what beings who can function that way might be like (see A398), thereby illustrating the functionalist strain in his thought very nicely. Concerning the other part of the claim, Kant will urge that how we must picture the mind tells us no more than the first part.

Note that neither UA nor the claim that we must picture the mind as one says anything about self-awareness. In the same way as commentators try to make self-awareness too central to TD, they try to centre Kant's attack on RPsy around misguided uses of self-awareness too much. Self-awareness does not figure in UA. Yet both UA and the conclusion drawn from it about how the mind can be pictured figure centrally in Kant's discussion of the Second Paralogism. So misuse of self-awareness cannot be the whole story about RPsy. By overplaying self-awareness, commentators neglect other interesting things going on in Kant's attack on the Paralogisms.

In addition to (1), the subjective deduction contains two other claims that fuel RPsy. Unlike (1), neither of these claims is made explicitly; rather, they are embedded in its underlying structure. They both pick up the claim made in (1) that when we think of the mind as a subject in the act of representing, we can picture it only as being one and noncomposite and identify two points of view from which this limitation also obtains. The first is picturing the subject from the point of view of what it would be like to be that subject, how would it be for that subject.[7] This is picturing a mind from the point of view of awareness^H, the point of view it has on itself when it is aware of itself on the basis of doing acts of representing and having representations. Kant described this point of view as the "transference of this consciousness of mine to other things" (A347 = B405), "put[ting] myself in his place, thus substitut[ing], as it were my own subject for the object I am seeking to consider" (A354). Thought of from this point of view, Kant found his options for picturing (imagining) a mind to be sharply constrained; again, the mind can be pictured only as numerically identical (A107), and again, picturing it as a unity precludes picturing it as a plurality (A344 = B402).

(2) From the point of view of what it would be like to be a subject of representations, we must picture the subject as being one and cannot picture it as a plurality of any sort.

The constraint in (2) on how a subject can be pictured is the same as the constraint in (1); it is just applied from a special point of view. Note that in those contexts in which we encounter this constraint, the picture we can form also gives us little with which to answer questions such as, 'One what?' or 'One in what way, by what principle of unity?' We examined this point in Chapter 2:5 and will return to it.

The constraint on how we can picture any subject from the point of view of what it would be like to be that subject also appears as a constraint on how I can picture myself as subject of my own representations.

(3) If I am aware of myself as subject, I must appear to myself to be one and cannot picture myself as a plurality of any sort.

Kant did not distinguish this third point of view from the first or second. I want to do so for two reasons. The first is my general desire to keep awareness as clearly distinct from self-awareness as possible, even in the special context of awareness of others that we are now considering. The second is that despite not separating these three claims, Kant gives RPsy one argument per claim in his analysis of the arguments for the Second Paralogism. That is, despite not separating them off, he gives my awareness of myself a separate role, different from the role he gives either to thinking of subjects having representations or to thinking of what it would be like to be a certain subject.

As Kant presents RPsy, its adherents found arguments for the idea that the soul is simple in each of (1), (2), and (3). He considers each of these claims, individually and in the order in which I have presented them, and shows how they each engender an illusion that the soul is simple, but also how none of them contains a single real reason to think that it is. This tripartite analysis is the topic of Section 4. Before we turn to it, we must first look at the extremely important ideas Kant put in his introductory remarks to the chapter as a whole, remarks that gain added importance from the fact that he changed not a word of them for the second edition.

3 The introductory remarks: the strategies of rational psychology

The introductory remarks (A341–8 = B399–406) deal primarily with what RPsy must do if it wants to remain a rational psychology. To be a rational psychology, it must make no use of observation and base itself entirely on pure reason alone. However, RPsy as Kant portrays it also appeals to our awareness of our own minds. Thus, Kant has two tasks in the introductory remarks: to examine the general strategies of RPsy, and to explain how it can appeal to direct awareness of self and still remain a *rational* psychology. Since Kant saw fit to leave these remarks entirely unchanged for the second edition, we may take them to be authoritative.

Kant begins by telling us that a paralogism is a formally invalid argument, and a transcendental paralogism is one for which there is a 'transcendental ground' giving rise to an unavoidable illusion that forces us to draw an invalid conclusion (see A402–3 and B410–11 for slightly different accounts of what a paralogism is).[8] RPsy's paralogisms are transcendental and, though Kant does not say so, we can already guess where the transcendental ground is apt to lie: in something to do with how the soul must function and/or be pictured. The illusion will be that the soul is a substance, simple and absolutely persistent; it will arise from taking how the soul must function and be pictured as a guide to its structure. Kant promises to render this illusion harmless.

Without any warning, Kant suddenly introduces 'I think'. He tells us that it is the sole text of RPsy, and the phrase immediately becomes the centerpiece of the whole chapter. All of this catches one a bit by surprise; the phrase has not been used before anywhere in the *Critique*. Though he does not say so, Kant is bringing to centre stage a topic that up to this point has been only a by-product of other discussions, namely, self-awareness. In Kant's primary usage, the phrase 'I think' expresses ASA. In TD, Kant's remarks on self-awareness are extremely scanty. His contribution to the topic was restricted to a few, to be sure very important, sentences that deal all at the same time with the claim we just examined about how we can picture the subject (A107), perceptive acts as the representational base of ASA (A108), a remark or two about the "bare representation 'I' " (A117n), and possibly a badly handled argument that synthesis of representations is required for ASA to be possible (A108, A113, A123). The chapter says nothing directly about what our awareness of ourselves is like or what we can and cannot learn from it. These are the topics Kant now brings to centre stage.

Suddenly introducing self-awareness as Kant does here probably seemed a smaller departure to Kant than it does to us (or at any rate, to me). As we saw in Chapter 3, Kant could run simple awareness and self-awareness together, nowhere more remarkably than in the concept of TA. He also held, as he says twice in the Paralogisms chapter (A347 = B405 and A353), that we can represent a subject of representations only from the point of view of what it would be like to be that subject, that is, from the point of view of self-awareness – 'I must put myself in his place'. Thus, introducing self-awareness at the beginning of the chapter on the Paralogisms may well have seemed to him to be simply taking up where TD left off. Running self-awareness together with what a subject must be like to be aware at all, to have representations, has unfortunate consequences in the chapter on the Paralogisms. It leads Kant to use 'I think' to refer both to self-awareness and to a thinking being as such. Yet it is far from self-awareness alone (claim (3) from the preceding section) that constrains how we can picture a mind or generates the illusion behind RPsy. As we saw, unity (claim (1)) does so, too, as does adopting the point of view a mind has on itself (claim (2)). Kant never makes these distinctions. Thus, it is possible to think that the whole Paralogisms chapter is about nothing but self-awareness – possible, but mistaken.

Strictly speaking, if RPsy is to be a *rational* psychology, it should not make any use of any kind of experience whatsoever, self-awareness included. It would seem that anything that experience could tell us about the mind would be experience sensitive, and so could be supported by some experiences and falsified by others. This would make anything experience could tell us not universal and not necessary – not *a priori* – and therefore outside of RPsy. In any case, Kant tells us later on in these introductory remarks, the properties that interest RPsy "do not in any way belong to a possible experience", and he offers simplicity, interestingly enough, as his example (A347 = B406). (Regrettably, he does not say what makes it beyond any possible experience, but his choice of simplicity as his example here indicates yet again that he viewed it as the root doctrine of rational psychology; see also B409–10, where a proof of simplicity is identified as the one real threat to the unknowability of the noumenal mind.) So if RPsy wants to prove that the soul is simple (as Kant thinks it must, simplicity being at the base of the other Paralogisms and necessary for immortality), then its psychology cannot depend on experience of any sort, even, one would think, awareness of self (A347 = B405–6). (If so, there would be a certain irony in the idea that the Paralogisms are based on nothing but self-awareness!)

Yet, says Kant, by being built on the single proposition 'I think', RPsy is built on a kind of experience – 'I think' expresses an experience (or at least, as Kant says later, a bare consciousness) of oneself. Kant tells us why this appeal is not illicit. The sort of awareness of self that 'I think' expresses, namely, ASA, is not experience sensitive; it contains no "special distinction or empirical determination" and it is not "empirical knowledge, but knowledge of the empirical in general" (A343 = B401). The picture of the soul it provides, the 'inner perception' of oneself (A343 = B401; unfortunate expression!), could not be falsified by any other experience. That is what I meant by saying that it is not experience sensitive (see Bennett's notion that this sort of awareness is not 'experience dividing' [Chapter 4:4]). The same is true of visualizing the soul from the point of view of what it would be like to be that soul. Here the resulting picture would not be sensitive to any experience that was imagined from the point of view of what it would be like to have it. Though RPsy cannot appeal to experience of objects (see, e.g., A784 = B812), it can appeal to ASA.

The 'experience' that awareness of self as subject gives us is not experience sensitive because each and every one of a person's representations provides this kind of awareness of self, or at least the representational base of it (see Chapter 4). That is why no judgement made on the basis of such awareness could be overturned by another experience: "Inner experience in general and its possibility, . . . in which no special distinction or empirical determination is given, is not to be regarded as empirical knowledge" (A343 = B401). Similarly, picturing a subject from the point of view of what it would be like to be that subject is not experience sensitive because it is picturing a subject from the same point of view on itself as I have on myself in the kind of self-appearance we are considering. Thus, RPsy can use both self-appearance as subject and pictures of other subjects from the point of view of what it would be like to be those subjects in their theories – and use them it does.

But there is more to RPsy taking 'I think' as its sole text than self-awareness, for RPsy as Kant presents it also uses something else. Indeed, the official basis for RPsy should be something else, something more like what we now call conceptual analysis, a point Kant makes a number of times (e.g., in The Amphiboly of Concepts of Reflection, A260 = B316ff.) And Kant does present RPsy as using conceptual analysis. The concepts it studies are those of a thinking being and of self-awareness. The concept of a thinking being is that of a being that can have experiences, have "perception in general" (A343 = B401). The concept of self-awareness is that of "inner experience in general and its possibility".

As I said, in the Amphiboly, Kant was well aware that what can be inferred from the concepts of a thinking being and self-awareness ought to be the official project of RPsy; he was aware of it in the current chapter, too. When he says, early in the introductory remarks, that 'I think' is the expression for "a thinking being, the object of that psychology that may be entitled 'the rational doctrine of the soul' " (A342 = B400), he is not using 'I think', here, as an expression for any form of self-awareness, ASA included. He is using it as a way of referring to thinking beings in general. This is shown most clearly in a passage near the end of the introductory remarks. In arguing that RPsy is appealing to something common to all subjects of representations, Kant says:

> The proposition 'I think' is here taken only problematically, not in so far as it may contain perception of an existent . . . but in respect of its mere possibility, in order to see what properties applicable to its subject (be that subject actually existent or not) may follow from so simple a proposition. (A347 = B405)

So how can 'I think' be the sole text of RPsy, then? Because Kant used the expression for two very different things: as a way of expressing ASA and as a name for a thinking being. RPsy based its doctrines on both: on what can be inferred from the concept of a thinking being as much as on what can be observed in ASA, the form of self-awareness that 'I think' expresses. The former is what the passage just quoted is about; here, Kant seems to be saying, RPsy is analysing the concept expressed by 'I think'.

Unfortunately, Kant does not distinguish the two kinds of investigation as clearly as he might. Consider, for example, the very sentence in which he first introduces 'I think'. First he calls 'I think' "the concept or . . . judgment 'I think' ". Then his very next words are, "as is easily seen, this is the vehicle of all concepts" (A341 = B399). A judgement is a vehicle of one's concepts? Kant has failed to distinguish the concept of the entity ('the concept or judgment') from the entity's awareness of itself. From this distinction flow two very different strategies.

Strategy A: Analyse the concepts of a thinking being and of self-awareness.
Strategy B: Study what self-awareness tells us about ourselves.

Only the second is an appeal to self-awareness, to how the self is pictured. In fact, Kant should have distinguished the subject's awareness of itself not only from its concept of itself, but also from the *concept* of self-awareness. Arguments from either concept would be good, old-fashioned conceptual analysis, first of the concept of a thinking being, then of the concept of self-awareness.

Using Strategy A, what could we infer about the nature of the soul from the mere concept of a thinking being? With the help of UA we could infer quite a lot. Consider all representations of which one is aware by having them (Kant's 'all our thought' [A341 = B400]). By UA, those representations will have a single, common subject, able to be aware of many representations simultaneously and, in many cases, of itself as their common subject. This concept of the subject is exactly the concept of a thinking being that Kant ascribes to RPsy: the "concept 'I', so far as it [this 'I'] is present in all thought" (A342 = B400). Later in the chapter, at the beginning of the Second Paralogism (A352–3), he unmistakably ascribes UA itself to RPsy. So the task of the conceptual analytic part of RPsy is to see what can be inferred from this concept of a single, common subject about the nature of this subject.

Now let us consider Strategy B. How could RPsy appeal to the way we picture the subject in the context of it having representations (claim (1)), from the standpoint that subject has on itself (claim (2)), or on the basis of how I am aware of myself (claim (3))? Historically, this kind of awareness of self as subject has always been by far the most common basis for investigations into the nature of the mind. Kant says that the picture of the subject that any of (1) to (3) yields is a "completely empty representation". And the essence of his attack on the way RPsy uses this empty representation is to say that they make the mistake of thinking that it is a representation of a completely empty, that is, simple, being.

Kant's summation of his view of RPsy's appeal to this representation of the subject is difficult. He says that its source is the completely empty representation 'I'; and we cannot even say that this is a *concept* but only that it is a *bare consciousness* which accompanies all concepts. Through this I or he or it (the thing) which thinks, nothing further is *represented* than a transcendental subject of the thoughts = *X*. (A346 = B404; my emphases)

Here is what I think Kant is trying to say. Though the words 'I think' look like a description of something, specifically of a subject of representations, they are not. The awareness of the subject that accompanies representations of objects ('all concepts') is so empty that the phrase in which we "express the perception of the self" (A342 = B401), namely, 'I think', is not really a 'concept', a description, at all. Thus, nothing useful can be deduced analytically from the meanings of its words. So much for Strategy A. However, how we picture the subject, even in self-appearance as subject, gives us nothing more. All we 'perceive' of the subject is that it is subject. This is not even a conceptualized, synthesized representation; it is merely a 'bare consciousness'. Given the emptiness of this bare consciousness, the subject

is known only through the thoughts which are its predicates and of it, apart from them, we cannot have any concept whatsoever . . . since any judgment upon it has already made use of its representation. (A346 = B404)

That is to say, all we can be aware of *about* ourselves are our particular representational states and their represented objects. Yet we must be *aware* of the subject in a way other than this, namely, as subject, as oneself. (We discussed both this idea and its connection to this passage in Chapter 4:1.) However, this representation of self as subject cannot contain any information *about* this self. So much for Strategy B. Thus, whether 'I think' is taken as expressing a concept to be analysed or a something represented to be studied, all it reveals about the mind is that this mind is the 'transcendental subject = *X*'. Obscure though the last passage is, it does contain an anticipation of the two major insights identified in Chapter 4:1 – that the representation of self provided by ASA is uniquely empty, a mere 'bare consciousness' – in it, 'nothing manifold is given' (B135); and that there is a way of referring to oneself that requires no identification of oneself, no use of concepts.

To summarize Kant's view of the data of RPsy more clearly than he himself did: 'I think' is the sole text of RPsy (A343 = B401). This text allows RPsy two strategies. Strategy A is to analyse the concept of a thinking being, a soul, a subject of representations, "in order to see what properties applicable to its subject . . . may follow from so simple a proposition. . . . 'I think' is . . . here taken problematically, not in so far as it may contain perception of an existent" (A347 = B405). Strategy B is to investigate the (quasi-)content of the picture we can form of a soul from the point of view of what it would be like to be that soul. This picture is quite empty, a bare consciousness, not even a synthesized representation. That these strategies of RPsy are tied in the closest possible way to the three claims from the subjective deduction we identified should be obvious. It could hardly be an accident that the two sources of RPsy parallel Kant's fundamental duality of concepts and intuitions. If the official project of RPsy is analysis of concepts, it really ought not to appeal to experience, not even experience-insensitive bare consciousness. However, nothing of interest can be analysed out of analytic propositions derived from the mere concept of a soul or self, so RPsy also draws in our awareness of what a mind appears to itself to be like. Kant presents a fine summary of this dual appeal to concepts and, if not full-blown intuitions, at least bare consciousness, at the end of his treatment of the First Paralogism:

> In the . . . proposition [I, as thinking being (soul), am substance], we have not taken as our basis any experience; the inference is merely from the concept of the relation which all thought has to the 'I' as the common subject in which it inheres. Nor should we, in resting it upon experience, be able, by any sure observation, to demonstrate such permanence. The 'I' is indeed in all thoughts, but there is not in this representation the least trace of intuition, distinguishing the 'I' from other objects of intuition. (A350)

That is to say, RPsy cannot infer that the soul is a substance from the concept of the mind as common subject of representations, nor can it rest the claim on the way the mind appears to itself. Because both strategies "exclude any admixture of [real, experience-sensitive] experience, we cannot . . . entertain any favourable anticipations in regard to [RPsy's] methods of procedure" (A348 = B406). Note that as yet Kant has not told us why we are prone to *the illusion that they do* reveal the structure of the soul. We will get to that topic in the next section.

4 The arguments for the Second Paralogism

The major premise of the Second Paralogism reads:

> That, the action of which can never be regarded as the concurrence of several things acting, is simple. (A351)

The minor premise then follows:

> Now the soul, or the thinking 'I', is such a being.

And the conclusion, of course, is that the soul is simple. Clearly, the strongest conclusion warranted by the first premise is that the soul must be *regarded* as simple. But Kant was after something more interesting than this rather obvious error. What sort of considerations lead people to accept the conclusion of awful arguments such as this Second Paralogism? What makes the idea that the soul is simple so appealing? Kant identifies three such considerations. The first three parts of his discussion attack these arguments and also try to diagnose why we might be seduced by them. I will label them as follows:

Unity argument. The first part of the discussion takes up the only argument that Kant actually attributes to RPsy (A351 to just before A354). I call it the unity argument (UA); it starts from the now-familiar idea that a "soul, or the thinking 'I' " must be unified to represent objects. Kant shows why this necessity does not demonstrate that the soul is simple.

He then turns to the task of diagnosing and dissolving the illusion behind the paralogistic inference, the 'illusion which cannot be avoided'. This is where transcendental designation makes its appearance, the idea that a certain form of reference to self is nonascriptive (see Chapter 4:1). Kant attacks two further arguments:

Representation argument. The first is an argument that some features of how a subject of experience must be represented seem to entail that it is simple (just before A354 to the end of the sentence beginning, "Thus the renowned psychological proof . . . " on A355). I call this argument the representation argument (RA).

Appeal to self-awareness. The second is an attempt to show that the soul is simple by appealing to how one does or must appear to oneself (from the sentence beginning "It is obvious . . . " on A355 to the end of the next paragraph [A356]). This I call the appeal to self-awareness.

It is important to lay out the stages in Kant's discussion in this way because it makes clear just how closely these arguments are related to the three claims from the subjective deduction examined in Section 2. Each argument is a natural over-interpretation of one of those claims. Kant concludes his attack with a discussion of a fourth and quite different topic, namely, *immateriality* (just before A357 to A361). Here his argument takes a new tack: even if the soul were simple, he argues, this would not be enough to prove that it is immaterial. Many of his notorious remarks about the unknowability of the soul vis-à-vis the knowability of (phenomenal) human beings are in this section (see Section 5).[9]

The unity argument

The only argument Kant represents RPsy as using to support the Second Paralogism is UA, cast in the form of a simple, powerful thought experiment. Taking the soul or thinking thing as its example, it is an argument for both the major and the minor premises. Distribute the parts of a thought – for example, the words of a verse – among several beings in such a way that no one being is aware of more than one part. So long as no one is aware of all of them together and at the same time, these parts would "never make up a thought", no matter how they were otherwise connected to one another (A352).[10] Thus, for something to be a thought, for its parts to be connected in the right way, its parts must all be had by a single subject. Now, the parts of a representation being distributed one-to-one over the parts of a composite subject would not be enough for them to be had by a single subject in this way (whatever way that is). Something more or different is required: the whole subject must be aware of all the parts as one representation, "a whole thought" (whatever that may be). So far, so good. But now RPsy makes a portentous move: the parts of a thought could not be had by a single subject in this way, it infers, if the subject were composite.

Therefore, the subject must be simple. Note that if this were true, any integration of function required of a subject could not be a matter of a system of parts working together.

It is clear that the attributes of the mind from which RPsy draws its conclusion are those laid out in claim (1):

(1) To represent a multiplicity of representations as the object of a single representation, they must all have a single common subject. Furthermore, when we think of a subject in the act of representing, we must picture it as being one and cannot picture it as a plurality of any sort.

And the argument RPsy used to support its conclusion is the argument Kant gave for (1), namely, UA. Nothing could make the close connection between the subjective deduction and the chapter on RPsy more clear. Kant of course accepts (1) and UA. So he has to focus on the portentous inference. It is invalid, Kant argues, because "the unity of the thought . . . may relate just as well to the collective unity of different substances acting together" (A353). And surely he is right. Knowing that parts of a representation need to be synthesized into a single intentional object by a single subject tells us little about what kinds of structure could 'realize' a subject with such abilities. Certainly it does not tell us that only a noncomposite structure could do so (see A398). Perhaps it is "impossible that the thought should inhere in the composite as composite" (A352), one piece of thought per each piece of the composite.[11] But that the soul be "absolutely simple" or an "absolute unity" is not the only alternative. Note that Kant's response to RPsy's misuse of UA is exactly the response a functionalist would make: how the mind functions does not dictate the structure of that thing, simple or composite.[12]

'Absolutely simple' and 'absolute unity' (as contrasted with 'unity') here mean 'not a composite of simpler components' or "contains no manifold of constituents external to one another" (B414). That is to say, these phrases mean simplicity. Now, Kant's point is that we have seen no reason to think that a composite subject could not have the unity required to synthesize representations and/or their objects into single representations. Nor need the parts of the resulting representation be thought of as distributed one-to-one among the parts of a composite subject. How the whole soul could have each of them is just as big a problem for a simple soul as for a composite one (cf. B415n). A soul must be a single epistemic system and have whatever is required to represent objects, functional integration being a plausible candidate. But whether or not it is composite is irrelevant:

> The . . . concept of simplicity vanishes; it is transformed into a merely logical qualitative unity of self-consciousness . . . which has to be present whether the subject be composite or not. (B413)

In short, RPsy has confusedly thought that to be a unity in the way a subject is a unity, a thing must be an 'absolute unity', that is, simple, not in any way composite.

What Kant had in mind when he spoke of unity – for example, in the notion just introduced of a 'merely logical qualitative unity' – is unclear. By 'unity' here did he mean simply being one or did he mean being one in the distinctive way in which subjects of representation are one? The latter would require not just being one but also unity of consciousness, being aware of a number of representations and/or objects as one object.[13] I think he clearly means the latter; functional integration of some sort would presumably be required, too, a topic in which Kant had strikingly little interest. (We touched on it in Chapter 2:4.) But it does not much matter which Kant had in mind; none would imply that the soul is simple. However, these distinctions are themselves of some interest in the context of RPsy, so we might keep them in mind.

If this is right, why did Kant write more? He wanted not just to show that we have no reason to believe that the soul is simple; he also wanted to diagnose and dissolve our inclination to do so. Note that Strategy A has dominated completely so far. But most of what gives the idea of simplicity its appeal grows out of Strategy B. So, having disposed of UA, he now asks, "Whence then are we to derive this proposition [of the absolute unity (i.e., simplicity) of the soul]?" (A353). Despite UA being the only argument for simplicity that he actually attributes to RPsy, he now turns elsewhere, to how we represent or picture the soul – what it appears to us to be like. Part of what gives UA its appeal as an argument for simplicity is that in thinking about the argument, we inevitably try to picture a composite self in the act of representing or being aware of a thought, and we find this hard to do. As Kant puts it, "We demand the absolute unity of the subject . . . only because otherwise we could not say, '*I* think' (the manifold in one representation)" (A353). That is to say, we cannot form a picture of ourselves except as a unity, a *single* subject of our representations. And the reason we 'demand' absolute unity, that we insist that the soul thus pictured is simple, is that our picture of the 'I think' somehow leads us to the idea that the unity we picture in it is incompatible with compositeness. Certainly the picture depicts no compositeness. This difficulty in picturing a composite subject and its contribution to the appeal of UA as an argument for simplicity is the reason I have kept the two of them together in (1).

How could the way we picture a soul generate an illusion that it is simple? One of Kant's clearest statements occurs only much later, in the appendix to the Dialectic:

> We . . . connect all the appearances, all the actions and receptivity of our mind, *as if* the mind were a simple substance. (A672 = B700; his emphasis)

However, an argument that the soul is indivisible had considerable currency in Kant's time – Descartes, Leibniz, and Mendelssohn all used it, and so did Reid – and it is to it that Kant now turns.[14]

> Although the whole of [a] thought could be divided and distributed among many subjects, the subjective 'I' [the 'I' pictured from its own point of view] can never be thus divided and distributed. (A354)

In what way could the 'I' not be divided and distributed? Kant was probably not aware of it, but there are two possibilities. A soul might not be able to divide into two or more souls, especially not from the point of view of that soul. This idea will take us to the heart of the argument for RPsy stemming from claim (2), which I call the RA and examine in the next section. Or a soul might not be able to divide into partial souls or parts of a soul. This idea, which Kant probably did not identify as a separate possibility, is interesting because it can readily generate an argument that the soul has no parts, and a soul with no parts would be noncomposite, that is, simple.

Try to picture a mind splitting into partial minds or mind parts. We picture (or imagine, if you prefer) representations (perceptions, memories, etc.), dispositions, and so on splitting into two groups had by two subjects, each aware of the representations and objects in one of the groups by having them without being aware of representations or objects in the other group, not by having them at any rate. But to be aware of a group of represented objects as one object – to be aware, not just of *A*, then of *B*, then of *C*, but of *A and B and C* together, as one intentional object – is to be a soul, not a partial soul or soul parts (see A108). If so, we have not pictured a soul splitting into partial souls or a bunch of soul parts. However, it is not easy to see how to divide up a soul so that it is *not* aware of groups of objects as a single object; what other model could we call on? If we cannot *divide* a soul into partial souls or soul parts, then it could not be *made* of parts either, and the soul must be simple. Joined with indivisibility in this way, UA becomes an interesting argument for simplicity.

It is easy to reply to this argument, of course: Who says a partial subject or parts of a subject have to continue to be aware of groups of objects, or even to have representations at all? However, suppose the argument works for beings that have representations. If it shows that even such beings could not be a partial soul or soul parts, that would still be interesting. To this argument, in either its unrestricted or its restricted form, Kant's reply would be the same as before. What we cannot picture is a poor guide to what is impossible. Whatever it is that guarantees that a subject who is aware of a group of representations in one representation will be a soul, not a partial soul or a soul part, would be functional and would not imply that such a soul has one kind of structure rather than any other, including a composite one. Thus, that a subject has what it takes to be aware of a group of representations in one representation gives us "no knowledge of the subject in itself, which as substratum underlies [the] 'I', as it does all thought" (A350).

What gives this twist on UA such plausibility as it has is also, I think, what deludes us into thinking that the unity we picture a subject to have (whatever sort of unity that is) is incompatible with compositeness. If the subject were composite, we should be able to make some sense of splitting it up into parts. Yet we have no idea of how to do so and no idea how whatever might result from doing so could still be a subject. Contrary to what RPsy may have assumed, it would not, of course, have to be a subject any longer; but we can still form no idea of what else it might be – what soul parts might be like. So we cannot picture a subject as composite. It would be easy to conclude with RPsy that this limitation reflects the way the soul is. We will see why it does not in the next section.

With his analysis of 'merely logical unity', Kant's functionalist colours really come clear. In fact, this reading of Kant on the mind can begin to make some very interesting sense even of the doctrine of the unknowability of the mind as it is. If the mind as it appears is limited to function and representation, and if function and representation do not dictate whether a mind is even one of anything else, then so long as we are restricted to function and representation, the mind as it is structurally really is unknowable. Let us pull together our results so far. Any subject aware of a group of representations and/or their objects in one representation must be one, minimally complete subject, not a partial one or parts of one. But this unity and minimal completeness as a subject is a 'merely logical unity'. What Kant meant is that nothing about what sort of being a subject consists in or is realized in is thereby determined. Indeed, a single, minimally complete subject of representation, *if individuated just by the fact that it is aware of a group of represented objects in one representation,* could be a partial person or a person part or even no whole number of persons *by any other criterion.*[15]

The representation argument

With the introduction of the issue of how we can picture the soul, Kant moves from the *concept* of the subject and its abilities to the subject's *representability,* to what we can picture happening to a subject in general and to ourselves in particular. This is a move from Strategy A to Strategy B, what the awareness I have of myself as subject reveals about my nature. The kind of awareness concerned is ASA, a form of representation or at least a bare consciousness of self. As Kant notes, we would expect that appeals to experience of any kind would be illicit as arguments for simplicity: "Absolute unity is quite outside [the] province [of experience]" (A353), but an appeal to ASA is legitimate, as we saw earlier. The difficulty in connection with UA over forming a picture of the soul as composite arises in connection with the second and third of the three doctrines we extracted from the subjective deduction, too – the ones to do with how we can represent a subject of experience and how a subject appears to itself – and Kant considers two further arguments for simplicity that arise out of their specific contexts. The first is what I call the representation argument (RA).[16]

Closely related to the strange idea that a subject of representation might be no whole number of persons, counted by any other criterion, is the even stranger idea, explored by Nagel, of a subject of representation who is not even a whole number of *subjects!* Nagel thinks that brain bisection patients become such creatures in certain laboratory situations, exhibiting too much duality (especially of ESA) to be one, but too much unity (especially behavioral) to be two. What makes the idea bizarre is that, as Nagel has put it, we cannot 'project' ourselves into the mental life/lives of such creatures, figure out how it would be with us if we were that being/those beings.[17] Neither doing so once nor doing so twice works. We can form no picture of what it would be like to be such a creature. This idea that I can picture a soul only if I can project myself into it has some appeal. How could I conceive of a being as a soul, a subject, if I could not figure out what it would be like to be that soul? For Kant, moreover, the only way we can picture a soul or subject is from just this point of view, what it would be like to be that soul: "If I wish to represent to myself a thinking being, I must put myself in his place" (A353). So for Kant if we cannot make sense of what it would be like to be some soul, we cannot picture that soul at all.

Nagel's claims connect to the side of the indivisibility argument concerned with dividing into two or more whole minds. It is also closely connected to RA. A very short argument, RA consists simply of the claim already considered that only if we picture a subject of representations as an 'absolute unity', that is, simple (A354), could we "say 'I think' " of it, picture it as one subject. This claim is an inference from (2).

(2) From the point of view of what it would be like to be a subject of representation, we must picture the subject as being one and cannot picture it as a plurality of any sort.

It interested Kant considerably.[18] RPsy of course infers that the constraint on how we can picture a subject described in (2) reflects the way it is.

Because Kant accepts RA, his response is to try to break the inferences. He does so in the course of analysing the indivisibility argument on A354. He will insist, of course, that from (2) we cannot infer that the soul is simple any more than we could infer this from UA. More interesting, he also diagnoses why we tend to over-interpret (2) in this way. From the mind's standpoint on itself, we do *appear to be* simple. Here, I think, we have the 'illusion which cannot be avoided' that we *are* simple. Is it true that I cannot picture a subject as composite? As we saw in the last section, Kant seems to think that we cannot picture splitting a subject up into parts ("The subjective 'I' can never be . . . divided and distributed" [A354]) and that it follows from this that I cannot picture it as composite. We can now strengthen this argument. To picture a subject in the way being talked about here is to project oneself into it. I cannot project myself into some being that is no whole number of persons, in the same way I cannot project myself into a plurality of beings. But a composite subject would be a plurality of beings.

Bennett has captured the first-person version of what Kant may have had in mind here thus: to think of myself as a plurality of beings is to think of *my* being aware of this plurality, "and that pre-requires an undivided *me*."[19] Bennett's point is nicely put, but he seems not to have noticed that it is by no means limited to picturing *oneself*. It applies to any picturing of what it would be like to be a subject. It works just as well, note, when cast in the third person: to think of a subject as a plurality of things is to think of it as possibly aware of this plurality, and that would require an undivided *it* to have this awareness. In short, Bennett's observation really elucidates and supports (2), not (3), which is restricted to self-awareness. This distinction alone would justify distinguishing (2) from (3), even if Kant did not himself do so. Bennett's not noticing that his observation applies to more than awareness of self might have been a source of his notion that the Paralogisms chapter is primarily concerned with self-awareness, a view we now know to be clearly wrong.

This sense of 'an undivided me' lends plausibility to the idea that a mind cannot divide into two or more whole minds. No one can think of him- or herself as more than one subject. In fact, no one can even think of him- or herself *becoming* more than one subject. Try for example to picture not merely going into but going through a fissioning machine! And the same is true in the third person. I can no more picture what it would be like for another mind to fission into two minds than what it would be like to be me to do it. In both cases, I can form no picture of what it would be like with that subject from the point at which he or she – one subject – begins to become two. Whether or not it is me is irrelevant. Unlike the earlier argument about splitting into parts, it is not clear why this sense of being one and undivided, this inability to project myself into a plurality or picture myself dividing into a number of subjects, should engender an illusion that I am simple and without parts. Why couldn't this sense of myself as one be a sense of an integrated system of parts of some sort? I myself see no reason why it could not be. However, RPsy did think that we would be unable to project ourselves into or picture a subject of representation dividing into two only if the subject were simple, or so Kant implies. His response is extremely penetrating.

To picture how it would be with a dividing or composite subject would be to project myself into it, and perhaps I cannot project myself into a subject in these situations, picture myself as a composite or as dividing. But that would merely be because appearing to myself to be a single subject is a requisite of thinking of myself at all; it is a "form of apperception which belongs to . . . every experience" (A354). And that is all. I "have no right to transform [this] . . . *merely subjective condition* [my being unable to think of me as 'we'] . . . into a concept of a thinking being in general" (A354). And surely Kant is right. That I appear to be one is no more indication that I am simple than that I am composite or anything else. What we can and cannot picture here is due to a kind of lens imposed by the conditions of picturing a self, not to the nature of the soul (its being noncomposite) (see A396).

At this point we need to introduce a distinction between ways of representing that Kant himself did not make. We can represent in descriptions or visualizations or both. Kant lumped the two together (see A107 for some examples), but in connection with RPsy it is helpful to distinguish them. In every case in which a representation of self leads RPsy astray, it is a visualization of the self, not a description of one. Thus, Kant's argument just quoted amounts to saying that though we may not be able to visualize one mind becoming two, such fission is certainly *possible* and therefore *describ-*

able. If we cannot *picture* a dividing or composite self, we can certainly *describe* such a self, well enough at least to make it seem just as possible as a noncomposite one. At the end of the introductory remarks, Kant says something that might seem to contradict the view I am attributing to him here: "We must assign to things, necessarily and *a priori*, all the properties under which alone we think them" (A347 = B405). I do not think there is any contradiction. Even if we must assign to something any property under which we think it, it does not follow that we must assign it every property and lack of property under which we visualize it. Compositeness would be such a property. If we are tightly constrained in how we can picture ourselves, we are less constrained in how we can describe ourselves.

The appeal to self-awareness

Kant turns at last to genuine self-awareness on A355. His attack on RPsy's appeal to self-awareness is the third part of his discussion of the Second Paralogism. Here RPsy argues in effect that

(3) If I am aware of myself as subject, I must appear to myself to be one and cannot picture myself as a plurality of any sort,

implies that the soul is simple. The argument for (3) is a simple appeal to self-awareness. Kant agrees: appearing to oneself to be simple is "involved in every thought" (A354). As he says a bit later, "We may [thereby] . . . profess to know that the thinking 'I', the soul (a name for the transcendental object of inner sense) is simple" (A361). He will again insist, of course, that the soul's actual simplicity is not thereby demonstrated. He does so in the two paragraphs on A355, and then again on A356, where he summarizes his response. In these passages Kant also finishes his diagnosis of our tendency to believe that the soul is simple. His argument is straight-forward: first he describes the manifoldlessness of self-appearance, then he introduces non-ascriptive self-reference to explain this emptiness. We should keep in mind that Kant himself did not distinguish (2) from (3), nor therefore the arguments of RPsy that stem from them. Many of the points he makes against the appeal to self-awareness are also and just as much points against RA.

Both paragraphs on A355 are exceedingly murky. The first is also puzzling. We find Kant asserting that an attribution of simplicity is "already involved in" reference to a self, in the same way as the *cogito* "asserts my existence immediately". But surely asserting my existence would be perfectly well founded, and his whole point is that an attribution of simplicity would not be, is it not? To remove the puzzle, we have to see that he is making a different kind of point altogether here, one not about how the subject is, but precisely the opposite, about how one appears to oneself, about what is built into that appearance. Rational psychologists thought they arrived at their belief that the soul is simple because they inferred the idea from other things that they know. The point Kant is making here is that this is precisely not the source of their idea. They did not infer it; they got it directly from the way the soul appears to itself: in a certain kind of self-appearance, we just appear to ourselves to be simple; this is what creates the illusion that we are simple. Now we can see why Kant made the comparison to existence. We do not infer that we exist, either; we directly appear to ourselves as existing. This point was an objection to RPsy, in Kant's eyes, because he believed that genuine simplicity could not be directly perceived, and thus would have to be inferred (A784 = B812).

What is it to 'appear to oneself to be simple'? Does one appear to oneself to be simple, and if so, why? What Kant meant is this. When we picture a subject, whether by self-appearance or by projecting ourselves into another subject, the representation does not depict any compositeness.

> '*I am simple*' means nothing more than that this representation, 'I', does not contain in itself the least manifoldness and it is absolute (though merely logical) unity. (A355)

This representation does not picture some other things, too, and as soon as we notice them, we begin to see that what we are dealing with is not a case of a rather featureless representation but some different phenomenon altogether. Take this 'absolute (but merely logical) unity'. Suppose that someone were to ask, 'What is this subject one of?' or 'In what way is it unified, integrated?' We would be stumped for an answer: "Of the absolute unity of this subject . . . I possess no concept whatsoever" (A340 = B398). Kant says 'absolute unity,' but I think the point extends to any unity of the subject: "This unity . . . is not the category of unity." (B131). We can say so little about our unity, among other reasons, because our representation of what it is like to be a subject depicts nothing at all about it except that it exists; the representation is completely empty. And that explains why we cannot picture a subject splitting, a point left hanging earlier: if our representation of a subject depicts no features, there are no features to split. As was suggested in Chapter 2:5, saying in what the oneness of space and time consists is difficult in exactly the same way.

In a fascinating passage late in the *Critique,* Kant uses a striking analogy to make the same point. Since commentators seem to have overlooked this passage, I will quote from it at some length:

> If I represent to myself the power of a body in motion, it is so far for me absolute unity, and my representation of it is simple; and I can therefore express this representation by the motion of a point – for the volume of the body is not here a relevant consideration. . . . But I may not therefore conclude that if nothing be given to me but the moving power of a body, the body can be thought as simple substance – merely because its representation abstracts from the magnitude of its volume and is consequently simple. The simple arrived at by abstraction is entirely different from the simple as an object; though the 'I', taken in abstraction, can contain *in itself* no manifold, in its other meaning, as signifying the soul itself, it can be a highly complex concept, as containing *under itself,* and as denoting, what is very composite. I thus detect in these arguments a paralogism. (A784 = B812)

Similarly, the unity depicted in a representation of a subject is a 'merely logical unity': the soul must indeed be one something, as must anything.

But that tells us nothing about what it is one of. If the unity pictured in a self-appearance contains no manifold, it is compatible with the self having any structure whatsoever. Merely being one no more determines structure than functional properties do, maybe even less. *A fortiori*, it does not entail simplicity. Kant's analysis here should be compared with his discussion of logical and real predicates at A598 = B626.

"Thus the renowned psychological proof is founded merely on the indivisible unity of a representation" (A355). This is how Kant begins the next paragraph, the last one I will consider. RPsy is founded on more than that, of course. As we have seen, it also relied on UA and what a soul must be like to synthesize representations and/or their objects. Nevertheless, ASA is a main source of the appeal of the idea that the soul is simple, and Kant's insight into why the picture we form when we are aware of ourselves in this way is so empty is of the first importance. Why is this picture of a subject so empty, a representation of simplicity only because it is a representation of no content at all? To explain this, Kant introduced the second of his great insights, the one into the nature of reference to self:

> In attaching 'I' to our thoughts [in using 'I' to refer to ourselves as subject of our thoughts] we designate the subject . . . only transcendentally, without noting in it any quality whatsoever – in fact, without knowing anything of it either by direct awareness or by reasoning [from the concept of it]. (A355)[20]

We discussed this insight extensively in Chapter 4, so here I can be brief. Transcendental designation is very similar to Shoemaker's self-reference without identification:

> My use of the word 'I' as the subject of [statements such as 'I feel pain' or 'I see a canary'] is not due to my having identified as myself something [otherwise recognized] of which I know, or believe, or wish to say, that the predicate of my statement applies to it.[21]

As I said in Chapter 4, I prefer to call this nonascriptive self-reference. The crucial point both Kant and Shoemaker are making is that one can be aware of oneself, and of oneself as oneself, without being aware of any property of oneself. As I also noted in Chapter 4, Kant says much the same about existence: we can be aware that something exists without being aware of any property of it (existence itself is not a property, a 'predicate' [A598 = B626]). Kant's name, 'transcendental designation' is appropriate; not only does this sort of reference to self not require any particular representation, but at least the potential for making such references is a part of an enormous number of representations, namely, all those that provide the representational base for ASA.

The self-appearance that would result from such an act of reference need not therefore depict any properties of oneself. That is the basic explanation of why it need not 'contain the least manifoldness.' (We examined it and another, deeper one in Chapter 4:1 and 3). It would not be wrong to say that one *appears* to oneself to be simple in nonascriptive self-reference. It could also be said that one appears to oneself to be part of the form, the framework within which everything of which one is aware is located, and not as a thing within that framework. Such a self-appearance could easily engender an illusion that one is simple. Nonascriptive reference to self may have other interesting properties, too, as we saw in Chapter 4:1; in particular, it is probably indispensable if I am to refer to myself as myself at all. I know of no one who has seen that Kant discovered nonascriptive self-reference except perhaps Strawson, as we noted in Chapter 3:4, N26 (Strawson's 'criterionless self-ascription' may refer to this phenomenon. If so, the choice of term was unfortunate; there is no ascription, criterionless or otherwise, in this form of reference.)[22]

Kant's neatest argument for why the soul's appearing to itself to be simple and without properties tells us nothing about its nature does not occur until the penultimate paragraph of the whole section on the Second Paralogism. There he points out that the way I appear to myself is of no service "in the comparison of myself with objects of outer experience" (A360). That is to say, the way I appear to myself tells me nothing about what sort of object to expect myself to be, what sort of object anyone observing me should expect to observe. This by itself is enough to show that "it does not suffice for determining what is specific and distinctive in the nature of the self".

As time passed, Kant seems to have become more and more worried by the kind of self-awareness that nonascriptive reference to self yields, that is to say, by ASA. In the first edition, ASA makes only brief appearances before the Paralogisms chapter, mainly in TD (e.g., on A108 and A113) and there is not a single passage in which Kant worries about its implications for knowledge of the mind as it is. In the second edition, by contrast, Kant obsesses about how the mind's knowledge of itself could be only representations in inner sense as early as B68, and ASA is front and centre from the beginning of TD. Kant devotes half of one section and the complete adjoining section to it later in the chapter (half of §24 and the whole of §25, B153–9; see Chapter 5:4 and 10:5). By contrast, except for the odd remark (B408 and B423n) and a sketch at the end (B429), ASA disappears in the chapter on the Paralogisms. This shift of location indicates a shift of emphasis. As time went by, in Kant's eyes not just the Paralogisms but ASA itself seems to have appeared to be an increasingly serious challenge to the doctrine that we do not know the mind in itself. The reason is that ASA seems to make us aware of *ourselves,* not just of highly doctored representations of ourselves. How otherwise would we know whose representations we have? To protect his general position, Kant had to argue that even ASA can be reconciled to the unknowability of the mind, and in §24 and §25 he tries to do just that (see, e.g., B155). We will examine these sections in Chapter 10.

ASA and its illusion-engendering lack of compositeness is central to all three of the arguments for simplicity. ASA is not the only source of the Second Paralogism, because the unity of consciousness plays a role, too, but ASA is even the source of a lot of the appeal of UA, the argument where the unity of consciousness figures most centrally. Kant thought that the only way we can picture a soul is by putting ourselves in its place (A354), by projecting ourselves into it. Thus, though picturing other subjects or the subject in general (claim (2)) is quite different from picturing oneself (3), any constraints on how I can picture selves of any sort will be manifestations of the constraints on how I can picture myself. We need not agree with Kant on this point, but it must surely be right for any constraints that arise in connection with (2), at any rate – it pictures other selves from the standpoint Kant is talking about, the standpoint of what it would be like to be that self; here we are certainly picturing other selves on the model of how we appear to ourselves. Kant's suggestion that the idea that the soul is simple is largely derived from the way each of us appears to him- or herself seems to me to be right. His remarkable insights into self-appearance and nonascriptive reference to self both diagnose why we might misread ASA this way and tell us what it actually reveals. That should have been enough to dispose of such misreadings for good; alas, Kant was not quite that successful. Even today philosophers still succumb to the siren call; Swinburne, Madell, and Chisholm have all done so.[23]

5 The fourth part of Kant's discussion

Kant's attack on the Second Paralogism has a fourth part. It begins just before A357 and goes to A361. Here Kant takes a dramatically different tack. He now argues that even if the soul were simple (and he has just gone to great lengths to show that we have no reason to believe that it is), this would not be enough to prove that it is immaterial (nor, implicitly, that immortality is possible). Some of Kant's most famous remarks about the unknowability of the soul and about its relation to empirical human beings are found in this passage. Commentators such as Ameriks who urge that Kant had a positive doctrine of immaterialism rest a lot of weight on it. Though he certainly accepted immaterialism as an item of faith, in Chapter 1:3 we saw powerful reasons to doubt that Kant's *theory* contained any such doctrine, so I will not examine the passage from A357 to A361 here.

In the second edition, the strategy of this passage – the strategy of granting RPsy its premises, for the sake of argument, to show that its conclusions still would not follow – became the dominant strategy of the attack on the Paralogisms. The long, famous footnote to B415 on fission and fusion is a prime example. On the basis of the first edition, Kant was in danger of appearing to *deny* that the soul is simple. All he wanted to show, of course, was that we have no *reason to believe* that the soul is simple, and his analysis equally shows that we have no *reason* (from theory or evidence) not to believe that it is. Nevertheless, perhaps to rule out even the faintest possibility of such a misunderstanding, Kant changed his strategy in the second edition. Rather than attacking the arguments for simplicity directly, he now concentrated on showing that even if the soul were simple, that would not prove either its immateriality or its immortality – unity is compatible with materialism (B415n), and we could still fade away by *elanguescence*(!) (B414). In the second edition, he also focuses almost exclusively on Strategy A, trying to get substantive conclusions out of concepts and analytic propositions about them, and relegates Strategy B to a minor part. As a result of these shifts, the discoveries about the mind that interest me so much in Kant's attack on the Second Paralogism no longer have any role to play and they disappear. For that reason, I will say little more about the second-edition version of the chapter.

Laying out the parts of Kant's attack on the Second Paralogism in the order in which he wrote them reveals how very closely they are tied to the subjective deduction. Of course, Kant does not carve up his discussion or identify the individual arguments as neatly as I have done. Nevertheless, the order is there: he attacks three arguments for the soul's simplicity, and each of them is a natural misinterpretation of one of the three claims defined in Section 2. These connections must have been at least one of the reasons for Kant's intense interest in the Second Paralogism. The danger that the doctrine of the simplicity of the soul posed for the idea that we know nothing about the mind lay in the heart of the subjective deduction. Perhaps one reason these connections have not been better explored is that there are important differences of emphasis between the two chapters. In the first edition, the subjective deduction is dominated by unity, the topic of claim (1), but exactly the reverse is true in the Paralogisms chapter – ASA and how the self can be pictured dominate, the topics of (2) and (3), and unity makes only one explicit appearance, the one in UA.

Three features of Kant's attack on the Second Paralogism are still relevant today, his use of functionalist arguments to demolish metaphysics of the mind, his account of what we appear to be like in ASA, and his discovery of nonascriptive reference to self, which Kant saw as partially explaining the peculiarities of ASA. His accounts of ASA and nonascriptive reference to self are among the genuine breakthroughs in the history of philosophy. We have already examined them in Chapter 4.

8

The Third Paralogism: unity without identity over time

To my mind, Kant's attack on the Third Paralogism surpasses all other short treatments of the implications for personal identity (identity over time) of the unity of consciousness and the sense of our persistence that goes with it. In brief, Kant shows that neither the unity of consciousness nor our sense of persistence as conveyed in memory and other ways reveals identity, and he lays the foundations of an argument that the unity of consciousness has little or no temporal depth at all. Memory specifically and temporal representation in general require unity of consciousness, and at least one major form of unity requires some forms of memory, namely, synthesis of recognition; but unity, memory, and temporal representation generally are quite compatible with a person being merely the latest in a series of minds or souls or subjects (A363n). Against our intuitions, Kant shows that even a memory of having an earlier experience and doing an earlier act is no proof that it was had or done by the person who now remembers having or doing it.[1] Equally, our sense that we have persisted for quite some time (normally, continuously since about age four or five) is quite compatible with not having persisted for anything like that long. Memory and the sense of having persisted require unity of consciousness, and this unity 'reaches back' into the past in a sense. However, this reaching back does not require identity. It is also, of course, not literally a reaching back, a point that will be crucial in Sections 3 and 5.

Demonstrating that much would guarantee Kant a place in the history of theorizing about personal identity, but he did even more. By paying close, if brief, attention to our sense of our persistence, to the way the earlier subject appears to us, Kant was able to do something no one else has done. He was able to diagnose why memories of a certain kind, namely, of having had experiences and having done actions, as well as some other representations represented as past, generate an illusion that the earlier subject whose experiences and actions one represents as having been had or done is guaranteed to be oneself. In addition, identity not being required for unity of consciousness here, Kant was able to show what is required. One of the reasons he was able to do all this is that he paid attention to the relationship between our sense of our persistence on the one hand and our awareness of ourselves and other things as objects on the other.

Others have redone some of this work. Of the various authors who have written on the subject, Derek Parfit's work is the most like Kant's.[2] Like Kant, Parfit has loosened the links between memory and identity, and he has argued that a current person could simply be the latest member of an on-going series of persons. However, Kant's account is superior to Parfit's in two respects. First, he was able to reconcile the possibility of looseness in persistence with tightness in the unity of one's consciousness across time, as displayed in memories of having had experiences and having done actions. One of the gaps in recent attempts to show that personal persistence could be a far looser matter than most earlier philosophers and theologians thought is that no one has paid much attention to this question. Kant did, in a way no one else has done. Second, Kant saw that the illusions of RPsy about identity across time arise from more things than a misinterpretation of a certain sort of memory. The first four sections of this chapter stick fairly closely to memory. The next three sections explore consequent issues and broaden the analysis. Does the unity of consciousness have temporal depth? Why did Kant say that time is in me (A362)? What is it to be a 'formal condition' of my thoughts (A363)? How do I identify myself known as subject with one of the objects of inner and outer sense? These sections are more speculative than the first four. In the final section, we examine Kant's own attitude to the simplicity of the soul and the nature of its identity.

1 Situating the Third Paralogism

Kant's actual statement of the Third Paralogism is singularly unhelpful as an indication of what he is going to go on to talk about. The parasyllogism he lays out runs as follows: 'That which is conscious of the numerical identity of itself at different times is in so far a *person*' (major premise); 'Now the soul is conscious, etc.' (minor premise); and 'Therefore it is a person' (conclusion) (A361). Numerous questions could be asked about what is going on here, not the least of which is what Kant means by 'person'. Bennett, Ameriks, and Powell have asked them all, so I will not do so again here.[3] The only phrase in Kant's statement of the Paralogism that actually says what he is going to talk about is this: 'conscious of the numerical identity of itself'. For that is Kant's topic: What is one's apparent awareness of one's own identity across time like, and what implications does this awareness have for one's actual identity? Though he does not say so here, memories of having experiences and doing actions that give one ASA (apperceptive self-awareness) of the earlier subject(s) and/or agent(s) as apparently oneself will be his main target.

Not only Kant's use of the term 'person' but his very statement of the topic parallels the way Locke put things:[4]

> We must consider what *person* stands for; which, I think, is a thinking intelligent being, that has reason and reflection, and can consider itself as itself, the same thinking thing, in different times and places. . . . [A]s far as this consciousness can be extended backwards to any past action or thought, so far reaches the identity of that person; it is the same self now it was then; and it is by the same self with this present one that now reflects on it, that that action was done.[5]

'Person' here means a subject of representation who persists, who exists at different times, and that is what Kant seems to mean by the term, too. (Kant uses 'person' somewhat differently at A355; there the term means roughly the same thing as 'subject' – persistence is not built into its very definition.)

To locate exactly what in the Third Paralogism was a threat for Kant, compare it with the second. The Second Paralogism is about simplicity, while the third is about identity. Why is the second not about identity, too? There certainly is such a thing as identity at a time. To explain this asymmetry, note first that unity of consciousness does generally go with identity at a time and therefore supports a positive thesis about this aspect of the mind. If a group of representations and/or their objects are unified by TA into a single intentional object, then, barring exceptional circumstances, they will have the same subject (for a look at these circumstances, see Chapter 4:3 near the end and Chapter 6:I:5), and it will be a mind, not a partial mind or mind parts or something that is more than one mind but less than two (see Chapter 7:4). However, first, knowing about identity at a time is no threat to the unknowability of the mind as it is, because being one mind in this way is compatible, *prima facie,* with being multiples or parts of a thing described in any other way (see Chapter 7:4). Identity at a time is a fascinating topic, one that has attracted more attention recently than for a very long time, due to the advent of commissurotomies (brain bisection operations) and growing interest in multiple personality disorder, but it is not much of a threat to the idea that we know nothing about the mind as it is. Second, identity at a time is largely irrelevant to immortality, the topic that is constantly in the background of the middle Paralogisms (A345 = B403 and A393). The soul's simplicity, however, is another matter. Not only would knowing the soul to be simple refute the doctrine of unknowability of the mind as it is, a topic of Chapter 7; simplicity itself is required for immortality – otherwise souls could end through disintegration. (In the first edition, Kant may have supposed that simplicity would also be sufficient. By the second edition, he was clear that it would not be sufficient: even a simple soul could fade away "by gradual loss . . . of its powers, and so . . . by *elanguescence*" [B414].) Thus, Kant could ignore identity at a time quite safely, and that is what he did (though the issue lurks in the background). Identity *over* time, however, is another matter; its connection to immortality could not be closer. Kant has to go after arguments that we know something special about our identity over time, and that is what the Third Paralogism is about.

The basis for the paralogistic conclusions that Kant attacks is the same in both middle Paralogisms: the unity of consciousness and our awareness of ourselves in ASA. In both cases, Kant tries to show that neither the unity of consciousness (the unity of TA, the unity that objects of representation have when these objects are represented in a single representation) nor our awareness of ourselves as the common subject of our representations and their objects gives us the slightest reason to accept RPsy's conclusion. In his attack on the Second Paralogism, Kant first considered unity and then followed with self-awareness. He reverses the order in his attack on the Third Paralogism; he leads off with self-awareness and takes up unity later, indeed only in the last paragraph of the discussion (A366).

To support immortality, personal persistence must have three properties. First, it must support true *personal* identity, that is to say, not persistence as some soul or other, even less some thing of some sort or other, but persistence as me, the person I am right now.[6] Second, it must be able to survive the death of the body. Third, what it supports must yield clear *identity,* not some loose situation where it is unclear whether the concept of identity applies or not. When we speak of something persisting as itself over time, we are often applying the concept of identity in a 'loose and popular sense', as Butler put it. Identity is both one to one and all or nothing: one thing cannot be two things and there are no degrees of a thing being itself. But there can be all degrees of certainty about applying the concept to something, from cases where no doubt about its applicability arises at all to cases where applying it or not seems to be purely a matter of decision or convention. Thus, I might speak of the bicycle in my garage as the bicycle I have had for fifteen years, even though I have replaced both wheels, changed the brakes, bought a new saddle and handlebars, and replaced the frame over the years. (And if I have also fixed and reassembled the parts I replaced? This is the famous Ship of Theseus problem.) Here, our popular manner of speaking notwithstanding, it is not clear that any bicycle is the bicycle I bought fifteen years ago. If I have reassembled the replaced parts from the bicycle, which current bicycle is the one I originally bought? Is it a matter for decision? Or is the one also two, violating transitivity? That problems such as these arise all over the place when we apply the concept of identity to persisting material objects (persisting, variously structured and related chunks of matter, to be strict about it) is well known. In the context of immortality, they pose a serious problem.

The problem is that I am not interested in surviving as some being or other, some being about whom some considerations may prompt a judgement that it is me but others not, some being for whom there is no clear sense in saying that it is me or that it is not me. I want to survive as me – full stop. Indeed, how could there be border-line cases for being me? How could it be a matter for decision whether some future person is me? Thus, when RPsy turned to identity across time, a basis for applying a concept of identity such as I had in connection with my bicycle(s) held no interest. It is not good enough to say there are some reasons for saying that a future soul is me, some reasons for saying it is not. What immortality requires is identity in what Butler called the 'strict and philosophical sense', persisting in such a way that the future being *is me,* full stop. Everything significant needed for the future being to be me is present, and anything significant that would detract from the future being being me is absent. Put into the epistemological mode, everything significant points to it being me and nothing significant or nothing at all points any other way.[7] Kant's terms for this were that the soul is 'incorruptible' (A345 = B403) and has 'absolute persistence' (B415). When we use the concept of identity in a loose sense, we are using it in such a way that questions could arise as to whether it is identity – being one and the same thing – that we are dealing with at all. Even the possibility of such questions arising with respect to the persistence of the soul beyond the death of the body and on into eternity has seemed to many philosophers and theologians to be intolerable. Very few commentators have seen how narrow and specialized the aim of the Third Paralogism is. It is not about, and thus Kant is not attacking, arguments for personal identity in general, for the idea that we persist as ourselves as such. In fact, he is clearly quite happy to accept approaches to personal identity based on observations and inferences in either outer or inner sense, approaches that parallel our approaches to the identity of other things. (Thus, he is not as far removed from Hume as is often thought; see Sections 4 and 6.)[8] He is attacking an argument that our persistence is 'absolute' and 'incorruptible', that is, that it is very special. Even commentators as insightful as Bennett, Ameriks, and Powell have not seen how limited Kant's target is – the idea that in persons identity is strict and absolute.[9]

To try to establish that personal identity is strict and absolute, utterly unambiguous, many philosophers have turned to the way one appears to oneself in ASA as the subject of past, now-remembered representations. In a certain form of memory of oneself, one may appear to have persisted in just such a strict and absolute way. The memory in question is memory of having had earlier experiences and done earlier actions. In such memory, earlier experiences and actions simply *present themselves* as experiences and actions one had or did. In such memory, both my identity with the earlier person who had the experience I remember having and also what this identity is like seems to be directly revealed. Kant's attack on the Third Paralogism is centred on this appeal to memory. Indeed, Kant may be suggesting that "the identity of the 'I' in the consciousness of all the time in which I know myself" (A365) is the only reason we believe that our identity over time is especially unambiguous.

In Chapter 7, we identified two strategies used by RPsy. Strategy A was analysis of concepts and Strategy B was appeal to ASA. As Kant presents RPsy's argument for the Third Paralogism, Strategy B is more prominent than Strategy A, but Strategy A is also in evidence. The concept analysed is that of the unity of consciousness. Though appeal to self-awareness dominates, unity is thoroughly enmeshed in memory, so to examine memory is also to examine unity. However, Kant deals with unity explicitly only in the very last paragraph of the section. Kant will argue, of course, that neither of these sources could lend any support at all to the idea that the soul has some sort of absolute (absolutely unambiguous) persistence.

2 The structure of Kant's discussion

Kant's attack on the Third Paralogism is only six paragraphs long. The reason it can be so short is that much of the groundwork has already been laid in TD and the attack on the Second Paralogism. Most of the text is a sustained commentary on a single idea, that I am aware both of my own identity over time and of what this identity is like. RPsy thinks that the persistence as myself that I am aware of is strict and philosophical, 'absolute persistence' (B415). Against this, Kant argues, the aspect of memory in question does not yield knowledge of identity at all, let alone knowledge that identity is absolute. The aspect of memory in question is awareness of 'myself' 'at different times' (A361), so awareness of 'myself' in memory is the phenomenon under examination. As I have already said, the unity of consciousness comes into the discussion near the end, too (A365).[10]

The question concerning memory is this: Does anything in how I remember myself at earlier times imply anything for my identity? Here we should correct a piece of terminological carelessness on Kant's part. Strictly, if I am aware of *myself* at earlier times, then of course it follows that the earlier remembered person was myself; it follows trivially. Interpreted literally, Kant is asking this: When I am aware of *myself* at different times, is it necessarily *always myself* of which I am aware? Since that is an absurd question, what Kant really had in mind must have been something different. I think what he meant to ask is this: When an earlier subject (mind, soul) appears in a memory to be me, perhaps even appears to be me in such a way that I could never tell that that subject (mind, soul) was not me, does this appearance imply that the earlier subject actually was me? And Kant's answer, in a word, is: no!

The first paragraphs of Kant's attack have a backwards order, though rhetorically an effective one. In the first paragraph, he reminds us of what we normally have to do if we want to determine whether some object has persisted. We have to adopt the standpoint of an outer observer and ask if the object in front of us is an object we have encountered in the past. Normally we answer this question by finding out if something has remained permanent or if there has been continuity running from the one to the other throughout the time in question. Then Kant shows why the way we appear to ourselves has led many people to think that we have parallel but even better awareness of our own persistence across time. In the second paragraph, Kant demonstrates that because the way we appear to ourselves as subject of representation is utterly different from the way objects of representation appear to us, the way we appear can do nothing to determine our identity across time. Then he argues in the third paragraph that this appearance of self is quite compatible with a total lack of identity with an earlier subject who nevertheless appears to be me. In fact, as he argues in the fourth paragraph, so far as anything this appearance of self could tell us, each of us could be the result of a process of flux in which "nothing [has been] permanent" (A364). So far as anything this appearance of self could tell me, the self I am now may have persisted for no significant amount of time at all.

These four paragraphs contain Kant's complete commentary on the Third Paralogism. In the two paragraphs that remain, Kant first offers a short comment on the peculiarity that across-time identity is arising only as late as the discussion of the Third Paralogism. Then, in the last paragraph of the section, Kant makes his only direct remark about unity, saying that we are free to continue using the idea that the soul persists over time in practical contexts, so long as we constantly remind ourselves that we mean no more by this than that the mind has unity; whether this unity corresponds to any real identity we cannot know. So far as what we can know is concerned, identity is a possible state of affairs in the soul as it is, not anything we can know in the soul as we are aware of it. Kant concludes this paragraph and his discussion with a brief, interesting recapitulation of why awareness of self in ASA cannot help us. In the language of Chapter 4, it is not experience dividing; ASA does not allow me to collect any information about myself. "If I want to observe the mere 'I' . . . I have no other *correlatum* to use in my comparisons [of myself with other persisting and changing things I observe] except again myself" (A366). So I can observe nothing that could indicate even something so basic as whether I, as I am aware of myself right now, am something that has persisted for some time or whether I am the end-point of a series of selves.

3 Does unity or memory require identity?

If the way earlier subjects appear when I call up memories of having experiences into my unified awareness of myself as the subject of my current experience can incline me to think that my identity is 'absolute', so can the way memories enter the activity of synthesis. (Note that these are both aspects of the unity of consciousness; as I said, that topic is never far from the Third Paralogism.) I have said little about the latter topic in this chapter. Some commentators think that TD contains an argument linking unity to identity via memory and synthesis. To represent anything, the story goes, I must remember the objects of earlier representations and I must remember them in a way that lets them enter my current unified awareness in the same way as my current representations do. I could remember earlier represented objects in this way only if I were the subject of those representations. Having unified global representations therefore requires that the subject of experience persist as itself over time. Indeed, Kant himself encourages this reading. He talks about "the numerical unity" of consciousness and apperception (A107), about "what has necessarily to be represented as numerically identical" (A107), and of the "original and necessary consciousness of the identity of the self" (A108). It is easy to take Kant to be arguing in these passages that identity across time is necessary for unified consciousness. Anyone who reads TD as containing such an argument will also expect it to be built into Kant's attack on the Third Paralogism. Paton is a good example; he thinks that Kant argued, both in TD and in his attack on the Third Paralogism, that for memory to play the role it plays in synthesis, the subject who had an experience now remembered and the subject who now remembers it must be one and the same subject. Moreover, he thinks Kant is right about this![11]

For anyone attracted to such a reading, it ought to give pause that Kant never actually mounts such an argument. In TD, he hardly mentions memory (his discussion of the synthesis of recognition is a rare exception and even there memory appears only by implication), and even more important, he says that unity of *consciousness* and *consciousness* of identity are what is required to connect past remembered representations to current ones, not unity of *the subject* or *actual identity*. He never argues that one and the same *mind* must *actually have had* the earlier and the later representations, only that it must *appear* to be this way. Here is how he put it in the unjustly neglected appendix to the Transcendental Dialectic:

> We . . . connect all the appearances, all the actions and receptivity of our mind, *as if* the mind were a simple substance which persists with personal identity . . . while its states are in continual change. (A672 = B700)

Indeed, in the long footnote in the preface revising the Refutation of Idealism, Kant flatly denies that we have any unmediated awareness of permanence in ourselves at all (Bxxxix, n). (He actually speaks of no *intuition* of permanence 'in me', but immediately extends the claim to all possible forms of awareness of self.) If TD had been based on an argument that identity itself is required, Kant would have needed to attack it as claiming knowledge of the mind in itself as much as anything in RPsy.[12] Nor is there such an argument in his attack on the Third Paralogism. There Kant does not mention unity at all until the last paragraph, and in connection with memory he deals not with how memory relates to synthesis but how a person appears in memory. If we look at what Kant actually said, it is hard to see how Paton got his reading off the ground.

Many, perhaps all acts of TA make use of memory, of course. As we saw in Chapter 6, to have certain sorts of representations we must be able to retain earlier representations and/or their objects, bring them forward, and synthesize them with current ones. This is the synthesis of recognition. UA contains a key example, that of retaining earlier words and connecting them to later ones so as to form a sentence. Put metaphorically, I must be able to span the whole group of earlier and later representations and tie them together into a single object of representation. However, the 'I' doing the spanning is me right now, of course, and what I am spanning is not earlier stages of my self, but memories. In order to synthesize earlier representations with current ones, we must be able to recall the earlier representations and recognize their relation to current ones. To do this requires that *our current memory* of the earlier representations belong to the same consciousness as the current representations; otherwise they could not all be accessed 'from the inside', as representations I have. Memories, however, are current representations, not past ones; I am not now directly aware of earlier stages of anything.[13] Now, when I remember having an earlier experience or doing an earlier action, it is *natural to think* that there must be 'one consciousness' linking the current memory to the earlier experience or action. We might even call the linkage that gives me this sense a kind of unity. If we do, this kind of unity would be a continuity of some sort, but need it be identity? In Kant's view, it need not be; continuity sufficient to "retain the thought of the previous subject and so hand it over to the subsequent subject" (A363) would be enough, and that does not require identity. The continuity in question yields what we could call a kind of unity, but it does not require identity. As I said earlier, it is very difficult to find even a *prima facie* argument for identity in the role of memory in synthesis.[14] It was not for nothing that Kant focused on self-appearance in his discussion of the Third Paralogism.

Surely, it will be objected, Kant did maintain that identity is required; in addition to the things we have quoted him as saying, he also said, did he not, that the apperceiving self must be the *common* subject of all the representations it can synthesize (A350)? My reply is the same as before – this requirement can be met without identity. To be sure, in memories of having the earlier representations, the person/persons remembered as subject of them will be *represented* as 'numerically identical' with the person doing the remembering, one 'common subject'. But how something must be represented is not necessarily the same thing as how it must be.

In general, far from trying to establish anything positive in the attack on the Third Paralogism, I think that Kant's aim was entirely sceptical: to show that, *so far as theoretical knowledge is concerned,* we can establish nothing whatsoever about which earlier person we were or which future person we will be (except what we can infer from the flux of inner sense).[15] For this task, Kant was right to focus on how we appear to ourselves in memory, it being difficult to find even a *prima facie* argument for personal identity in the role of memory or other kinds of retention of representations and/or their objects in synthesis. In the way (an) earlier self/selves seems/seem to appear in our memories, philosophers such as Butler, Leibniz, and Reid have thought they could find the most breath-taking revelations about personal identity. To see how an idea like Paton's can arise, we have to look more closely at the way subjects of experience appear in memory.

I get an impression of an identity of subject in cases where an earlier representation or its object is available to me *because I remember having had the earlier representation or having been aware of the object.* Here I will remember the earlier representation and/or the represented object 'from the inside', as I remember representations I had and objects they represented. (We also used the metaphor of 'from the inside' in Chapter 6:I:5.) It is important to note that this is not the only way an earlier representation or its object could enter my current experience. It could just pop into my head; someone could tell me about it; I could see a film of it or read a report about it; and so on.[16] Such objects would be just as thoroughly within the unity of my current awareness and just as available for synthesis as an earlier object there as a result of memory. Yet such objects would not create any impression that the earlier subject of the original representation of them was me. It is when I retain an earlier representation and/or object *because I remember having the representation or being aware of the object*[17] that an impression is created that the subject of the earlier representation was me. (*Mutatis mutandis,* retaining awareness of an earlier action by remembering doing the action will also create an impression that it was me who did it.)

Some might argue that I am not entitled to use the word 'remember' in the way I have been doing here. Saying that I *remember* the earlier experience as though I had it *entails* that it was me who had it – I can only *remember* having an experience that *I* had (with the emphasis on the second 'I'). To meet this objection Shoemaker coined the term 'quasi-remember', which Parfit shortened to 'q-remember', the form in which it is now usually used.[18] Q-memories are exactly like memories except that it is not ruled out as a matter of definition that I might q-remember having an experience that someone else had. Far from entering into niceties like these, Kant does not even use the term 'remember'. He speaks of "my consciousness of myself at different times" (A363). So I am simply going to ignore scruples about the literal meaning of 'remember' and use it to include what would now more exactly be called q-memory.

We find Kant's analysis of what memory of an earlier subject of representation 'from the inside' actually tells me about my identity with that subject in the first and second paragraphs of his discussion of the Third Paralogism. He shows how the form an earlier subject takes in my memory can lead me to be certain that I am that subject, and his diagnosis is extremely interesting. Begin with the first paragraph. As I said earlier, Kant urges that to determine whether a normal object has persisted, I will see if there is any permanence and continuity in the objects of various representations I have had and am having. Now, to do this, I must ascribe these representations to myself, as something that has persisted, common to them all, across the time in which they occurred. "This being so, the personality of the soul [its identity through time] has to be regarded not as inferred [from any other information, by any criteria, etc.] but as a completely identical proposition of self-consciousness in time" (A362). It will just seem that the common thing to which I ascribe these representations, namely, me, has remained the same thing throughout all the time in which I ascribe these representations. Note that I do not *infer* that these representations are mine, either the current ones or the earlier ones; for any earlier representation I remember having or any earlier action I remember doing, if I remember having or doing it, it will simply *appear to me* to be a representation I had or an action I did. That is not something I infer. In the same way, Kant told us earlier (A354), we do not infer that we are simple; we just appear to ourselves to be simple. For Kant, such appearances are not to be trusted.

Whether he or she was me or not, whoever actually had the remembered experience or did the remembered action certainly does appear when I remember having the experience or doing the act in question. Two points now become vital. First, such a past subject or agent will be represented in my memories of having experiences or doing actions *from the same point of view as I represent myself to myself right now, namely, from the point of view of being that subject or agent.* Right now I represent myself to myself from the point of view of *being that self,* represent that self as me, 'from the inside'. I represent myself from the point of view of what it is like to be me. Similarly with the earlier subject or agent. I represent the earlier subject or agent from the point of view of what it would have been like to be that subject or agent, too (what it was like, if the subject was me). In short, I represent the earlier subject or agent as me. This creates the central illusion of the Third Paralogism. The reason it is an illusion is that I will think that the earlier person who had the experience I remember having or did the action I remember doing was me *whether that he or she was me or not.* When I retain an earlier representation in the way required to remember the object of that representation 'from the inside', its *subject* will appear simply as me. I have been dealing with real memories, at least to the extent that their object or content is veridical, but acts of imagination, hallucinations, being told about something, and so on can reinforce the point. In representational states like these, a subject will still appear – an imagined or hallucinated one – and that subject will still appear as me – even though there neither is nor was any such subject! That is how much a representation of an earlier subject as oneself tells us about identity.[19]

Nevertheless, that the earlier subject or agent actually was me is something I will 'automatically assume', as Parfit puts it. The result is that I think that "I can *trace* my identity, quite independent of the identity of my body".[20] Instead of 'automatically assume', Kant said, "In my own consciousness, identity of person is unfailingly met with" (A362). This may appear to be an over-statement – the illusions of RPsy are not *impossible* to resist – but as Kant makes clear in the next paragraph, he means the *appearance* of identity is unfailingly met with:

> The identity of the *consciousness* of myself at different times is . . . only a formal condition of my thoughts and their coherence, and in no way proves the numerical identity of my subject. Despite the logical identity of the 'I', such a change may have occurred in it as does not allow of the retention of its identity, and yet we may ascribe to it the same-sounding 'I'. (A363; my emphasis)

Despite the words that belie his meaning, I think Kant's point is clear. He and Parfit are saying the same thing. They also draw the same inference: even if I will automatically assume that it was me who had an earlier representation I now remember having, it does not follow that it was me.

'Whatever I may assume, surely I could check to see if the earlier remembered subject or agent actually was me?' No, you might not be able to do so. The reason why not is also to be found in the preceding paragraph. As in present awareness of self, in a memory of an earlier subject, transcendental designation is the kind of reference used to refer to that subject (see Chapter 4:1). Thus, nothing *about* the subject need appear, no distinguishing feature or mark of any kind. The earlier subject will simply be referred to as me and thus will simply appear to be me – whether or not that appearance is correct. Even if I am the last in a series of substances, the

> last substance would . . . be conscious of the states of the previously changed substances, *as being its own states,* because they would have been transferred to it *together with the consciousness of them.* (A364; my emphases)

Moreover, and this is the crucial point so far as reconciling the unity demands of TD with the sceptical arguments of the attack on the Third Paralogism are concerned, someone else appearing in one of my q-memories *as though* he or she were me, appearing in such a way that I will automatically assume he or she is me, is just as good – so far as synthesizing the earlier q-remembered representation or action with current representations is concerned – as the earlier person actually being me. For unity of consciousness, I must q-remember earlier representations and actions *as though* they were mine (A672 = B700) – but they need not have been. Moreover, what matters to us is not identity per se, what matters is the transcendental unity of our consciousness and the continuities, memories, and so on that sustain it.[21]

To bring out the full genius of Kant's argument, compare the situation with respect to identity across time with identity at a time. Is it possible to be aware of a group of current representations and/or their objects on the basis of having them, as a global object of representation, and yet for these representations to be had by more than one subject? Put the question in the first person and the present. Could I be aware of a group of current representations on the basis of having them and yet those representations be the representations of more subjects than me? I think we would agree that they must all be had by me, or at least by me; perhaps we could imagine strange circumstances that might incline us to say that some or all of them are had by other people, too (me being wired to other people in certain ways, for example; see Chapters 4:3 and 6:I:5). But they must also be representations of mine. Why? Because if these representations are united as one global object on the basis of someone being aware of them by having them, that is *sufficient* (or as close to sufficient as we get in this life) for the subject of each of them being the subject of all of them. That is what it is to be one subject. Synchronically, unity of consciousness goes with identity of subject. The genius of Kant's argument is that he saw that the same is *not* true across time. To achieve unity of consciousness across time, I must retain representations of earlier objects of representation and combine them with current ones. UA is built on a good example of this, words being things we encounter one at a time and sentences being objects of single unified acts of awareness. However, it is possible for me to retain representations of earlier representations and/or objects that were originally had by someone else. They will just appear to have been had by me.

The two ways in which temporal unity of consciousness can engender an impression of identity are independent. My retaining an earlier representation in a way that allows for synthesis and it appearing to be me who had an earlier experience are quite different from one another. Retaining an earlier representation by having a memory of having had it will also be retaining it in a way that allows for synthesis but even this is not true in reverse. I can retain many earlier objects of representation in a way that allows for synthesis without having any memory of them.

4 Kant and Hume versus Butler and Reid, and Strawson, too

In attributing the Third Paralogism to RPsy, presumably Kant had in mind such philosophers as Leibniz and Wolff. But the rationalists were by no means the only ones to think that memory reveals our identity over time to be strict and absolute. Many philosophers and theologians in the English tradition have held the same view, Butler and Reid being two leading examples.[22] In fact, Kant's commentary on the Third Paralogism could be read as a commentary on their work; as we will see, Kant sometimes even used the same phrasing. What makes this parallel particularly interesting is that though Butler had written some time earlier, Reid and Kant were almost contemporaries (b. 1710 vs. 1724), and Reid wrote his most influential work, *Essay on the Intellectual Powers of Man* (1785), only four years after Kant wrote the first *Critique* (1781). Moreover, Reid's first book on the mind and one that contains many of the same opinions as the later work is from 1764 (*An Inquiry into the Human Mind on the Principles of Common Sense*). I know of no evidence directly linking the two philosophers, but the parallels even in phrasing between Reid's assertions about personal identity and Kant's way of stating the views he will attack are extremely striking.

As we saw, the way the subjects of experiences I now remember having and actions I remember doing appear in those memories to be me can easily create an illusion that I know something special about my identity. Butler got caught by it:

> Every person is conscious, that he is now the same person or self he was as far back as his remembrance reaches: since when any one reflects upon a past action of his own, he is just as certain of the person who did that action, namely, himself, the person who now reflects upon it, as he is certain that the action was at all done.[23]

As Butler saw it, this 'consciousness of self' also ascertains to me that my identity is strict and philosophical. It caught Reid, too:

> The conviction which every man has of his Identity, as far back as his memory reaches, needs no aid of philosophy to strengthen it, and no philosophy can weaken it without first producing some degree of insanity [!!]. . . . My personal identity . . . implies the continued existence of that indivisible [i.e., simple] thing which I call myself.[24]

Not only does Reid espouse the view Kant attacks, his analysis takes up the same topics as those Kant chose for the Paralogisms: Reid argues for simplicity, and links strictness of identity to it. It might sometimes appear that Kant succumbed to the illusion himself. For example, talking about changes in a person, he asks:

> Can a man be conscious of these changes and still say that he remains the same man (has the same soul)? The question is absurd, since consciousness of such change is possible only on the supposition that he considers himself in the different states as one and the same subject. (*An* Ak. VII:134n)

However, I do not think so. He is just noting once more what Butler and Reid did not see, that our suppositions and what is the case here can be two different things.

According to Reid, our confidence that what we have characterized as memory of an earlier subject 'from the inside' reveals our identity with that earlier subject can be weakened only at the cost of insanity. Kant, like Parfit two hundred years after him, begs to differ:

> The identity of the consciousness of myself at different times is . . . only a formal condition of my thoughts and their coherence, and in no way proves the numerical identity of my subject. Despite the logical identity of the 'I', such a change may have occurred in it as does not allow of the retention of its identity, and yet we may ascribe to it the same-sounding 'I', which in every different state, even in one involving change of the subject, might still retain the thought of the preceding subject and so hand it over to the subsequent subject. (A363)

This passage could easily have been written as a direct response to Butler and Reid. There are even parallels in the phrasing. To be sure, the earlier subject will appear to be me. Moreover, in appearing to be me, I will refer to it using the same word 'I' that I use to refer to myself right now, and I will think that I am referring to the same being. (These two points encompass, I think, what Kant meant by "the logical identity of the 'I' ".) Since this appearance and this reference give me nothing that I could use to check them, I might even have to take them to be correct (unless I can somehow suspend judgement, which is what Kant seems to recommend). At any rate, that they are correct is something I will automatically assume. But I could be wrong. Memory 'from the inside' does not require identity.[25]

It is even more helpful to relate Kant's position on the Third Paralogism to Hume. Some aspects of the subjective deduction can be read as an answer to Hume, even though Kant never mentions him by name in connection with the mind.[26] We should follow this suggestion with caution, however. If Kant *answered* Hume, that does not mean that he *rejected* Hume. In fact, as I see it, Kant did not reject Hume's view of the mind. On the contrary, he accepted Hume's conclusions, as far as they went. He just thought Hume had missed something, namely, the unity of consciousness. For Hume, the mind is just a group of representations, abilities, and so on, held together by certain patterns of "subjective necessity (that is, from *custom*)" (B127). Kant replied, first, that it is not contingent that these representations and so on be tied together. On the contrary, global representations represent other representations and/or their objects, so the former could not exist without the latter.[27] Second, for global representations to exist, the representations being unified must have a common subject, must belong to one consciousness. Third, without these unities, ASA, the awareness of oneself as the common subject of these representations, could not exist. Since contemporary cognitive science and philosophy of mind tend to be Humean on these issues and pay little attention to any of Kant's three additions – synthesis, unity, and ASA, the self-awareness that unity makes possible – Kant's additions to Hume should also be of great interest to contemporary thinkers.

However, and this is a crucial point, *Kant did not reject Hume's story about the mind.* He supplemented it. The same is true of Hume's account of personal identity. Hume's account is radical inner-sense empiricism: what we can know about our persistence is what we can infer from the flux and flow of representations, memories in particular. To this, Kant adds just one point: we also have a unified consciousness, and it reaches backwards and forwards in time. All representational states, memories included, must belong to this single consciousness if they are to be 'something to us', and the memories within this unified consciousness do give us a sense that the single common subject we are aware of in ASA has persisted, and persisted as itself, for some time. Leibniz and others stressed both points, so Hume should not have missed them, but do we know more about our identity over time than Hume allowed? Kant's answer is no, we do not. Remarkably enough, despite adding unity and its temporal dimension to Hume, Kant's account of what we can know about our own identity is *exactly the same as Hume's.* We can know what we can infer from the 'continual flux' (A382) of inner sense (from what Kant called the physiology of inner sense [A347 = B405 and A381]), and what we can infer from the standpoint of the outer observer (A362) – and nothing more. Neither our unity at a time nor our memories of having experiences and doing things at earlier times need tell us anything about our identity over time. Hume should not have overlooked unity or the appearance memory gives us of having persisted for some time; but adding them to his story does not affect his conclusions. If we want to add the unity and the appearance memory gives us of unity over time to Hume, the only other thing we need to add is an explanation of how his sceptical conclusions could possibly still be right – which is what Kant adds.

Thus, Strawson is certainly wrong to suggest that Kant wanted to reject Hume in favour of some account in terms of bodily and other causal continuities such as Williams' or Shoemaker's.[28] This reading is both anachronistic and unwarranted. *So far as knowledge of our identity is concerned,* it would be far closer to the truth to say that Kant wanted to reject Descartes and Leibniz – and other absolutists like Butler and Reid – in favour of Hume. Hume missed the unity of consciousness and the special features of memory, but so far as knowledge of personal identity in inner sense is concerned, he was right.

> For in what we entitle 'soul', everything is in continual flux and there is nothing abiding except (if we may so express ourselves) the 'I', which is [i.e., appears to itself as] simple [and, we may add, abiding] solely because its representation has no content, and therefore no manifold. (A381)

Perhaps Hume should have seen, as Kant did, that the 'standpoint of the outer observer' also plays a role, indeed has epistemic priority, but he was totally correct in his main points, that the way the 'I' appears to itself in its memories tells it nothing about which earlier being(s) it was, and that to make these judgements we must rely on inferences from what we observe, just as we do in all other cases. As Bennett once said, Kant is not attacking judgements of identity based on the data of inner sense (which is what Strawson has Kant doing and himself does in *Individuals*); Kant had almost the same (qualified) respect for the 'physiology of inner sense' as Hume had (A347 = B405 and A381–2).[29] Kant is attacking judgements of identity made on the basis of no data at all, just a bare consciousness of what seems to have been me earlier in the memories I have. As I will suggest in Section 5, what we take to be an abiding 'I' is nothing more than sheerest appearance, a mere artefact of how we remember experiences and actions when we remember them as had and done. For all we know, this appearance of an abiding 'I' could correspond to no real, abiding object of representation at all.

To be sure, unity of consciousness represents in a temporal dimension. For many *X*s, awareness that *X* is *F* requires awareness that *X was F;* it also requires an expectation that *X* will continue to be *F, ceteris paribus.* As we will see, this temporal dimension is not at all like what we might expect (Section 5); but whatever it is like, Kant argued that it does not require that I, the subject of that awareness, have persisted as myself. Temporal representation does require some form of causal continuity, the continuity required for retention of objects of earlier representations. However, an earlier subject could be connected to a later subject by many types of continuity without necessarily being the same subject, so the continuity required for retention is compatible with absence of identity. There is nothing about the unity of consciousness that requires identity over time.

Once again we see the functionalist strain in Kant's thought. In order to represent at all, both the mind and the representation must have a certain unity and be the end-point of certain continuities. But such unity and continuity is characterized functionally. From the facts that the mind is the end-point of continuities and functions so as to achieve unity in its representation, from the fact too that the mind is the common subject of all its representations, nothing whatsoever follows concerning its nature or its across-time identity. In the same way as the unity of consciousness demonstrated by UA in the Second Paralogism "may relate just as well to the collective unity of different substances acting together (as the motion of a body is the composite motion of all its parts)" (A353) and thus does not entail simplicity, so the unity of consciousness and continuity across time could be achieved by

> a whole series of substances, of which the first transmits its state together with its consciousness to the second, the second its own state together with that of the preceding substance to the third, and [so on]. (A364)

Nothing the functioning of the mind can tell us settles anything one way or the other.

Of course, whether we actually do persist is another matter. That it cannot be shown that I persist as myself does not entail that I do not thus persist; on this, Kant would have insisted. The whole point of his attack on *arguments* for personal identity was to leave it open for us to accept on *faith* that we not only persist, but persist in a way sufficient for immortality. Kant certainly wanted to show that immortality could only be a matter of faith, but he also wanted to ensure that it did remain open to faith.

5 To what extent is the unity of consciousness diachronic?

We now need to take another look at the unity of consciousness, the awareness of a number of representations as a single global object of a single representation. What I say will also apply to the transcendental unity of apperception synthesizing these diverse representations *into* a single global object. What happens when it is earlier and later representations that get unified? We have seen that it is difficult to find so much as a *prima facie* argument in Kant that personal identity is required to achieve this form of unity. If the temporal dimension of these unities does not rest on identity, why have so many philosophers thought otherwise, and what does it rest on?

If the unity of consciousness is a matter of multiple representations and/or their objects being recognized together in a single act of awareness as a single global object, it is not clear that it has to have any more temporal depth than the depth of the specious present. Contrary to Kitcher, for example, who thinks that the unity of consciousness is primarily diachronic and made up of the continuities that support memory and so on, what get tied together in a global object are *currently occurring* representations and represented objects. Suppose a memory of something I saw yesterday enters a global object. Neither yesterday's object nor yesterday's perception of it enters. What enters is the content or object of a memory; the memory exists now, not then. Anything that is the object of a representation I am having or an act I am doing may enter a global object, including other representations, representations of other people, things I read about, imaginings, fictional events and entities, and so on. But these representations are all currently existing; not a single one of them is an event or object from the past. There must be various continuities from the past to the present, of course; both q-memories and dispositions require causal continuities. But causal continuity is not unity of consciousness, objects of representation being tied together as one object, and what I synthesize with current representations are *current* representations. It is the *representations* of earlier objects *as they appear in current memory* that I synthesize with current representations, not earlier objects themselves. Though the unity of our consciousness gives us the impression that it has a large diachronic dimension, that dimension is really synchronic unity that contains remembered representations and objects. In fact, it seems that the unity of consciousness hardly extends across time at all.

What creates the impression that the unity of consciousness not only represents but has great temporal depth is that earlier representations and represented objects enter my current awareness from the point of view I would have had on them had I experienced them. In addition, the actual object of my memory is something that existed or happened earlier, and it is the representation of this object that is synthesized with represented current objects. These two things together create an illusion of great temporal depth, indeed of identity across time in the subject(s) of the various representations. This is the illusion that I can actually span the whole period from the time of the original representation to the present and be aware of past and present together. It is typically the representation of the object of the memory that enters a global object, not the memory itself, and the object is represented as something past. Thus, the unity of my awareness appears to extend both across my current experience and also back in time. Nevertheless, the unity of consciousness does not actually have that temporal depth. It uses continuities that have temporal depth, but it itself does not.

To what extent did Kant accept all of this? It is hard to know. On the one hand, he certainly did not *articulate* any view that unity lacks temporal depth. On the other hand, however, he did say, for example, that "we can conceive a whole series of substances . . . such that one communicates to the other representations together with the consciousness of them" (A364). Clearly, then, the unity of consciousness could have at least very little temporal depth for him. At any rate, he certainly did not hold, contrary to what Paton and others have argued, that the unity of consciousness requires identity in the subject(s) of the temporally diverse representations that can be synthesized in it.[30] In memories of having earlier experiences, memories whose subjects I appear to be able to span in a single act of awareness, the remembered subject will *appear* to be me; there will be "identity of the *consciousness* of myself at different times" (my emphasis), but this appearance "in no way proves the numerical identity of my subject" (A363).

In the literature on Kant on the mind, the dominant image of Kant is that he pictured the mind as a serial processor, dealing with bits of information one at a time and linking them forwards and backwards to other bits. Though Kant himself sometimes gives this image credence – for exampe, at A99 and in the Second Analogy (we discussed this appearance in Chapter 6:I:6) – I think that it is exactly the wrong image. I think Kant saw the mind as a massive *parallel* processor, with everything present before it linking to everything else present before it at the same time. The mind links no representations forwards and no representations back; what it links are current *representations* of past and future events and objects – *current* representations. This point, if I am right, may help to make the idea that the mind itself just is a global representation more palatable when we finally explore it in the next chapter. It will be objected that global representations have only a short and ever-changing life. We will also consider that objection in the next chapter, but note that exactly the same is true of the mind, at any rate of that aspect of it of which we are directly aware, representational consciousness. The idea that Kant may have seen the subject of experience as anything this fleeting may look absurd, but I will try to show in the next chapter that it not.

That we are aware only of currently existing representations may help to explain Kant's bewildering claim that the objects of outer sense are not represented in time. ("Time cannot be outwardly intuited." "It cannot be a determination of outer appearance" [A23 = B37 and A33 = B49].) This explanation will lead us into the murky sayings of the second paragraph of Kant's attack that we postponed earlier. If we are directly aware only of current representations and can only represent, not directly be aware of, anything earlier (or later), then we are not directly aware of more than one point in time at a time, and can only infer all others. If so, in objects of outer sense, we could never be directly aware of change, temporal duration, and so on but could only infer these states, too. If all that is so, the objects of outer sense, *as we are aware of them,* would be nontemporal: if we never intuit more than one point in time, then we never intuit temporal depth in them. Of course, the same analysis would also seem to apply to the objects of inner sense, in flagrant violation of the standard assumption about Kant that Waxman calls "the assumption of a transcendentally real succession of representations in inner sense."[31] Instead, the temporal order of representations would also become an ordering we impose on them by applying the form of intuition called time to them. Represented representations would be as distinct from representations in themselves as represented objects are from objects in themselves (see Chapter 1:3). Time would become the form of *representing,* not of *representations.*[32] This would also explain why Kant thinks that it takes some real cognitive work to achieve consciousness of "my own existence as determined in time" (B275), the conviction behind the Refutation of Idealism. As Guyer points out, this view of time also connects to the seemingly paradoxical realism that breaks through in the Refutation.[33] However, to explore these ideas properly would take us far afield.

6 Unity as the form of thought: 'time is . . . in me'

So far, I have treated the Third Paralogism and Kant's attack on it as though they were exclusively concerned with memory, specifically memory of having experiences and doing action. That is not the whole story. The class of representations that engender the illusion of 'absolute persistence' is a good deal broader than memories. Indeed, the illusion is contained in all representation of time of any sort whatsoever. Memory is just a special case of this broader problem. I focused on it first because it by itself has lead generation after generation of philosophers and theologians astray, but it is still just a special case. Kant sums up the general feature of representing time that seems to him to cause the problem in the phrase, "In the apperception *time* is represented, strictly speaking, only *in me*" (A362). What did he have in mind?

In Kant's view, not just judgements of identity but conceptualized representations of any sort require that we locate items in time and at various points in time. The way Kant then handles this requirement might make it appear that he merely has some exotic feature of transcendental idealism in mind: "All time is the form of inner sense" (A362), so time is merely a form I impose on my representations and their objects – locating something in time is merely relating something to something else within myself. If so, "in the whole time in which I am conscious [Kant says 'of myself', but the point holds for anything of which I am conscious], . . . I am to be found as numerically identical in all this time" (A362). I think Kant has something less parochial in mind, however. To see what, we have to trace the steps we take to fix temporal location.

Representations come to us. Being representations I am having, if I am aware of them at all, they will come as *my* representations; part of what they represent is that they are mine. (As I urged in the theory of the representational base, whatever a representation is about, it generally or always contains everything needed on the side of representations to be aware of oneself, the subject who has it.) When these representations are represented as temporally distributed (synthesis of apprehension), the 'me' they all belong to will be represented as temporally extended. These representations all being presented as 'mine', I will automatically take the references to a 'me' in them to refer to a "permanent element" to which these representations are "related as determination[s]", and "I will refer each and all of [these] successive determinations to this numerically identical self in all the times (*in aller Zeit*)" (A362). Having *represented* these various appearances as mine, they appear as representations of a continuing substantive subject; thus, "In my own consciousness . . . identity of person is unfailingly met with."

This exercise in inflated representation construction holds no implications for what my persistence is actually like, however; that is what RPsy failed to see. To demonstrate this, Kant shows that one's representation of time also behaves in a peculiar way in one's own representational system. The parallel goes like this. As I represent it, "the 'I' . . . accompanies, and indeed with complete identity, all representations at all times in my consciousness" (A362–3). If representations I have all appear to be 'in me', so does time. Whatever time may actually be, any *representation* of the time of an object will appear as mine. That is to say, in any represented point of time, I will also appear. One is reminded of Wittgenstein: "The world is my world".[34]

One might think that any illusion engendered by what we have just said about represented time could be easily cleared away. The claim simply trades on an ambiguity between *representations* of time, which may indeed always appear as 'mine', and the time represented; there is no need to represent myself as at the latter. This will not dispose of the point that Kant is after, however. In any representation of time I have, I will appear as the bearer of that representation (if I am aware of having it at all). To begin to see what Kant is after, first consider a point he does not make: the same is just as true of far distant represented times and represented times of fictional entities and worlds. If I represent the Big Bang or Tolkien's Middle Earth, I appear just as much 'in' these representations as I do in the act of seeing the computer in front of me. Yet I do not represent myself as existing at the Big Bang or in the fictional world and time of Middle Earth. Thus, the point has nothing to do with the represented time of *objects;* it concerns only the times *representations* are represented to be at. Now, it is indeed true that at any time at which I represent a representation of mine as occurring, I will also represent myself as occurring. Representations come to me as mine; I appear in everything in my 'field' of representations. Thus, I will represent the time of all my representations as inside the time-span of myself – as '*in me*'. Kant then goes on to show why there is no succour for RPsy in this point, why an outer observer "will draw no inference . . . to the objective permanence of myself" (A363).

One of his arguments is to be found in the very first paragraph of his discussion of the Paralogism. As he puts it there, all judgements of identity I make – that some earlier thing *A* is the thing *B* now before me and also that it is not – are judgements *that I make.* All judgements of identity I make presuppose a unified conscious subject. If so, I am making no similar judgement about myself, not at any rate so long as I stick to the same standpoint.[35] Thus, this unity of myself in all my representations at all times is a 'logical identity', a mere "formal condition of my thoughts and their coherence", of them all being something to me (A363). This 'merely logical unity' (A355, A398, B413) tells us nothing about what our actual existence, location, or persistence is like. "I exist as an intelligence which is conscious *solely* of its power of combination" (B158; my emphasis).

We can also give some content to Kant's use of 'form' here. In the same way that time is the form of my representations, he seems to want to say that my appearing to be the single common subject of my representations is part of the form of them (space, too, for representations of 'outer' objects [A266 = B322–A268 = B324]). Each and every one of my representations simply appears as one of *my* representations. Moreover, in the same way as my representations are represented as having a determinate location within what Kant calls the "individual unity" time, they are also represented as having a location within the unity of my represented self. A subject and time are common to representations not as common properties that representations share, but as a single something within which representations are located. This is what Kant meant, I think, when he referred to awareness (the global representation of a global object) as the "subjective form of all our concepts" and, we could add, representations (A361). In connection with the subject, we are not, of course, talking just about temporal location. Representations are also located in conceptual, volitional, and emotional dimensions in a categorially structured cognitive system. In the second edition, Kant explicitly says that time (and space, too), on the one hand, and the subject, on the other, are all *singular* representations (B136n). This is not the way an object *in* time and space is represented. (We examined the kind of unity involved here in Chapter 2:5.) In other places, he speaks of the unitary subject as a form and as a subjective form (A361) of representations (A110, A125, A346 = B404), or apperception (A354), and the subjective form of concepts (A361). In the same way, Wittgenstein said, "The subject does not belong to the world: rather, it is a limit of the world."[36]

It is desperately easy to over-interpret the way the representations that I have appear as mine – this is what gets RPsy into trouble. As Kant put it in the second edition,

> The unity of consciousness, which underlies the categories, is here mistaken for an intuition of the subject as object. (B421)

It goes with this error:

> There is nothing more natural and more misleading than the illusion which leads us to regard the unity in the synthesis of thoughts as a perceived unity in the subject of these thoughts. (A402)

Put these errors about self-appearance and synthesis together and RPsy is on its way.

Return now to memory. How does Kant's analysis of represented time connect to the analysis of the kind of memory we discussed earlier, memory of having earlier experiences and doing earlier actions? I think this way. Such memory is a special case of representing representations as located in time; in such memory, we represent certain representations as *past*. The same analysis applies to them – they appear simply as *mine*, as representations *I* had, actions *I* did – but with this extra feature: in them I seem to have the most direct possible kind of access to an actual earlier subject as me. We have seen why that is an illusion, but now that we have seen Kant's broader analysis, another question arises: Was I right to take Kant to be talking about *memory* in this section at all, or was he talking only about placing representations in time? I will stick by what I have said: the latter is his general project, but he dealt with memory as a special case of it. I can cite two kinds of evidence. First, memories are a very important form of representations-located-in-time and so would willy-nilly have been included in Kant's analysis. Second, and more conclusively, however, Kant himself included them. In the footnote to A363 in which Kant lays out his famous thought experiment to show that the unity of consciousness is quite compatible with a current subject being merely the last in a series of subjects, he says that this last subject "would . . . be *conscious* of all the states of the previously changed substance" (my emphasis). What could this consciousness be but memory?[37]

To close this section, let me emphasize again something that I stressed in Section 1. Kant is not saying anything about normal assessments of personal identity. Indeed, outer observers are not the only ones who can do more than one can do oneself on the basis of the way one appears to oneself as subject. One can do more oneself, too. For example, I could see what Hume-like inferences I can draw about continuities and so on from the 'continual flux' in myself as I introspect this flux. This would be physiology of inner sense (A347 = B405 and A381–2), and it is a rich source of information about myself. I could also be my own outer observer and make the same observations about causal and bodily continuities that anyone else could make, by looking in a mirror, for example. And so on. All I cannot do is infer anything useful from the way I appear to myself as subject. In a *Reflexion* that Allison also notes, Kant remarks that not only is time in me, but also I am in time – the former as form of inner sense, the latter as an object of inner sense.[38] I could be my own observer – place myself as an object in my experience – in both inner and outer sense. As Kant makes very clear in the appendix to the Transcendental Dialectic (A690 = B718), he has no objection to determining personal identity empirically. What he objects to is any attempt to short-circuit such empirical work by appealing to the fact that my representations appear as mine.

Behind Kant's obscure remarks on the representation of myself and "time . . . in me" may stand the baffling question of the difference between an asymmetrical, personal point of view on the world and the symmetrical, third-person or no-person, God's-eye point of view. The latter is Nagel's view from nowhere.[39] On the question of how to relate them, Kant has little to say. On the special question of which yields knowledge of oneself, however, he was clear. The standpoint of the outer observer is the standpoint of objective validity on persons; indeed, he seems to imply that the standpoint of ASA cannot even come into conflict with it (A363). As to the apparently in-between case of ESA, observing the flux and flow of inner sense is equivalent to taking the standpoint of the outer observer for Kant, because nothing is being used that could not also be made available to an outer observer.

7 Identifying the subject with an object

One implication of what was said in the preceding section is that the subject does not, *as subject,* have a location within the world of its objects of representation. Rather, the subject appears *throughout all* its representations. As just indicated, Kant was aware that we are also aware of ourselves as objects within our world(s). The difference between these two ways of being aware of oneself stands behind most classical formulations of the mind–body problem (though not some recent ones, as we will see shortly). The difference can be shown in a number of ways. Here is one about as far removed from academic philosophy as possible. Think first of the background sense of ourselves we have, made up of our sense of confidence, doubt, anxiety, frustration, and so on. Here one is aware of oneself as subject. (That we have such a background sense of self may indicate that our awareness of ourselves as subject in ASA is less empty than Kant thought it is, though not in any way that reveals our nature or structure.) Now compare this sense of oneself to narcissism – one's attitude of attraction or repulsion, fondness or disgust for oneself. Here one is aware of oneself as an object, the object of these attitudes. Looking at oneself in a mirror or reading one's writings for what they may indicate about oneself would be illustrations of this second way of being aware of oneself.

Here is another example. I am looking in the mirror and I say,

(1) It looks to me as though there is something growing on my nose.

'It looks to me' is clearly about me as subject. The 'my' in 'my nose' refers to me as a perceptible, middle-sized object, namely, the organism whose image I am seeing in the mirror. How do I know that the thing doing the looking is the thing reflected in the mirror? Consider one more example. Over the past couple of decades, some primates have been trained to use the American Sign Language equivalents of 'I' and its cognates. Do they know that the object doing the referring is the object being referred to? What would be the difference between this knowledge and merely knowing that (the equivalent of) 'I' is the appropriate term to use of a certain object, in the way that 'the food tray' is the appropriate term to use of a different object? Here there would be no knowledge that the object in question is the thing doing the referring. But what would be the difference?[40] These two ways of being aware of oneself raise a new question: How am I able to identify myself as subject, something that appears in any representation, with myself appearing as the object of only a few representations?

Kant was aware of this identification, even between self as subject and an extended object, a body or human being (A359–60). He was also aware of how it is possible for us to find it puzzling

> how the I which I think, is distinct from the I that it, itself, intuits, and yet, as being the same subject, can be identical with the latter; and how, therefore, I can say: 'I, as intelligence and *thinking* subject . . . am given to myself beyond that which is in intuition, and yet know myself, like other phenomena, only as I appear to myself, not as I am to the understanding' –

Unfortunately, his only response to it is some hand waving:

> these are questions that raise no greater nor less difficulty than how I can be an object to myself at all, and, more particularly, an object of intuition and of inner perceptions. (B155)[41]

This response is quite inadequate. If the way we appear as subject is so totally different from how objects of representation appear, our ability to identify subject with object demands explanation. If the subject is a form of all representations, identifying this subject of every representation with any object of only a few representations ought to be a bit like identifying space with a chair located in it.

How we can identify subject with object is a question that arises in the work of other philosophers, too. In 'Persons', for example, Strawson says that we must be able to identify subjects of representation with persons, the latter understood in his work as objects that are embodied – middle-sized objects of representation. The issue also arises in Dennett's "Where Am I?"[42]

Dennett's thought experiment depicts the puzzles to do with identifying subject with object very vividly. In this thought experiment, Dennett's brain and his body are separated but remain interconnected via radio links. And the question is, Where is Dennett? That is to say, with which part of his body is he, the subject of his representation, to be identified, so far as location is concerned? (Later in the paper Dennett raises other questions, too, to do with the effect of duplications of various kinds on our sense of our own identity, but these I will not explore.) Not surprisingly, Dennett identifies himself with his overall body, not his brain. But this puzzles him. Is not the brain the centre of the self?

The general shape of the solution to *this* puzzle seems clear and has already been sketched by Strawson. We identify ourselves as subject with the body (the object) on which we are dependent for representations of the world – the body whose location is the centre of my perceptual point of view, the body that controls my perceptions (a complicated matter, as Strawson has shown),[43] my pains, my proprioceptive sense, my consciousness, the existence of psychological states for me to introspect, and the body over whose actions I can exert control merely by an act of will – that is the body that I will treat as me. If this body is split up, as in Dennett's thought experiment, then I will go with the part of it that exhibits the most salient of these linkages, of which, as a matter of contingent fact, the location from which I get my perceptions of the world is probably first. (We tend to think of ourselves as located behind our eyes, I think, because our eyes are at the point at which perspectival perception is 'widest'.) And if I lose these linkages to one part, then I will switch (faster than the speed of light, Dennett says!) to the other, so long as I still have similar linkages to it.

Whether or not that is the approach to take to Dennett's puzzle, it does not touch ours. For our puzzle is over how it is *so much as possible* for us to make these identifications, a problem that arises for both Strawson and Dennett. Given that I can identify with some body, Strawson may be able to tell us how I identify with one body rather than another. But how can I identify with any body at all? How is it even possible for me to know that the body at the centre of my point of view and of whose states I am proprioceptively aware is *my* body? In Wittgenstein's way of putting it, what makes it possible to identify the 'I' with the eye, the geometrical eye, as he calls it, with the physical eye?[44] Strawson's description of the 'technology' of picking which body is me leaves the question of how I can identify with *any* body completely untouched, in much the way Descartes' choice of the pineal gland as the royal road between the brain and the mind leaves untouched the question of how such a road is even possible.

Note that the question of identifying subject with object is not just the mind–body problem over again. First, subject–object identification can arise entirely within the mental, between ASA and awareness of myself as an object in inner sense. Consider

(2) I hate myself for doing that.

Here 'I' refers to me as the subject of this feeling and of many other feelings and other representational states. However, 'myself' is the object of the feeling, only one representational state. How is it possible for me to take the subject of all representation as the object of this one representation? Second, though the problem of identifying the subject with an object may well underlie many classical formulations of the mind–body problem, the problem is no longer usually conceived as a problem about the relation of the subject to the human brain or body, but about the relation of particular mental states (part of Kant's inner sense) to the brain or body (part of outer sense). Indeed, Kant conceived it in this way, too (A386–88). In Kant's version of the problem, the mind appears as subject of representations of both kinds of object, inner-sense mental ones and the outer-sense bodily one. Thus, Kant saw the mind–body problem as an object–object problem; the subject–object distinction is a feature of both sides (A402).

A special form of the subject–object problem does raise a mind–body problem that is current now, or should be. How can we map awareness of self as subject onto the brain? The problem is this. Awareness of self as subject is awareness of oneself as the subject of a number of representations represented together as a single object of representation. Where is this state of unitary awareness to be located? In the brain (or the cerebral cortex) as a whole? In some localized part of the brain? The problem is that we have great difficulty imagining a self-monitoring function that will do what awareness of self as subject has to do, namely, be aware of a multitude of representations and objects, be aware of oneself as the common subject of these representations, and know that the subject of these representations is me (or in the case of memory, at least appears to be me). Indeed, it seems impossible even to describe this function without merely repeating over and over what we want rather to understand: being aware of myself, knowing that it is myself and the common subject of my representation of which I am aware (see Chapter 4). The elusiveness of an informative description here is related to Dennett's problem of the little man, which we considered in Chapter 2:1 and to which we will return next chapter.[45] Such a function would have to be unitary, unifying, and self-recognizing. Lacking a conception of any such function, we have no idea how to go about mapping it onto or replacing it in favour of functions of the brain. This problem presents both a subject–object problem – how can I identify myself as subject with self-monitoring activities of a brain? – and a traditional mind–body problem – how can the mind's being aware of itself as the subject of its representations be related to activities of the brain? This particular mind–body problem, namely, how does the mind as a whole relate to its material 'substratum', to use Kant's term (A350), has generally been ignored by contemporary researchers.

One response to the subject–object problem is to argue that it is a pseudoproblem. Wittgenstein once said that when looked at in a certain way, personal experience has no neighbour. Kant seems to have looked at it this way. On this view, if one were aware of oneself only as subject, one would think of oneself as utterly different from anything, except perhaps space and time.[46] One Wittgensteinian approach to these appearances is to undermine Kant's whole way of conceiving the subject of experience, to argue that awareness of self as subject is simply mismodelled if it is thought of as any form of awareness of an entity – the noncognitivist option mentioned briefly near the end of both Chapters 3 and 4. Using 'I see . . . ' is not referring by using an indicator; it is performing some completely different linguistic act. Unfortunately, at this point the Wittgensteinian story tends to go vague. Even for Kant, the awareness we have of ourselves as subject is as useless and vacant as any awareness could be; it allows us to distinguish self as subject from objects of representation, including the self as object (A342 = B400), but nothing else, certainly not anything that could come into competition with anything we know of ourselves as object. However, awareness of self as subject is still a kind of representation and can give rise to genuine cognitive questions. For example, I see someone in a mirror (perhaps dimly or distortedly) and wonder if the person reflected in the mirror is myself, the person doing the seeing. If awareness of self as subject is pretty strange, noncognitivism is not the answer. As well as identifying oneself as subject with represented objects, "in making a judgment like 'I feel pain' one is aware of [no] thing less than the fact that one does, oneself, feel pain," as Shoemaker has said in a passage we also quoted in Chapter 4.[47] Awareness of self as subject may not be representation of an object, but it is not cognitively vacuous either.

As I said, Kant was aware of the problem of identifying subject with object, but he never did anything with it. At B155 and again at B422 he tells us that there is no problem, but that is mere hand-waving. The account he gives on B156 is just a complicated restatement of the fact that we do it. The remarks he makes on the topic at B422 are even less helpful. In short, Kant has nothing to explain how I know that I am seeing myself, rather than someone else, in a mirror, how I know that it is my hands currently putting letters into my computer rather than someone else's, and so on. Nor does anyone else.

8 Results and attitude

About two decades ago, something like a consensus emerged among many philosophers about personal identity, primarily because of Derek Parfit. Strictly speaking, there is no such thing as personal *identity*. Transitivity can never be guaranteed, a condition of identity being one to one, and judgements of identity can never be securely all or nothing; however good the reasons for affirming that a later person is an earlier person, there will always be reasons for denying it. Memories fade, other continuities weaken, and relevant similarities diminish as bodies and personalities change. Thus, strictly speaking, we should not talk about personal *identity* and switch instead to some other sort of survival concept, one that does not require that the relationship be one to one and all or nothing. Kant did not mount this argument or anything like it, but he actually went further than Parfit in other ways. He showed that perennially popular arguments for an extreme form of the opposite view are worthless, and he diagnosed why many people have nevertheless been seduced by them.

His account of how, in memories of having earlier experiences, an appearance – that a subject of earlier experiences was me – is entirely consistent with the subject of the earlier experience having been someone else is just an anticipation of Parfit. Parfit could have written everything Kant said in the footnote to A363, for example. (That in itself is noteworthy; the footnote is two hundred years old.) But Kant's theory of why these earlier subjects appear in these memories to be me and yet might not be provides a diagnosis of why these appearances incline us to the illusion that we persist in a strict and philosophical way, a diagnosis that goes further than anything in contemporary philosophy. As we have seen, the theory is largely an application of the theory of the representational base of nonascriptive reference to self explored in Chapter 4. Kant's conclusions are very similar to Parfit's; the difference is that Kant can explain them. Thus, Kant's ideas do not just anticipate Parfit's position, they still have something to contribute to it.

As well as these insights into personal identity and memory, Kant also laid the foundation for some new insights into the temporal dimension of the unity of consciousness. Exploring these foundations leads us rapidly, as we have seen, to begin to wonder if the unity of consciousness actually has temporal depth at all, its representation of itself in memory as having such depth notwithstanding.

What in the end was Kant's own attitude to the conclusions of the Paralogisms? The two crucial conclusions were that the soul is simple and that it persists in some absolute way across time. The *arguments* used by RPsy to support the conclusions of the Second and Third Paralogisms were based on ideas he himself accepted, so he could hardly reject them; but he could reject the idea that they offered any *support* for the doctrine that the soul is simple or that it has absolute persistence, and this he did. The urge to over-interpret synthesis and self-awareness, as RPsy did, is "an illusion which cannot be avoided." However, "it may . . . be rendered harmless" (A341 = B399). But what was his attitude to simplicity and absolute persistence themselves? That is more complicated. He certainly thought that so far as rational considerations go, we have no reason to believe that we have either characteristic. To this extent, his attitude was sceptical. But it is vital to understand that he was not seeking to disprove the substance of the claims themselves. His aim in the Paralogisms chapter was entirely negative, merely to show that certain views could not be supported rationally. Nor, however, could they be *attacked* rationally. In fact, he had no positive goal whatsoever – his theory of mind, insofar as he thought one could be given, had already been given in TD. This is a point worth emphasizing; a great many commentators have believed just the opposite, that Kant's attack on the Paralogisms contains some sort of positive theory. Paton, Strawson, Henrich, Ameriks, and Powell are all examples, Henrich and Ameriks in particular.

Recall why the 'dialectical inferences' of the Paralogisms interested Kant. Their claims to knowledge of the mind as it is in itself threatened his fundamental doctrine that it is unknowable. And recall why Kant defended this view. He thought that we have practical, moral reasons having nothing to do with argument or evidence in the usual sense for accepting the immortality and therefore, he presumed, the simplicity and absolute persistence of the soul. On the one hand, even the barest possibility of theoretical knowledge on the matter would reduce the force of such practical arguments to insignificance; on the other, the absence of any possibility of theoretical knowledge would leave them the field. That is precisely the result Kant's attack was designed to bring about, as Kant himself says late in the chapter: "It is [thus] possible that I may find cause, on other than merely speculative grounds, to hope for an independent and continuing existence of my thinking nature, throughout all possible change of my state", including bodily death (A383). Indeed, Kant argued in the second *Critique,* belief in the soul's immortality is one of three Postulates of Pure Practical Reason (the other two being belief in freedom of the noumenal will and belief in God).[48]

Kant almost certainly accepted that the soul is simple and persists absolutely – as an article of faith. In fact, on B419 he actually says that it is simple, though unfortunately he also seems to say that the idea can be proved, that it follows from apperception. But this slip notwithstanding, it was imperative that there be no reason (evidential or theoretical) to believe either idea. Kant tried to show that there is not and why there is not. But that is all. It is interesting to note that Kant looked at simplicity one more time later in the *Critique,* in the context of indivisibility in the Second Antinomy. There he argues once more that we have no reason to believe that the soul is simple. But now his approach is diametrically the opposite of the approach he adopted against the Paralogisms. Rather than arguing that we have no grounds for the idea, he now says we have too many: two air-tight arguments that unfortunately contradict each other, one for and one against. Still, the result is the same and it is still purely negative. Again all he wants to show is that we have no theoretical reason to believe, one way or the other.[49]

9

The second-edition subjective deduction: self-representing representations

1 Homunculi and self-representing representations

Representational models of the mind have trouble accounting for the thing that has representations. Their picture of the mind is usually Humean, in which nothing but representations and transformations of representations have a place. It is difficult to build an account of the subject, the thing to whom representations represent, out of these resources – difficult, but perhaps not impossible. In the second edition, Kant at least opened the way to a possible solution to this problem that stays within the ambit of representations. Traditionally, philosophy and cognitive science have concerned themselves with how representations represent, how they are representations *of* something. In this chapter, we are going to focus on their representing *to* someone.

The representational model of the mind in one form or another has been so dominant for the past four centuries, at least in European philosophy and its offshoots, that even those who do not accept it always end up discussing it. Representational states are, minimally, states or processes that contain or convey information about some other states or processes or objects, real or imagined.[1] In the representational model, mental states are treated as representations (information-bearing states), propositional attitudes are viewed as consisting in computational relations among representations, and mental activity is a matter of performing transformations on representations.[2] There is nothing in any of this that Kant would have rejected. Throughout its history, the model has usually been given a realist reading, in which representations are taken to be real events (either material or immaterial) hidden away in a realm not visible on the surface of the body, but it need not be, as witnessed by Dennett's recent instrumentalist version in which representations are simply postulates that explain behaviour. By temperament if not by necessity, Kant would have been a kind of realist about representations. Even if we are aware of representations only via representations of them, not as they are in themselves, Kant would have held that representations exist and exist as representations. As was argued in Chapter 1:3, however, he could have accepted almost any view of what representations are in themselves, including instrumentalism.

In a number of ways, Kant went further with the representational model than contemporary philosophers have done so far. Since he nevertheless was a representationalist, the additions he made to the basic, Humean model that holds sway ought to be of some interest. Most of Kant's additions were on the topic of the mind as a whole: its nature, functioning, and awareness of itself. On this topic, leading representationalists have gone no further than Hume. In Fodor or Pylyshyn, for example, the mind as a whole is nothing beyond an assembly of representations; they say little or nothing about synthesis, unity, or representation of self, certainly nothing to match the sophistication of their accounts of mental contents and functions. The leading alternatives to representational realism such as Dennett's or the Churchlands' do no better. On the mind as a whole, Kant still has things to teach us.

The additions Kant made to the model are fairly radical. In the first edition he introduced the twin ideas that I have called the global object and the global representation (his general experience), ideas we have examined in earlier chapters. Then in the second edition he at least opened the way to a radical representationalism about the mind itself. It will be the topic of this chapter. The fundamental idea behind this radical representationalism is that the mind itself, the thing that has global representations, itself is these global representations, at least so far as we can know what it is at all. The mind not only has representations; so far as we can know it, it is a representation. (Saying that the mind *is* what it *has* may sound peculiar. I think the peculiarity is merely skin-deep, no more serious than the peculiarity of saying that something both *has* and *is* the molecules that make it up.) Kant never developed the idea that the mind is a representation or even articulated it fully; clear indications that he held it appear only in the second edition, and at that only in TD. But the evidence there is significant. In addition to this direct evidence, another reason for ascribing the view to Kant is that it ties various elements of his theory of mind together in an elegant way, as we sketched in Chapter 2. This will be the topic of Section 7.

The idea that the mind is a representation, insofar as we can be aware of it, connects to Fodor's and Dennett's notion of a self-representing representation. Fodor and Dennett introduced this intriguing notion as a way of getting around positing homunculi (Dennett's exempt agents)[3] to satisfy the need for something to which representations represent. We introduced the problem in Chapter 2:1. A representation is not only a representation *of* something, it also represents *to* someone, so we need an account of this someone. If the someone is not itself a representation or collection of representations, however, then it is external to the system of representations. But if it is external to the system of representations, then even a complete theory of this system of representations will not provide any account of this subject who has the representations. We end up with an undischarged homunculus, an exempt agent, on our hands, and the mystery is as big as when we started. As a way out, Fodor and Dennett are trying to describe representations that could "understand themselves", represent to themselves – representations that are both representation and subject of representation.[4] If representation and subject are one, however, the mind could itself be a representation.[5]

As I will argue in Sections 5 to 7, Kant held to all of this. However, he had a way to make the idea plausible. If replacing homunculi with representations is to make any progress, representations do indeed have to represent to themselves; in this Fodor and Dennett are surely right. But the idea of a self-representing representation seems at first glance to be bizarre. How could the thing that has representations, the thing to which representations represent, itself be a representation? Among other things, surely that would be to do away with the subject! Since the idea also looks very much like an idea Hume might have had, any suggestion that Kant may have espoused it will seem doubly bizarre, given his implicit critique of Hume. Needless to say, I do not think that the idea is bizarre for either reason.

Note first that we are not talking about self-awareness here; we are talking about representations representing *to* themselves, not being *of* themselves or their subject. Now consider Hume. About his notion of the mind as a bundle of mental states, everyone immediately asks, What ties these states together? What has these states? What understands them, forms attitudes to them, acts on what they contain, and so on? In response to such questions, Hume has nothing to offer but patterns of association (see B127). However, he did not think that he *needed* to offer more than that, either. On his own terms, Hume may have been able to dispatch the subject this way; he may have assumed as Descartes probably did that representations can represent without representing *to* anything. In fact, Hume may have assumed that none of the three aspects of a representation – content, the representation itself, and attitude to content – requires representing *to* anything. If so, he could consistently posit representations while denying that there is anything that has them. (We examined intrinsic representing briefly in Chapter 2:1.) At the very least, Hume's attempt to maintain that the mind is nothing more than a bundle of associated mental states is not obviously incoherent.

Kant, Fodor, and Dennett have a different picture of representations, however, one that bars Hume's way out. For them, representations can represent *only* to something. If so, there must be something to which they represent. This is what creates the problem of the little man, the undischarged homunculus, and motivates the idea of representations that represent to themselves. Fodor's and Dennett's idea is not without promise – as they point out, computers represent without there being anything more than various representations for them to represent to – but in one respect they have not gone beyond Hume. Though they at least see the problem, they have nothing to explain how this happens. The reason is that, like Hume, they have no account of how individual representations combine into larger representational units.

This gap creates a problem. As we have seen a number of times, my representations represent or can represent

(i) their contents,
(ii) themselves, and
(iii) me, their subject.

As we have now added, my representations also represent *to something,* namely

(iv) to me.

To display what Fodor and Dennett have left out, take my seeing the computer screen in front of me. This act of seeing does not represent to itself. Among other things, it is only one among many representations, and my representations represent to something common to a great many representations. Fodor and Dennett have nothing that allows them to account for this fact: How do multiple representations represent to the same thing? Without this, there is no hope for a picture of the mind as a system of self-representing representations.

The trouble is, Fodor and Dennett have not identified any plausible candidate for the role of self-representing representation. (Dennett does not develop his new notion of the self as a series of virtual captains in this direction, so it is hard to say whether it has potential.) Thus, their notion of self-representing representations seems as bizarre as Hume's bundle theory and in much the same way. How could a representation be represented *to* in the way a mind is? Since they see the need to account for representations representing to someone, they have a problem. It might be thought that the problem is with the very idea of a self-representing representation, but perhaps it is not. Perhaps we just need to identify the right kind of representation and understand how it could represent to itself in the right way. That is exactly what I think Kant shows us how to do. The most striking thing about a subject of experience is that each of us is *one* of them. Two central features of being one subject are that (a) each of us is aware of a great many objects of representation at one time in a global object, and (b) on the basis of this awareness, each of us is able to launch single, integrated courses of action, which we are also aware of as the object of a single representation. Thus, a self-representing representation apt to be a mind would also have to be

(v) unitary,

and this unitary representation would have to be

(vi) aware of a great many objects of representation at the same time in a global object and able to launch single, integrated courses of action.

Fodor has always thought of self-representing representations as things we have many of, representations in the plural, as though a multiplicity of particular representations is the whole story about representations. So has Dennett, at least until recently. (It is hard to tell how his new model would fit here.) Any representation worth anything as a model of the mind, however, would have to be unitary and able to represent a multiplicity of representations in one representation. Multiplicity cannot be the whole story; we are also unitary.

One place in which the unity of the mind shows up is in ASA; we are aware of ourselves as the *single, common subject* of a great many representations at the same time, not just of one representation at a time. Thus, any representation that could be a mind must also be able to be

(vii) aware of *itself* as the single, common subject of a great many representations.

Finally, a point on which all parties agree, a representation that could be a mind would have to be able to

(viii) manipulate representations.

The Fodor–Dennett candidates for a self-representing representation cannot do half these things, but Kant offered one that can: the global representation, with its global object. In earlier chapters, we examined this notion's potential to explain some of the unifying functions of the mind. To be a serious candidate for being a subject of experience, a mind, we can now see that, in addition, it would also have to be able to represent itself, as common subject and *to itself,* and in addition it would have to be able to manipulate the included representations. If we can find a way to allow a global representation to be both self-representing and self-manipulating in this way, it would be all we could ask for in a representation that could be its own subject.

Could a global representation have these additional features? Did Kant advance such a view in the second-edition TD? Before we take up these questions, let us first examine the new TD itself, focusing on the subjective deduction. We will see that Kant now simplifies the doctrine of synthesis and introduces some twists in the central argument linking the unity of apperception and consciousness (some kind of consciousness) to use of the Categories to link experiences under concepts.

2 The second-edition Transcendental Deduction

Kant completely rewrote TD for the second edition. The rewriting begins earlier than is sometimes realized, not at the beginning of Section 2 but at the end of Section 1, where Kant added three paragraphs on Locke and Hume. Because Kemp Smith interpolated the first-edition TD between these new paragraphs and the new Section 2, they are often ignored. They should not be, because they show that in the second edition Kant explicitly cast TD in the form of a response to Locke and Hume. Though his official philosophical target in the Dialectic continues to be rationalism, he now aims TD at empiricism. He accuses Locke of philosophical enthusiasm: on the one hand, Locke thought that all concepts are derived from experience, but on the other hand, he thought they could be used to establish all manner of transexperiential (= necessary) truths. By contrast, he tells us, Hume, who proceeded more circumspectly, managed to achieve something of lasting value. He raised a sceptical doubt about whether knowledge has any foundation more secure than mere custom and found a powerful argument to back up his scepticism. Kant urges that mathematics and the 'general science of nature' are enough to prove that Hume had to have been wrong. But that is not the same as knowing *where* he was wrong or *how* mathematics and science could be more than the mere custom that he said they were. Kant continues to take the credentials of mathematics and physics for granted, and his project continues to be to find out how such knowledge is possible; he just makes empiricism his explicit target.

Kant then launches into his analysis. The repetitions of the first version are now gone; equally, there is no longer a Section 3. The new Section 2 consists of twelve subsections. Two groups of them are devoted to the mind. The first occurs right at the beginning of the section (§15 to §18; B129–40), the second near the end (last half of §24 and §25; B153–9); we looked at the details of the structure and placing – in the second case, the very peculiar placing – of these passages in Chapter 5:4. The first passage contains the new subjective deduction. As in the first edition, it consists of an argument that synthesis under concepts is required for unity of consciousness, though with some interesting changes. Then, after switching to the objective deduction for a while (§19 to half-way through §24), he returns to the mind in the last half of §24 and §25. This passage is quite unlike anything in the first edition; the topic is what exactly we are aware of when we are aware of ourselves. This topic was barely touched on in the first edition, and only in the chapter on the Paralogisms, not TD. (§24 also elaborates the doctrine of synthesis introduced in §15.) Finally, Kant argues (§26 and §27) that "all possible perceptions, and therefore everything that can come to empirical consciousness . . . must . . . be subject to the categories" (B164–5). §26 also contains some further elaboration of the doctrine of synthesis.

The structure of the objective deduction in the second version of TD has been the object of intense study, as has the question of what exactly Kant can be said to accomplish in it.[6] Fortunately, we do not need to consider those questions here. On the subjective side, the second TD differs from the first primarily in putting self-awareness and specifically ASA right at the centre of things. Strangely enough, however, many of the riches in Kant's investigation of this form of self-awareness disappear. The same is true of many other interesting details; Kant now paints in much broader strokes overall. In addition, he now largely blurs the distinction between synthesis of individual objects of experience and synthesis of a multiplicity of objects into a single global object, talking simply about 'synthesis of the manifold', which presumably includes both. This makes the question of what sort of representation Kant is taking as the starting point of TD even harder to settle than it was in the first edition.

On some issues the second version of TD is much less helpful than the first (that is the main reason I have focused on the latter up to now). The treatment of synthesis is thinner and far more scattered, and as I just said, he runs synthesizing individual objects of experience and synthesizing a group of individual objects into a global object together. The concept of apperception, though still a concept for a faculty or capacity (B133n), is now firmly and unambiguously linked to representation of self, that is to say, to self-awareness of some sort. With the abandonment of the distinction between the synthesis of one object and that of many objects, the useful distinction between apperception *sans phrase* and transcendental apperception goes – in the first edition, Kant generally used the former term for the activity of synthesizing individual objects and reserved the term 'transcendental apperception' for the activity of synthesizing many objects into a global object; now he calls the whole range of unifying activities that are necessary to have representations transcendental apperception (TA) (also 'pure' and 'original' apperception). (However, he is now somewhat clearer about the distinction between pure and empirical apperception.) Most of the remarks about the referential machinery of ASA and the peculiar kind of access that the use of this machinery generates are dropped. And it is far harder to decipher how he has structured the subjective deduction.

3 §15: synthesis in the second edition

Allison's view of where TD starts in the second edition is shared by many others: "The real starting point of [TD] is . . . the transcendental unity of apperception . . . at the beginning of §16".[7] That is to say, §15 is not really part of TD and §16 is not connected to it in any significant way. This view cannot be correct. Just as in the first edition, the deduction begins with Step (1), representation of objects and the acts of synthesis required to do so. This step is taken in §15, the first part of Section 2. Kant now lumps representation of individual objects and of global objects together, and the focus is on the general activity of synthesis, though in a much simplified form, not on representation of objects, but the basic step is the same. (As we saw in Chapter 6:I:4, Kant says less about representation of objects even in the first edition than its being the official starting point there would lead one to expect.) All that remains of the threefold division in the doctrine of synthesis, at least at this point in the argument, is the abstract idea of what Kant now calls combination in general. The refinements of the threefold division do not appear until §24 and §26. Moreover, Kant drops all his arguments for the necessity of synthesis (counting units, forming a triangle out of three lines, a physical object out of impenetrability, etc.) and simply asserts that without synthesis we cannot have objects of representation with any diversity of elements. The *a priori* element in synthesis is prominent; since synthesis is an act of cognition (understanding), he tells us, not receptivity (sensibility), all experience has a nonexperiential, cognitive component, even sensible representation. Unlike other representations, our representation of acts of synthesis "cannot be given through objects". (It is given, presumably, by doing acts of synthesizing, as we discussed in Chapter 4.) Prior to a filling of sense experience, acts of synthesis are indistinguishable (equipollent, *gleichgeltend*), presumably because they all do the same job. Kant's thought must be that they get their diversity from the diversity in the sensible material they work on. Most of these claims are familiar.

§15 concludes with a paragraph that is not so familiar, on the unity of acts of synthesis. First, Kant makes a claim about unity and synthesis that is portentous for his overall view of the mind, as we will see in Section 5. He says that synthesis is a matter of adding a representation of unity, a *representation* of unity, to a representation of a manifold. This claim heralds his new radical representationalism. The activity of synthesis, which is about finding a way to make our concepts and principles fit our experience, now becomes a matter of finding a way to make a representation, the representation of unity, fit another representation, the representation of the manifold. This is an interesting new twist. Second, this paragraph makes a number of new points about the unity of synthesis, which Kant also calls the unity of apperception and the unity of consciousness, points that are echoed throughout the new TD. Kant says, for example, that this unity is "not the category of unity". The idea seems to be that having one consciousness, engaging in single acts of synthesis or apperception, is more than simply being one or single. The unity of being one in these ways is more than and different from the unity of being one table. Recall that we also defined the unity of consciousness (Chapter 2:4) as more than being one aware being; it includes awareness of a number of particulars as one, as a group. Is this what Kant has in mind? We examined this notion of unity in Chapter 2:5. In a footnote to B133 and again on B135, Kant distinguishes analytic from synthetic unity. Apparently analytic unity is simply being one; anything must be one in some respect, must be itself. By contrast, synthetic unity is some special form of unity or unification or integration that a mind and its system of representations must have to be a mind. This special unity is what is 'not in the category of unity'; we cannot talk about its oneness in the way we can talk about the oneness of other things. Not being an instance of the category of unity, this synthetic unity is difficult to characterize.

How many kinds of synthesis does Kant now recognize? Judging by the opening subsections of the new TD, the answer might easily seem to be just one. The details of the various kinds of synthesis so meticulously distinguished at the beginning of TD in the first edition now play no role. However, Kant does retain these various kinds of synthesis (apprehension, reproduction, recognition); they just do not appear until later in the chapter (in §24 and §26). Even there, though synthesis of apprehension and synthesis in imagination are both mentioned by name, synthesis of recognition in a concept, the crucial form of synthesis, is not. Nevertheless, the three different forms of synthesis in general and synthesis of recognition in particular are very much at work in the chapter. For example, in §18, the distinction between empirical and transcendental unity of apperception or consciousness is built on the distinction between synthesis of reproduction and synthesis of recognition. In §20 Kant speaks of the 'functions of judgement' and says that the categories are those functions of judgement. This is surely the synthesis of recognition in a concept in a new guise. He draws a new distinction between a "synthesis of the manifold of sensible intuition, which . . . may be entitled *figurative* synthesis" and a "synthesis which is thought in the mere category in respect of the manifold of an intuition in general, and which is entitled combination through the understanding" (B151). The former seems to take in synthesis of apprehension and reproduction and the latter is again synthesis of recognition in a concept. Kant is trying to merge his old terminology with a new one, not entirely successfully. The new notion of figurative synthesis is only part of it. Far from reducing the number of different kinds of synthesis, Kant adds a whole range of new ones, and they cut the phenomena up in new ways. In a note added to the introduction to Section 3 of the Principles of Pure Understanding, for example (A162 = B201), he goes so far as to distinguish synthesis of composition (of homogeneous elements) from synthesis of connection (of diverse elements that belong to one another), and then he divides each of these up in several further ways.

In addition, Kant makes much more of the distinction between productive and merely reproductive imagination than he did in the first edition; he seems to have found his old notion of reproductive imagination to be inadequate. He now says that reproductive imagination is merely empirical (B152), meaning presumably that behind it stands an *a priori* form for images as there is an *a priori* form of intuition (space and time, the pure form of intuitions) and an *a priori* backing to recognition or judgement (the Categories). Though less cogently laid out, the doctrine of synthesis is not only alive and well in the second edition but even becomes more complicated. Thus, anyone who holds that the subjective deduction in the second edition does not begin from representation of objects or give synthesis an important role is missing something.

4 §16 and §17: the new version of the central argument

As we will recall, in the first edition the central argument of the subjective deduction was repeated three times, once starting on A107, a second time starting on A116, and a third time starting just before A120. In the second edition the whole argument appears in §16, with a reprise in §17. §17 adds little to what is said in §16, but §16 requires virtually line-by-line examination.[8] (§18 is concerned with an aspect of the mind, too, specifically with the distinction between empirical apperception and TA, but this topic is largely independent of §16; see Chapter 10:3.) In general outline, the argument of §16 follows the same three steps as the argument in the first edition. It begins with

(1) representation of individual objects;

argues that

(2) such representations and/or their objects or some vital subclass of them must 'stand along side one another in one experience' (A108), and that this requires synthesis by TA into one experience in one consciousness;

and then infers that

(3) TA must use concepts to do so (Kant's particular interest is the causal ones).

Step (1) is the topic of §15, already examined. We will now take up the second-edition version of step (2). The blur around this second step is far more intense in the second edition than it was in the first. There are two reasons for this.

The first is that exactly what restriction Kant thinks he is imposing on the class of representations that enter step (2) is even less clear here than it was in the first edition. Clearly not all my representations get to enter (2) (which by itself refutes simple self-ascription readings), only those that are something to me (see Chapter 6:I:5). The new problem is that, in the second edition, Kant switches before long from talking about *representation* of objects to talking about *judgement* of objects. Is Kant making the same move here as the move from representations *simpliciter* to representations that are something to someone? I think he is; I think he held that we can make judgements about all and only representations and represented objects that are something to us, but I am not sure. The main reason why the blur around (2) intensifies in the second edition, however, is that Kant now links (1) to (2) via a claim about the conditions of representations belonging to one *self*-consciousness, rather than to one consciousness, that is to say, via LP′, in the terminology of Chapter 6:I:5, rather than LP. This in turn requires an extra substep, to get from self-consciousness to the claim about synthesis into 'one experience' of one consciousness. In fact, (2) proper does not even appear in the first paragraph of §16, which is entirely taken up with LP′. The first sentence of that paragraph is very famous:

> It must be possible for the 'I think' to accompany all my representations; for otherwise something would be represented in me that could not be thought at all, and that is equivalent to saying that the representation would be impossible, or at least would be nothing to me. (B131–2)

This sentence is clearly related to LP:

(LP) Representations can represent something to me only in so far as they belong with others to (can be connected in, can be taken up into) one consciousness.

There are two differences. One is trivial: the order of the clauses is reversed. The other is not. Rather than tying representations being something to me to their belonging to one consciousness, Kant now ties them to the possibility of 'I think' accompanying them – whatever that means. This new idea is LP′:

(LP′) Representations can represent something to me only in so far as it is possible for " 'I think' to accompany them," for them to "stand together in one universal self-consciousness". (B131 and B132)

I take being something to me and being something that could 'be thought at all' to be equivalent.[9] It is also likely that a representation standing with others in one self-consciousness and it being possible to accompany it with 'I think' are equivalent. If so, the only difference between LP and LP′ is that one consciousness has been replaced with "one universal self-consciousness". For a representation to represent something to someone, suddenly 'I think' must be able to accompany it; it has a "necessary relation to the 'I think' ". The root notion in all these locutions seems to be the idea that for a representation to be something to someone, the person having it must be able (a) to become aware of having it, and therefore (b) to become aware of him- or herself as the common subject of this and other representations.

What could have led Kant to think this? If he thought that LP, the need to belong to one consciousness, worked in 1781, why had he stopped thinking that it was enough by 1787? As we saw in Part II of Chapter 6, the picture is actually far from straightforward even in the first edition. It being so obvious that we have ASA, unified awareness of oneself as subject, by 1787 Kant may have come to feel that if he could deduce a need to apply the Categories from it, he would have a particularly convincing argument. Indeed, he may have half-felt this all along. If he could, in addition, make representation of objects necessary to having ASA, then he would have both the power of the first-edition strategy and whatever independent power ASA as a separate starting-point could provide. He would have combined the two Henrich–Guyer starting-points into a single argument. Perhaps he also had his refutation of idealism in mind and wanted his new refutation of scepticism (for that is what the idealism he had in mind really is) to start from something that had been central to the deduction of the Categories. Perhaps, too, he thought it more obvious that ASA is a *unified* consciousness – ranges over a diversity of representations – than that consciousness of objects is. (One point in favour of this conjecture is that animal representation, empirical apperception – in short, nonunified consciousness of objects – was a recurring worry for him.) Or perhaps we just do not know. As Guyer points out, Kant did begin deductions from ASA a number of times, and we may simply have to leave it at that.[10] Indeed, acute readers from his time to ours have taken ASA to be either his primary starting-point (Henrich) or his only one (Strawson).

What makes the introduction of self-awareness really baffling is that Kant does not go on to deduce the Categories from it. He still deduces them from unified consciousness of objects, that is to say, from (1), just as he did in the first edition. So far as the argument from (1) to (3) is concerned, all that inserting self-consciousness does is face him with added complications: to get from (1) to (2), he needs two extra steps, the move from (1) to LP′ and something to get him from LP′ to (2). The latter something goes like this: it is possible "for the 'I think' to accompany all my representations" "only in so far . . . as I can unite [these] representations in *one consciousness*" (B133), which is what he does in the second paragraph. We might call this supplementary claim LP^2:

(LP^2) For it to be possible for 'I think' to accompany representations, for them to stand together in one self-consciousness, they must stand together in one consciousness.

In the third paragraph, Kant pulls it all together (B134). I will change the order of his sentences and attach my labels:

[LP′] The thought that representations . . . one and all belong to me, is equivalent to the thought that I [can at least] unite them in one self-consciousness.

[LP^2] [This is possible] only in so far as I grasp the manifold of representations in one consciousness. . . . For otherwise I should have as many-coloured and diverse a self as I have representations of which I am conscious. . . .[11]

[2] [But grasping the manifold in one consciousness, or, therefore, uniting it in one self-consciousness], though not itself the consciousness of the *synthesis* of the representations, . . . presupposes the possibility of that synthesis.

The only fly in the ointment is that I have to say that he misplaced [2]. Instead of putting it where I put it, he placed it earlier, immediately after the sentence I labelled LP′. That is why I had to put a long insertion at the beginning of the sentence as I placed it. Otherwise, the argument is complete and in order.

Let me break the flow of my analysis for a moment to identify one major way in which my account here differs from accounts like Strawson's and Allison's. I have treated Kant as arguing that (3) is a necessary condition for (2), as part of an argument laying out a nested series of necessary conditions. By contrast, they both think that Kant holds what Allison calls a 'reciprocity thesis' between (2) – or at least a self-consciousness-enriched version of (2) – and (3). Strangely enough, Allison's actual development of the claim is seriously flawed. If there is a relationship of reciprocity between (2), or enriched (2), and (3), it would have to be that each is necessary for the other, so that the other is sufficient for the first. But Allison says (on p. 146) that the thesis is that "[a synthetic unity of] representations of objects is necessary for unity of consciousness, and the unity of consciousness is *sufficient* for [such] representation of objects"! This inference is indeed sound; but the result is not a reciprocity thesis! Setting this problem aside, what about the thesis itself? If we take (2) to be talking about unity of *consciousness,* then the reciprocity thesis is probably correct, though all Kant cares about is that (3) is necessary for (2). But if we take (2) in the enriched form, the thesis is not just unnecessary and implausible, but it is unclear that Kant ever held it – which brings us back to the problem of how Kant brought self-consciousness into the argument, and why.

The whole business of inserting self-awareness into LP to create LP′ and then forging LP^2 to bridge the ensuing gap is remarkable – all this finagling just to get to (2), something he did in one easy step in the first edition!

Instead of the structure (1), LP, (2), (3), we now have (1), LP′, LP^2, (2), (3). One wants to ask, Why bother with this extra complication? Kant still deduces the categories from (2), not from either LP′ or LP^2. He still urges that we need a 'conjoining' or 'uniting' of the manifold of representations (a conjoining into, presumably, 'one knowledge' in the language of A108, one global object) for them to be in "*one consciousness*" (B133). The same is true at B137: "All unification of representations demands unity of *consciousness*" (my emphasis).[12] Why not just stick with LP and go straight to (2)? Another way to express the bafflement is to ask, why, in the first sentence of this paragraph, does Kant say that "a synthesis of representations . . . is possible only through *the consciousness* of this synthesis" (B133; my emphasis)?[13]

A tiny change made it easy for Kant to switch to LP': whereas the argument in the first edition is impersonal, in the second edition it is couched in the first person – it is all 'I' this and 'me' that. First-person statements are exceedingly slippery; the mind slides back and forth between awareness and self-awareness and it is hard to stay clear about the difference. If Kant had any *justification* for making the switch, and I am not sure he had, it has to be found in his careful claim that for a representation to be something to someone, to belong with others in one consciousness, only the *possibility* of attaching 'I think' is required; only the *possibility* of being aware of having the representation and of myself as its subject is required.

Even this weak condition does not attach to all representations a person has, only to representations that are something to that person. A representation may be too fleeting or too unconnected to anything else in a representational system to become anything to its bearer. Both representations I have and representations that are something to me are mine; but Kant is interested only in the latter. This distinction frees Kant to argue that a representation being something to me requires more than just having it.[14] The ultimate 'something more', of course, is synthesis with other representations. This distinction between having a representation and a representation being something to someone is extremely impressive. As I said in Chapter 6:I:5, that by itself is enough to show that Kant's target is deep-running psychological conditions of cognitive life as we know it, not a relatively trivial issue like the conditions of a representation being mine.[15] We discussed what makes a representation something to someone in Chapter 6:I:5. It has this property when its possessor can use its objects, and/or the representation itself, in his or her cognitive activities. A representation being something to someone is very much like recognizing its object in a concept, something that requires synthesis; a representation can be something to me only if it is or can be cognitively related to other representations had by me. If a representation I have is isolated from and does not influence other representations I have, it is nothing to me. It may still represent, contain awareness of its object, it may even represent to something (e.g., to my brain), but it would not represent to me. By itself, "empirical consciousness, which accompanies different representations, is . . . diverse and without relation to the identity of the subject" (B133), without relation, that is to say, to the 'connected whole of human knowledge' (A121) of that subject. Kant illustrated the kind of connections among representation needed here in many ways, but perhaps none better than the way words are unified with other words to make sentences, an example central to UA in Chapter 7. The example is perfect because, as Frege insisted, words have meaning only in sentences. Word representations get combined into larger representations than sentences, of course – paragraphs, chapters and even whole books. (Indeed, if Wittgenstein, Quine, Davidson et al. are right, the smallest possible representation with semantic content may be a whole language.) Representations of words and so on get combined with representations of many other things, too. All such acts of combination are acts of synthesis.

But what has happened to the possibility of attaching 'I think'? Indeed, what has happened even to simple ESA, awareness of representations? Why does Kant insert the possibility of attaching 'I think' before inferring the need for synthesis from being something to someone? As I have re-created the argument, we do not need even awareness of representations for them to be something to us, let alone the possibility of attaching 'I think' to them. If we need to *recognize* anything at all for a representation to be something to us cognitively, at most it is the object and the connections represented between this object and others. We do not need to recognize the representation itself, or that we are having it. Nor would recognizing it be *sufficient* for it to be something to me, Kant argues at B134; its object must still be represented as connected to other objects. Otherwise, recognizing objects would yield "as multi-coloured and diverse a self as I have representations." (This of course would not be something of which I could be aware; there would be no single 'I' to be aware of anything. These claims hold, so far as I can see, for both awareness$^{RR\text{-}CC}$ and awareness$^{RR\text{-}CS}$ of objects [see Chapter 3:1], but I will not pursue the details of that claim here; we touched on aspects of it in Chapter 6:I:5.) So why, for a representation to be anything to me, must it be possible to attach 'I think' to it? Why must it be "possible for me to represent to myself the identity of the consciousness of these representations" (B133)? Why does so much as the bare possibility of self-awareness enter the picture?

The first and most striking point is that Kant nowhere gives even the appearance of an argument for the claim that representations could be something to someone only if that person could attach 'I think' to them. He must have thought that the idea, once stated, would be intuitively obvious! This observation suggests the possibility of confusion. Kant might be confusing a person being able to make some cognitive use of a representation with recognizing the representation itself, or assuming that the only way a representation could be of cognitive use is if a person recognizes it. However, these suggestions seem unlikely. First, Kant is not talking about actual recognition as one's own, merely the potential for it. The recognition could clearly be absent (he must have awareness$^{RR\text{-}CS}$ in mind) – "even if I am not conscious of [the representations as mine]" (B132). Second and directly following from the first point, Kant knew perfectly well that synthesized, unified representing could go on in the absence of any recognition that one is having the representation. Here we can cite not only the remark just quoted from B132 but also the remarks on A113 and A117n that we examined in Chapter 6:II:1. We will return to them.

In fact, so far as the central argument of the subjective deduction is concerned, I cannot see that Kant has any basis whatsoever for linking even potential self-awareness to a representation being something to someone. He does not need the idea and he has no argument for it. Since Kant knew perfectly well that recognition of an object does not require awareness either of the representation of the object or of oneself, his introducing even the possibility of self-awareness is puzzling. Something we have not yet thought of must be going on. The first point to notice is that Kant actually insists on very little in connection with self-awareness. One can clearly have the *possibility* of attaching 'I think' without actually being aware of oneself. If so, merely having the representational base for ASA might be enough. Since, as I argued at the end of Chapter 6:II:2, even having a *representation* of self would not guarantee that one is aware of oneself, the mere possibility of attaching a *representation* of 'I think' might fall far short of *being aware* of oneself (see Section 6 of this chapter).

After the famous 'It must be possible . . . ' sentence and before the restatement of the same idea near the end of the paragraph, Kant interpolates some extremely important remarks on the status of 'I think'. As we will see shortly, these brief remarks are a pivotal text for Kant's emerging radical representationalism, but they can also help us here. Kant tells us that 'I think' is both a representation and an act. As a representation it has the fascinating property of being able to act. As an act, it is spontaneous pure apperception and does not belong to sensibility. Thus, having "a necessary relation" to 'I think' is having a relation to an act of TA, an act that also yields a representation of self, 'I think'. This act represents various things and properties of these things as its object, but the representation of self it contains would be the nonascriptive 'bare consciousness' of self of the introduction to the Paralogisms. The idea seems to be that when an act of TA generates a representation of some object, a representation of the actor also results, a representation expressed by 'I think'. When Kant said that representations have a relation to 'I think' and "can stand together in one universal self-consciousness" (B132), he may well have meant no more than that.

What is it for acts of TA to generate the representation 'I think'? 'I think' refers to the self as subject, "representations . . . combined in one apperception through the expression common to them all (*allgemeinen Ausdruck*), 'I think' " (B138).[16] (See A382: "The 'I' is . . . the . . . form of consciousness".) Start with this question: What is apperception doing linked to an *expression?* Recall my argument in Chapter 4 that when one is aware of multiple representations as a single global object, one has the representational base for ASA, awareness of oneself as the common subject of these representations. In the first edition, we saw Kant arguing that representations are something to me when I am aware of them as part of a global object and that global representations provide the representational base of ASA. Is Kant now adding something more to this first-edition idea when he says that I must be able to attach 'I think' to them? I think he is. (Whether he knew it is another matter.) He now seems to be saying that global representations not only provide the representational base for ASA, they themselves *actually are a representation of oneself as common subject.* In my view, this representation is what Kant calls 'I think'. However, having such a representation does not mean that we are aware of ourselves; we have many representations of which we are unaware, including many representations of self (when asleep, in memories not currently before us, etc.).

If I am right, Kant's view on possible versus actual self-awareness would now go like this: when representations of objects are synthesized into global objects, we are given everything we need for ASA not just so far as the representational base is concerned but *so far as actual representations of self are concerned.* So if we do not have actual ASA, the reason must be elsewhere – some conceptual apparatus needed for recognizing the representation is missing, or we need to shift our attention or whatever. (Kant knew of the role of attention in awareness [B156n].) We will say a bit more about this expansion of the Chapter 4 notion of the representational base again briefly in Section 6, but even on the little just said, we can see that it might allow the Strawsonian claim that any coherent 'course of experience' "must be, potentially, the experience of a self-conscious subject" to take on some precision.[17] Kant himself, of course, did not formulate this new development or its relation to his first-edition idea of the representational base in the way I have. In addition and most unfortunately for his readers, he plunks the idea that apperceptive acts of synthesis always yield an 'I think' representation down in the middle of the subjective deduction. He should not have done so. Not only is it not a necessary part of the subjective deduction, it could not be a transcendental or *a priori* claim at all. It is a good, old-fashioned empirical hypothesis, though a very abstract one. And it is interesting. In fact, it is part of an entirely separate line of analysis, one new to the second edition.

5 The mind as representation

This new line of analysis concerns the nature of the mind. Kant's remarks on this topic are even briefer and sketchier than his remarks on representations being something to me or on the representation 'I think', and the latter are sketchy enough. Thus, my reading of them will of necessity be speculative, more speculative than anything I have said so far. I have suggested a number of times that a new and radical representationalism of the following sort appears in the second edition. The mind, the self, the understanding, the thing that thinks not only has representations; it is a representation. It is to this claim that we now turn. As will be clear, the global representation, first introduced by Kant on A110 (his 'general experience') has to be the representation at issue. A global representation is the result of synthesizing a multitude of representations and/or their objects into a single intentional object, representations that are all 'something to me'. A global representation is unitary in the way awareness is, and therefore in the way minds are – their system of awareness at any rate. If we could find a way to think of it as also representing *to itself* and able to manipulate various parts of its content and use aspects of this content to guide action, it would be all that Fodor and Dennett could ask for in a representation that represents to itself. If in addition we can think of it as representing *itself* to itself, as well as its objects, it would be a serious candidate for being what the mind is. First let us ask, What is the evidence that Kant thought of the mind as a global representation?

Here we must be careful. For Kant, theories about the nature of the mind are inferences from how the mind appears to us (and what else could they be?). Whether the mind really is the way we infer it to be is something we cannot know; we simply cannot know whether even our best theory of the mind as it appears to us (in outer as well as in inner sense) captures what it is really like. If Kant held that the mind is a global representation, he meant, or should have meant, that this is the best account we can give, based on how it appears to us, of what it is. I emphasize this point because, as we will see in Chapter 10, Kant seems to have believed that we can *be aware of* the mind as it is. However, he never seems to have thought that we can *know* it other than as it appears to us. I need to make two other preliminary points, though I will not discuss these points until Chapter 10 either.

First, even if the mind is a global representation, it does not follow that what we are aware of when we are aware of this representation exhausts what it is. Who knows what other properties the substrate that 'realizes' this representation might have? We know our representations only as we represent them, not as they are (see Chapters 1:3, 6:I:5, 8:5), and like everything else, all we can know about them as they actually are is what we can infer from the way they appear to us. As we saw in Chapters 1:2 and 7:4, Kant's view of the relation of the appearing mind to its noumenal substrate is very similar to the view of contemporary functionalism, except that the latter talks about mental functions relating to the *physical* structures that realize these functions. The one object that is both can equally well be described as either. This may also be the way to answer those like Waxman who claim that "the representing mind cannot itself be representation".[18] 'The mind is a global representation' and (just to take an arbitrary possibility!) 'the mind is a brain' can be complementary descriptions. Second, it will be objected that if the mind is a representation, then, since we have knowledge of representations, we would have at least some knowledge of the mind as it is. The short answer to this objection is contained in what I have already said: we are aware even of representations only as we are aware of them, not as they are. A better answer would point out that Kant distinguished between being aware of something and having knowledge of it (B158; the curious are referred to Chapter 10:5).

If Kant did mount a theory of the mind as global representation, the same first paragraph of §16 on which we focused in the preceding section is again the crucial text. Recall once more the famous first sentence of that paragraph:

> It must be possible for the 'I think' to accompany all my representations; for otherwise something would be represented in me which could not be thought at all, and that is equivalent to saying that the representation would be impossible, or at least would be nothing to me. (B131–2)

As I mentioned in the preceding section and in Chapter 6, this sentence is often taken to mean something like the following:

> For a representation to be anything to me, I must be able to ascribe that representation to myself; and to do that, I must be aware of myself, that I am having the representation.

All the passage actually says, however, is this:

> For a representation to be anything to me, it must be accompanied by (or, Kant also says, have a necessary relation to) something called 'I think'.

Does 'I think' have anything to do with self-ascription? Given Kant's sophistication about reference to and awareness of self, I would have thought that if he had had self-ascription in mind here, he would have said so. As I said in note 15, he does mention self-ascription in both editions (A122 and B138), so he was clearly capable of talking about it by name when he wanted to. Moreover, he clearly did not have *actual* self-ascription in mind – later in the same paragraph he explicitly allows the possibility of representations being mine "even if I am not conscious of them as such" (B132). But did he have self-ascription in mind at all? For all its fame, perhaps the first sentence of §16 has been misinterpreted.

Everything hangs on what Kant meant by 'I think'. Contrary to the view that takes the expression to be straightforwardly about self-ascription or ASA, it is actually far from clear what Kant meant by the term. As we saw in the preceding section, he seems to take 'I think' to express a representation of self and to take being accompanied by 'I think' to be equivalent to standing together in one (act of) self-awareness, but that is not a big help. Kant's next-but-one sentences are interesting, though they are seldom noticed:

> All the manifold of intuition has . . . a necessary relation to the 'I think' in the same subject in which [it] is found. But this *representation* . . . I call . . . *pure apperception*. (B131–2; first emphasis is mine)

If we look closely, we can see something emerging in this passage that is new and interesting. Considered together, the two sentences just quoted are saying that 'I think' is both an act of TA and a representation. Kant says 'I think' is a representation in the first edition, too (A350), but there he would have said that representations have a necessary relation to a *subject* (unified etc.) if they are something to their possessor. Now he is suddenly saying that they have a necessary relation to a *representation* of the subject, 'I think'. Kant might better have said 'a representation *expressed by* 'I think', but the important point is that being related to a mind is suddenly being related to a *representation!* Even more surprisingly, Kant next says, "This representation is an act of spontaneity, . . . pure apperception" (B132). Pure apperception seems to be another name for TA, and TA is the act that ties representations and their objects together into one global representation. Suddenly the act that ties representations together is itself a *representation!*

Now we can begin to see what Kant may really have been saying in the famous 'I think' sentence. For a representation *R* to be something to someone, *R* must have a relation to another representation, 'I think', the relation of being accompanied by the latter. Why? Not because self-ascription must be possible; this representation 'I think' is what has *R!* What synthesizes *R* and relates it to other representations in a global object is a *representation.* (The reason I found the new theory of synthesis as the imposition of a representation of unity on other representations sketched in §15 so interesting earlier is that it could very well have been an anticipation of these claims.) There is still one puzzle: Why does Kant refer to this busily apperceiving representation as 'I think'? Why the link to self-awareness? We will tackle that question in the next section.

To summarize the story so far. As Kant now sees it, acts of apperception are acts of a representation, a global representation having a global object; the mind is nothing more nor less than this active representation. This idea that the mind is activity has a long history. It was first articulated by Aristotle and is still alive today in the foundations of functionalism. To see the appeal of the idea, consider the parallels between a mind and a global representation. A global representation contains all its particular representations as its object. So does a mind. TA is the main cognitive power that global representations have. TA is the main cognitive power of the mind. The way particular intentional objects stand together in a global representation is precisely the way they stand together in a mind; indeed, their standing together in a mind simply is their standing together in a global representation. Far from being strange and shocking, I think it is actually quite plausible to suggest that the mind, the thing that has representations, is itself a representation – a representation that has representations, a global representation. I think Kant is on to something important.

In addition to the remarks from §16 that we have just examined, there are a number of other pieces of textual evidence for the claim that Kant now thought of the mind as a representation. The first clue that this was now his view is found in §15, just before the passages from §16 just quoted. There Kant tells us, as we saw, that synthesis is itself a matter of representations – of adding a representation of unity to a representation of a manifold. "Combination is . . . the *representation* of unity . . . which . . . , when added to the representation of the manifold, first makes possible the concept of the combination" (B131; my emphasis).[19] On this account, synthesis seems to be something like superimposing one image on another. B136 and the note to it also contain an indication that Kant now thought of the mind as a representation. Here Kant tells us that when representations come into relation to space and time, many representations are contained in a single representation ("*viel Vorstellungen als in einer... enthalten*"); space and time are single representations. In a parallel fashion, Kant seems to be saying in §15 and §16, when the mind has a representation *R, R* comes to be contained in another representation 'I think'. This business of representations being located in representations may look like simple-minded imagism but it is not. Kant can easily maintain that locating representations in time or synthesizing representations into global objects is a matter of relating representation to representation without backing down from his insistence that there are metrics of space and time and a lot of conceptual machinery of judgement operating in the background. Indeed, all this background machinery could itself be representational. Nor need representations and the activities they engage in all be open to introspection, available in inner sense. The need for metrics, machinery of judgement, and so on is a supplement to radical representationalism, not a refutation of it.

The most powerful reasons for attributing radical representationalism to Kant are found in §16 and §17. The cumulative effect of assembling in one place the remarks that point to radical representationalism in these two subsections is considerable. In addition to the remarks in §15 about synthesis being a matter of adding a representation of unity to a representation of the manifold, in §16 Kant says, as we have already seen, that 'I think' is a representation and that acts of pure apperception are acts of this *representation.* He also links being anything to me to having a relation to this representation: to be anything to me, a given representation "has a necessary relation" to the representation 'I think'. And in §17, he speaks explicitly of "the act of the apperception 'I think' ". Together, these remarks indicate that Kant now thought of the unified mind within which representations occur as itself a representation.

There is little direct evidence of a representational account of synthesis in the first edition TD, though there is a hint of it in the chapter before TD, 'The Clue to the Discovery of all Pure Concepts of the Understanding' (A67 = B92–A83 = B109), the so-called metaphysical deduction (B159). Even in the first edition, however, Kant presented the mind itself as an empowered representation at least three times. In the remarks on A110 in which he introduces the general experience, he says that this general experience is the form of experience; but the form of experience is a key feature of what *has* experiences, the subject. In a strange remark near the end of A117n, he says that the single self-consciousness in which all empirical consciousness must be combined and "the collective unity of which it makes possible" is "the bare representation 'I' ". This remark reads like a direct precursor of the remarks we have been examining in §16, and it is bewildering on any other construal. And in the introduction to the Paralogisms, he says that the judgement 'I think' is the "vehicle of all concepts" (A341 = B399).

If Kant now thought of the mind as a global representation, how did he picture this mind as representation, and how did he think of its relation to other representations? It is plausible to turn again to the model of space and time as the form of intuition containing particular intuitions (see B136n) and suggest that Kant now thought of the relation of the mind to its representations on the same model. On this model, as space and time are the form of intuitions, the mind or global representation would be the form of representations (see Chapter 3:6). Representations come into relation with space and time by being 'contained' in a representation that provides a temporal and/or spatial matrix. Representations would come into the requisite relation to the 'I think' by being related to other representations in a conceptually structured global representation. Support for ascribing this parallel to Kant may be found in the fact that he called all three, space, time, and the mind, 'forms' of knowledge (see A117n last sentence, A346 = B404, A354). He also thought of space and time as representations of a special singular sort (A32 = B48 and B136n), and he clearly thought of the mind as having the same special singularity. So he may have thought of it as a representation, too, certainly in the second edition.

There are some obvious objections to the view I am exploring here. The mind is active, does things, and representations do not do anything; they are done to. So how, it will be asked, could Kant even think of the act of pure apperception that ties all representations together into a global representation as itself a *representation?* In reply, I would say that the idea of representations with the power to engage in spontaneous acts of judgement, to interrelate and manipulate component representations, sounds a lot stranger to us than it probably did to Kant.[20] We are children of empiricism and think of representations as something that happen to us, not something that we actively make or do. Kant, however, thought of representations as active sense seekers, as activities that seek to unify experience within the constraints of what experience allows. He had no trouble granting even remarkable powers to representations; the activity of synthesis being a representation of unity added to other representations is a leading example. Space and time are representations or representation-like (intuitions are representations; see B156n). Yet space and time do work: they organize other representations. For idealists, including transcendental idealists, everything is representations; thus, for them, representations have all possible powers. In computers, representations are not passive; they control the transformation of other representations. Why should they be passive in us? Given all this, the idea that the activities of the mind might be done by representations is certainly not preposterous.

A second objection is internal to Kant. Kant was drawn to the view that the soul is simple (see Chapter 2). He was adamant, of course, that we have no reason to think that the soul is simple; that was the whole point of his attack on the Second Paralogism. He seems to have thought, however, that simplicity of soul is required by morality and that we have good *practical* reasons to believe in it. That would seem to pose a problem for my reading. The idea that the soul so much as could be simple would seem to be in some tension with the idea that it is a representation, even an active one. But are these two ideas in tension? For Kant, psychological acts are simple, and so are global representations. That a global representation ties a whole representational system together does not entail that it itself is composite. Thus, the soul's being a representation would not rule out its being simple; and that is all Kant requires. The soul's being a representation would not *require* that either it or its noumenal substrate be simple either, of course. Kant insisted that this, too, remain an open question.

The last objection I will consider is both the most obvious and the most important. Even if a person has (or is) only one global representation at a time, global representations have only a short and ever-changing life. Our judgement as to how long might vary, depending on our view of the specious present and so on, but all will agree they do not last very long. Surely, it will be objected, that is not true of their subject! Minds last for a relatively long time. So the mind cannot be a global representation. On the one hand, is it so clear that global representations do not last for long? How do we measure the length of a representation? Certainly a global representation is in a state of constant change, but so is the mind, and how do we decide when one of either of them ends and a new one begins (see Chapter 8)? On the other hand, is it so clear that I do last a long time? I am noninferentially aware of myself only in the present (whether as the object or via having a representation), and I am not directly aware of myself as I was – if I was – nor as I will be – if I will be. I can only remember, anticipate, or infer my relationship to subjects at other times, and we saw in the preceding chapter that (an) earlier subject(s) could appear to be me in my (q-)memories even if (it) they were not. The same is true, *mutatis mutandis,* for (an) anticipated and inferred one(s). From what I am directly aware of in myself, I have no reason to think that I have lasted or will last any longer than my current global representation.

The unity of consciousness and, therefore, the unity of global representations and the unity of the mind do have a diachronic dimension. They rely on continuities of certain kinds, those that support memory and psychological dispositions. It is important to remember, however, that both minds and global representations can *represent* a longer span of time than they *occupy*. Indeed, in memory 'from the inside' (see again Chapter 3), they can represent acts of *witnessing events* and *having representations* that occurred before either the mind or the representation existed. In short, neither how short a time global representations last nor the way memory reaches back intentionally into the past poses an insuperable objection to the idea that the mind is a global representation. In fact, I think the contemporary image of the self that comes closest to Kant's is Dennett's notion of the self as a *virtual captain,* a short-lived coalescence of various representations into a representation of oneself, a representation that *behaves* like a substantial self but is in fact just representations (which is why Dennett calls it virtual).[21] This 'self' has links forwards and back only because it contains anticipatory representations and memories 'from the inside' of an ever-shifting but seamless web of anticipated and remembered captains. Memories and anticipations exist now, obviously, not in the past or future.

The model of the mind as an active representation also fits perfectly with an important belief of Kant's that I have discussed too infrequently (see, e.g., Chapter 4:2), the belief that the mind is a self-legislating and spontaneous initiator of autonomous action.[22] The most important part of this idea for Kant was his conviction that the mind can reach conclusions and initiate actions on the basis of 'rational' requirements dictated by its system of concepts and principles, not just on the basis of nonrational causal forces. Here, what makes a mind a mind is that it engages in a certain distinctive form of action, a form of action whose whole medium and material is through and through representational. This picture first appears in the *Critique* as late as the solution to the Third Antinomy, long after TD and the chapter on the Paralogisms are finished. The idea that the mind is characteristically a self-legislating actor does not entail that it is nothing but active representations, of course, but anything nonrepresentational will be epiphenomenal.

Early in §16, Kant says that for a representation to be anything to me, it must have a necessary relation to a representation that is a spontaneous act of pure apperception. If, as I have said, he had the global representation in mind, we can readily see why. For a representation to be anything to me, I must be able to recognize and use it. Thus, it must be 'combined with' other representations I have. Both recognition and combination are done by and are part of a global representation. If I am a global representation, then when recognition and combination are done by me, they are done by a global representation. In fact, for Kant, everything interesting of which we can be aware in a mind is done in, by, or to representations. Of course, the mind has a material 'substrate', but this substrate and anything else the mind is, over and above representation, does not appear.

6 Self-representation and self-awareness

In this section I want to explore a grab-bag of three further issues related to the idea that the mind is a global representation. The first is the question left earlier: even if Kant thought that the mind is a global representation, why did he think that a global representation represents itself, in the way expressed by 'I think'? The second is the puzzle about how Kant could say that apperception is self-consciousness, that representations must belong to one self-consciousness, and yet leave it open whether the mind is actually aware of itself. The third is the question with which I began this chapter: Can we make room in a representational theory of the mind for the fact that representations represent to someone?

As we saw in Section 4, Kant seems to have expanded the idea that representation of objects provide the *representational base* of awareness of itself into the idea that they actually *represent* the self, though of course we need not be aware that the latter is being represented. It is now relatively easy to see why he thought that the global representation I am must represent me. If global representations represent themselves and if I am a global representation, then that global representation represents me. (Again, I need not know it; only *potential* self-awareness is at issue.) If a global representation represents me, it would be appropriate to call the representation 'I think'.

The idea that global representations represent themselves can also help us resolve some of the puzzles about how Kant saw the relationship between TA and self-awareness, to come to our second topic. Here is a sample. Even in the second edition (B133n), apperception is a faculty of judgement; yet it is also a kind of self-awareness (B68 and B132). Apperception is a kind of self-awareness; but it is possible to apperceive without being aware of oneself doing so or of the results of doing so. All representations that are something to me have "a necessary relation to the 'I think' . . . " and "belong to one universal self-consciousness"; yet they can be something to me "even if I am not conscious of them as such" (B132). In the first edition, too, it is possible to apperceive without being self-aware: "Representations belong to the totality of a possible self-consciousness" (A113) – a merely possible self-consciousness. Similarly, "Whether this representation ['I think'] . . . ever actually occurs does not here concern us" (A117n). How can apperception be self-consciousness, yet awareness of self be optional? Finally – a different form of the same puzzle – at A108 and elsewhere, Kant runs *being* one subject and awareness of it together.

One way to resolve these tensions is to say, with Strawson, that like the 'course of experience', apperception also includes not actual self-consciousness but only a 'potential' for it.[23] In addition to the general problems with this move examined in Chapter 6:I:5 and 6:II:2, applying it to apperception faces the decisive objection that Kant does not say that apperception is a potential for self-consciousness; he says it is self-consciousness (B132; see B68: "This consciousness of self (apperception) is the simple representation of the 'I' "). Another way is to argue that Kant does not mean that every act of apperception must yield self-consciousness; he means that apperception is an act of a self-conscious *being*, whether or not self-consciousness is present in every case. This might work for Kant saying that the mind need not be aware of itself or a representation in every case in order to have representations, but for Kant's flat declarations that apperception is self-consciousness, it does not work any better than Strawson's move. If the mind is a global representation, another and better tactic becomes available.

Kant's remarks about self-consciousness make sense only if he does not mean actual, full self-awareness (awareness[RR-CS]; empirically actual consciousness, in the sense of A117n). On the view that the mind is a global representation, we can make this distinction because we can distinguish between *representations of self* and *awareness of self.* A mind can represent itself to itself without being aware of doing so in many different ways, as I said earlier – in memory, during sleep, while I am totally absorbed in some activity, and so on. Distinguishing between representations of self and awareness of self in this way thus immediately resolves the puzzles just delineated. If Kant means the representation 'I think' by 'apperception', then he could easily have thought that my acts of apperception are self-aware in the sense that they represent me and yet hold that I need not be aware of myself. One can have representations of oneself of which one is unaware. If so, one could represent oneself as 'I think' without being aware of doing so. That would resolve the puzzles nicely.

There would then be no difficulty at all in Kant maintaining as he does in the first paragraph of §16 that a representation of self, 'I think', must accompany any representation that is anything to me and yet that I need not be aware of having the representation it accompanies. Equally, my representations could have a *necessary relation* to 'I think' without my being aware of having them. Even if the 'I think' representation is the mind, I need not be aware that I am this representation. We can also explain why a representation must be related to 'I think' to stand in one self-consciousness now. By a self-consciousness Kant would be seen to mean a being that represents itself. That is the *same* as containing the representation 'I think'. (Yet it is still not the same as actually being aware of itself.) Does representation of other things require self-awareness, then, or not? The answer, we can now see, is yes and no. To represent objects (those that are something to me, at least), I must *represent* myself; but I need not be aware of doing so. This distinction is the key, I think, to solving many puzzles about self-awareness in Kant.

Finally, could a global representation represent to itself? It can *represent* anything a mind can represent – objects, itself, and its subject (of course, if the mind is a global representation, the latter two collapse into one) – but *to itself*? To discharge the self/homunculus, it must be able to do so. Here the best I can offer is an argument from ontological parsimony, Occam's Razor. There is nothing more mysterious about a global representation representing to itself than about me representing to *myself*. The phenomenon is pretty mysterious and philosophers tend to hide other mysteries under it (e.g., the mystery of intrinsic representation), but saying that it is a matter of a representation representing to itself not only would not deepen the mystery, but would reduce the number of mysteries by one. Instead of two mysteries, the mystery of representation and the mystery of the subject of representation, we would have only one, the mystery of representation.

How is it so much as possible that representing to myself consists in a global representation representing to itself? I do not see a *special* problem here. A global representation is 'one consciousness' of a multiplicity of representations, and I am not aware of myself as anything more than that. Indeed, to the extent that I appear to myself to be anything at all, I do appear to myself to be a representation. I appear to myself to be a being that is aware of objects and itself, and that is just the way a representation appears. Why need *me* being aware of *myself* as the common subject of *my* representations be anything more than a global representation presenting *itself* to *itself* as the common subject of what *it* represents. It might be objected that I *know* I am me, but a global representation does not know, surely, that it is it! Well, if it is me, then it does know that it is it – and me! (It need not know itself *as* a global representation, of course.) There is a deeper source of resistance to the suggestion I am making. If it is mysterious how I acquire the awareness of a being (the being who is in fact me) *as me,* surely positing that I am a global representation makes these even more mysterious. More mysterious? I do not see how, but I would agree that it leaves it just as mysterious. Thus, on this point the suggestion seems to make no progress. So far as *this* puzzle is concerned, that is true. If the analysis of Chapter 4:1 is right, nothing is going to remove this mystery. Moreover, that the suggestion cannot answer an epistemological question should not blind us to the contribution it can make to the ontological one.

7 Mind as representation: final considerations

As a reading of Kant, a number of additional considerations favour the idea that the mind is a global representation, a representation that also represents itself. First, Kant was an idealist, at least about the knowable. Everything that can be known consisted for him of representations. But he thinks that we know some things about the mind – for example, that it exists, is unified, is active, and has contents. If so, at least these aspects of the mind must be representational.

Second, the idea that the mind is a representation was around in Kant's time. Descartes may have held a version of it (see Descartes' reply to Hobbes' objections to the *Meditations*). On Kant's reading of Leibniz's notion of minds as monads, "simple beings endowed with representations" (A283 = B340), Leibniz too held something close to the same idea. To a first approximation, Kant kept Leibniz's representations, did away with the simple substance, and substituted a simple global representation. (Whether that is a real substitute or just Leibniz's idea in different dress is another matter.) That is to say, the idea would not have appeared to be as peculiar to Kant as perhaps it does to us.

Third, the idea fits nicely with the doctrine of the unknowability of the noumenal mind. Arguing for this claim and dealing with some objections to it is a main task of Chapter 10:4–5.

Finally, as I said at the end of Chapter 2, the idea that the mind is a global representation allows Kant to integrate synthesis, unity, and ASA into one neat package. Here is how. To synthesize a collection of representations and/or their objects into a global object, Kant believed, these representations must all be the representations of a single, unified mind; they must have a common subject (A350). If the single, unified mind *is* a global representation, that ties synthesis and unity together. Now for ASA. The crucial part of the notion is that each of us is aware of him- or herself as the common subject of a great many representations, the same subject of each of them. For it to be possible for us to do so, these representations must be united in a global representation. If the subject *is* this global representation, then being aware of this representation *just is* to be aware of oneself; that is to say, the theory of ASA and the theory of the global representation are parts of a single theory. If the mind is a global representation, any possible mystery is also removed from the fact that the global representations, acts of synthesis, and the subject of representation are all unified in the same way. In fact, the idea would be a 'supreme unifying principle' of a Kantian theory of mind. Of course, as well as the representation, we must also posit something that 'realizes' this representation/mind, but we have to do that no matter what theory of mind we adopt. Moreover, as Dennett and the Churchlands argue, this something need not be at all 'mindlike' – propositional or sentential. Once we accept this, the idea that the mind, so far as we (now) know it, is a representation becomes more palatable.

How palatable? The most I have shown is that the idea is not obviously absurd and that it fits at least some of the things a theory of mind has to be able to explain. There are certain things it does not explain. As we saw earlier, it does not explain how I know, when I am aware of myself, that I am aware of *myself.* This, as I said, I do not think we can explain. It also does not explain the ascriptionlessness of self-reference or the barrenness of ASA. These latter can be explained, as we saw in Chapter 1, by the semantics and epistemology of ASA. But the idea does fit and/or explain some other things, as we have seen, and it has the additional advantage of parsimony. As we will see in the next chapter, it also helps us to interpret some of Kant's more puzzling remarks on the nature and knowledge of the mind. From none of this does it follow, of course, that Kant embraced the idea. I have certainly not shown conclusively that he did, but I think the evidence I have assembled is at least suggestive.

In this chapter we have explored four main theses. The first two were LP′ and LP^2:

(LP′) Representations can represent something to me only in so far as it is possible for 'I think' to accompany them.

(LP^2) For it to be possible for 'I think' to accompany representations, for them to stand together in one self-consciousness, they must stand together in one consciousness.

The mind, the self, the understanding, the thing that thinks, not only has representations; it is a representation.

One can have a representation of oneself of which one is unaware; thus, one can have representations of oneself without being aware of oneself.

Each of them deserves more attention than it is receiving at the moment. To my mind(!), the idea that the mind is a global representation and the distinction between having representations of oneself and being aware of oneself are especially worthy of attention. If philosophy and cognitive science began to explore ideas such as these, we might begin to regain some of the sense of ourselves as a whole that we have lost, some sense of the kind of thing we are. We might also begin to regain some sense of what it is to be one of that kind of thing, of our ability to synthesize and integrate vast ranges of individual representations of objects, and of being the common subject of such representations.

10

Nature and awareness of the self

The task of this chapter is to examine the second set of remarks on the mind new to the second-edition TD, the ones beginning half-way through §24 and running to the end of §25 (B153–9). The most interesting thing about these remarks is that Kant seems to indicate in them that we are directly aware of our actual selves, not just representations of self, apparently in flagrant violation of his doctrine of the unknowability of the noumenal mind. In my view, not only do these remarks not violate his claim that we have no knowledge of the mind, they are of real interest in their own right. Before we turn to them, I want to look at an important challenge to all standard readings of Kant's view of the mind, and also to mine. On all standard readings, Kant at least saw the mind as a single entity in some significant sense. (Even a global representation is a single entity: it is individuated, meets clear criteria for identity at a time, and comes complete with important unity and continuities over time.) The challenge comes from Patricia Kitcher. Kant's real view, she tells us, was that there is no subject, not in any sense that entails that it is a significantly unified entity. Kant's 'I' is nothing more than a contentually interconnected "system of diverse states":

> In conceiving of mental states we must think of them as belonging to a continuing interdependent system, hence we talk about a continuing consciousness or I, we use the representation 'I'. . . . [However,] . . . there is in fact no inner intuition of a self.[1]

The reason there is no inner intuition of a self is that there is no self to intuit.

1 What the subject is and what we can know about it

A good way to situate the resulting disagreement is to start with the basic distinction between the subject (self, soul, mind, thing that thinks) as it appears to itself in the manifold and diverse representations of inner sense (perceptions, emotions, desires, etc.) and the subject as it is, the thing that has these representations. In addition to diverse representations in inner sense and an unknown noumenal nature, the subject of experience also has transcendental properties – its unity and its ability to synthesize (apperception) – that seem to hover in between. They are not intuitable as objects in inner sense, yet we are aware of them. In fact, we can be aware of them in two ways: by inferring that we need these properties to have the kind of representations we have and, for some of them at least, by acts of ASA. The awareness of these properties seems to hover between the phenomenal and the noumenal because it seems pretty clearly to be more than phenomenal awareness of representations and their objects in inner sense, and the more is in the direction of being knowledge of the mind as it is. This gives rise to two questions: Can we know enough about the mind for a disagreement such as the one between Kitcher and the standard view to arise, and if so, about what aspect of the mind do they disagree? Consider the first question first.

At first glance, Kant's views on what we can know about the mind look quite unequivocal:

> If anyone propounds to me the question, 'What is the nature (*Beschaffenheit*) of a thing which thinks?', I have no *a priori* knowledge wherewith to reply. (A398)

All we can know of the mind is how it appears to us. However, this remark may be saying less than it appears to be. Kant made the remark in the context of the Paralogisms. He may be saying no more than that we know nothing of the mind's structure or composition – whether it is simple or composite, for example, or whether it persists in some special way. Knowing nothing of something's composition or persistence is quite compatible with knowing other things about it, in particular things about its functioning. (Kemp Smith translates '*Beschaffenheit*' as 'constitution'. That word would give added plausibility to what I have just said. Unfortunately, a word as specific as 'constitution' may not be warranted, only a general word like 'state' or 'nature'.) Kant's doctrine of the unknowability of the noumenal is confusing and in its generality is probably best left for separate investigation.[2] Let us remind ourselves, however, that it is actually far from clear that Kant wanted to bar *all* knowledge of the mind as it is. He certainly thought that any awareness of the mind *as the object of a representation* falls short of revealing the mind as it is, at least as far as we can know; representations are highly doctored artefacts of the mind's sense-making activities, and there is no guarantee, to say the very least, that they correspond to the way anything actually is. But what about properties that we infer, properties the mind has to have in order to do what it does? Though Kant seems never to have addressed the topic directly, it is hard to see how he could have viewed these functional necessities as mere features of the mind as it is represented to itself. In his system, propositions describing these necessities have to be about the mind as it is. Yet we are directly aware of some of these properties in ASA (unity and acts of judgement – apperceptive synthesizing activities) and can infer others. Furthermore, that our representations might never *describe* the mind as it is does not entail that we are never *aware* of the mind as it is. In fact, as we will see later, Kant seems to suggest that we are aware of the mind as it is.

Taking my view for present purposes as representative of the standard view, when I say that the subject of experience is a global representation and Kitcher says that, in a certain good sense, there is no subject of experience, what aspect of the mind are we disagreeing about? There are three options: the representational states of inner sense, the substrate that underlies them, or the bearer of the transcendental properties revealed in ASA and acts of judgement or inferred as functional necessities. I think we both have mainly the third aspect in mind. If what I have said about propositions about the mind's necessary features is correct, however, talk of the mind's transcendental properties is also talk about the underlying substrate – functional, not structural, talk, perhaps, but still talk – so we are also disagreeing about the second. Indeed, even if what we disagreed over was the mind's representations, we would still be disagreeing about an aspect of the mind as it is; representations are properties of *the mind,* the mind as it is, not a representation of the mind. Representations are real states and have a nature, which like any other nature may or may not be well represented by our representations of them; yet only the latter would not tell us *anything* about the mind as it is. In short, a disagreement about whether there is a subject and, if so, what it is like is really a disagreement about all three aspects of the mind, representations, substrate, and transcendental properties. In addition, representations and transcendental properties can themselves be represented and not just by doing acts but also as objects of inner sense (see Chapter 4:5). If so, we are also disagreeing about an aspect of the-mind-as-represented.[3]

This disagreement between Kitcher and me about the existence of a subject in Kant is the topic of Section 2. Then in Section 3 we will turn to Kant's texts. Recall that Kant discussed the mind in two places in the second-edition TD. The first runs from §15 to §18. We still have §18 of that discussion to consider; it is the topic of Section 3. The second is the strange discussion that begins without warning half-way through §24 and continues to the end of §25. We examined its peculiarities in Chapter 5:4; now we will consider what it says about our awareness of our actual selves and how to reconcile this with the unknowability of the noumenal mind, in Sections 4–6.

2 Is a subject merely a formal requirement?

The transcendental aspect of the mind is its being unified and having the ability to apperceptively synthesize. In addition to the two positions just mentioned, that it is a global representation and that there is no such thing, there is a third and more traditional position – that the mind is a simple, persisting substance. We have seen Kant deny that we have any reason to believe that the mind is *or is not* any such thing, either as we are aware of it or as it is (Chapters 7 and 8). So it is startling to find Kitcher saying that "unlike Descartes, Kant conceives of [the] self not as a simple substance, but only as a system of informationally interdependent states".[4] Kant did not think that the mind is not a simple substance! To the contrary, he insisted that the mind *could be* just that. He just insisted that we have no *theoretical reason* to believe one way or the other; the question has to be settled on practical grounds. He himself probably held – on practical grounds, as an article of faith – that the mind is simple and persisting: a noncausal, self-legislating, simple substance. If he held that so much is even possible, that would seem to be fatal to Kitcher's view.

Nevertheless, in so far as we can be aware of what it is like, we are not *aware* of the mind as simple *or* persisting *or* substantial. For the mind as we *know* it (are either directly or inferentially aware of its properties), that leaves the other two possibilities: that it is a global representation or that there is no such thing. If Kitcher does not see Kant modelling the mind as a global representation, a single unified consciousness that uses transcendental apperception to unite diverse representations and/or their objects into one global object, then how does she see him modelling it? To repeat, "In conceiving of mental states we must think of them as belonging to a continuing interdependent system, hence we talk about a continuing consciousness or I, we use the representation 'I' ". The 'I' is nothing more than a contentually interconnected "system of diverse states",[8] an ensemble of particular representations synthesized from and in turn synthesized into other, contentually related representations. Kant's subject, far from being the agent of the transcendentally apperceptive faculties that do this work, is merely a *product* of them; the self is a *result* of synthesis, not the agent of it! Equally, the various activities of synthesis are blind, subpersonal processes, either undirected or directed merely by blind, subpersonal algorithms.[6] The ghost of Hume casts a long shadow over Kitcher's reading: at the representational level at least, the mind consists in total of nothing more than particular representations of particular internal or external events and states of affairs tied together by relationships of contentual interdependence. Kitcher thinks Kant supplemented Hume's bundle theory to an even smaller extent than I do (see Chapter 8:4).

If the mind is nothing more than an ensemble of particular representations, then what is going on when we refer to it? One answer, and I think Kitcher's, is that, for Kant, postulating a subject of experience is merely a formal requirement of having and thinking about representations, roughly on a par with putting 'It' in 'It is raining'.[7] All that a mind actually consists of is representations. They can include a *representation* of oneself as subject, but such a representation either represents nothing or misrepresents the ensemble, representing it *as* a single subject; for as Kitcher reads Kant, a judgement having a subject is in reality nothing more than its belonging to a contentually interconnected system of mental states.[8]

At first glance, a few passages in Kant might seem to support a 'subject as formal requirement' reading, for example, A354. There Kant speaks of 'I think' as a "formal proposition of apperception," which must be taken as (taken as referring to?) "a merely *subjective condition* of that knowledge". Also at A354, Kant notes that a person must think of him- or herself as one and indivisible, and then says, "We have no right to transform [this] . . . *merely subjective condition* . . . into a concept of a thinking being in general". 'Subjective condition' sounds very much like 'formal requirement', a condition of the representation of oneself that is no guide to how one actually is. Then at A398 he says that "the 'I' in 'I think' . . . is only the formal condition, namely the logical unity of every thought." However, these remarks are not expressing views even remotely like Kitcher's. The question is, Whatever we might take the words to mean now, what did *Kant* mean by terms like 'formal condition' and 'subjective condition'? Certainly nothing in the slightest like the purely conventional or arbitrary condition imposed on sentences like 'It is raining' by syntactic form. Kant's formal conditions are conditions on an intuitional, conceptual, and recognitional system that is able to represent objects. Representations being located in time, the Categories applying to them, their having a single common subject – these are the kinds of thing Kant meant by 'formal condition' (A266 = B322–A268 = B324). And the latter, that thoughts require a single, unified conscious subject, is also what Kant meant by 'subjective condition'. For him, calling something a formal condition or a subjective condition implies the very opposite of their having no existence in fact. Formal conditions are conditions to do with the *form* of representation (see Chapter 8:6). The term 'subjective condition' has an added twist. When Kant says that the way we appear to ourselves, namely, as simple and without parts, is a subjective condition of representation (A354), what he means is that though we cannot but represent ourselves as being that way, we may not actually be that way. Here again, however, Kant does not mean to imply that I have no reality or am nothing more than this appearance and my particular representations.

The statement on A398, " 'I think'... is only the formal condition, namely, the logical unity of every thought, in which I abstract from all objects", may appear to be a little awkward for my reading. But does Kant mean that 'I think' is only a condition of proper semantic form or some such? Or does he mean that 'I think' refers to some real form or framework of experience, but one that we tend to over-interpret as a representation of a simple, persisting substance (Chapter 8:6)? If A398 is making the former claim, it would be the only passage in the whole *Critique* saying such a thing. Thus, I think we should conclude that it is making the latter one: "This 'I' is... the... *form of consciousness,* which can accompany the two kinds of representation [intuition and concept]" (A382; my emphasis). When Kant called the unity of the subject 'a merely logical unity,' he certainly had something in mind (see Chapter 7:4), but not that there is no subject. To the contrary, Kant clearly thought that the subject of experience is *something* more than its particular mental states, though of course we might disagree about what more.

With Kant's meaning of 'formal condition' clarified, let us return to the main issue, Kitcher's claim that for Kant the "continuing consciousness or I" is nothing but "a continuing interdependent system", about which "we use the representation 'I' ".[9] Kitcher offers strikingly little to justify this attribution. Furthermore, far from entailing that there is no substantial mind, the proposition that the mind is a continuing interdependent system of mental states implies that there *is* a mind, namely, this continuing system. When we use "the representation 'I' ", as we are using it, it may be referring to this system *quite unmisleadingly.* I clearly have no quarrel with the idea that the mind is a continuing interdependent system of representations; I too think that Kant saw the mind as such a system. Kitcher just overlooked some central properties of such a system: unified recognition of multiple objects of members of the system in a single act of apperception as a single global object, and the system's ability to be aware of itself as itself and as the single common subject of the representations in the system it is. Add these to her account, and it would be close to mine – and to Kant's, I would argue. The problem with Kitcher's account is not that she sees the mind as a system of contentually interdependent states, the problem is that she has a far less unified conception of such a system than Kant had and undersells the self-activating, initiating powers that Kant thought a unified global representation has. In the language of §18, to which we will turn shortly, informationally or contentually interdependent states would be something like the empirical unity of consciousness, but representation of objects also requires the transcendental unity of apperception. Kitcher seems to think that there are only two alternatives. Either Kant held that the mind is a simple substance or he accepted that it is a mere bundle of diverse states, non-Humean only because the items in the bundle are tied together by bonds of contentual dependence, and the 'self' is not the initiator of activity in the bundle but a product of it. As we have seen, there is a third alternative: he could also have held that the mind is a global representation, an active, unified self-representing representation.

An unenriched Kitcher-like account has problems with other things Kant said, too. We have already mentioned his conviction that a substantial, simple, and persistent mind is at least possible. It is hard to see how a system of informationally interdependent states could be such an entity, but a global representation could; at any one time, there is only one per person, and it could be simple (noncomposite) in itself, whatever the complexity of its object. Nor can I see that it could not be a substance; even if its persistence consists entirely of the causal continuities supporting memory and dispositions, that would be enough. It is also hard to see how informationally interdependent states without enrichment could be aware of themselves collectively as the single common subject of those states. Kant also attributed active, spontaneous, determining powers to the mind, powers of synthesizing, concept-using apperception (see, e.g., B153) If such powers are powers of the 'I' (and how could powers like these be entirely subpersonal?), that would be hard to reconcile with the 'I' being a diverse system (even harder if it is a mere formal condition). As Pippin has pointed out, Kant's granting the mind spontaneous, active powers raises a real problem for most simple information-processing construals of Kant's model of the mind, though not necessarily for all materialist accounts, as we saw in Chapter 1:3.[10]

In this regard, Allison has a curious in-between position.[11] On the one hand, he understands the unity of the mind and its active powers in a way that Kitcher does not and sees that ASA gives us awareness of single, unified acts of apperception, not just of diverse members of a system. On the other hand, however, he still insists that awareness of such acts is not awareness of an actor, because for Kant there is no such actor, only the act. My response to such a mixed position is this. To be aware of the act *just is* to be aware of the actor; the actor being a global representation, act and actor are two aspects of the same thing. As I mentioned in Chapter 4:4, part of what leads Kitcher and Allison to their strange reading is that she ignores and he misinterprets Kant's distinction between being aware of something as the object of a representation and being aware of oneself via performing acts of apperception. Kant certainly denies that we represent ourselves as an object when we are aware of ourselves as subjects. However, Kitcher and Allison misinterpret this to be denying that we are directly aware of ourselves at all, when what Kant actually meant was that we are directly aware of ourselves but in a different way, namely, via acts of transcendental (nonascriptive) designation (A355). Saying that our awareness of ourselves is different from normal representational awareness is not the same thing as saying that we have no direct awareness of ourselves at all.

To close this section, let me consider two objections whose failure is informative, one to Kitcher's position and one to mine. The objection to Kitcher's position is the obvious one that if my mind is merely diverse mental states, there could be no warrant for referring to these representations as *my* representations, representations that *I have,* and so on. Strawson mounted a version of this objection in his attack on what he calls the no-ownership theory.[12] The response is simple. Any account of the mind must, of course, make room for ascription of psychological states and reference to self with its peculiar semantics. But if someone wants to object that a bundle is just not the right *kind* of individual to be the object of acts of nonascriptive self-reference and so on, then I would invite him or her to tell us what is the right kind of individual. Since no one can do that, the objection fails. A bundle is a perfectly good, if somewhat sloppy individual, so representations could be ascribed to it, and we have no more reason to say that it could not be aware of itself as itself than that a simple, persisting substance could not. *Some* kind of thing has to be able to be aware of itself, because we are aware of ourselves and we are some kind of thing. But no one has any clear idea of what the limits are on *what* kind(s) of thing. Of course, Kant thought that Humean bundles need to be supplemented even to be conscious, let alone aware of themselves, but now we are back to the objection that we considered earlier in this section and found potent.

The other objection is to the mind as a global representation. 'This view is wrong in principle', it might go. 'To have the kind of unity you have been talking about, the mind would have to be a structure that *has* representations, not a thing that itself merely *is* representations'. I do not see why. Everything we know of minds, whether our own or others, whether directly or by inference, is representational. Of course, we now think that we have pretty good reason to believe that this representational system is material, namely, the brain (or the brain in a world). But in that case, the brain is not just a nonrepresentational something-we-know-not-what that has representations as properties; it *is* representations, in part. Nor would what I am saying violate the unknowability of the noumenal mind. There is a great deal we do not, maybe even cannot, know about the microstructure and relationships of this brain/representational system, and direct awareness of representations and inference to the functions required to have them is not apt to take us very far. Moreover, we can never be *certain* that we know even the things we think we do know. Nor do the recent claims that the brain is a nonsentential connectionist machine threaten what I am saying. If the brain is nonsentential, then so is our representational system. To summarize, I do not see that we need postulate anything other than something representational – in particular, a global representation – as the thing that has representations; but on the other hand, there is no reason why a global representation could not be a material object such as the brain. (On this general topic, also see Chapters 1:3 and 10:4–5).

Kitcher's neglect of the unity of consciousness and so on may be the result of neglecting something else in Kant. So far as Kant's view of the empirical unity of consciousness or representations is concerned, her reading may well be adequate; indeed, she adds a wrinkle, that empirical representations are not only associated but also contentually dependent. However, the empirical unity of consciousness is just an "association of representations" (B139–40); Kant distinguished it from the transcendental unity of consciousness and apperception. Kitcher ignores this distinction and that may be one of the sources of the gaps in her account. Kant's best account of the distinction is in §18, the mind-boggling but mercifully short subsection entitled 'The Objective Unity of Self-Consciousness'.

3 §18: empirical versus transcendental apperception; foundationalism

The distinction between empirical and transcendental apperception is about two things. The first is a contrast between freedom we have and freedom we do not have in how we relate our representations to one another, a contrast closely related to the issue of foundationalism. The second is a contrast between two kinds of unity in interrelated representations. Epistemology has been moving in an antifoundational direction for many years. Many philosophers now believe that representations can be related to one another in a never-ending variety of different ways, indeed that our representing activities can themselves be carved up into representations in a never-ending variety of ways and that no one way is privileged, canonical. Everything is perspectival; versions reign supreme. Kant was as well aware as anyone that representations can be tied together in different ways. Like Hume, he called this activity 'association', and once we get over the threshold of structure needed to have representations at all, he was as empiricist about what kinds of association we can set up or find among our representations as any associationist psychologist or contemporary epistemologist. He called the activity of tying representations together in the different ways left open to us 'empirical apperception', and the awareness of them and/or their objects that results is 'empirical knowledge'. As we saw in Chapter 6:I:5, he also thought that it is possible to have representations, or at any rate sensations, without tying them together to any great degree at all, certainly not by recognition of relations among them. He thought animal experience was like this.

But Kant was aware of something else. Before we get the opportunity to start exploring the endless variety of associations, we must first have representations to explore. We must also have the capacity to recognize associations among them, that is to say, to be aware of multiples of them in single acts of recognition. The possibility of variability and optionality rests on a foundation of unity. Moreover, for this recognitional unity to be possible, we must be able to organize the raw manifold of intuitions into representations under concepts, and there are sharp constraints on the concepts that can do the job. As Kant saw it in his doctrine of the Categories, we must always use concepts of number (we must be able to individuate representations and/or their objects), concepts of quality (we have to be able to discern at least some properties in what we are representing), concepts of modality (we have to be able to decide whether what we are representing exists or is just imagined), and concepts of relation (we must be able to discern at least some relations, indeed some causal relations, connecting the objects of our representations). Perhaps the kind of representations animals have are open to having any concepts whatsoever applied to them or their objects, but being able to recognize and think about representations has nothing like those degrees of freedom. Though we have a great many options in how we can apply most concepts to most objects, to use any optional concepts at all, we must first use some about which we have no option. We examined the details of this story in Chapter 6, especially the problems that arose for Kant over the concepts of relation, but it is hard to find anything objectionable in this minimal foundationalism. (Kant's more ambitious hopes for Euclidean geometry and Newtonian physics are entirely another matter, of course.) The activity that achieves recognitional unity under concepts is TA; the distinction between empirical apperception and TA is of a great deal more than merely historical interest.

Let us start with empirical apperception. 'Empirical apperception' and 'empirical consciousness' are terms for optional acts of synthesis open to us on the basis of what is suggested by our representations ('the evidence'), what we feel like imagining, what we are dreaming, and so on. Empirical apperception is the activity and empirical consciousness is the result of synthesis under "empirical laws, the laws, namely, of association" (B152). Empirical association also seems to be the business of reproductive imagination (see A118), after intuitions are placed within the forms of intuition, space, and time, and perhaps after the synthesis of apprehension (see Chapter 6:I:3). Syntheses of reproductive imagination can be achieved in many different ways, as many as the ways that one can tie objects together by patterns of association. TA enters the picture in the following way. Associative syntheses can come about in at least two different ways. One is automatically, under the causal influence of mere 'feeling and desire'.[13] The other is as the result of a deliberate process of recognition and connection. (Deliberate does not necessarily mean introspectible.) The latter requires TA and is a realm of nonoptionality. Before we can deliberately explore associations by acts of judgement (e.g., generate and test hypotheses), we have to be able to recognize the items being explored and so connect them to other such items as to recognize the totality of them as a single, unified object of representation. These acts of recognition proceed by the application of the Categories and they are not optional; that is one reason why Kant called them transcendental.

If there are concepts or propositions that must be applied to perform these acts of recognition, they would have a strong claim to be foundations of representational knowledge. One way to see what these concepts are is to see that Kant is arguing in effect that in order to recognize something, it must be *individuated*. In addition to temporal and, in many cases, spatial placement, this requires the application of concepts. Individuation uses at least two and probably three of the four classes of Categories, namely, quantity (number and quantifiable magnitudes), quality, and probably modality (existence status). It is not completely implausible to say that we need to apply some relational concepts, too. From the perspective of our current antifoundationalism, all this is very interesting. As well as the boundless conceptual freedom for which contemporary epistemology propagandizes, perhaps there is also an unvarying abstract framework within which this freedom must be exercised. Kant says strangely little about individuation, at least by name. The only place where he discusses the subject explicitly is in the appendix on The Amphiboly of Concepts of Reflection, in the context of the argument that Leibniz confused conceptual and sensible representations (examined briefly at the end of Chapter 6:I:5). Nevertheless, the notion is central to the argument of TD.

Kant's main point in §18, then, seems to be something like this. Our synthetic activities must individuate particular representations and unify them as global representations. We can do so, however, in a virtually limitless number of different ways. Once we have satisfied the constraints of individuation and unification, only "circumstances or empirical conditions" limit us in what we can do (B139). Moreover, to achieve the degree of unity necessary for a global object, every possible synthesis need not be performed. We can see a number of things as the object of a single representation and yet remain uncertain about a great many of their relationships and features. Probably some representations can coexist without being connected at all; the defense mechanisms of psychoanalysis, the existence of unidentified contradictions in our beliefs, slips betwixt what we believe and what we do, and so on, all attest to this. Nevertheless, if I am to recognize and judge at all, my representations must be located in time and combined with others in a global representation. Thus, the transcendental–empirical distinction marks the balance between the necessity of unity and of individuating particular representations, on the one hand, and the huge range of different ways of combining representations that these necessities still leave open, on the other.

This distinction gives rise to a question. On which side does science fall? Is it a body of nonoptional propositions or a body of optional ones? The empiricist tradition opted for the latter view, but Kant himself restricted the range of possible combinations much more sharply than that. He also restricted them more sharply than I have done. As we saw in Chapter 6, he had a particular axe to grind about 'synthetic *a priori*' knowledge, in the form of mathematics, Euclidean geometry, and Newtonian physics, and so tried to argue that the framework within which we have conceptual freedom had to be a Euclidean and Newtonian one. This is one of the ideas that motivates commentators like Cassirer to see the distinction between intuition and synthesized, conceptualized global representations as a distinction between a rhapsody of impressions and a system of representations that instantiate a true scientific theory.[14] It is important to see that we can abandon Kant's excessive enthusiasm for Euclid and Newton and yet still retain the more abstract claim about the need for a framework of quantities, qualities, existence statuses, and relations. The distinction between empirical and transcendental apperception is designed to capture this mix of freedom and constraint. Empirical apperception captures the idea that different patterns of combination are possible, transcendental (pure, original) apperception the idea that some pattern of association using the concepts just mentioned must nevertheless be achieved if we are to have representations that can be recognized and judged at all – one moreover that yields a unified, global object. It is very important to understand that transcendental and empirical apperception need not be different acts; one apperceptive act could satisfy the requirements of both kinds of apperception. (I should also note that Kant gave a rather different account of the distinction in the *Anthropology* [*Ak* VII: 134n].)

This claim that there is an element in apperception that is transcendental, that is, nonoptional, is what Kant added to Hume's epistemological story. Hume urged that representations and their patterns of association are purely contingent. For the representations Hume had in mind and for the kinds of associations he identified, Kant agreed; but, he argued, Hume had overlooked the fact that they must also be unified. This requires another kind of representation, namely, a global one, and another kind of association, namely, recognition under concepts. (On occasion, Kant also used the distinction between apperception and inner sense to capture this distinction, e.g., on B154.) We can now see more clearly what Kitcher missed in Kant's view of the subject of experience: the recognitional, unifying aspect of apperceptive synthesis, the peculiar unity that subjects have, in which diverse representations are united as a single representation in a single unified consciousness. This unified representation or consciousness, I have argued, is what I am, is me. These activities also being what is spontaneous and self-legislating in the subject, Kitcher managed to miss a great deal of what mattered most to Kant about the mind.

4 §24 and §25: self-awareness and the noumenal mind

With the clarifications of the preceding sections in place, we can now turn to the question with which I opened the chapter: When I am aware of myself in ASA, am I aware of my mind itself or am I aware merely of a representation that may neither present me to myself as I am nor even make me aware of my actual self? It seems intuitively obvious that I am aware of my actual self, however correct or incorrect my beliefs about it may be. I am certainly aware of global representations, so if I am a global representation, I am aware of the mind as it is, the noumenal mind. It does not follow, of course, that I am aware of *everything* about this global representation/mind, but *any* awareness of the mind as it is would still appear to be in violent conflict with Kant's general theory of the limits of representational knowledge and particularly his two central claims that (1) we do not know ourselves as we are and (2) we are immediately aware only of our representations. Whatever exactly Kant was denying when he denied that we have knowledge of things as they are, he clearly intended this denial to apply to ourselves, too. Yet my reading entails that he held that we are aware of our actual selves. As we shall see, some remarks in §24 and §25 of the second-edition TD certainly seem to say just that. These same remarks also seem to delineate a clear, though also clearly confined, exception to (2). The full extent of the exception is closely connected to a tension in Kant's thought between his official idealism and a lifelong sympathy with a certain form of realism. Guyer has documented this tension extensively. (Indeed, before his work, the tension was not even widely known.)[15] In the rest of this chapter, we will confine ourselves to the place of this exception in Kant's theory of self-awareness.

Kant held that representations of oneself are just as 'theory-laden' and prone to error as representations of the world (see, e.g., B68). This notion is enjoying considerable popularity right now, thanks to the Churchlands and others. Kant's general view of representations was that a lot of activity of the mind goes into making them what they are. This activity is governed by the mind's own imperatives, not necessarily by patterns in even our intuitions, let alone in what is intuited. Representations are thus highly processed appearances that may not represent things as they are at all. Now even of representations in general we might want to distinguish being aware of something from describing it, being aware of what it is like. When Kant ruled out *knowledge* of things as they are, did he intend to rule out *all* direct awareness of them or only awareness of what they are like? That is to say, did he intend to rule out all direct epistemic contact with things as they are, period, or did he intend to say only that representations may give us a picture of things that is entirely incorrect, or at least a picture that we can never have any reason to accept as correct? Another form of the question is to ask, Even if we can never know that the *sense* of our concepts and sentences corresponds to the way things are, did Kant intend to rule out that we ever *refer* to anything as it is? Kant used the terms 'immediately given' (or better, unmediatedly given; '*unmittelbar . . . gegeben*') (A375) and 'immediate consciousness' (*unmittelbare Bewußtsein*) (B277n) for what I am calling direct epistemic contact. 'Immediate awareness' is as good a term for this intuitively clear but descriptively elusive phenomenon as any. Whether or not there is any real difference between immediate awareness of something (reference to it) and awareness of what it is like in general, for Kant there is with respect to representations of self in ASA.

Appearing to oneself as the intentional object of a representation (taking up an attitude to oneself, seeing oneself in a mirror, etc.) raises no problem for Kant's general theory of representation. In these cases intuitions are involved, and where intuitions are involved, I am aware of myself only via highly doctored representations that may very well not be representing me as I am. I have the same immediate awareness or lack thereof of myself when I am aware of myself as the object of a representation as I have of things in general as they are. The interesting questions arise about awareness of myself as myself, of myself as subject. Here is one of the things Kant said about it:

> In the synthetic original unity of apperception [the representational base of ASA], I am conscious of myself, not as I appear to myself, nor as I am to myself, but only that I am. (B157)

Kant says the same thing in virtually the same words on B423n. That is to say, I am immediately aware of *myself*, that it is *me* who is, not just of some representation of myself. (The 'just' is important; even if I am immediately aware of myself, I am still aware of myself by having a representation, of course; immediate awareness of myself *is a representation of myself.* To be sure the representation is nonintuitive and contains no sensible or analogous manifold [though it is not supersensible], but it is still a representation.) Kant advanced the same view in the first edition, too. At A108, he says that the mind is *aware* of its identity, that is to say, does not just infer it. Similarly, at A354, he tells us that the 'I think' "asserts my existence immediately". The 'bare consciousness' of A346 = B404 (a passage that remained the same in the second edition) is likely a version of the same idea. We are aware of our actual selves. Yet Kant was also at pains in both editions to insist that we *know* nothing about our self as it is. He goes on:

> I have no *knowledge* of myself as I am but merely as I appear to myself. (B158)

This is an interesting state of affairs.

The most important passage in the *Critique* for this issue of awareness of one's actual self is the strange passage that begins with three asterisks half-way through §24 of the second-edition TD and runs to the end of §25 (B153–9). Nothing like it exists in the first edition. I speculate that Kant added it in the second edition because he knew that he was not going to be discussing ASA in the chapter on the Paralogisms, except incidentally, and felt that the topic was too important to be left out altogether, precisely because of the *prima facie* danger it posed for the doctrine of the unknowability of the noumenal mind. And this doctrine is indeed one of the two main topics of the passage. (The other is the question of how one identifies oneself as subject with oneself as object already examined in Chapter 8:7.)

Of what am I aware when I am aware of myself as subject? There are four possibilities:

(1) my mind as it is, the noumenal substrate of myself and my representations,
(2) a global representation which the mind is, so that being aware of this representation is being aware of my mind, whether or not this gives me any knowledge of what I am like,
(3) a highly processed representation, whether the global representation or some other, which does not give me immediate awareness of my mind as it is and may well not represent me as I am, and
(4) nothing; when I think I am aware of myself as subject, all that I am aware of is a ensemble of particular representations in inner sense. The rest is an illusion generated by the formal requirements of experience.

In recent decades, every one of these positions has been attributed to Kant by one commentator or another – every one except (2). Sellars and Walker urge (1) on us; one is immediately aware of oneself as one is. Chisholm and Waxman opt for (3); one is immediately aware merely of a representation that presents nothing outside itself. In Kant's jargon, the self as we are aware of it is a mere appearance. Kitcher tries to pin (4) on Kant, obviously, as do Allison and nonreferentialists such as Rosenberg and Powell; one is not aware of even the little offered by (3).[16] The difference between (3) and (4) is subtle, because there will be some kind of representation of oneself as subject in both cases. One important difference is that advocates of (3) hold but advocates of (4) usually deny that 'I' and its cognates are referring expressions, and we have already rejected it for that reason. Granting that Kant could avoid flagrant inconsistency (something that many have not been willing to grant him), if we take (1) to be Kant's position, we would need to insist that, for him, this awareness gives us no *knowledge* of the mind unless the texts absolutely rule this out. That would leave us with (1), (2), or (3). For reasons given in Chapter 9, I think that (2) is Kant's position. However, (2) is also a version of (1), if the remarks in Section 1 about representations being a feature of the mind as it is are right, so in advocating (2) I am also advocating a version of (1).

The problem for commentators who ascribe standard versions of (1) is to see how Kant could have meant what he said. Sellars is representative of this position.[17] They do not pay enough attention to the implications of transcendental designation – the difference between awareness via acts of apperception and awareness via intuition-based representations, as well as between immediate awareness of something and knowledge of it. The same is usually true, interestingly enough, of commentators who ascribe (3) or (4) to Kant. Waxman is one of the few commentators who pays much attention to B157 and the pages around it. Of being "conscious, of myself, . . . that I am"

(B157), he says that "just like any other phenomenon, it is a mere representation and so must, in its turn, be referred to a transcendental ground in the faculty-endowed mind." He then introduces the strange notion of a nonintuitive *intellectual phenomenon* to account for the consciousness of which Kant here speaks.[18] Behind this reading is Waxman's fundamental conviction that Kant could not allow *any* form of immediate awareness of anything that is, only of representations, so he could not have been allowing it in the special case of ASA, a conviction that suffuses his whole book. Even Guyer, who goes further than anyone else in the direction of finding an important realist strain in Kant's thought, stops short of ascribing immediate awareness of anything other than representations to Kant.[19] Commentators just cannot believe that Kant could ever have abandoned or said things inconsistent with his professed (but never argued) conviction that we have immediate awareness only of representations. (This conviction is expressed more clearly in the first-edition discussion of the Fourth Paralogism than anywhere else in the first *Critique*.)

Part of the reason why even commentators like Waxman and Guyer draw back from ascribing belief in any form of immediate awareness to Kant, even immediate awareness of oneself, is that they have a strong and clearly justified conviction that Kant wanted symmetry between knowledge of self and knowledge of the world. As Waxman demonstrates with great persuasiveness against Strawson and others,[20] Kant insisted that we have no better awareness of ourselves than we do of things other than ourselves, not even of the temporal order of our representations (see Chapter 8:5). I agree that Kant wanted to maintain such a symmetry, but I think he went further in the direction of immediate awareness on both sides than Waxman or Guyer think he did. The 'world' side will have to await another occasion, but on the 'self' side, I take Kant exactly at his word when he says, "The soul in transcendental apperception is *substantia noumenon*".[21] Moreover, I think he was not only right on his own terms to say so, he was on to something important.

To solve the problem that faces commentators who ascribe (1) and to change the minds of those who ascribe (3) or (4), we have to understand what Kant is really saying on B157 and throughout §24 and §25. The first move is to bring back the notion of transcendental designation (see Chapters 4 and 7), the nonascriptive form of reference to self in which one refers to oneself as oneself without "noting in [oneself] any quality whatsoever" (A355). It yields awareness of self in which "nothing manifold is given" (B135). Even though Kant mentions it explicitly not even once in the second edition, the notion is clearly at work on B157 and throughout §24 and §25. That Kant fails to mention it by name can only be considered astonishing. Kant does keep his old distinction between awareness via apperception and awareness via intuitions or appearances (B153), and that is what he uses to introduce us to an awareness of self that is not an appearance of self. "Consciousness of self" is awareness of no more than acts of apperception: "I exist as an intelligence which is conscious solely of its power of combination"

(B158–9), of "the activity of the self" (B68), but it is awareness of *self.* In this awareness of self, I am aware of myself merely as myself. As he told us clearly both in the first edition and early on in the second-edition TD but fails to reiterate here, in awareness of oneself by doing acts of apperception, "nothing manifold is given" (B135). Even though the 'consciousness of myself' of which Kant speaks is plainly full recognition, full awareness$^{RR\text{-}CS}$ as we called it in Chapter 3:1 (see the next paragraph), the emptiness of this kind of self-awareness will allow Kant to save his claim that we have no *knowledge* of the self.

Yet Waxman, Chisholm, and Kitcher all insist that Kant's view was either (3) (Waxman and Chisholm) or (4) (Kitcher). Even Walker, who believes that Kant espoused the implausible version of (1), claims that, in doing so, he made an awful slip, which opened a floodgate to knowledge of the noumenal.[22] What have these commentators missed? Various things. As we have just seen, one is the use Kant makes of his notion of transcendental designation. Another from the immediate context of B157 is that they misinterpret the words that follow Kant's claim that I am aware that I am. "This *representation* is a *thought*", he says, "not an *intuition*". Everything hangs on how we interpret the word 'thought' here. It is tempting to think, even hope, that Kant meant 'inference' by it. If he had, the claim that we do not know the noumenal mind is safe, and one or the other of (3) or (4) has to have been his view. However, it is clear that he did not. First, if he had meant 'inference', the whole passage at B157 would have been so obviously compatible with the unknowability of the noumenal and the passivity of inner sense as hardly to be worth saying, let alone emphasizing. Second and more conclusively, in the surrounding sentences the evidence that Kant meant some form of immediate awareness is unmistakable. In B155, by 'something thought' Kant means something 'given to myself', but given to myself 'beyond intuition'; he does not mean something inferred. 'Thought' in this sense is "consciousness of self" (B158) and of its "power of combination" (B159) and the "spontaneity" of it (B157n). In fact, it is the immediate but non-intuitional awareness we get when we "designate the subject . . . transcendentally, without noting in it any quality whatsoever" (A355). There is nothing inferential in that; it is a form of awareness$^{RR\text{-}CS}$, and one is aware of oneself, not just a representation.

Waxman does not think Kant meant something inferential by 'thought', either, but he still does not think Kant meant any form of immediate awareness. He thinks 'consciousness of self' here is still a phenomenon; that is to say, it is not an immediate awareness of anything other than the representation itself. However, it is not an intuitive phenomenon; it is an *intellectual* one! Though Kant, interestingly enough, could characterize the superrepresentational knowledge of things other than ourselves for which he argued in the Refutation as 'intellectual intuition',[23] I think Waxman's account is flying in the face of so much of what Kant says that we would need very strong reasons to accept it. Kant did, after all, say "I am conscious of myself, *not* as I appear to myself" (B157). In fact, I think Waxman misses the real genius of Kant's remarks. In the remainder of this section, we will look at the evidence that Kant was talking about immediate awareness of oneself in B157–9 and some putative evidence against the idea. In the next section we will examine the distinction between 'bare consciousness' and 'knowledge' of something that seems to me to contain the real genius behind what Waxman mislabels as 'intellectual phenomenon' and that Kant himself once mislabelled as 'intellectual intuition'.

Later Kant says that "I am conscious of my own existence as determined in time" (B275) – conscious of *my own* existence, not just the existence of an appearance. He makes the same point even more unmistakably in the long footnote to the second-edition preface: "I am conscious of my own existence in time . . . , and this is more than to be conscious merely of my representation" (Bxl, n). This consciousness is the 'thought' presenting myself of B157, the consciousness of self of B158, the bare consciousness of A346 = B404. This awareness does not involve a sensible modality (B429): eyes, ears, etc.[24] Nor does it involve any sensible or analogous intuition: images, appearances, objects of representations, and so on, or any spatial or temporal positioning (B158–9). Thus, Kant cannot call it appearance or phenomena, so he calls it thought. (Note that *he* does not call it 'intellectual phenomenon'.) By 'thought', however, here he means a kind of immediate awareness, the kind that one gains by doing, not by sensing: doing synthetic acts of representing, not sensing objects (Chapter 4:2). This 'thought' is the immediate awareness we have of our synthesizing activities. Like immediate awareness of self, our awareness of our synthesizing activities tells us virtually nothing about them: "Nothing but the unity of the act . . . as an act . . . is conscious to itself . . . without sensibility" (B153). This 'consciousness' of the unity of the act no more gives me *knowledge* of the act of representing than referring to myself using 'I' gives me *knowledge* of myself. However, it is still immediate awareness of the act. Waxman argues that even in passages like this one, Kant does not *have* to be taken to be talking about awareness of the act itself.[25] Perhaps, but that does seem to be what he is talking about, and if we can take him this way without doing violence to anything else in this theory, why should we not do so?

A particularly clear and forthcoming statement of Kant's belief that one is aware of one's actual, noumenal self in this 'thought', not just an appearance, occurs in the passage in the discussion of Third Antinomy cited in an earlier chapter:

> Man, . . . who knows all the rest of nature solely through the senses, knows (*erkennt*) himself also through pure apperception; and this, indeed, in acts and inner determinations which he cannot regard as impressions of the senses. He is thus to himself, on the one hand phenomenon . . . and on the other hand, in respect of certain faculties the action of which cannot be ascribed to the receptivity of sensibility, a purely intelligible object. (A546 = B574)

The word 'knows' (*erkennt*) is unfortunate here, given that at B157 Kant denies that we have knowledge of ourselves. Otherwise, however, Kant is again saying that we are aware of our actual self, but not via 'impressions of the senses'. Both ideas at work here, that we are aware of our actual self and that it comes by doing acts of experiencing, play an indispensable role in Kant's thought. They are both crucial, for example, in the Third Antinomy. Without either of them, Kant's whole attempt to reconcile the possibility of free will in reality with determinism at the level of appearance would instantly collapse. Likewise, the first, combined with the idea that our immediate awareness of ourselves gives us no knowledge of ourselves, plays an indispensable role in the Refutation of Idealism.

As I said earlier, Kant could not have believed (4), that ASA makes us aware of nothing at all. Kitcher claims to present some evidence that this *was* his view. Such evidence would also help Waxman. Kitcher's evidence is that Kant retreats from the view that we are aware of the actual self ((1) or (2)) as often as he maintains it.[26] She then cites A103 and B134 as examples of retreat. Neither of them shows any sign of retreat. All either passage says is that we need not be aware of the self *to have representations of objects*! (As we saw in Chapter 3:3, Kant allows this in other places too, e.g., A117n and B132.) They say nothing about awareness of one's actual self at all. Kitcher also cites A381, the passage from the concluding section of the first-edition Paralogisms chapter that we have seen before:

> In what we entitle 'soul' everything is in continual flux and there is nothing abiding except (if we may so express ourselves) the 'I', which is simple solely because its representation has no content, and therefore no manifold, and for this reason seems to represent, or (to use a more correct word) denote, a simple object. (A381–2)

Yet this passage immediately goes on to say that our awareness of this 'I' is not via intuitions of it and thus does not give us knowledge of it. That is to say, Kant precisely *avoids* saying that we are not immediately aware of the soul! What he focuses on are its introspected *qualities;* because they are not fixed and abiding, he says that these could not give us *knowledge* of the soul. In short, not a single passage Kitcher cites actually favours her reading. By contrast, there are a number of passages that favour (2) as the right reading. It takes a grasp of his insights into transcendental designation and ASA, however, to see how he could say that we are immediately aware of ourselves without contradicting himself.

5 Why immediate awareness of the noumenal mind is not knowledge

Having shown that neither (3) nor (4) could be right, let us now see if we can help advocates of (1) with their problem. My variant of (1), position (2), faces the same problem: How could Kant have meant what he said when he said that we are immediately aware of the mind as it is? How can Kant possibly have said this without doing violence to his theory that we do not know even the mind as it is? Curiously enough, whether we *are* aware of ourselves as we are was not even an issue for Kant on B157. He took that for granted; we are aware not just of appearances but also of at least some apperceptive acts of recognition and judgement. For him, the important issues were two. First, how can this fact be reconciled with the equally vital fact that "we intuit ourselves only as we are inwardly *affected* [by ourselves]" (B153)? Second, as he was at pains to insist in both editions, "it would be a great stumbling block, or rather would be the one unanswerable objection, to our whole critique" (B409) if we had knowledge of the self as it is. Can awareness of one's self as it is be squared with the doctrine that we know nothing about it?

Here is how Kant sets out what he has to reconcile. He puts his positive claim like this:

> I, as intelligence and *thinking* subject, know (*erkenne*) myself as something *thought* (*gedachtes Object*), in so far as I am given to myself beyond that which is in intuition,

but then goes on:

> and yet know myself, like other phenomena, only as I appear to myself, not as I am to the understanding. (B155)[27]

I do not merely infer myself, I am given to myself – but I am given 'to the understanding' as 'something thought', not to sensibility as an appearance or phenomenon. The first 'know', the one in the first line of the passage quoted, muddies the water, but otherwise Kant's position is clear. Awareness of oneself as subject, of oneself simply as oneself, is nonascriptive – so it is not knowledge, awareness of qualities. But it is still a 'bare consciousness' (A346 = B404; see B158). Only awareness via intuitions in inner sense of one's actual self would give one knowledge of oneself of the sort Kant wants to proscribe. Awareness of oneself as subject gives one no intuitions, no awareness of properties, so it is not proscribed, indeed is not *knowledge* at all. Kant concludes:

> Consciousness of the self is thus very far from being a knowledge of the self. . . . For knowledge of myself I require, besides the consciousness, that is to say, besides the thought of myself, an intuition of the manifold in me, by which I determine this thought. (B158)[28]

This 'consciousness of the self' is what transcendental designation yields – nonascriptive awareness of myself as myself gives me, or need give me, no awareness of any of my 'qualities' whatsoever.

That is why immediate awareness of myself in ASA does not require intuitions, not because it is some bizarre 'intellectual phenomenon' as Waxman suggests. That is also why it gives me no knowledge of myself. Indeed, it is so little a knowledge of myself that nothing in it could even conflict with any knowledge of myself, as the chapter on the Paralogisms argues. 'Concepts without intuitions are empty'; so is immediate awareness of myself in ASA. Waxman worries that any immediate awareness of anything as it is, oneself included, would require some sort of 'migration' of information from the superrepresentational beyond to my representations.[29] As we can see, there is no danger of that, because awareness of myself as myself *contains* (virtually) no information. Put another way, Waxman's worry is that any immediate awareness of anything would open a communication channel from the superrepresentational beyond to the realm of representations.[30] Nonascriptive awareness of self may or may not *open* a channel of communication to my actual self; whichever, nothing comes down it, except perhaps the peculiar pseudofact that it is myself of which I am aware (and perhaps that this self is cognitively active). Immediate awareness of myself is thus quite compatible with not knowing myself as I am. Contrary to Walker, no noumenal floodgates are opened.

In summarizing our discussion, two things are clear. First, in ASA one is aware of oneself, indeed of oneself as oneself, not just a highly processed appearance whose object appears as oneself; immediate awareness via apperception is different from what any intentional object could give us. Second, ASA gives us no *knowledge* of ourselves. Immediate awareness of one's noumenal self is thus compatible with complete lack of knowledge of it. Laid out this way, Kant's position plausibly accommodates two powerful convictions. It accommodates the Churchlandian intuition that incorrigibility is mythology, that we can be just as wrong about ourselves as about anything else, and it accommodates the conviction shared by philosophers as different as Descartes and Shoemaker that I have immediate awareness of my actual self, at least that I am and that it is me that is.

6 Why did Kant claim that we are immediately aware of the noumenal mind?

When it would have been so easy for Kant to stick with the opposite view, why did he accept, indeed apparently take for granted, that in awareness of self as subject one is aware of one's actual self? Kant himself does not tell us what his reasons were, but one can think of a number of possibilities. The first is this. I can wonder if I am really aware of anything that appears as the object of an experience. Maybe my eye-sight has suddenly gone haywire; maybe I am a brain in a vat; maybe this feeling feels like pain only because I am so tired; maybe I no longer know what 'jealous' means; and so on. As the Churchlands and others have argued, I can have just as many doubts and be just as wrong about states of myself as about states of any other thing.[31] But I cannot be wrong that it is me of which I am aware, not when I am aware of myself as subject. This awareness of myself as myself is not prone to those errors; it has Shoemaker's "immunity to error through misidentification."[32] As I argued in Chapter 4:4, I have this immunity only when I am aware of myself as the subject of an experience I am having. I can doubt and be wrong about anything that appears as the object of an experience, including even myself *when I appear as object*. When I am aware of myself as subject, however, I cannot. Here I am aware of myself on the basis of having experiences and doing actions. Whatever being I am aware of as subject when I am aware of representations by having them and as agent when I am aware of actions by doing them will be me. Indeed, being aware of a being in this way likely *is what it is* for that being to be me. With awareness of self as subject, there is no room for any slippage between how things are and how things appear to be. (There may still be room for doubting and wondering, but it would take too long to explore that bypath.)

Kant did not actually advance this argument, though he assembled many of the pieces of it (see Chapter 4:4). He did advance another one. Perceptions and apparent perceptions of the normal kind – the sensible and analogous contents of inner sense – are not only subject to all manner of error, they are clearly in part at least the result of activities of one's own mind. It is hard to see how a representation of oneself as subject could be the result of mental processing in the same way. How could I have a skewed or distorted picture of simply being me? This representation does not represent properties, so there is nothing for the mind to manipulate or distort. *How* one appears to oneself may be subjectively conditioned and subject to error, just as the Churchlands insist. But merely appearing to myself as myself is not, not when I am aware of myself as subject. For Kant, this absence of manifoldness is extreme. Awareness of oneself as subject is nonspatial and even nontemporal. ("Time is . . . in me" [A363] – awareness of oneself as oneself is not time dividing; see Chapter 8:6.) Indeed, this awareness is not conditioned by any form of experience at all (B157n). In short, there is nothing that could change the presentation of oneself as subject from being a correct, if utterly barren, presentation to being a mistaken one. If so – and this is a vital point – we have suddenly run out of reasons for saying that the presentation of self as subject is mere appearance. Where could it go wrong?

There is one more possible reason why Kant simply took for granted that we are aware of our actual self, that awareness of myself as myself is not just awareness of another intrapsychically generated representation. If someone tells me that I do not have immediate awareness of objects around me, I can form at least some idea of what he or she might mean. I might think, for example, that all experience of objects is corrigible. But if somebody tells me that I do not have immediate awareness of myself, I would immediately invite the person to tell me what he or she means by 'immediate awareness' here. I have no idea what is being denied. What would the contrast be? Generalized, the thought here is the following. If no representation could present an actual object even in principle, the statement 'We are not aware of actual objects, only appearances' would cease to have any use. What would we be missing, what would awareness of actual objects be like? This is a version of an old problem with sense-data solipsism – if one's representation even of oneself is merely a sense-datum that gives one no immediate awareness of anything outside itself, then the very contrast between sense-data and anything else collapses. The points I have made in this and the preceding paragraphs also seem to me to be a further and decisive reason for rejecting Waxman's idea of an intellectual phenomenon.

Though Kant was no slave to Cartesian preoccupations, I suspect he simply took it as obvious that when I say 'I think', I could not be wrong that it is me doing the thinking. I may not be thinking, but I could not be wrong that it is me doing whatever I am doing (nor, therefore, that I exist).[33] He accepted Descartes' argument, *cogito ergo sum*, for existence (A355), why not for accuracy in who it picks out as existing? As we saw in Chapter 4:I, Kant also gives what seems to be at least a precursor of the argument that I must be aware of myself as subject to know that any property described non-token-reflexively is a property of me (see A346 = B404 and B422). This further forecloses on any possibility for error. In addition, it is at least hard to imagine being aware of something as the subject of an experience that I am having *(in fact* having; I need not know that I am having it) without being aware of that thing as me. Kant may have had some inkling of this point, too; he always runs awareness of being a subject and awareness of the 'I think', of oneself as subject, together as equivalent. All of this lack of room for error about awareness of myself as myself leaves little room for any notion that I do not have immediate awareness of my actual self.

Kant says, "I am conscious of myself, not as I appear to myself, nor as I am in myself, but only that I am" (B157). This sentence summarizes his whole position. I am not aware of myself as a manifold of intuitions, an object of representation. Nor am I aware of what I am like – of what a realized global representation is actually like. All I am immediately aware of in myself is – being me, the common, unified representation of my representations. I am aware that it is me, that I am, perhaps that I am cognitively active – and that is all.

All this gives further reason for thinking that of the available options about the nature of the mind, the idea that the mind is a global representation was Kant's best choice. We know that representations exist and that they have the unity of a single representation. We do not *know* that any other mental kind of thing exists. From the point of view of ontological simplicity and parsimony, then, the idea that the actual mind, the mind as it is, is a representation would be the best option. Ontological plurality of the sort found in Descartes, Leibniz, and sense-data solipsists alike would be replaced by ontological neutrality and at least the possibility of ontological unity. In addition, if the mind is a representation, that would maximize the chances that the mind's representations of itself, the mind's representations of this representation, correspond to the mind as it is, at least in broad and abstract outline. Of course, we could still never know. Yet, because a global representation could be spontaneous and self-legislating, the possibility of free will and of immortality, the possibilities Kant most wanted to protect, would remain safe. As will be obvious by now, the idea seems to me to have considerable appeal.

7 Coda: the mind in the two versions of the deduction

The first block of chapters in which we attempted to construct an overview of Kant's model of the mind as a whole, Chapters 1–4, ended with a purely exegetical coda. There would be a certain symmetry to ending the second block of chapters, Chapters 5–10, in the same way. Our exegetical question here will be, How does the second edition's model of the mind as a global representation relate to the model laid out in the first edition, in which the capacity to synthesize is not treated as a power of a representation? To begin with, the contrast is not this clear, as we have seen. In the first edition the power to synthesize is certainly a power of a noumenal apparatus "which as substratum underlies the 'I' " (A350), a substratum about which we know, or at any rate know that we know, nothing. However, Kant also laid out the notion of the global representation (general experience) in the first edition (A110). Equally, he certainly kept some notion of the noumenal mind in the second edition. If so, any change was simply in the extent to which Kant thought that the "abiding and unchanging 'I' (pure apperception) which forms the correlate of all thoughts" (A123), so far as we are aware of it at all, itself simply *is* a global representation. Here there was at the least a change of emphasis; Kant much more clearly views the mind as a global representation in the second edition than in the first. And there is a corresponding shift in the doctrine of synthesis; in the second edition, it becomes an activity of adding representations to representations (B130–1).

Perhaps connected to these shifts, the expression 'I think', which appears for the first time in the first edition only as late as the chapter on the Paralogisms, is front and centre from the beginning of TD in the second. In general, self-awareness, or at least self-representation, is far more prominent in the second edition than in the first. As we saw in Chapter 9:4, it even appears as a principle linking representation of objects to the need to use categorial concepts; nothing like this is to be found in the first edition. By the second edition, Kant may also have been toying with a notion of self-representation in which one can represent oneself without being aware of oneself, a possibility we considered in Chapter 9:6. Nevertheless, as we also saw, the fundamental strategy of the subjective deduction otherwise remained the same in both editions and the fundamental concern remained the same: to identify the mental constraints on representation of objects. There is no clear way in which representation of objects requires self-awareness.

There is also a shift in the second edition in the direction of realism. The idealist doctrine that we are immediately aware of only our own representations has exclusive possession of the first edition, officially at least, and the manifestations of realism that suddenly appear in TD and the Refutation of Idealism in the second edition sit pretty badly with this official idealism – a tension that is at the very least well buried in the first edition. This tension is never resolved in either edition of the first *Critique*, which is why I said the shift was 'in the direction of', not 'to' realism in the second edition. In this chapter, we have examined one of these two manifestations, the one expressed in the idea that we have a direct consciousness of ourselves that is nevertheless not a knowledge of ourselves, the one found in §24 and §25 of TD. The ideas out of which the shift are built were all there in the first edition – the idea of being aware of oneself via acts of representing rather than as an object of representation and the idea of 'transcendental designation', that is to say, nonascriptive reference to self. However, in the second edition, Kant uses them to generate the realism about our awareness of ourselves that we have examined in this chapter. The other manifestation of this realism appears in the new Refutation of Idealism: awareness of "other things outside me" (B276), "an external thing distinct from all my representations" (Bxli, n), that is to say, awareness of things other than oneself in *both* the empirical and the transcendental sense, is necessary for a certain kind of awareness of self. There is nothing like this claim in the first edition, not explicitly anyway. As we have just seen, Kant was at pains to argue that this realism is compatible with the unknowability of the mind as it is; nothing like this argument is to be found in the first edition either. One of the most curious things about Kant's theory of representations is that his immense sophistication about how representations are generated and what they are like was married, officially at least, to a view of what we can be immediately aware of, namely, representations alone, that is simplistic and unattractive and probably committed him to solipsism. But that is a story for another occasion.

One strange change in the second edition is the disappearance of the doctrine of transcendental designation, at least on the surface. Kant's important analysis of unity, composition, memory, temporal representation, and identity worked out in the course of refuting and diagnosing the Second and Third Paralogisms also disappeared. Many other things stayed pretty much the same, however, in particular the three vital doctrines of synthesis, of the unity of consciousness and apperceptive action, and of apperceptive self-awareness. As was said at the beginning of Chapter 1, from these and the doctrine of the mind as global representation there is still much to be learned.

8 Concluding remarks

When working with empirical cognitive scientists, I have often been struck by their inclination to stick to topics that are manageable, even at the risk of leaving major issues unexplored. The good sense of this strategy for an empirical scientist is obvious. Philosophers impose no such restriction on themselves – certainly Kant did not; to avoid the problem that not a great deal is known about some of the things we consider, we carefully keep our work at a high and conceptual level of abstraction. The problems with this approach are obvious, but it has a corresponding advantage: we are free to take the whole of the mind for our province, not just those parts of it that can now be understood.

Here Kant can still teach us. However far we are from understanding the empirical details, the abstract conceptual map of the mind that he left us contains a great deal that has not been superseded by subsequent work. His theories of our capacity to synthesize representations, of the special unity that allows us to do so (the unity of consciousness and apperception), of the peculiar features of our awareness of ourselves as opposed to our psychological states (apperceptive self-awareness), and of the nonascriptive form of reference by which we gain this awareness (transcendental designation) still have much to offer us. Indeed, I think that even some of his critical work still has ideas from which we can benefit. In particular, Kant's analysis of how the diachronic aspect of the unity of consciousness does not require identity of person or mind, the analysis he sketched in the course of refuting the Third Paralogism, may be both brief and obscure, but it still goes beyond what contemporary research on the topic has achieved. The same is true, though less obviously true, of the implications of his work on synchronic unity for issues of individuation. Yet not only his contributions but even his topics are often neglected in contemporary writings. That is true *a fortiori*, of course, of his more exotic views such as the idea that the mind not only has but is a global representation and his theory, built on the idea of a global representation, of what we have called the representational base to explain the peculiarities of reference to and awareness of self.[34]

It should be relatively easy for contemporary workers to reconnect with Kant. Despite the forbidding face of his prose and his reputation as a died-in-the-wool antimaterialist, in a number of ways he is surprisingly accessible. First, though he was indeed hostile to materialism, that was as a matter of faith, not doctrine. Whatever his faith, his model of the mind was and had to be studiedly neutral ontologically, for the reasons we have given. The same is true of contemporary functionalism, of course – only one of many parallels between the two bodies of doctrine. Second, the background picture of the mind that he brought to his work will be congenial to many contemporary workers. Kant thought of the mind as a system of representations and functions for manipulating representations. And he thought of its awareness of itself as largely on a par with representational awareness in general; self-awareness has some special features, lack of manifoldness in particular, but these peculiarities rest on a foundation of broad underlying similarity with other kinds of representation. Since that is also the dominant contemporary view, anything Kant is able to contribute to it should be easy to incorporate. In general, I think contemporary workers should be paying more attention to Kant. As a general theorist of awareness, Kant, as I said earlier, is still a great deal more than a mere earlier stage in our intellectual history.

Notes

1. The contemporary relevance of Kant's work

1 William James, *Pragmatism* (Cambridge, Mass.: Harvard University Press, originally published 1907), p. 269.
2 Patricia Kitcher, *Kant's Transcendental Psychology* (New York: Oxford University Press, 1990).
3 Karl Ameriks, *Kant's Theory of Mind* (Oxford University Press, 1983); Kitcher, *Kant's Transcendental Psychology;* C. Thomas Powell, *Kant's Theory of Self-Consciousness* (Oxford University Press, 1990); Wayne Waxman, *Kant's Model of the Mind* (New York: Oxford University Press, 1991); Henry Allison, *Kant's Transcendental Idealism: An Interpretation and Defense* (New Haven, Conn.: Yale University Press, 1983); Paul Guyer, *Kant and the Claims of Knowledge* (Cambridge University Press, 1987); and Richard Aquila, *Matter in Mind* (Bloomington: Indiana University Press, 1989). Unless otherwise indicated, references to these authors will be to the works cited here.
4 The best-known example in our own time of the strategy of insisting that Kant submit to the authority of contemporary orthodoxy is P. F. Strawson, *The Bounds of Sense* (London: Methuen, 1966).
5 See Powell. Because of our natural inclination to take identity to be about similarity (and, I would add, about a relation of one thing to another: 'These two chairs are identical'), Perry prefers to talk about individuation and to call the relation that makes two person-stages stages in the life of one individual a 'unity relation'. This usage does two things. It helps to produce a clearer way of talking about what philosophers have called 'personal identity', and it provides the clearest possible illustration of how the notion of unity has come to be tied to the notion of identity ("Introduction: The Problem of Personal Identity", John Perry, ed., *Personal Identity* [Berkeley: University of California Press, 1976]).
6 References to the *Critique of Pure Reason* will be included in the text. 'A' refers to the pagination of the first edition of 1781 and 'B' to the second edition of 1787. (There were later editions of the *Critique,* but these were the only two that Kant prepared himself.) I will use Norman Kemp Smith's 1927 translation, *Immanuel Kant's Critique of Pure Reason* (London: Macmillan, 1963), except where otherwise noted. A reference to only one edition means that the passage in question appeared only in that edition.
7 Unity is not the only topic on which Kitcher misses things in Kant. She also fails to discuss Kant's claims that apperception yields the special kind of self-awareness that I am calling ASA, and thus misses the interesting insights he offers into this peculiar form of self-awareness.
8 Strawson, *The Bounds of Sense,* p. 32; for his current view, see "Sensibility,

Understanding, and the Doctrine of Synthesis", in Eckard Förster, ed., *Kant's Transcendental Deductions,* pp. 47–68 (Stanford, Calif.: Stanford University Press, 1989).

9 Later, Strawson says something even harsher about Kant's views on synthesis, that they "belong neither to empirical psychology nor to analytical philosophy of mind" (*The Bounds of Sense,* p. 97). So far as I can see, he offers little by way of reason for saying this.

10 The word 'formal' is Wilkerson's: "The unity of consciousness . . . is a formal unity consisting simply of the formal fact that experiences are mine". *Kant's Critique of Pure Reason* (Oxford University Press, 1976), p. 52. It is not clear what he means by it (any more than it is clear what Allison means by his apparently cognate term 'logical' [p. 144]). Presumably they would draw on Kant's use of such terms as 'formal subject' and 'logical subject'. However, by these terms Kant meant something to do with form, something to do with general nature, function, or essence, not some alternative to how the mind really is.

11 Kant, *Anthropology from a Pragmatic Point of View,* trans. Mary Gregor (The Hague: Nijhoff, 1974) (Ak. VII:140–1), second-to-last emphasis mine. (The Akademie pagination is included in this translation; *Gesammelte Schriften,* ed. Koniglichen Preussischen Akademie der Wissenschaften, 29 vols. [Berlin: de Gruyter, et al., 1902–]). Hereafter I will cite the work in the text as *An,* followed by a page reference to the Akademie edition.

12 The question of the natural and the normative in Kant's theory of the mind is thoroughly explored by Gary Hatfield in *The Natural and the Normative* (Cambridge, Mass.: MIT Press / Bradford Books, 1990). On this issue, it is interesting to put two views of Kitcher's together. On the one hand, she argues that Kant meant to be talking about real properties of the mind when he discussed synthesis and unity, not just formal requirements of some kind (chap. 1 and p. 94). Yet she also argues that 'Kant's real self' is nothing more than a unification resulting from representations being contentually interconnected, a process that requires at most a purely formal self, not a real one (pp. 122–3; see her "Kant's Real Self", in Allen Wood, ed., *Self and Nature in Kant's Philosophy* [Ithaca, N.Y.: Cornell University Press, 1984], pp. 111–45). I introduce this issue in the next chapter and discuss it more extensively in Chapter 10.

13 Kitcher, p. 25.

14 D. C. Dennett, *The Intentional Stance* (Cambridge, Mass.: MIT Press / Bradford Books, 1987), p. x. See also idem, "Toward a Cognitive Theory of Consciousness", in *Brainstorms* (Montgomery, Vt.: Bradford Books, 1978), especially p. 149, where Dennett amusingly makes the same complaint about cognitive psychologists. Dennett goes on to say that he himself has such a theory. It is now available, in idem, *Consciousness Explained* (Boston: Little, Brown, 1991). I will touch briefly on why the theory he presents in this book cannot at any rate do the whole job in Chapter 2:1. It is worth noting, however, that he says virtually nothing about the mind's various kinds of unity (though he has lots to say about varieties of disunity) and makes only one brief and somewhat dismissive remark about the form of self-awareness I call ASA (p. 428n). Other philosophers have studied aspects of ASA (not under that name, of course) – for example, Castañeda (one of the people Dennett dismisses) and Shoemaker. We will examine the issue in Chapter 4.

15 Jerry Fodor, *Modularity of Mind* (Cambridge, Mass.: MIT Press, 1983), p. 107; my remarks on the term 'isotropic' draw on pp. 103–19.

16 Here I am talking about inner sense (psychological states) as though it contrasts with outer sense (objects, events, and so on represented as located in space). In the passages from which I am quoting here, Kant talks the same way, but his considered view was that outer sense is *part* of inner sense, the part that represents objects, events and the like in space. On this way of thinking, Kant's strictures about empirical psychology would not apply to inner sense per se, but to representations (as opposed to their objects) and to such objects of representations as are nonspatial. (If I think about a pain or an emotion, the pain or emotion is an object of thought but a nonspatial one.) We will take a brief look at the vexatious concept of inner sense in Chapter 4.

17 Kant, *The Metaphysical Foundations of Natural Science* (1786), trans. with intro. by James Ellington (Indianapolis, Ind.: Library of Liberal Arts, 1970) (Ak. IV). This translation includes the pagination of the Akademie edition; for the remainder of the current discussion, I will refer to the work in the text, using this pagination.

18 In addition to the reasons I have just given for why we have no clear sense of what Kant thought about the mind, another reason has been the state of scholarship on the topic until recently. Until 1990, Karl Ameriks' book was the only full-length study in English of Kant on the mind. This book has some serious problems. It deals only with the chapter on the Paralogisms, and it makes the mistake of thinking that Kant is presenting a positive theory there. (Kant actually tries to prove that no positive theory of the mind's composition is even possible.) In addition, Ameriks says little about synthesis or synchronic unity, or even Kant's contribution to our understanding of ASA. Yet Kant's ideas on the latter appear more clearly in the first-edition chapter on the Paralogisms than anywhere else.

19 Some people, e.g., Owen J. Flanagan, even refer to this method as the method of transcendental deduction, apparently intending to honour Kant as its originator (*The Science of the Mind* [Cambridge, Mass.: MIT Press / Bradford Books, 1984], p. 180). What makes this curious, the intention to honour Kant notwithstanding, is that Kant himself used the term 'transcendental deduction' for something entirely different. He used it not as a name for his method but as the name for an argument: the *deduction,* in the crucial section of the same name(!), that use of certain concepts is necessary for experience to have an object. Yet Flanagan even says that Kant himself called his method transcendental deduction! Kant devised his deduction by using this method, but he did not call the method a deduction. He called it transcendental argument.

20 Wilfred Sellars, " . . . this I or he or it (the thing) which thinks . . . " (Presidential Address, Eastern Division of the American Philosophical Association, 1970), *Proceedings of the American Philosophical Association* 44 (1970–1), reprinted in *Essays in Philosophy and Its History*, pp. 62–90 (Dordrecht: Reidel, 1974). Sellars gives one of the earliest accounts of functional classification, in a Kantian context, in *Science and Metaphysics* (New York: Humanities Press, 1968). Patricia Kitcher, "Kant's Real Self", in Allen Wood, ed., *Self and Nature in Kant's Philosophy*, pp. 113–47 (Ithaca N.Y.: Cornell University Press 1984) (see also pp. 111–12 of idem, *Kant's Transcendental Psychology*); Dennett, *Brainstorms,* pp. 111 and 122–6; Ralf Meerbote, "Kant's Functionalism", in J. C. Smith, ed., *Historical Foundations of Cognitive Science,* pp. 161–87 (Dordrecht: Reidel, 1989); Powell, esp. pp. 200–6. Robert Pippin has mounted an interesting objection to certain forms of this reading of Kant in "Kant on the Spontaneity of

Mind", *Canadian Journal of Philosophy* 17 (1987), pp. 449–76, arguing that Kant's claims about the spontaneity of the mind would be difficult to reconcile with a view of the mind as a set of information-processing functions. I look at this argument briefly in Section 3.

21 See, e.g., Colin Martindale, "Can We Construct Kantian Mental Machines?" *Journal of Mind and Behaviour* 8 (1987), pp. 261–8.

22 Hilary Putnam in his recent work is a partial exception (*Representations and Reality* [Cambridge, Mass.: MIT Press, 1988]); Saul Kripke may be another ("Naming and Necessity", pp. 334ff., in G. Harman and D. Davidson, eds., *Semantics of Natural Languages*, pp. 253–355 [Dordrecht: Reidel, 1972]) and also published with changes, as *Naming and Necessity* (Cambridge, Mass.: Harvard University Press, 1980).

23 As he says at B420, "If materialism is disqualified from explaining my existence, spiritualism is equally incapable of doing so; and the conclusion is that in no way whatsoever can we know anything of the constitution of the soul" – *know* anything; we can only believe. (Kant is here talking about knowing whether the mind could exist without a material world, but I think he would apply the argument he gives more generally.) Much the same could be said about the passage on immaterialism in *What Real Progress Has Metaphysics Made in Germany Since the Time of Leibniz and Wolff?* (1804), trans. T. Humphrey (New York: Abaris, 1983). Commentators such as Ameriks (chap. 2) and Henry Allison ("Kant's Refutation of Idealism", *Monist* 72 [1989], pp. 190–208), who find theoretical arguments in Kant for accepting immaterialism, rely on very dubious texts. And how do they think Kant reconciled immaterialism with the doctrine of the unknowability of the mind as it is?

24 R. C. S. Walker, *Kant* (London: Routledge & Kegan Paul, 1978), p. 108.

25 Ameriks is actually right to think that Kant believed that the mind is immaterial; but as an article of faith – he did not think there was any *theoretical* support for the view.

26 Dennett, "Two Approaches to Mental Images", in *Brainstorms,* pp. 174–89.

27 See note 20.

28 Or perhaps they are nowhere. As Dennett notes, if 'the order that is there' has the same sort of abstractness as a centre of gravity has, it may be difficult to say where it is (*The Intentional Stance,* p. 39). The phrase 'order that is there' is Elizabeth Anscombe's (*Intention* [Oxford: Basil Blackwell, 1957, 2d ed., 1963], p. 80). Dennett also uses it in "Reply to Arbib and Gunderson" in *Brainstorms,* pp. 23–38, at 28.

29 Some Wittgensteinians have claimed that whatever the 'I' in a sentence like 'I am puzzled by your comments' is doing, it is not reporting or expressing an awareness of something, not an awareness at any rate at all similar to what the rest of the sentence is reporting. What Wittgenstein actually had in mind is not easy to determine, as the widespread bewilderment about remarks like §404 in the *Philosophical Investigations* (Oxford: Basil Blackwell, 1953) illustrates. He and Kant would have agreed this far: awareness of oneself is very different from awareness of external objects; but doubtless their reasons for believing this would have been very different, too.

30 Jay F. Rosenberg, " 'I Think': Some Reflections on Kant's Paralogisms", *Midwest Studies in Philosophy* 10 (1986), pp. 503–32.

31 The only exception known to me is Dennett, and he is only a partial exception. In *Consciousness Explained* he attempts to undermine the picture of the mind

as what he calls a Cartesian theatre. However, he too continues to view self-awareness as a process of representing something, analogous to perception. He just wants to do away with the idea that being aware of these or any other representations requires a Cartesian theatre.

32 I owe my sense of just how fervent an antimaterialist about the mind Kant was to Lorne Falkenstein.

2. Kant's theory of the subject

1 For a short, accessible account of some of this work, see Paul M. Churchland and Patricia Smith Churchland, "Could a Machine Think?" *Scientific American* 262 (Jan. 1990), pp. 32–7. See also Daniel L. Schacter, "Memory", in Michael Posner, ed., *Foundations of Cognitive Science,* pp. 683–726 (Cambridge, Mass.: MIT Press, 1989).

2 By the time of her book, Kitcher had become very aware of the ambiguity of the term '*Vorstellung*', an ambiguity mirrored perfectly in the Latin-derived word 'representation'. Thus, she turned to 'cognitive state' and 'the contents of a cognitive state', which do capture the distinction between intentional state (or act) and intentional object between them. Even in her book, however, she does not apply the distinction to Kant, not in the way I do at any rate.

3 Paul M. Churchland, *Matter and Consciousness* (Cambridge, Mass.: MIT Press, 1984; 2d ed., 1988). See also idem, "Eliminative Materialism and the Propositional Attitudes", *Journal of Philosophy* 78 (1981), pp. 61–90.

4 Dennett, *Brainstorms,* p. 12. Even in this gender-sensitive time, I will continue to refer to the subject thus postulated as the little man; being only part of a whole person, it would not in fact be either man or woman but just a homunculus. Dennett examines and endorses the argument against intrinsic representations in "Evolution, Error and Intentionality", *The Intentional Stance,* pp. 287–322. For arguments running in the opposite direction, see Fred Dretske, *Explaining Behaviour* (Cambridge, Mass.: MIT Press, 1988), chap. 3, and Jerry Fodor, *Psychosemantics* (Cambridge, Mass.: MIT Press, 1988), chaps. 3 and 4.

5 If we were now to go on to give the sort of functionalist account of what it is to represent and mean something – of intentionality – that has become pretty much standard, that something's representing something is a matter of its playing a certain role in the functioning of an organism, then the argument against intrinsic representations would become even stronger. I will not pursue this question of what a representation is here, or the question of what Kant thought a representation is. He did not spend a lot of time trying to describe how representations work in nonrepresentational language. For what he did have to say about the nature of a representation, see Chapter 6.

6 This distinction between being a subject and full personhood may go some way toward explaining some of Sacks' remarkable patients who seem to be borderline for personhood but clearly remain subjects and have experiences. (See *The Man Who Mistook His Wife for a Hat and Other Clinical Tales* [New York: Harper & Row, 1970] and many subsequent books and articles.) I owe this observation to Tim Kenyon.

7 M. Minsky, *The Society of Mind* (New York: Simon & Schuster, 1985). The notion of a production system has been around for a while (A. Newell, "Production Systems: Models of Control Structures", in W. G. Chase, ed., *Visual Information Processing,* pp. 463–526. [New York: Academic Press, 1973]), but in

the last few years it has really come into its own: see, e.g., A. Newell, *Unified Theories of Cognition* (Cambridge, Mass.: Harvard University Press, 1990). For Act*, see J. Anderson, *The Architecture of Cognition* (Cambridge, Mass.: Harvard University Press, 1983). A good review paper is A. Newell, P. S. Rosenbloom, and J. E. Laird, "Symbolic Architectures for Cognition", in Posner, ed., *Foundations of Cognitive Science,* pp. 93–132. As we saw in Chapter 1, Dennett first noted the need for a theory of awareness in *The Intentional Stance,* p. 257. There he also advocated looking at the functioning of whole brains. His response to these suggestions is the multiple drafts model laid out in *Consciousness Explained.*

8 Dennett, *Brainstorms,* p. 101; see pp. 122–5. The problem of 'discharging the little man' was articulated as long ago as the time of Leibniz; it is far from being a newly discovered problem.

9 Dennett's attempt to discharge the little man in *Consciousness Explained* is a version of homuncular functionalism. Like Kant's, this approach is a kind of representational theory. I will say a bit more about the differences later in this section and take up the question again in Chapter 9.

10 P. S. Churchland, *Neurophilosophy* (Cambridge, Mass.: MIT Press, 1986); P.S. Churchland and T. J. Sejnowski, *The Computational Brain* (Cambridge, Mass.: MIT Press, 1992).

11 D. Dennett, "Reflections: Real Patterns, Deeper Facts, and Empty Questions", *The Intentional Stance,* pp. 37–42; idem, "Real Patterns", *Journal of Philosophy* 89 (1991), pp. 27–51. See also W. Lycan, ed. *Mind and Cognition* (Oxford: Blackwell's, 1990), chap. 4.

12 D. Dennett, *Brainstorms,* p. 124.

13 By Kitcher in "Kant's Real Self". I discuss this attribution in Chapter 10:1.

14 Jerry Fodor, *The Language of Thought* (New York: Crowell, 1975), p. 74n; Dennett, "A Cure for the Common Code", in idem, *Brainstorms,* p. 101.

15 I would like to thank Tim Kenyon and Michael Blake for helpful comments on an earlier draft of this section.

16 That Kant used these terms as interchangeably as I am implying has been denied. Allison, for example, maintains that while '*Vorstellung*' was Kant's term for representational states in general, he reserved '*Erfahrung*' for a representation that yields "knowledge by means of connected perceptions (*Wahrnehmungen*)" (B161; see also A110 and A177 = B218) or, more simply, "knowledge of objects" (B1) (pp. 148–52 and 166ff.). Guyer, on the other hand (pp. 80–3), presents powerful evidence that '*Erfahrung*' is multiply ambiguous in Kant. Let me say two things about this issue: First, by 'experience' (*Erfahrung*), Kant often did not mean individual experiences in the normal sense, but 'one single experience' (A110), 'one consciousness' (A177 = B218), that is to say, something more like my global experience than like representations of the normal sort. (That may be what is behind the B161 passage just quoted.) Second, Allison's brief quotations may not support as sharp a distinction as he thinks. Though he has in mind the kinds of objects for which there is an order in the objects of experience different from the order of the experiences and/or our associations among them, Kant often meant no more by the term 'object' than 'object of thought' or intentional object, something far weaker than "an entity which exists as more than an object of thought", an object in the 'weighty' sense. (Allison takes this term from Strawson but expands it to include internal objects that actually exist as more than objects of a representation [p. 136].) Most commentators note that Kant had two different terms for what Kemp Smith translates as 'object', namely '*Objekt*' and '*Gegen-*

stand'. Allison thinks that these terms mark the distinction he needs here, between a merely intentional object (*Objekt*) and a 'weighty' object (*Gegenstand*) (p. 27 and p. 135n32). I tend to think that which kind of object Kant is referring to when he uses these terms is often just unclear. (Kant used '*Gegenstand*' in the phrase I just quoted from B1, but he also uses it, for example, in the well-known remark at A104 where he says that sensible representations "must not be taken as objects capable of existing outside our power of representation", where he is clearly talking about intentional objects.)

Sometimes Kant does indeed draw such distinctions among representations, perceptions, and experiences, and between intentional and 'weighty' objects. In the *Prolegomena to Any Future Metaphysics* (1783), trans. P. Carus, rev. with intro. L. W. Beck (Indianapolis, Ind.: Library of Liberal Arts, 1950), for example, he distinguishes judgements of perception from judgements of experience, and it is clear that the latter are more objective than the former in some way. Similarly, at A320 = B376–7, Kant says "the genus is representation *(Vorstellung)*" and then lists all of perception, sensation, knowledge, intuition, and concept as nested species and subspecies! The trouble is, he does not make distinctions like these consistently. Because of their connection to the vexed issue of what Kant thought about objectivity, "knowledge of objects", these questions of terminology have received a lot of attention. Fortunately, I do not need to worry about them here. Given this and given also that Kant's use of experience terminology is at least variable and imprecise (as Kitcher also notes, p. 16), I will skirt the terminological puzzles and treat roughly similar terms as interchangeable wherever possible.

17 Allison uses the latter phrase (p. 138).

18 A. Treisman and G. Gelade, "A Feature-Integration Theory of Attention", *Cognitive Psychology* 12 (1980), pp. 97–136; A. Treisman, "Features and Objects in Visual Processing", *Scientific American* 255 (Nov. 1986), pp. 114B–125.

19 Anscombe, *Intention;* Dennett, "Brain Writing and Mind Reading", in *Brainstorms,* pp. 39–52, at 39; Richard Wollheim, *The Thread of Life* (Cambridge, Mass.: Harvard University Press, 1984).

20 Allison, pp. 139–40. Dieter Henrich, *Identität und Objektivität* (Heidelberg: Carl Winter Universitäts, 1976). (References to Henrich will be to this work unless otherwise noted.)

21 Henrich, pp. 54–8; Allison, pp. 139–40.

22 Imagination is often not included in this account. Waxman mounts a powerful argument in *Kant's Model of the Mind* that Kant saw it as just as essential as the other two.

23 Fodor, *Modularity of the Mind.* Fodor does, of course, introduce the notion of global, isotropic features of the mind. The trouble is, he does nothing with them, indeed argues at least half-seriously that they are beyond the reach of cognitive science. See Fodor's 'First Law of the Non-Existence of Cognitive Science', discussed briefly in the preceding chapter. See, too, Patricia Smith Churchland, "Consciousness: The Transmutation of a Concept", *Pacific Philosophical Quarterly* 65 (1983), pp. 80–95, and Flanagan, *The Science of the Mind,* pp. 200–2.

24 Fodor makes a clear distinction of levels similar to mine in *Modularity of Mind.* He distinguishes vertical, encapsulated modules from horizontal, unifying higher cognition. This good start notwithstanding, he does not go on to say much about the unity of these unifying aspects.

25 Dennett, *The Intentional Stance,* p. 89.

26 J. Bennett, *Kant's Dialectic* (Cambridge University Press, 1974), p. 83. I have paraphrased slightly. We will have occasion to refer to this remark again (Chapter 7).
27 L. Wittgenstein, *Tractatus Logico-Philosophicus* (1921) (London: Routledge & Kegan Paul, 1961), remark 5.62.
28 Discussions with John Leyden helped clarify the analogy (see also note 25, p. 278).

3. Kant's conception of awareness and self-awareness

1 To be fair, Dennett has gone both ways on the issue of distinguishing self-awareness and simple awareness. In "Consciousness", he explicitly distinguishes them and includes both under the concept of consciousness (in Richard L. Gregory, ed., *The Oxford Companion to the Mind* [Oxford University Press, 1987], pp. 161–4), and his early distinction between awareness$_1$ and awareness$_2$ could be seen as a step in the same direction (*Content and Consciousness* [London: Routledge & Kegan Paul, 1969)], pp. 118–19; see also *Brainstorms,* chap. 2). In *Consciousness Explained,* however, he no longer distinguishes them, returning to a point of view he held as far back as his first book, *Content and Consciousness.* (The title is really distinguishing *self*-awareness, Nagel's 'what it is like to be something', from content). He did the same in "Toward a Cognitive Theory of Consciousness" and "Conditions of Personhood", both in *Brainstorms* and, it seems, in the passage just quoted.
2 Dennett, *Content and Consciousness,* pp. 118–19; see also idem, "Reply to Arbib and Gunderson", in *Brainstorms,* chap. 2.
3 Dennett, "About Aboutness", *The Intentional Stance,* pp. 205–8.
4 This distinction between the intentional and the subintentional can usefully be compared to Dennett's distinction between the personal and subpersonal. As he characterizes the subpersonal, it is a level of description in which things are described in nonintentional, nonrepresentational language (see, e.g., Dennett, *The Intentional Stance,* pp. 61–3). The same is true of my subintentional. However, there is something curious about Dennett's characterizations of the subpersonal. The natural home for the idea is not the nonintentional but the nonconscious, psychological states of which we are not aware. For that reason, I prefer the term 'nonintentional' to characterize things described nonintentionally. My term 'intentional' is then free to range over both Dennett's personal states and that portion of his subpersonal states that are intentional but not available to awareness. Indeed, states that are intentional but not available to awareness are central to my argument in this section.
5 As R. L. Gregory reports, the behaviour of even pigeons and fish exposed to optical illusions can be explained only by invoking such notions (*Eye and Brain* [London: World University Library, 1966], p. 137).
6 Kant lays out these distinctions in the appendix on The Amphiboly of Concepts of Reflection, in the course of an argument against Leibniz's rationalist conceptualism. I will say a further word about the Amphiboly at the end of Chapter 6:I:5. My distinction a few sentences back between qualitative and conceptual relations may cause eyebrows to be raised. Are not qualitative distinctions always conceptual ones for Kant? No, they are not. We may need to use concepts to recognize them, and conceptual distinctions may always be qualitative ones, but the argument of the Amphiboly is precisely an argument that there are qualitative

differences that could not be recognized by concepts alone. In addition, Kant's distinction in TD between the synthesis of apprehension and reproduction, on the one hand, and the synthesis of recognition *in a concept,* on the other, seems to rest on the same distinction. Even if the former two kinds of synthesis require the use of concepts, even the use of the Categories, as Kant may have argued in the second-edition version of TD, that would not entail that qualitative differences are *nothing but* conceptual ones.

7 Dennett, *Consciousness Explained,* contains a number of important discussions of this distinction between the properties of a representation, the properties it represents, and the properties it in turn is *represented* as having. See chap. 6 in particular. A later paper with M. Kinsbourne, "Time and the Observer: The Where and When of Consciousness in the Brain", *Behavioral and Brain Sciences* 15 (1992), pp. 183–247, contains what Dennett calls an industrial-strength version of the same analysis.

8 D. Rosenthal has explored a similar suggestion, "Two Concepts of Consciousness", *Philosophical Studies* 49 (1986), pp. 329–59.

9 Dennett puts this ability at the centre of what he calls awareness$_1$, the companion to awareness$_2$ already introduced: "*A* is aware$_1$ that *p* at time *t* if and only *p* is the content of the input state of *A*'s 'speech centre' at time *t* ("Reply to Arbib and Gunderson", in *Brainstorms,* p. 30). Dennett seems to think that awareness$_1$ and awareness$_2$ between them exhaust the notions of awareness and self-awareness. Clearly, I disagree. Indeed, here I am using input to the speech centre to explicate a concept of awareness, not a concept of self-awareness.

10 Allison, chaps. 12 and 13; Powell.

11 There may have been more excuse for his doing so than there is for us. In a very interesting paper, K. V. Wilkes has explored a little of the history of the term 'consciousness' in the sense of self-awareness. She makes clear that at the time Kant wrote the first *Critique,* the term 'consciousness' used in this way was less than a hundred years old and did not have a stable usage ("____, yishi, duh, um, and consciousness", in A. J. Marcel and E. Bisiach, eds., *Consciousness in Contemporary Science*, pp. 16–41 [Oxford University Press, 1988].

12 This unclarity also clouds the TD, at least in the first *Critique*. Note that the question here is not whether Kant thought simple awareness, or perhaps simple conceptualized awareness, *requires* ESA or ASA. That is a separate question, one indeed that already takes for granted that they can be distinguished. It also arises in the TD, of course.

13 Strawson, *The Bounds of Sense,* Part II:II.

14 Kant to Marcus Herz of May 26, 1789 (*Gesammelte Schriften,* Ak. XI:52; translated in *Kant's Philosophical Correspondence, 1759–1799,* ed. and trans. Arnulf Zweig, pp. 150–6 [Chicago: University of Chicago Press, 1967],). This idea that animals can be aware while lacking the cognitive capacities that shape our experience raises some questions about the status of the claims of TD about the necessary cognitive conditions of experience – all experience or just experience of a certain sort? Unfortunately, precisely because the animal experience Kant speaks of occurs in the absence of these cognitive capacities, what Kant says in this letter also leaves open the most interesting question about self-awareness, namely,. Is the kind of experience shaped by cognitive capacities possible in a creature without self-awareness? We will examine both issues in Part II of Chapter 6.

15 Leibniz, *The Principles of Nature and Grace,* sec. 4. Another work in which

Leibniz makes the same distinction in almost the same words (something not uncommon in his work) is the *Monadology*, also written in 1714 (Philip P. Weiner, ed., *Leibniz: Selections*, pp. 525 and 535 [New York: Scribner's, 1951]).

16 Jonathan Bennett, *Kant's Analytic* (Cambridge University Press, 1966), p. 105.

17 Paul Guyer, "Kant on Apperception and *A Priori* Synthesis", *American Philosophical Quarterly* 17 (1980), pp. 205–12. Ameriks does a masterful job of showing that Guyer is wrong in "Kant and Guyer on Apperception," *Archiv für Geschichte der Philosophie* 65 (1983), pp. 174–84.

18 Jay Rosenberg, *The Thinking Self* (Philadelphia: Temple University Press, 1986), p. 10.

19 Kitcher, "Kant's Real Self", p. 141.

20 Kitcher, p. 107.

21 Ibid., p. 86. Guyer (p. 148 and n. 11) seems to think that a claim that we must make judgements about mental states, that is to say, about representations, is the "fundamental premise" of the deduction and attributes recognition of this fact to Kitcher's "Kant on Self-Identity", *Philosophical Review* 91 (1982), pp. 41–72, at pp. 53 and 65. In response, I would urge all of the following: Kitcher seems to have changed her mind by the time she wrote her book; her earlier view is not true to a lot of what Kant says; on this point, the same is true of Guyer; her later view is close to Kant's view. I provide arguments to back the claims that I am making dogmatically here in Chapter 6.

22 As I noted at the beginning of Chapter 2, Kitcher used to ignore this distinction between act and object (e.g., in "Kant's Real Self", pp. 141–2). As a result, her early work on Kant often seems out of focus.

23 One philosopher who does think Kant distinguished between awareness and self-awareness is Waxman (*Kant's Model of the Mind,* pp. 18–19 and 218). His account is highly original and quite different from mine. Kant distinguished three kinds of synthesis, apprehension, reproduction, and recognition, as well as a precursor to them all, synopsis. Waxman thinks synopsis and apprehension are the realm of consciousness, reproduction and recognition the realm of self-consciousness (p. 218)! By contrast, I think Kant wanted to distinguish simple awareness of the world from awareness of self all the way up. Indeed, for the higher forms of synthesis, I think Waxman makes exactly the same mistake as Strawson, Bennett, and others do. (Waxman also seems to think that intentionality does not arise before the two higher syntheses, but we would have to go far into the complexities of his account to explore this strange idea.)

24 Fodor's discussion occurs in *The Language of Thought*. A. J. Marcel and E. Bisiach, eds., *Consciousness in Contemporary Science* (Oxford University Press, 1988), is perhaps the most important of the more recent collections. From a more single-mindedly psychological point of view, the three-volume collection *Aspects of Consciousness,* ed. G. Underwood and R. Stevens (New York: Academic Press, 1979–82) is also interesting. P. S. Churchland's "Consciousness: The Transmutation of a Concept", *Pacific Philosophical Quarterly* 65 (1983), pp. 80–95, is an early example of the same interest. Since making the quoted remark, Dennett himself has tackled a whole range of problems to do with the self and awareness of ourselves and our states in *Consciousness Explained*.

25 Patricia Smith Churchland is one example (*Neurophilosophy,* p. 307). Paul Churchland is another (*Matter and Consciousness,* p. 74). Indeed, he not only urges, in line with the tradition, that self-awareness is simply one kind of per-

ception, perception of oneself, he argues for similarities between awareness of self and awareness of the external world that are stronger than anything in the tradition.

26 Sydney Shoemaker, "Self-Reference and Self-Awareness", *Journal of Philosophy* 65, no. 20 (Oct. 3, 1968), pp. 555–67, at 558. Among commentators on Kant, Strawson has come closest to seeing that Kant was using a notion very similar to Shoemaker's notion of self-reference without identification, at least in the chapter on the Paralogisms. But Strawson calls the phenomenon in question 'criterionless self-ascription' (*The Bounds of Sense,* p. 165). This term obscures more than it reveals; what is in question is not ascription but reference.

27 Ludwig Wittgenstein, *Blue and Brown Books* (Oxford: Basil Blackwell, 1964), pp. 66–70. This is the passage from which Shoemaker derived the inspiration for his idea of self-reference without identification. What Wittgenstein meant by the passage is open to a variety of interpretations. We will return to the topic in Chapter 4.

4. Kant's theory of apperceptive self-awareness

1 It is remarkable because Powell's book is called *Kant's Theory of Self-Consciousness*. The reference to Jay Rosenberg is to his paper, " 'I Think': Some Reflections on Kant's Paralogisms".

2 In German the last phrase reads, *'etwas von ihm zu kennen, oder zu wissen'*. Kemp Smith translates it, 'without knowing anything of it either by direct acquaintance or otherwise', but this is clearly inadequate. The 'reasoning' in question is the form of analysis characteristic of rationalism, something much like conceptual analysis as understood in the 1960s and 1970s, or so I will argue in Chapter 7.

3 Shoemaker, "Self-Reference and Self-Awareness", p. 558.

4 Ibid; T. Nagel, "Physicalism", *Philosophical Review* 74 (1965), pp. 339–56. Hector-Neri Castañeda has argued persuasively that no description can be substituted for 'I' (see his " 'He': A Study in the Logic of Self-Consciousness", *Ratio* 8 [1966], pp. 130–57, and later work). Since then, a selection of philosophers who have written on the topic are G. E. M. Anscombe, "The First Person", in Samuel Guttenplan, ed., *Mind and Language*, pp. 45–65 (Oxford University Press, 1975); John Perry, "The Problem of the Essential Indexical", *Nous* 13 (1979), pp. 3–21; J. L. Mackie, "The Transcendental 'I' ", in Zak van Straaten, ed., *Philosophical Subjects: Essays Presented to P. F. Strawson* pp. 48–61 (Oxford University Press, 1980); Robert Nozick, *Philosophical Explanations* (Cambridge, Mass.: Harvard University Press, 1981), chap. 1.II, "Reflexivity"; and Roderick Chisholm, *The First Person* (Brighton: Harvester, 1981). Chisholm's account of the first person has a strong Kantian flavour.

5 Note that the phrases just cited are from no earlier than the Paralogisms chapter, but are all from the first edition. This illustrates two things that I will discuss in Chapter 5: that Kant seems not to have developed his theory of reference to self until he needed it to attack rational psychology and that when he moved the discussion of ASA to TD for the second edition, he stripped off a lot of detail. A stripped-down version of his theory can also be found in "The Psychological Idea", §46 of the *Prolegomena* (Ak. IV:333–4).

6 I use the term 'nonascriptive reference of self' and discuss the phenomenon in

"Imagination, Possibility and Personal Identity", *American Philosophical Quarterly* 12 (1975), pp. 185–98, at 188.

7 Shoemaker, "Self-Reference and Self-Awareness", p. 560.

8 Hilary Putnam, "The Meaning of Meaning", in his *Mind, Language and Reality: Philosophical Papers,* Vol. 2 pp. 215–71, at p. 265 (Cambridge University Press, 1975).

9 Shoemaker, "Self-Reference and Self-Awareness", pp. 566–7. This also speaks against the idea of a separate '*Ich-Vorstellung*'.

10 Though Allison talks about the awareness of self that apperception gives and distinguishes it from awareness of one's representations, he says little about A355 and nothing about transcendental designation. The same is true of Powell, who even has a whole chapter comparing Kant's work on the 'I think' to the views of Anscombe, Mackie, and others on the uses of 'I'. Similarly, in " 'I Think': Some Reflections on Kant's Paralogisms", Rosenberg does not mention A355 at all.

11 Wittgenstein, *Blue and Brown Books,* pp. 66–70. Actually, though Shoemaker attributes the core of his treatment to Wittgenstein, it is not clear that Wittgenstein is making the same point he and Kant are making. Certainly in his later writings Wittgenstein maintained that uses of 'I' and cognates that are apparently self-referential are in fact doing something altogether different. But that I cannot go into here. What Wittgenstein meant in the passage in question from the *Blue Book* is a complex and controversial question. My claim could be put thus: Kant anticipated what may be one thread in it, and Shoemaker later found the same idea in it.

12 Allison makes this abundantly clear in chap. 11 of his book. In Chapters 6 and 9, I will argue that the standard image of TD makes it look far worse than it is.

13 "Whatever the origins of our representations, whether they are due to the influence of outer things, or are produced through inner causes, whether they arise *a priori,* or being appearances have an empirical origin, they must all, as modifications of the mind, belong to inner sense" (A98–9).

14 The German of the first part is, "*Wie aber das Ich, der ich denke, von dem Ich, das sich selbst anschauet, unterschieden . . .* ". Kemp Smith translates this, "How the 'I' that thinks can be distinct from the 'I' that intuits itself . . . ". In addition to changing his translation, I have removed his emendations. We will come back to the very important distinction between being 'given' to oneself and knowing oneself in Chapter 10:5.

15 If I were aware of acts of global representing as objects of other representations, there would always be one act of global representing of which I could not be aware at all, the last one. Strangely enough, Powell seems to think that Kant held this view (p. 5 and throughout)! He does not discuss the passages just cited.

16 See Sellars, " . . . this I or he or it (the thing) which thinks . . . " and Pippin, "Kant on the Spontaneity of Mind".

17 Allison makes something like the opposite point. Taking acts of TA already to be acts of self-awareness, he argues that to perform these acts of self-awareness is to unite the manifold (p. 142).

18 Kant was aware of the phenomenon of attention, but seems to have discussed it only once in the *Critique,* in a note to B156.

19 Discussions with Richard DeVidi saved me from some errors here. Undoubtedly, some people will think that I have not fixed all of them.

20 L. Wittgenstein, "Notes for Lectures on 'Private Experience' and 'Sense-Data' ", ed. Rush Rhees, *Philosophical Review* 77 (1968), pp. 271–320. In using the term,

Wittgenstein probably meant to raise a question about whether what it applies to is anything remotely like a normal representation. I will not pursue this question here.

21 Allison argues that the unity of the subject is the "form or prototype" for the unity "that pertains to concepts" (p. 144). He fails to note that our awareness of the unity of the subject, in turn, comes from our awareness of the unity of our acts of apperception.

22 The qualification about nonsensible intuition is required because in the second edition Kant allowed, or pretended to allow, that there might be beings who in their awareness of themselves as subject could be aware of themselves as object – could be aware of features of themselves, distinguish themselves from other beings – without being aware of any other intentional objects, via an intellectual or nonsensible intuition. Of course, none of Kant's conclusions about the necessary conditions of representing objects would hold of anything that could do this. He may have introduced this idea so as to leave at least a possibility of an omniscient Knower open.

23 An obscure remark in the attack on the Third Paralogism may be making the same point: "In the apperception, time is represented . . . only in *me*" (A362). Part of what Kant may have meant here is that my representations that locate something in time or that are themselves located in time will also represent myself. We examine this remark in Chapter 8:6.

24 Bennett, *Kant's Dialectic,* p. 80. He uses the notion only in the context of imagining one's own nonexistence, but it has possibilities much wider than that, as we will see in Chapter 7:4.

25 Interestingly enough, Shoemaker also says something similar about the self as object ("Self-Reference and Self-Awareness", pp. 563–4).

26 Ibid., p. 560.

27 Allison, p. 282; Jay Rosenberg, *One World and Our Knowledge of It* (Dordrecht: Reidel, 1980), p. 77; Kitcher, pp. 189, 195, 197; Powell, chap. 6.

28 Shoemaker, "Self-Reference and Self-Awareness," p. 563.

29 Allison, p. 275–6.

30 Castañeda, " 'He': A Study in the Logic of Self-Consciousness".

31 Sydney Shoemaker, "Persons and Their Pasts", *American Philosophical Quarterly* 7 (1970), pp. 269–85. Ludwig Wittgenstein, *Blue and Brown Books,* pp. 66–70, which is where we also find Wittgenstein drawing a distinction between "the use of 'I' as subject" and its use as object using exactly Kant's terminology. Anscombe ("The First Person") and Mackie ("The Transcendental 'I' ") have both taken this feature of 'reference' to self to be an indication that it is perhaps not reference at all. Strawson thinks it is genuine reference but puts the immunity down merely to the rules governing our practice of reference to self ("Reply to Mackie"). I agree with him on the first point but, as what immediately follows makes clear, think that there is more to the immunity than that. Mackie's paper and Strawson's reply are both in Zak van Straaten, ed., *Philosophical Subjects: Essays Presented to P. F. Strawson.*

32 Powell offers a very interesting discussion of immunity to error (pp. 221–2). He raises doubts first about whether immunity to error through misidentification is unique to first-person reference, referring to Gareth Evans' similar suggestion (*Varieties of Reference,* ed. J. McDowell [Oxford University Press, 1982]), and second about whether such immunity is as good a reason to think uses of 'I', etc., are nonreferential as Anscombe urges in "The First Person". For my part, I think

that *there is* something special about first-person contexts, but that this *does not* argue against uses of 'I' in such contexts being referential. His doubts notwithstanding, Powell himself ends up hesitantly favouring nonreferentialism (pp. 232–3).

33 I owe this point to Richard DeVidi.

34 Kitcher plays with the idea that Kant may have distinguished three different selves – noumenal, empirical, and thinking (p. 22)! Being both empirical and necessary for the empirical, the thinking self bridges the other two. In my view, Kant thought there is only one self, so there is nothing to bridge.

35 The German of the first part is "*Wie aber das Ich, der ich denke, von dem Ich, das sich selbst anschauet, unterschieden . . .*". As I said in note 14, Kemp Smith translates this, "How the 'I' that thinks can be distinct from the 'I' that intuits itself . . .". Kant makes a similar remark about the 'I' of apperception and the 'I' of inner sense being one in the *Anthropology* (*An* Ak. VII:134n).

36 One place is in connection with a fascinating discussion of mental images. See Dennett, "Two Approaches to Mental Images", in *Brainstorms,* pp. 174–89. Another is in idem, *Consciousness Explained,* most of which is devoted in one way or another to undermining the idea of what he calls the Cartesian theatre.

5. The mind in the *Critique of Pure Reason*

1 Guyer (p. 434) says that Feder was the villain. Apparently the troublesome passages were introduced by him into Garve's original review.

2 Even the attack on the Fourth Paralogism seems to me to be only a partial exception. I try to say why in "Reality and Representations: Kant's Refutation of Idealism", unpublished manuscript.

3 *Prolegomena,* §19 (Ak. IV:298).

4 Allison also remarks on Kant's untroubled acceptance of the objective validity of normal sensible experience (p. 136).

5 Allison also notes Kant's focus on sifting the good from the bad, rather than worrying about whether there is any good at all (see, e.g., p. 168). Ernest Cassirer has perhaps emphasized objectivity as the absence of subjectivity most strongly, focusing on Kant's distinction between rule-governed judgement about objects and a mere rhapsody of perceptions (A156 = B195 and *Prolegomena* §39 [Ak. IV:323–4]). I think Cassirer overloads the notion of representation of objects, making it come out too much like quantitative theory in science, and correspondingly overloads the notion of bare intuition, making it come out too much like what I am calling representation of objects, but he is right to emphasize the role of absence of subjectivity and whim as defining characteristics of objective knowledge for Kant (*Kant's Life and Thought* [1918] [New Haven, Conn.: Yale University Press, 1982], chap. III:2, pp. 145–50).

6 Kant used the terms 'objective deduction' and 'subjective deduction' only this once in the *Critique.* Nevertheless, they mark a useful distinction. We will examine what Kant included in them in the next chapter.

7 I explore the relationship of *a prioricity* and necessity in Kant's thought and specifically the interesting question of whether and if so where and how he argued for the necessity of the propositions of mathematics and physics, in "Kant's *A Priori* Methods for Recognizing Necessary Truths", in Philip Hanson and Bruce Hunter, eds., *Return of the A Priori, Canadian Journal of Philosophy,* Supp. Vol. 18 (1993), pp. 215–52.

8 Note, parenthetically, that the idea that propositions can acquire some element of necessity from using the Categories and Principles to generate them works better for relational concepts such as cause and effect than it does for any of the other three. What sort of necessity could be found in the quantitative concepts of everything being one, some, or all of something, or in the qualitative concepts of reality, negation, and limitation (whatever exactly Kant means by these concepts), or in the modal concepts of being possible, actual, or necessary?

9 Guyer, p. 11. See the whole of Part I of his book, especially pp. 21–4.

10 As I noted in Chapter 2, Kant had two different terms for what Kemp Smith translates as 'object', namely, '*Objekt*' and '*Gegenstand*'. If we were to follow Allison and take these terms to mark a distinction between merely intentional objects ('*Objekt*') and objects in a more 'weighty' Strawsonian sense ('*Gegenstand*') (p. 27 and p. 135–32), it would be natural to expect Kant to use '*Objekt*' in the passage just quoted. In fact, he uses '*Gegenstandes*'. This may mean that he thought even 'weighty' objects are mere representations, or it may simply mean that Allison is wrong, at least in this case.

11 Walker, *Kant,* pp. 76.

12 P.F. Strawson, *Individuals* (London: Methuen, 1959), chap. 3.

13 I explore Kant's proof of the necessity of the propositions of mathematics and physics in "Kant's *A Priori* Methods for Recognizing Necessary Truths". For an interesting account of what the notion of a *quaestio juris* meant to Kant, see Henrich, "Kant's Notion of a Deduction and the Methodological Background of the First *Critique*", in Eckart Förster, ed., *Kant's Transcendental Deductions,* pp. 29–46 (Stanford, Calif.: Stanford University Press, 1989). The most extensive discussion yet written of the relationship between normative considerations and psychological facts in Kant's work is the one in Hatfield, *The Natural and the Normative.*

14 In "Some Remarks on Logical Form", *Proceedings of the Aristotelian Society,* Supp. vol. 9 (1929), pp. 162–71, Wittgenstein writes of a system of representation having or lacking "the right logical multiplicity" to allow "reality" or some aspect of it to be "projected into our symbolism" (p. 166).

15 Walker, *Kant,* p. 77. Guyer, pp. 94–5. The famous note in *The Metaphysical Foundations of Natural Science* (Ak. IV:474n) is the best-known comment on this issue.

16 Henrich, p. 70; Guyer, p. 26 and the whole of Part II.

17 Kitcher thinks Kant said that the subjective deduction is inessential only because he was mixing up an abstract characterization of the necessary powers and features of the mind with an account of how these powers and features are realized in specific beings (pp. 13–14 and 65). I see no warrant for explaining away his remark in this way.

18 Strawson, *The Bounds of Sense,* p. 117; see also p. 98.

19 Ibid., p. 165. Bennett, *Kant's Dialectic,* stns. 27 and 33–4.

20 Roderick Chisholm, "The Loose and Popular and Strict and Philosophical Senses of Identity", in Norman S. Care and Robert M. Grimm, eds., *Perception and Personal Identity,* pp. 107–25 (Cleveland, Ohio: The Press of Case Western Reserve University, 1969); Sydney Shoemaker and Richard Swinburne, *Personal Identity* (Oxford: Blackwell, 1984).

21 Even contemporary commentators can be misled on this point. Kitcher, for example, says that "unlike Descartes, Kant conceives of [the] self not as a simple substance, but only as a system of informationally interdependent states" ("Kant's

Paralogisms", *Philosophical Review* 91 [1982], pp. 515–47, at 527). Kant did no such thing; he just thought we cannot *know*, one way or the other.

22 As I mentioned in Chapter 1:3, Karl Ameriks is one writer who claims that Kant argued for the mind's immateriality. H.J. Paton is an example of someone who held that Kant had positive views about the mind's diachronic identity ("Self Identity", in his *In Defence of Reason* [London: Hutchison, 1951]). Guyer has held the same view (see e.g. "Kant on Apperception and *A Priori* Synthesis") and views the possibility of self-ascription over time as a requisite of apperception. (For my view, see Chapters 6:I:5 and 6:II:2). The third point of view is Kitcher's ("Kant's Paralogisms", p. 527; see chaps. 4 and 5 of her book). The term 'contentually' occurs on p. 117.

23 Kitcher is an advocate of the latter reading, in "Kant on Self-Identity" and "Kant's Paralogisms". Walker, *Kant* p. 134, insists with regret on the former one.

24 Even a commentator as recent as Kitcher can still say that Kant replaced the Fourth Paralogism and his attack on it with "cursory reflections about materialism" (p. 183). I disagree on two counts: the topic of the new discussion of the Fourth Paralogism does not replace that of the old – materialism is one of the things at issue in the first edition, too – and Kant's comments are not cursory.

25 See Brook, "Reality and Representations: Kant's Refutation of Idealism".

6. The first-edition subjective deduction

1 This is Kitcher's view, too (p. 95). However, I am puzzled by other things in each of their accounts. Kitcher is very hostile (this page and elsewhere) to the idea that Kant also used the second strategy, which I find puzzling. Guyer, on the other hand, wants to make the picture even more complicated. He says that there is a second split in the strategies Kant employs. Sometimes the premises from which he begins are contingent propositions, as I have assumed throughout, but sometimes they are propositions that he takes to be synthetic *a priori*. This split cross-classifies with the conditions of objects/conditions of ASA split, for a total of four distinct strategies. For my part, I do not see much evidence that Kant ever takes the propositions from which he begins the deduction to be synthetic *a priori*, in the first *Critique* at any rate, but it would take us too far afield to go into this issue here.

2 Bennett, *Kant's Analytic*, p. 100. Bennett actually extends this judgement to both versions of TD, saying that attempts to "canonize the whole text . . . have been derisible", but he is more scathing about the first version than the second.

3 Henrich, pp. 44–6. Walker lists some of the other places where Kant did a transcendental deduction (*Kant*, p. 77), and Guyer discusses some of them in detail. See, too, the papers in Eckart Förster, ed., *Kant's Transcendental Deductions* (Stanford, Calif.: Stanford University Press, 1989).

4 Whether the second-edition TD even contains a subjective deduction has been disputed. As is well known, Kemp Smith denied it (*A Commentary on Kant's Critique of Pure Reason* [London: Macmillan, 1918]). But that was because (i) he took the subjective deduction to include little if anything other than the doctrines of synthesis and the faculties, and (ii) he missed how often and how centrally synthesis still figures in the second edition, perhaps because he isolates it from the rest of Kant's theory of experience.

5 In the second edition, Kant seems to argue explicitly that these concepts must

be used to have experience of any kind, even the most apparently unconceptualized (§26). In the first edition, he may have held that concept usage arises only at the level of recognizing what is represented in a representation.

6 Kitcher, chaps. 3 and 4, particularly pp. 72 and 77. Kitcher's position is more hedged and nuanced than I have indicated (see, e.g., p. 80). Waxman has an arresting version of this idea. He claims that the raw material of representations is a "formless primary . . . sensation", which is quite incapable of being a "channel of communication between our faculty of representation and the world of things in themselves" (*Kant's Model of the Mind,* p. 288). It is important to see that it does not follow from this that the world has no form, or even that our synthetic constructions could never parallel it (though we could never observe any such parallel, of course).

7 Letter of July 1, 1797 (Ak. XI:514).

8 For both the last two points, see, e.g., Kitcher, pp. 75–9.

9 Ibid., p. 104. The second unity is not required for all representations of objects, and this restricts the generality of the conclusions Kant can draw from it. Kant never got this problem clearly into focus and Kitcher follows him in this (see Section 5).

10 Kitcher does see that Kant is concerned with the conditions of unity in us as we are, that he is not attempting to determine "the limits of our concept 'same person' ", and that is important (p. 131). She just has a one-dimensional vision of unity.

11 It might be worth clarifying the relationship of this distinction between the two unities to Kitcher's distinction between judgement and representation. They do not run in tandem. In fact, they cross-classify: representation of both individual objects and of multiples would involve both judgement and representation.

12 Wilkerson, *Kant's Critique of Pure Reason.*

13 Allison mentions "representation of a manifold as a single complex thought", and the need for "discrete representations being unified in the thought of a single subject" (p. 138), but he says little about the form of recognition involved.

14 A recent article by Irvin Rock and Stephen Palmer, "The Legacy of Gestalt Psychology", *Scientific American* 263 (Dec. 1990), pp. 84–91, introduces this work.

15 My account of intuitions puts me at odds with the commentators who take intuitions to be worked-up, conceptualized particulars. Sellars i he best-known example ("Some Remarks on Kant's Theory of Experience", *Journal of Philosophy* 64 [1967], pp. 633–47, reprinted in his *Essays in Philosophy and Its History* [Dordrecht: Reidel, 1974], pp. 44–61). I think this reading runs a risk of confusing intuitions with appearances; however, I also recognize that my view flies in the face of at least a few texts, e.g., B44 and A320 = B376–7. I have to view these texts as aberrations. One reason for not worrying about these texts is that Kant can also write as though intuitions were sense-data in the empiricist sense – already well-formed images of which the mind can become aware in their original form. At A120, for example, he talks of presynthesized appearances becoming conscious perceptions, conscious objects of experience. The appearances he has in mind here seem to be unprocessed intuitions. Yet in other places he is just as clearly aware that it is impossible to be aware of presynthesized intuitions. Chapter 2 of Kitcher's book, "The Science of Sensibility", is devoted to intuitions and the forms of intuition, time, and space. Lorne Falkenstein has published a series of papers and is preparing a book on the topic ("Spaces and Times: A Kantian

Response," *Idealist Studies* 16 [1986], pp. 1–11; "Is Perceptual Space Monadic?" *Philosophy and Phenomenological Research,* 49 [1989], pp. 709–13; "Was Kant a Nativist?" *Journal of the History of Ideas* 51 [1990], pp. 573–97; "Kant's Account of Sensation", *Canadian Journal of Philosophy* 20 [1990], pp. 63–88; "Kant's Account of Intuition", *Canadian Journal of Philosophy* 21 (1991), pp. 165–93; "Kant, Mendelssohn, Lambert, and the Subjectivity of Time", *Journal of the History of Philosophy* 19 [1991], pp. 227–51).

Sometimes it seems as though there are two Kants. There is the immensely sophisticated Kant, who can postulate theoretical entities and events, but there is also a Kant who can slide into clichéd caricatures of his own better views. We can find the same tension in the doctrine of the unknowability of the noumenal. Here the tension is between the idea that, check our theories as we might, in the end we can never *guarantee* that they reflect the world as it is, a very sophisticated position, and the flat assertion that the world as it is is unknowable, a mere caricature of that position. Hakam al Shawi first suggested this duality to me.

16 Bennett makes a similar point in his discussion of Kant on objectivity (*Kant's Analytic,* pp. 130–4).

17 In *Kant's Model of the Mind,* Waxman develops a rich and novel account of the role played by synopsis and apprehension in the genesis of representations of objects, taking synopsis to be a concept for a pretemporalized and prespatialized contribution of sense, and apprehension to be a similar contribution of imagination (chaps. 5 and 6). His account is both so complicated and so different from anything else in the recent literature that it would take a long discussion to examine it. One comment I can make is that he may be overloading the concept of synopsis, given, as he himself notes, that the two remarks about it near the beginning of the first-edition TD seem to be the only references to it in the whole of Kant's corpus. Most notably, in the second edition it disappears completely.

18 Kitcher devotes a long discussion to the question of whether concepts enter into temporal and spatial synthesis, indeed argues in chap. 6 that the second step (§26) of the two-steps-in-one proof that Henrich finds in the second edition is an attempt to argue that we must apply the Categories to achieve temporal and spatial synthesis.

19 Ibid., p. 134.

20 Waxman makes a convincing case that Kant intended the imagination, both reproductive and productive, to have a far more central place in his model of the mind than most commentators have given it. It is now widely believed that imagination plays a larger role in the generation of both hypotheses and testing procedures than was allowed by the old empiricist theories of scientific reasoning. And how could it be otherwise? – we are possibility entertainers. Kant's sensitivity to the role of imagination in cognition may merit further study, fragmented and incomplete though it is.

21 We examined Leibniz's view briefly in Chapter 3:3.

22 A futile hope, one would think; however, this peculiar idea plays some role in Kant's attack on the first Paralogism.

23 Letter to Herz, May 26, 1789 (Ak. XI:52); B134. Could a mind still be aware of the subject of these representations? I think so; it just could not be aware of the subject of one of them as the subject of another of them, it could not form them into a single global object, so it could not be aware of itself as their common subject (see Chapter 4:3).

24 In addition, TA is necessary, as he tells us in A108, for awareness of oneself as

the common subject of this experience. I will come back to Kant's strange slide to self-awareness here in Part II.

25 I have changed Kemp Smith's 'in me' to 'to me' and relocated the phrase. The German seems to support either phrase, and only the latter captures the parallel with Kant's assertions about representations otherwise being nothing to us and so on (A120). In "Spaces and Times", Falkenstein puts this requirement that representations 'belong with others in one consciousness' to work to show that standard thought experiments claiming to show that multiple, unconnected spaces and times are possible assume that it is satisfied and rapidly unravel when we imagine situations in which it is not.

26 Guyer says the "concept of an object" (p. 26) – the concept of what is needed for a representation to have an object.

27 Despite the fact that he only mentioned self-ascription once in TD in the first edition (A122) and focused on awareness, not self-awareness, Strawson and Wilkerson both think that such a claim is somehow implicit in what he says. More recently and very surprisingly, Guyer too has urged that the possibility of self-ascription is central to one form of the deduction, picking up on a few remarks on the topic scattered through the *Critique* ("Kant on Apperception and *A Priori* Synthesis").

28 Ameriks is one commentator who has seen that Kant is interested in the conditions of representations being something to someone, not just the conditions of them belonging to someone ("Kant and Guyer on Apperception", p. 183). In the same paper he shows that the possibility of self-ascription was not a general requirement of representing objects for Kant.

29 Kitcher, p. 117.

30 Strawson discusses some mixed dependencies like these in the early pages of "Persons", in *Individuals*, chap. 3. See Wittgenstein, *Philosophical Investigations*, §253.

31 In the second edition, Kant says "nothing to me" (B132). Note that (a) the idea stayed the same in both editions, but (b) Kant switched to the first-person singular. Both points are significant, as we will see in Chapter 9:4.

32 A similar rejection of the idea that Kant is making merely the trivial point that all my experiences are mine is a key move in Kitcher's rejection of the antipsychological, or what she calls the 'logic' or 'formal', reading of Kant (chap. 1 and pp. 92–5). Her analysis and mine make contact at another point, too. She too believes that Kant imposed an implicit restriction on the kinds of representations and objects that can be synthesized. She thinks, however, that the restriction is that they not go through outer sense (p. 121). This will not work. If I become aware of many representations of bodily states at all, it is not by having them (I mean the unintrospectible ones such as representations of temperature that the brain uses to regulate oxygenation), yet it need not be via outer sense either.

33 As is well known, Anscombe argues that such vagueness and generality are a mark of intentionality ("The Intentionality of Sensation: A Grammatical Feature", *Analytical Philosophy,* 2d series, ed. R. J. Butler [Oxford: Blackwell's, 1965], pp. 158–81, at 159).

34 Phenomenologists have spent a great deal of time exploring various relationships between individual representations and unified consciousness, as well as the introspective manifestations of same.

35 It is also possible that there are synthesis requirements on representations, es-

pecially representations that are cognitively and/or behaviourally effective, of which we lack awareness[H] and of whose objects we lack awareness[RR], requirements in addition to and even quite unlike those required for the representation to be taken up into a global representation. That is a possibility Kant did not even consider.

36 Kitcher discusses the loss of generality resulting from the 'belonging' requirement twice (pp. 112–14 and 134–5). Due to her failure to separate the two kinds of synthetic unity (p. 104; see Section 2, this chapter), she does not do so in my terms. She examines a different loss of generality, namely, a restriction to spatiotemporal objects in chap. 6; see p. 173.

37 Kitcher, "Kant's Paralogisms", p. 541.

38 A point Kitcher misses in her book, p. 152.

39 David Hume, *A Treatise of Human Nature,* ed. L. A. Selby-Bigge (Oxford University Press, 1962), p. 253.

40 Kitcher, p. 152. She repeats the claim on p. 201.

41 J. M. D. Meiklejohn identifies apperception with self-awareness in a footnote to his translation of the *Critique of Pure Reason* (London: Everyman's Library 909; Dent, 1934), p. 94. The phrase from Walker is from *Kant,* p. 80. Allison's view is a little more complicated. On p. 137 he seems to adhere to the orthodox view, with a Strawsonian qualification that TA is only the possibility of self-awareness; see also pp. 72 and pp. 145–7. Anyway, if TA is only the possibility of self-awareness, of what is it the actuality (see Section 2)?

42 Guyer, p. 83. I think a similarly close reading would raise doubts about Guyer's claim that A113 identifies TA with self-awareness, too.

43 Kitcher, p. 117. As I said earlier, I think this gap occurs because Kitcher sees connections among representations as primarily a diachronic affair.

44 As I said earlier, he may also have linked them in the footnote to A117. The actual phrase is "consciousness of myself as original apperception". This does not entail that apperception *is* consciousness of myself; it could just be something I am aware of in myself when I am conscious of myself. But Kant was probably identifying the two. A similar ambiguous remark occurs near the end of the footnote. Note, however, that if TA is self-awareness, Kant tells us that it need not be *actual* (empirical) self-awareness.

45 My translation of the last sentence differs slightly from Kemp Smith's. In [3], he has, "The original and necessary consciousness of the identity of the self . . . ". But the German is, "*also ist das ursprüngliche und nothwendige Bewußtsein der Identität seiner selbst . . .*". '*Seiner*' can mean something like 'on the side of' as well as 'of'. Though my rendering makes Kant's remark less obviously a remark about self-awareness, it is still far from clear what it means.

46 Guyer, pp. 83–4. Kitcher, pp. 105–8 and 144. Kitcher thinks that the synthesizing power sense is primary (p. 127). Given the second edition and the *Anthropology,* I think Kant gave neither sense primacy, because he conflated them. Guyer, by contrast, captures the full duality in all its awkward glory, even if he starts off with a reading more centred on self-awareness than the text of A107 supports.

47 Guyer has claimed that Kant conflated the two systematically ("Kant on Apperception and *A Priori* Synthesis"). I see no evidence for this assertion, which would be a harsh criticism if it were true. Ameriks shows that none of the evidence Guyer himself cites supports the claim ("Kant and Guyer on Apperception").

However, Ameriks himself seems to conflate self-awareness with the form of recognition that I earlier called recognition in a concept and certainly with recognition in consciousness (p. 184), and seems to assume that Kant did, too.

48 Guyer, pp. 26, 39–41, 85, pt. II, sec. 5.

49 Strawson, pp. 97–111. Jonathan Bennett, *Kant's Analytic,* p. 105; Patricia Kitcher, "Kant's Real Self", p. 141; see pp. 139–47. Kitcher disparages the idea on p. 95 of her book.

50 Strawson, p. 117; see p. 98.

51 If we say, with Descartes, that all awareness of objects requires self-awareness, we would have to allow that any animal not aware of itself could not be aware of anything else either! That can be said; indeed, Descartes may have said it. It just forces us onto the desperate expedient of maintaining that what goes on in animals is not awareness or perhaps is awareness 'in a different sense', a strategy Kitcher once adopted ("Kant's Real Self", p. 141).

52 The letter to Herz of May 26, 1789 (Ak. XI:52), makes the point about animals lacking unity. It also supports my point about self-awareness in the animals that have it: us.

7. Kant's diagnosis of the Second Paralogism

1 To give just a sampling of this literature in the English language and the past twenty-five years alone, there has been Strawson, *The Bounds of Sense;* Sellars, ". . . this I or he or it (the thing) which thinks . . . "; Bennett, *Kant's Dialectic;* M. Wilson, "Leibniz and Materialism", *Canadian Journal of Philosophy* 3 (1974), pp. 495–514; Ben Mijuskovic, *The Achilles of Rationalist Arguments* (The Hague: Nijhoff, 1974); Wilkerson, *Kant's Critique of Pure Reason;* R. M. Chisholm, *Person and Object* (London: Allen & Unuin, 1976); Ameriks, *Kant's Theory of Mind;* Kitcher, "Kant's Paralogisms" (rewritten as chap. 7 of *Kant's Transcendental Psychology*); and Powell, *Kant's Theory of Self-Consciousness.* In addition, R. E. Butts, *Kant and the Double Government Methodology* (Dordrecht: Reidel, 1984), includes a long discussion of the Paralogisms. Bennett, Wilson, and Butts all explore the history of the Paralogisms, and Butts also offers some fascinating insights into their broader, nonphilosophical context: dogmatic theology, spiritualism, paranormal epistemology, etc.

2 Kant discussed a fourth paralogism but it is commonly thought not to parallel the other three. I have reservations about this view; I examine them, the problem of what Kant is saying against the Fourth Paralogism, and the relationship of this attack to the second-edition Refutation of Idealism in "Reality and Representations: Kant's Refutation of Idealism." As to the First Paralogism, it seems to me that it sets the stage for both the Second and the Third Paralogism, and Kant's critiques of both of them reflect back on and develop material from his attack on the first, but that it contains little not handled better in the second and third. Kitcher says that "the first and third Paralogisms appear to cover exactly the same territory, the permanence of the I" (p. 194). I think this is a bit too simple – the First Paralogism does more than that. Nevertheless, I do not think that it warrants separate treatment.

3 Kemp Smith (*A Commentary to Kant's Critique of Pure Reason,* pp. 245 and 456), Strawson, Sellars, Bennett, Kitcher, and Powell all emphasize the relation. Kitcher sees in a general way that the danger posed by the Paralogisms resides in TD itself (p. 183).

4 Kitcher also recognizes that misinterpretations of what I am here calling UA are behind the Paralogisms (p. 192). As well as the central role of UA in the Second Paralogism, it is also at work in the first. Kant may have thought that to be one subject in this way also requires what Nagel calls functional integration, a topic we touched on in Chapter 1 ("Brain Bisection and the Unity of Consciousness," *Synthese* 22 [1971], pp. 396–413). If so, he managed to make this thought no more explicit in the Paralogisms chapter than he did in TD.

5 Strangely enough, Kitcher attributes to Kant the view that there are no necessary limits on how anything can be represented (p. 265). The statement of Kant's just quoted directly refutes that attribution.

6 As I said earlier, (1) might have to be modified if the group of representations were spread across time (see Chapter 8).

7 The phrase 'What it would be like to be that subject?' is taken from T. Nagel's "What Is It Like to be a Bat?" *Philosophical Review* 83 (1974). I prefer the variant 'How would it be for that subject?' as Nagel has suggested that he does too (p. 440n). I have changed the mood of both phrases. Nagel asked, 'What *is* it like . . . '. I ask, 'What *would* it be like . . . '. The reason is that, for creatures without self-awareness, there is nothing that it is like to be that creature. But there might still be something it would be like if they were aware of themselves. Again the distinction between awareness and self-awareness proves to be crucial to getting a clear grasp of something.

8 Practically every commentator spends some time trying to puzzle out how the analysis Kant gives of each Paralogism relates to the syllogistic argument for each of them with which each analysis begins. That investigation being purely exegetical and often none too rewarding, I will forgo it. Kemp Smith's, Bennett's, Ameriks', Kitcher's, and Powell's accounts of these relationships are among the most interesting.

9 The first part is the first four paragraphs, the second is paragraphs five to seven, the third is paragraphs seven to nine, and the fourth is made up of the rest of the section. Norman Kemp Smith identified these separate parts as long ago as 1918 (*Commentary*), though he combined the second and third into one. Few commentators have paid much attention to Kemp Smith's partitioning; nor did he himself give it much significance. However, Powell has recently breathed new life into it. In my view, he is the only commentator in recent times to see the true range of different arguments Kant considered in his attack on the Second Paralogism. The only one Kant actually attributed to RPsy was UA; the others arose in the course of his attempts to diagnose how RPsy could be convinced of something as unlikely as the mind being simple.

10 William James' version of this argument is entertaining: "Take a sentence of a dozen words, and take twelve men and to each one word. Then stand the men in a row or jam them in a bunch, and let each think of his word as intently as he will; nowhere will there be a consciousness of the whole sentence" (*Principles of Psychology,* i, 160; quoted by Kemp Smith, *Commentary,* p. 459).

11 Following Wilson ("Leibniz and Materialism", p. 510), I have modified Kemp Smith's translation slightly. He has "what is essentially composite".

12 For a different reading of Kant's claim that all the parts of a single representation must be had by a single subject, see Patricia Kitcher, "Kant's Paralogisms", pp. 542–3. She models the claim on the Fregean dictum that words have meaning only in the context of a sentence, rather than on the conditions for being aware of words as parts of a single object of experience as I do. However, she too sees

Kant's reaction to rational psychology's use of the claim as a functionalist one (see esp. pp. 191–2 of her book). In a nice move, she shows that Kant's refutation of RPsy here works equally well against recent arguments of Vendler, Nagel, and Searle (see chap. 7).

13 It might be worth recalling the account we have given of being aware of representations as one object (Chapter 2:4). To be aware of them as one object is to be aware of them in such a way that to be aware of any of the representations involved is also to be aware of others of them and of at least some of them as a group.

14 That Kant's critique of the Paralogisms could just as accurately have been aimed at Reid as any of the philosophers usually identified as a target has not been recognized. Moreover, Reid and Kant were near contemporaries (b. 1710 and 1724, respectively). We will return to the relationship between Reid's doctrines and Kant's critique of RPsy in Chapter 8:4.

15 By the phrase 'no whole number of persons', I mean something that is either too much to be one but too little to be two, or (the sort of case Nagel discusses in "Brain Bisection and the Unity of Consciousness") something to which the criteria for being one apply contradictorily, so that there is some reason to say the thing in question is one person and some reason to say that it is two – or three.

16 The passage just quoted helps to resolve a terminological question. At A347 = B406 Kant used the word 'simplicity' in making the point he here makes about absolute unity, as we saw earlier. This parallel is another indication that he meant the same thing by the two terms. On A784 = B812 he finally combined them into 'absolute simplicity'.

17 Nagel, "Brain Bisection and the Unity of Consciousness", p. 412.

18 At A344 = B402 he says that even across time we can *picture* ourselves only this way. That this constraint on how I can picture myself across time is compatible with my in fact being the result of a composite of beings over time is a central part of what Kant argues against the Third Paralogism of RPsy, as we will see in the next chapter.

19 Bennett (*Kant's Dialectic,* p. 83) attributes this argument to Descartes and he is surely right. Although the issue of historical models for the Paralogisms is much debated, Descartes not only held that the soul is noncomposite (without parts) and indivisible, he held that it is indivisible in both the ways I have defined. In addition, he argued for these claims using both UA and the appeal to self-awareness (R. Descartes, *Meditations,* VI; in *Philosophical Works,* trans. E. S. Haldane and G. R. T. Ross, Vol. 1, p. 195 [Cambridge University Press, 1970]).

20 In German the last phrase reads '*etwas von ihm zu kennen, oder zu wissen*'. Kemp Smith translates it 'without knowing anything of it either by direct acquaintance or otherwise', but this is clearly inadequate. See note 2 to Chapter 4.

21 Shoemaker, "Self-Reference and Self-Awareness", p. 558. Wittgenstein, *Blue and Brown Books,* pp. 66–7. As I said in Chapter 4, what Wittgenstein meant on these pages is controversial.

22 Strawson, *The Bounds of Sense,* pp. 165–9.

23 In addition to Chisholm, Swinburne, and Madell, there are traces of the idea even in Bernard Williams' treatment of indefinability (see "Imagination and the Self" and "The Self and the Future", both in *Problems of the Self,* pp. 26–64 [Cambridge University Press, 1973]). I discuss Chisholm and Williams in "Imagination, Possibility and Personal Identity".

8. The Third Paralogism

1 If 'remembers' in the sense used here *implies* identity, as some think, the terminology I have used to make this claim would have to be modified. The term 'q-memory' has been introduced for this purpose. We will return to this issue.

2 Derek Parfit, "Personal Identity", *Philosophical Review* 80 (1971), pp. 3–27; and idem *Reasons and Persons* (Oxford University Press, 1984).

3 Bennett, *Kant's Dialectic,* sec. 31. Ameriks, chap. 4. Powell, chap. 4.

4 Powell explores this parallel, too (pp. 157–62).

5 John Locke, *Essay Concerning Human Understanding* (1689), ed. A. C. Fraser, bk. 2, chap. 27, p. 188 (New York: Dover, 1959). Powell has noticed the parallel, too, though he seems not to see how detailed it is and how deep it goes (p. 157).

6 As Powell points out, that is why *consciousness* of self plays a much larger role in the attack on the Third Paralogism than in the attack on the second (p. 141). Just being simple would be metaphysically interesting, whether or not we are aware of it, but for *personal* identity, not just continuing to be me but also being *aware* of it matters.

7 Powell also differentiates the ontological from the epistemological, in the form of a distinction between the grounds and the criteria for identity (p. 148). I have explored the idea that personal identity is strict and philosophical and some recent thought experiments that have been held to support it in "Imagination, Possibility and Personal Identity". The thought experiments in question are different from the ones Kant explores but have some of the same roots in self-awareness. There are important problems with talk about senses of 'identity', of course. Here I just try to avoid them; I say something about them in the paper just mentioned.

8 See A363, also the appendix on the Amphiboly (A263 = B319), A690 = B718 of the appendix to the Dialectic, and *Prolegomena,* §48.

9 Bennett, sec. 31–8 of *Kant's Dialectic.* Bennett misses some other things, too – for example, Kant's diagnosis of why the way the mind appears to itself in ASA generates an illusion that personal identity is special in this way. Indeed, he tells us that he has no idea why Kant thinks that a subject will inevitably attribute identity with some earlier subject to itself (pp. 93–102). Powell touches on the relevant points and even mentions Butler (p. 162), but seems to miss their significance. Ameriks seems to imply that Kant himself believed that personal identity is 'strict and philosophical' (p. 149). He may be right, but not for the reasons he gives. If Kant held the view, it would have been as an article of faith on practical grounds, not on intellectual grounds (see Section 8).

10 For an account of how it is legitimate for *rational* psychology to appeal to a form of *experience* in this way, see Chapter 7:2.

11 Paton, "Self-Identity".

12 Ameriks has a good discussion of this issue, pp. 139–42.

13 Lorne Falkenstein has pointed out to me that I may appear to be assuming the transcendental reality of time in my remarks about *current* representations, *current* memories, etc. In response, I would suggest that for Kant current representations are simply the representations one is having. These are the representations that make us aware of themselves and their objects by themselves, not or not just as the object of another representation.

For some suggestions about how to develop the account of the relation of memory to current experience farther than I have taken it, see Strawson, *The Bounds of Sense,* p. 111. Like many others, however, he takes memory to be more central to current experience than I do or Kant does, as I read the latter at least.

14 Kitcher sees this point, or comes very close to doing so (chap. 5). Rather than longing for 'strict' or 'absolute' sameness of subject over time, she is content with a subject who simply consists of the kinds of continuities of content and causality that link earlier to later representations in synthetic processes. Kant would have had no quarrel with her good, inner-sense enterprise. It would not yield the sort of conclusions about either the subject or its identity that the Patons of this world want.

15 Ameriks sees Kant's analysis as more sceptical and as generating less positive doctrine than many, but I go further than even he does.

16 Earlier experiences can reach into the present to become synthesized with current experiences via more channels than memory or quasi-memory. Consider, for example, the way in which earlier experiences (including earlier wishes and fantasies) shape current wishes, expectations, fantasies, fears, etc. by setting up dispositions. This is more like Kant's associative reproduction than it is like memory; indeed, it need not involve memory at all. Wollheim discusses such inputs to synthesis, though not in these terms, in *The Thread of Life.* For an earlier discussion in a rather different vein of the various ways earlier representations can enter current ones, see Shoemaker, "Persons and Their Pasts", pp. 269–71.

17 Shoemaker introduces a special notion of 'witnessing' to capture this idea of remembering something in the way I remember objects of representations I was aware of by having them ("Persons and Their Pasts", pp. 269–71).

18 Ibid.; Parfit, "Personal Identity".

19 Parfit gives a good account of the distinction between veridical q-memory, as he calls it, and imagination, hallucination, being told about something, etc., in "Personal Identity".

20 L. Wittgenstein, "Notes for Lectures on 'Private Experience' and 'Sense-Data' ", pp. 264–5; Parfit, "Personal Identity", p. 15. As I said, Bennett claims to have no idea why Kant thought that a subject must attribute identity to itself at different times (*Kant's Dialectic,* pp. 93–102). We now see why.

21 Though I came to my thoughts about the Third Paralogism independently, both Ameriks (pp. 141–3) and Powell (pp. 133–4, 169) make the point that the necessity of representations *appearing* to have had a common subject does not entail that they have had one. (So much for new ideas about Kant!) However, neither of them gives an account of Kant's Parfit-like explanation of how memory is able to produce the curious result that other minds could appear in my q-memories to be me. (Other kinds of representations can, too, as we will see in Section 6.) Perhaps the person who has come closest to seeing Kant's point here is Georges Rey, who notes that Kant tried to block the move from the transcendental unity of apperception to the identity of the person (G. Rey, "Survival", in Amélie Rorty, ed., *The Identities of Persons,* p. 62 [Berkeley: University of California Press, 1975]). He also urges that what matters to us is not identity. Kant would not have agreed with him about that (see Section 8).

22 Joseph Butler, "Dissertation I: Of Personal Identity", in his *Analogy of Religion* (1736) (London: Dent, 1906); Thomas Reid, *Essays on the Intellectual Powers*

of Man (1785) (Cambridge, Mass.: MIT Press, 1969), essay 3, chap. 4: "Of Identity".

23 Butler, "Of Personal Identity", p. 324.

24 Reid, *Essays,* pp. 200 and 203.

25 I discuss Butler and the doctrine that personal identity is strict and absolute further in "Imagination, Possibility and Personal Identity".

26 Kitcher presents persuasive evidence for the proposition that Kant knew a good deal more about Hume's sceptical arguments concerning the mind than has generally been credited (chap. 4). Kant does mention Hume by name in the second-edition TD (B127) and in the *Prolegomena,* of course, just not in connection with personal identity.

27 Kitcher makes this noncontingent link the basis of her account both of Kant's answer to Hume and of his own account of synthesis and unity. I think Kant would say, certainly I would say, that she leaves something out.

28 Strawson, *The Bounds of Sense,* p. 164.

29 The reference to Bennett is to material that he left out of *Kant's Dialectic* in the end. The reference to Strawson is to *Individuals,* chap. 3: "Persons". Powell makes some interesting remarks about Hume and Kant (p. 138). He suggests that whereas Hume saw Butler, the rationalists, etc. as reaching over-inflated conclusions as the result of habit or custom, Kant saw them as doing so because they misinterpreted the self as it appears in unified consciousness. Unfortunately, he does not describe the misinterpretation.

30 Paton, "Self-Identity".

31 Waxman, *Kant's Model of the Mind,* p. 18.

32 Allison articulates the same distinction (p. 270), but I do not think he would want to draw Waxman's radical conclusions from it. Dennett makes a similar point about the ordering of representations (*Consciousness Explained,* pp. 136–38). Indeed, he begins chap. 6 with a highly apposite quote from Kant: "I can indeed say that my representations follow one another; but this is only to say that we are conscious of them as in a time-sequence" (n. to A37 = B54). We looked at this view of Dennett's earlier in Chapter 3:1.

33 Guyer (p. 324) quotes *Reflexion* 6312, written in 1790. Kant says there that we "construct time as the mere form of the representation of our inner condition", and Guyer connects this view to a realist streak in Kant by noting that Kant further argues that "there must really be something outside us", i.e., something other than ourselves and our states, with which we have some kind of immediate contact; otherwise, "the representation of something outside us could never come to be thought" (Ak. XVIII:612–3). I take up this topic in "Reality and Representations: Kant's Refutation of Idealism".

34 Wittgenstein, *Tractatus Logico-Philosophicus*, 5.62.

35 Powell also discusses this argument (p. 134).

36 *Tractatus,* 5.632.

37 In a commentary on an earlier version of part of this chapter, Lorne Maclachlan argued that Kant's attack on the Third Paralogism has nothing to do with memory, memory being an empirical matter. For the reasons I have just given, I think he is far from entirely right about this; moreover, RPsy can use the kind of awareness of previous subjects given by the kind of memory we have been dealing with, or so I argued in Chapter 7. However, Maclachlan's challenge forced me to sharpen my understanding of the broader structure of Kant's attack considerably and I am grateful to him for mounting it.

38 *Reflexion* 5655 (Ak. XVIII:314), cited by Allison, p. 270.
39 Thomas Nagel, *The View from Nowhere* (New York: Oxford University Press, 1986).
40 Paul Wallich ("Silicon Babies", *Scientific American* 265 [Dec. 1991], p. 132) quotes Patrick Hayes as asking the same question about Lenant's CYC, the huge knowledge base being built to give artificial knowledge systems something like the same belief base as ordinary people, or at least babies.
41 The German of the first sentence of this passage is, "*Wie aber das ich, der ich denke, von dem Ich, das sich selbst anschauel, unterschieden . . .*". Kemp Smith translates this, "How the 'I' that thinks can be distinct from the 'I' that intuits itself . . .". In addition to the changes I made, I have removed his emendations. We also looked at Kemp Smith's translation of this passage in Chapter 4, note 14.
42 Reprinted in Dennett, *Brainstorms,* chap. 17.
43 Strawson, *Individuals,* pp. 90–4.
44 Wittgenstein, *Blue and Brown Books,* p. 63.
45 Dennett, "Intentional Systems," in *Brainstorms,* pp. 3–22, at 12.
46 L. Wittgenstein, "Notes for Lectures on 'Private Experience' and 'Sense-Data' ", pp. 241, 253, 255–6. As I mentioned near the end of Chapter 4, Wittgenstein even used the terminology of subject and object, distinguishing the use of 'I' 'as subject' and its use 'as object' (*Blue and Brown Books,* pp. 66–70). He also noted that the concept of the self behaves in some respects like the concept of space ("Notes", p. 256). On this conception, one's world might well be quite solipsistic. Indeed, some of the things Kant says in the first-edition Fourth Paralogism may imply solipsism, a possibility I consider in "Reality and Representations: Kant's Refutation of Idealism".
47 Shoemaker, "Self-Reference and Self-Awareness", p. 563.
48 *Critique of Practical Reason* (1788), trans. Lewis White Beck (Indianapolis: Library of the Liberal Arts, 1956), p. 137 (Ak V:132).
49 For more on this 'double method' for justifying the acceptance of propositions, see Butts, *Kant and the Double Government Methodology.*

9. The second-edition subjective deduction

1 We examined this notion of information briefly in Chapter 3:1. Many philosophers have noted that it is neither as clear nor as neutral as it might appear to be.
2 Jerry Fodor is currently the leading exponent of this model (see *The Language of Thought*). Fodor uses it to support what is now a very conservative position, that normal psychological discourse corresponds to actual structures in the brain and has and will continue to have a central role in our understanding of mind, and that our psychological states are independent of the world – in all, a rather Kantian model.
3 Dennett, "A Cure for the Common Code", in *Brainstorms,* p. 101.
4 Ibid.
5 Dennett's new theory of the self as a 'virtual captain', a coming together of an assemblage of representations ('memes') that somehow come to generate a representation of the whole system and at least a feeling of being in charge, is his latest attempt to give substance to the idea of a self-representing representation.

I will consider it again later; it is closer to Kant's view than it might appear to be.

6 Henrich's two-steps-in-one-proof analysis seems, broadly speaking, to have won the day ("The Proof-Structure of Kant's Transcendental Deduction", *Review of Metaphysics* 22 [1969], pp. 640–59, and *Identität und Objektivität*). Unfortunately, all that victory has done is throw the weight of controversy onto what is going on and what is accomplished in each step. Practically every commentator on Kant has something to say about this matter; it would take a whole book just to review their various ideas.

7 Allison, p. 137.

8 One of the few commentators to give §16 the sort of close reading I think it needs is Allison, though even he thinks that TD starts here, not in §15, as we saw (p. 137). Allison lays out many of the same pieces of the subjective deduction as I do, but he assigns value to them differently from me and assembles them into a somewhat different reconstruction of Kant's argument. The differences are complicated and, in places, subtle. To discuss them properly would take a great deal of space. I will not try to do so in any comprehensive way here.

9 Linking not being something to me and being impossible as he does, Kant toys with the idea that being something to me is a condition of a representation existing at all. This phenomenalist idea is expressed even more clearly in the first edition: "Since [an appearance] has in itself no objective reality, but exists only in being known, [if it is nothing to us,] it would be nothing at all" (A120). If this move worked, it would suit Kant's purposes wonderfully. There would be no problem of the relational categories not applying to representations that do not 'belong to one consciousness' – because there would be no such representations! Unfortunately, I do not see that it works.

10 Guyer, p. 28.

11 Kemp Smith has "as I have representations of which I am conscious *to myself*", but there is weak warrant for 'to myself' in the German ("*als ich Vorstellungen habe, deren ich mir bewußt bin.*").

12 Allison reads Kant's 'consciousness' on B137 as meaning 'self-consciousness' (p. 145). I see no basis for this reading; indeed, I think it is plainly wrong.

13 This phrase "and is possible only through the consciousness of this synthesis" is actually a little less clearly a remark about awareness of oneself (ASA) or of one's representations (ESA) than it looks. The words 'consciousness of . . . ' ('*Bewußtsein dieser . . .*') are ambiguous. They could mean 'consciousness that has as its object . . . ', or they could mean only 'consciousness of the type found in . . . '. Only the second makes good sense in the context, though the first is a more natural way to read the English translation. On the second reading, Kant's argument contains nothing new; it is still a straightforward inference from (2) to (3).

14 Allison thinks that the contrast is not between a representation being mine and a representation being something to me, but between a representation being mine and its "function[ing] as a representation, represent[ing] some object" (p. 137). I think all representations represent 'some object' (in the 'logical', not the 'weighty', sense of object that Allison is talking about at this point). What else is there for them to do? If so, Allison's distinction is trivial. However, not all my representations are 'something to me' in Kant's sense.

15 Given the importance that Strawson, Wilkerson, and others place on self-ascription and its possibility, I should perhaps note that Kant does talk about

self-ascription – once in the first edition (A122), and once in the second-edition subjective deductions: "All *my* representations . . . must be subject to that condition under which alone I can ascribe them to the identical self as *my* representations" (B138). Likewise, on B134 Kant talks about the conditions of *calling* all my representations mine. The possibility of self-ascription may, however, merely be a consequence of what really interested him; the possibility of self-ascription is provided by a representation being something to me. None of this changes the fact that being something to me is his main way of getting from his starting point (representation of objects) via the unity of consciousness to the Categories. Moreover, the fact that Kant *could* name self-ascription when he wanted to makes it likely that when he does *not* do so, he was talking about something else. We will look at self-ascription again briefly in Section 5.

16 Kemp Smith has "the general expression".

17 Strawson, p. 117. We discussed his notion in Chapter 6:I:5 and 6:II:2.

18 Waxman, *Kant's Model of the Mind,* p. 272. Waxman's argument is that "the faculty of representation whose peculiar constitution determines the objects of representations as transcendentally ideal cannot itself be transcendentally ideal". True; but on Waxman's own analysis, representations *as they are* are not 'transcendentally ideal' either. Indeed, on his analysis, representations in themselves are not even temporal (p. 18).

19 My translation; Kemp Smith has the representation of unity *adding itself* to the representation of the manifold, but there seems to be no warrant for that in the German. In the German it merely *comes* to the manifold ("*sie zur Vorstellung des Mannigfaltigen . . . hinzukommt*"); what brings it there is not specified.

20 However, Dennett's memes engage in activities of judging (*Consciousness Explained;* see, e.g., p. 239). I owe this point to Christopher Viger.

21 *Consciousness Explained,* p. 228.

22 The most interesting discussion of this strain in Kant's work on the mind is still Sellars' " . . . this I or he or it (the thing) which thinks . . . ". See also Pippin, "Kant on the Spontaneity of Mind".

23 Strawson, *The Bounds of Sense,* p. 117; see p. 98.

10. Nature and awareness of the self

1 The first quote is from Kitcher's book, p. 195, the second is from her "Kant's Paralogisms", p. 527. See also "Kant's Real Self", pp. 118–21, and "Kant on Self-Identity", pp. 41–72. Though Allison puts more emphasis on unity than Kitcher does, in other respects he would seem to agree with what she says here (see p. 282 of his book). I think Powell, Rosenberg, and others who claim that Kant thought that uses of 'I' are nonreferring or refer to a function of unity, not a thing, would also agree.

2 I attempt to do so in "Reality and Representations: Kant's Refutation of Idealism".

3 As the preceding two paragraphs will make clear, I think Kitcher's claim that Kant's transcendental self, the being that does the thinking and apperceiving, "must be phenomenal" (p. 22) grossly oversimplifies a complicated and conceptually rich issue.

4 Kitcher, "Kant's Paralogisms", p. 527.

5 The first quote is from Kitcher, "Kant's Paralogisms", p. 527; the second is from her book, p. 195.

6 Kitcher, pp. 122–3; 'subpersonal' is a phrase of Dennett's and means, roughly, 'not introspectible and not open to deliberate control'; see "Toward a Cognitive Theory of Consciousness", in *Brainstorms,* chap. 9, and note 4 to Chapter 3 above.

7 My reason for thinking that this would be Kitcher's answer is that she espouses a view that uses of 'I' are nonreferential (pp. 185, 195, 197).

8 Kitcher, idem, p. 195; "Kant's Paralogisms", p. 527.

9 Kitcher, "Kant's Paralogisms", p. 527. She has laid out the theory behind this view more fully in "Kant on Self-Identity", pp. 41–72.

10 Pippin, "Kant on the Spontaneity of the Mind", pp. 449–76. Pippin also says some interesting things about what Kant meant by spontaneity and why.

11 Allison, p. 290.

12 Strawson, *Individuals,* chap. 3, p. 96.

13 Letter to Herz, May 26, 1789 (Ak. XI:52). I will not go into the question of whether such automatically generated associations would count as full reproductive syntheses. Presumably they would not at least be *productive* syntheses.

14 Cassirer, *Kant's Life and Thought,* chap. 3.

15 We discussed this issue briefly in Chapter 5:1 and in Chapter 8, note 33.

16 Walker (*Kant,* p. 134) views Kant as making a regrettable slip. Sellars (" . . . this I or he or it (the thing) which thinks . . . "), correctly in my view, views him as saying exactly the right thing. Roderick Chisholm attributes the third position to Kant in *Person and Object*, pp. 41–6, and Waxman does so in *Kant's Model of the Mind,* chap. 8 (all references to Waxman hereafter will be to this book). Walker thinks this is the view Kant should have taken. Kitcher ascribes the fourth position to Kant on p. 195 of her book and in "Kant's Paralogisms", p. 527. Allison ascribes this view to Kant in chap. 13, pp. 282 and 290. Of these discussions, Sellars' strikes me as by far the best, largely because he sees the true character and significance of the inner sense–apperception distinction, the only one of the six who does. (Allison is also aware of the importance of the distinction, but mischaracterizes this aspect of it.)

17 Sellars, " . . . this I or he or it (the thing) which thinks . . . ".

18 Waxman, p. 283. This conviction that we are immediately aware only of representations, not even the mind as it is, in turn supports Waxman's belief that the representing mind as it is "cannot itself be representation" (p. 272). If the representing mind were representation, then, granting that we would be immediately aware of the representation(s) concerned, we would have some form of immediate awareness of the mind.

19 Guyer focuses his analysis on the Refutation of Idealism (pp. 327–8). It was written at about the same time as §24 and §25.

20 Waxman; see, e.g., p. 278.

21 Kant says this in the well-known *Reflexion* 6001 (Ak. XVIII:420–1). I explore the 'world' side in "Reality and Representations: Kant's Refutation of Idealism". As I try to show there, Kant gives reason to think that he may, at times at least, have entertained the idea that acts of reference to things other than ourselves reach all the way out to them, make us immediately aware of them, too. We then 'clothe' these references in a 'sense' – in judgements *about* the object. Category and theory laden, these judgements are not a mirror. Shaped by the resources of the mind, they are the mind's best effort to find order in the manifold that these acts of reference generate. Even if we are immediately aware of *objects,* we have no unshaped awareness of any of their *features.*

22 Walker, *Kant,* p. 134.

23 *Reflexion* 5653 (Ak. XVIII: 306).
24 It does not involve intellectual *intuition,* either. Kant allows that intellectual intuition is possible, but insists that we do not have it (perhaps God does; that may be why Kant allows that it is possible). Yet we do have immediate awareness of ourselves in ASA; so this 'thought of the self' cannot be intellectual intuition.
25 Waxman, pp. 280–1.
26 Kitcher, "Kant's Real Self", p. 119n.
27 I have taken out Kemp Smith's interpolations, which are unnecessary, and altered his translation.
28 Kant repeats the point on B277.
29 Waxman, p. 280.
30 Ibid., p. 288.
31 Paul M. Churchland, *Matter and Consciousness,* pp. 76–9.
32 Shoemaker, "Persons and Their Pasts", p. 269.
33 This fact points to a problem for any account such as Waxman's: If my awareness of myself as myself is not awareness of *myself,* why should I think of any ground that underlies what I am aware of as *me?* Could it not just as well be Spinozan absolute substance, or Hegelian absolute spirit, or Lucretian atoms, or anything else you like? Waxman himself raises the issue, but ducks it (pp. 288–9).
34 In these summary concluding remarks on what still is living in Kant's work on the mind, I do not give references to the places in the book where his various contributions have been discussed. To have done so would have made the section virtually unreadable. For those who would like to be reminded of the discussions in question, I hope the section headings in the Contents will suffice.

Bibliography

Works by Immanuel Kant

References to Kant of the form 'Ak. N' and 'N:xx' are to *Gesammelte Schriften*. Ed. Koniglichen Preussischen Akademie der Wissenschaften, 29 vols. Berlin: Walter de Gruyter et al., 1902–.

Anthropology from a Pragmatic Point of View. Trans. Mary Gregor. The Hague: Martinus Nijhoff, 1974 (Ak. VII).

Critique of Practical Reason (1788). Trans. Lewis White Beck. Indianapolis, Ind.: Library of the Liberal Arts, 1956 (Ak. V).

Critique of Pure Reason (1781 and 1787). Trans. Norman Kemp Smith as *Immanuel Kant's Critique of Pure Reason*. London: Macmillan, 1963.

Kant's Philosophical Correspondence, 1759–1799. Ed. and trans. Arnulf Zweig. Chicago: University of Chicago Press, 1967. Kant to Marcus Herz of May 26, 1789 (Ak. XI:52). Kant to Beck of July 1, 1797 (Ak. XI:514).

The Metaphysical Foundations of Natural Science (1786). Trans. with intro. by James Ellington. Indianapolis, Ind.: Library of Liberal Arts, 1970 (Ak. IV).

Prolegomena to Any Future Metaphysics that Will Be Able to Come Forward as Science (1783). Trans. P. Carus; rev. with intro. L. W. Beck. Indianapolis, Ind.: Library of the Liberal Arts, 1950 (Ak. IV).

What Real Progress Has Metaphysics Made in Germany Since the Time of Leibniz and Wolff? (1804). Trans. T. Humphrey. New York: Abaris, 1983 (Ak. XX).

Other works

Allison, Henry. "Kant's Refutation of Idealism". *Monist* 72 (1989), pp. 190–208.

Kant's Transcendental Idealism: An Interpretation and Defense. New Haven, Conn.: Yale University Press, 1983.

Ameriks, Karl. "Kant and Guyer on Apperception". *Archiv für Geschichte der Philosophie* 65 (1983), pp. 174–84.

Kant's Theory of Mind. Oxford University Press, 1983.

Anderson, J. *The Architecture of Cognition*. Cambridge, Mass.: Harvard University Press, 1983.

Anscombe, G. E. M. "The First Person". In Samuel Guttenplan, ed., *Mind and Language*, pp. 45–65. Oxford University Press, 1975.

Intention. Oxford: Blackwell, 1957; 2d ed. 1963.

"The Intentionality of Sensation: A Grammatical Feature". In R. J. Butler, ed. *Analytical Philosophy*, 2d series, pp. 158–81. Oxford: Blackwell, 1965.

Aquila, Richard. *Matter in Mind*. Bloomington: Indiana University Press, 1989.

Bennett, Jonathan. *Kant's Analytic*. Cambridge University Press, 1966.

Kant's Dialectic. Cambridge University Press, 1974.
Brook, Andrew. "Imagination, Possibility and Personal Identity". *American Philosophical Quarterly* 12 (1975), pp. 185–98.
"Kant's *A Priori* Methods for Recognizing Necessary Truths". In Philip Hanson and Bruce Hunter, eds., *Return of the A Priori. Canadian Journal of Philosophy,* supp. vol. 18 (1993), pp. 215–52.
"Reality and Representations: Kant's Refutation of Idealism". Unpublished manuscript, Carleton University.
Butler, Joseph. "Dissertation I: Of Personal Identity". In his *Analogy of Religion* (1736). London: Dent, 1906.
Butts, Robert. *Kant and the Double Government Methodology*. Dordrecht: Reidel, 1984.
Cassirer, Ernst. *Kant's Life and Thought* (1918). New Haven, Conn.: Yale University Press, 1982.
Castañeda, H.-N. " 'He': A Study in the Logic of Self-Consciousness". *Ratio* 8 (1966), pp. 130–57.
Chisholm, Roderick. *The First Person*. Brighton, Sussex: Harvester Press, 1981.
"The Loose and Popular and Strict and Philosophical Senses of Identity". In Norman S. Care and Robert M. Grimm, eds., *Perception and Personal Identity,* pp. 107–25. Cleveland, Ohio: The Press of Case Western Reserve University, 1969.
Person and Object. London: Allen & Unwin, 1976.
Churchland, P.M. "Eliminative Materialism and the Propositional Attitudes". *Journal of Philosophy* 78 (1981), pp. 67–90.
Matter and Consciousness. Cambridge, Mass.: MIT Press, 1984; 2d ed., 1988.
Churchland, P.M., and Churchland, P.S. "Could a Machine Think?" *Scientific American* 262 (Jan. 1990), pp. 32–7.
Churchland, P.S. "Consciousness: The Transmutation of a Concept". *Pacific Philosophical Quarterly* 65 (1983), pp. 80–95.
Neurophilosophy. Cambridge, Mass.: Bradford Books/MIT Press, 1986.
Churchland, P.S., and Sejnowski, T.J. *The Computational Brain*. Cambridge, Mass.: MIT Press, 1992.
Dennett, D.C. *Brainstorms*. Montgomery, Vt.: Bradford Books, 1978.
Consciousness Explained. Boston: Little, Brown, 1991.
Content and Consciousness. London: Routledge & Kegan Paul, 1969.
The Intentional Stance. Cambridge, Mass.: Bradford Books / MIT Press, 1987.
"Real Patterns". *Journal of Philosophy* 89 (1991), pp. 27–51.
Dennett, D.C., and Kinsbourne, M. "Time and the Observer: The Where and When of Consciousness in the Brain". *Behavioral and Brain Sciences* 15 (1992), pp. 183–247.
Descartes, René. *Meditations*. In E. S. Haldane and G. R. T. Ross, trans., *Philosophical Works,* vol. 1, pp. 131–200. Cambridge University Press, 1970.
Dretske, Fred. *Explaining Behaviour*. Cambridge, Mass.: MIT Press, 1988.
Evans, Gareth. *Varieties of Reference*. Ed. J. McDowell. Oxford University Press, 1982.
Falkenstein, Lorne. "Is Perceptual Space Monadic?" *Philosophy and Phenomenological Research* 49 (1989), pp. 709–13.
"Kant, Mendelssohn, Lambert, and the Subjectivity of Time". *Journal of the History of Philosophy* 19 (1991), pp. 227–51.

"Kant's Account of Intuition". *Canadian Journal of Philosophy* 21 (1991), pp. 165–93.

"Kant's Account of Sensation". *Canadian Journal of Philosophy* 20 (1990), pp. 63–88.

"Spaces and Times: A Kantian Response". *Idealist Studies* 16 (1986), pp. 1–11.

"Was Kant a Nativist?" *Journal of the History of Ideas* 51 (1990), pp. 573–97.

Flanagan, Owen J. *The Science of the Mind*. Cambridge, Mass.: MIT Press, 1984.

Fodor, Jerry. *The Language of Thought*. New York: Crowell, 1975.

The Modularity of Mind. Cambridge, Mass.: MIT Press, 1983.

Psychosemantics. Cambridge, Mass.: MIT Press, 1988.

Förster, Eckart, ed. *Kant's Transcendental Deductions*. Stanford, Calif.: Stanford University Press, 1989.

Gregory, Richard L. *Eye and Brain*. London: World University Library, 1966.

Gregory, Richard L., ed. *The Oxford Companion to the Mind*. Oxford University Press, 1987.

Guyer, Paul. "Kant on Apperception and *A Priori* Synthesis". *American Philosophical Quarterly* 17 (1980), pp. 205–12.

Kant and the Claims of Knowledge. Cambridge University Press, 1987.

Hatfield, Gary. *The Natural and the Normative*. Cambridge, Mass.: MIT Press, 1990.

Henrich, Dieter. *Identität und Objektivität*. Heidelberg: Carl Winter UniversitätsVerlag, 1976.

"Kant's Notion of a Deduction and the Methodological Background of the First *Critique*". In Eckart Förster, ed., *Kant's Transcendental Deductions*, pp. 29–46. Stanford, Calif.: Stanford University Press, 1989.

"The Proof-structure of Kant's Transcendental Deduction". *Review of Metaphysics* 22 (1969), pp. 640–59.

Hume, David. *A Treatise of Human Nature*. Ed. L. A. Selby-Bigge. Oxford University Press, 1962.

James, William. *Pragmatism*. Cambridge, Mass.: Harvard University Press, 1907.

Kemp Smith, Norman. *A Commentary on Kant's Critique of Pure Reason*. London: Macmillan, 1918.

Kitcher, Patricia. "Kant on Self-Identity". *Philosophical Review* 91 (1982), pp. 41–72.

"Kant's Paralogisms". *Philosophical Review* 91 (1982), pp. 515–47.

"Kant's Real Self". In Allen Wood, ed., *Self and Nature in Kant's Philosophy*, pp. 113–47. Ithaca, N.Y.: Cornell University Press, 1984.

Kant's Transcendental Psychology. New York: Oxford University Press, 1990.

Kripke, Saul. "Naming and Necessity". In G. Harman and D. Davidson, eds., *Semantics of Natural Languages*, pp. 253–354. Dordrecht: Reidel, 1972. Republished with changes as *Naming and Necessity*. Cambridge, Mass.: Harvard University Press, 1980.

Leibniz, Gottlieb. *The Principles of Nature and Grace*, sec. 4, and *Monadology* (both 1714). Trans. Robert Latta. In Philip P. Weiner, ed., *Leibniz: Selections*, pp. 525 and 535. New York: Scribner's, 1951.

Locke, John. *Essay Concerning Human Understanding* (1689). Ed. A. C. Fraser. New York: Dover, 1959.

Lycan, William, ed. *Mind and Cognition*. Oxford: Blackwell, 1990.

Mackie, J. L. "The Transcendental 'I' ". In Zak van Straaten, ed., *Philosophical Subjects: Essays Presented to P. F. Strawson*, pp. 48–61. Oxford University Press, 1980.

Marcel, A. J., and Bisiach, E., eds. *Consciousness in Contemporary Science*. Oxford University Press, 1988.

Martindale, Colin. "Can We Construct Kantian Mental Machines?" *Journal of Mind and Behaviour* 8 (1987), pp. 261–8.

Meerbote, Ralf. "Kant's Functionalism". In J. C. Smith, ed., *Historical Foundations of Cognitive Science*, pp. 161–87. Dordrecht: Reidel, 1989.

Meiklejohn, J. M. D., trans. *Critique of Pure Reason*. London: Everyman's Library 909, Dent, 1934.

Mijuskovic, Ben. *The Achilles of Rationalist Arguments*. The Hague: Nijhoff, 1974.

Minsky, Marvin. *The Society of Mind*. New York: Simon & Schuster, 1985.

Nagel, Thomas. "Physicalism". *Philosophical Review* 74 (1965), pp. 339–56.

"Brain Bisection and the Unity of Consciousness". *Synthese* 22 (1971), pp. 396–413.

The View from Nowhere. New York: Oxford University Press, 1986.

"What Is It Like to be a Bat?" *Philosophical Review* 83 (1974), pp. 435–50.

Newell, A. "Production Systems: Models of Control Structures". In W. G. Chase, ed., *Visual Information Processing*, pp. 463–526. New York: Academic Press, 1973.

Unified Theories of Cognition. Cambridge, Mass.: Harvard University Press, 1990.

Newell, A., Rosenbloom, P. S., and Laird, J. E. "Symbolic Architectures for Cognition". In Michael Posner, ed., *Foundations of Cognitive Science*, pp. 93–132. Cambridge, Mass.: MIT Press, 1989.

Nozick, Robert. *Philosophical Explanations*. Cambridge, Mass.: Harvard University Press, 1981.

Parfit, Derek. "Personal Identity". *Philosophical Review* 80 (1971), pp. 3–27.

Reasons and Persons. Oxford University Press, 1984.

Paton, H. J. "Self Identity". In his *In Defence of Reason*, pp. 99–116. London: Hutchison, 1951.

Perry, John. "Introduction: The Problem of Personal Identity". In John Perry, ed., *Personal Identity*, pp. 3–30. Berkeley: University of California Press, 1975.

"The Problem of the Essential Indexical". *Nous* 13 (1979), pp. 3–21.

Pippin, Robert. "Kant on the Spontaneity of Mind". *Canadian Journal of Philosophy* 17 (1987), pp. 449–76.

Powell, C. Thomas. *Kant's Theory of Self-Consciousness*. Oxford University Press, 1990.

Putnam, Hilary. "The Meaning of Meaning". In his *Mind, Language and Reality: Philosophical Essays*, vol. 2, pp. 215–71. Cambridge University Press, 1975.

Representations and Reality. Cambridge, Mass.: MIT Press, 1988.

Reid, Thomas. *Essays on the Intellectual Powers of Man* (1785). Cambridge, Mass.: MIT Press, 1969.

An Inquiry into the Human Mind on the Principles of Common Sense (1764). Edinburgh: Bell Publishers, 1814.

Rey, Georges. "Survival". In Amélie Rorty, ed., *The Identities of Persons*, pp. 41–66. Berkeley: University of California Press, 1976.

Rock, Irvin, and Palmer, Stephen. "The Legacy of Gestalt Psychology". *Scientific American* 263 (Dec. 1990), pp. 84–91.

Rosenberg, Jay F. " 'I Think': Some Reflections on Kant's Paralogisms". *Midwest Studies in Philosophy* 10 (1986), pp. 503–32.

One World and Our Knowledge of It. Dordrecht: Reidel, 1980.

The Thinking Self. Philadelphia: Temple University Press, 1986.

Rosenthal, D. "Two Concepts of Consciousness". *Philosophical Studies* 49 (1986), pp. 329–59.

Sacks, Oliver. *The Man Who Mistook His Wife for a Hat and Other Clinical Tales.* New York: Harper & Row, 1970.

Schacter, Daniel L. "Memory". In Michael Posner, ed., *Foundations of Cognitive Science,* pp. 683–726. Cambridge, Mass.: MIT Press, 1989.

Sellars, Wilfred. "Some Remarks on Kant's Theory of Experience". *Journal of Philosophy* 64 (1967), pp. 633–47. Reprinted in his *Essays in Philosophy and Its History,* pp. 44–61. Dordrecht: Reidel, 1974.

Science and Metaphysics. New York: Humanities Press, 1968.

"... this I or he or it (the thing) which thinks ...". *Proceedings of the American Philosophical Association* 44 (1970–1), pp. 5–31. Reprinted in his *Essays in Philosophy and Its History,* pp. 62–90. Dordrecht: Reidel, 1974.

Shoemaker, Sydney. "Persons and Their Pasts". *American Philosophical Quarterly* 7 (1970), pp. 269–85.

"Self-Reference and Self-Awareness". *Journal of Philosophy* 65, no. 20 (1968), pp. 555–67.

Shoemaker, Sydney, and Swinburne, Richard. *Personal Identity.* Oxford: Blackwell, 1984.

Strawson, P. F. *The Bounds of Sense.* London: Methuen, 1966.

Individuals. London: Methuen, 1959.

"Sensibility, Understanding, and the Doctrine of Synthesis". In Eckart Förster, ed., *Kant's Transcendental Deductions,* pp. 47–88. Stanford, Calif.: Stanford University Press, 1989.

Treisman, A. "Features and Objects in Visual Processing". *Scientific American* 255 (Nov. 1986), pp. 114B–125.

Treisman, A., and Gelade, G. "A Feature-Integration Theory of Attention". *Cognitive Psychology* 12 (1980), pp. 97–136.

Underwood, G., and Stevens, R., eds. *Aspects of Consciousness.* New York: Academic Press, 1979–82.

Walker, R. C. S. *Kant.* London: Routledge & Kegan Paul, 1978.

Wallich, Paul. "Silicon Babies". *Scientific American* 265 (Dec. 1991), pp. 125–34.

Waxman, Wayne. *Kant's Model of the Mind.* New York: Oxford University Press, 1991.

Wilkerson, T. E. *Kant's Critique of Pure Reason: A Commentary for Students.* Oxford University Press, 1976.

Wilkes, K. V. "___, yishi, duh, um, and consciousness". In A. J. Marcel and E. Bisiach, eds., *Consciousness in Contemporary Science*, pp. 16–41. Oxford University Press, 1988.

Williams, Bernard. *Problems of the Self.* Cambridge University Press, 1973.

Wilson, Margaret. "Leibniz and Materialism". *Canadian Journal of Philosophy* 3 (1974), pp. 495–514.

Wittgenstein, L. *Blue and Brown Books.* Oxford: Blackwell, 1964.

"Notes for Lectures on 'Private Experience' and 'Sense-Data' ". Ed. Rush Rhees. *Philosophical Review* 77 (1968), pp. 271–300.

Philosophical Investigations. Oxford: Blackwell, 1953.
"Some Remarks on Logical Form". *Proceedings of the Aristotelian Society,* supp. vol. 9 (1929), pp. 162–71.
Tractatus Logico-Philosophicus (1921). London: Routledge & Kegan Paul, 1961.
Wollheim, Richard. *The Thread of Life*. Cambridge, Mass.: Harvard University Press, 1984.

Index of passages cited

Critique of Pure Reason

Passages from material new to the second edition

General index

LaVergne, TN USA
16 October 2009

161056LV00003B/11/A